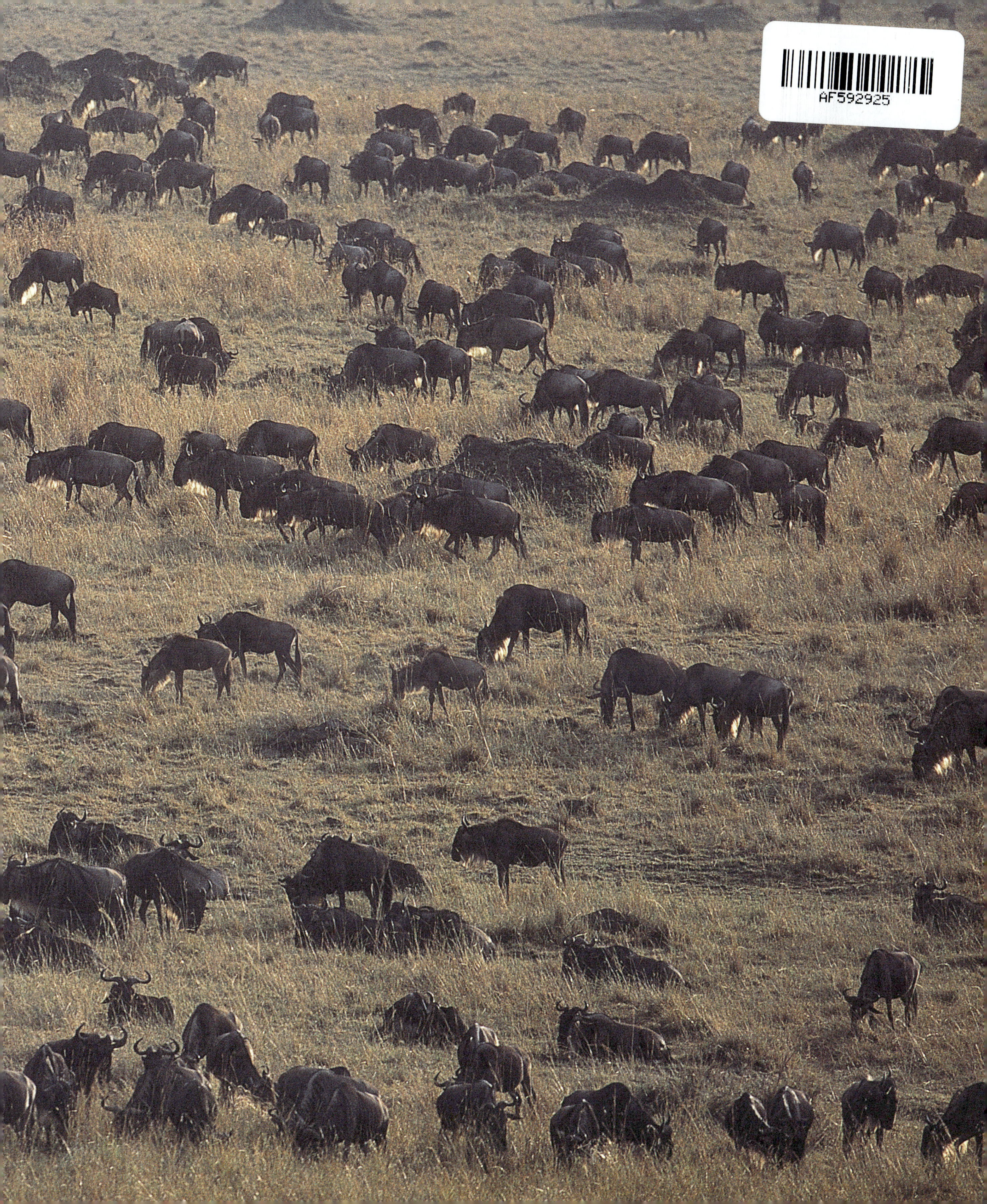

The Circle of Life

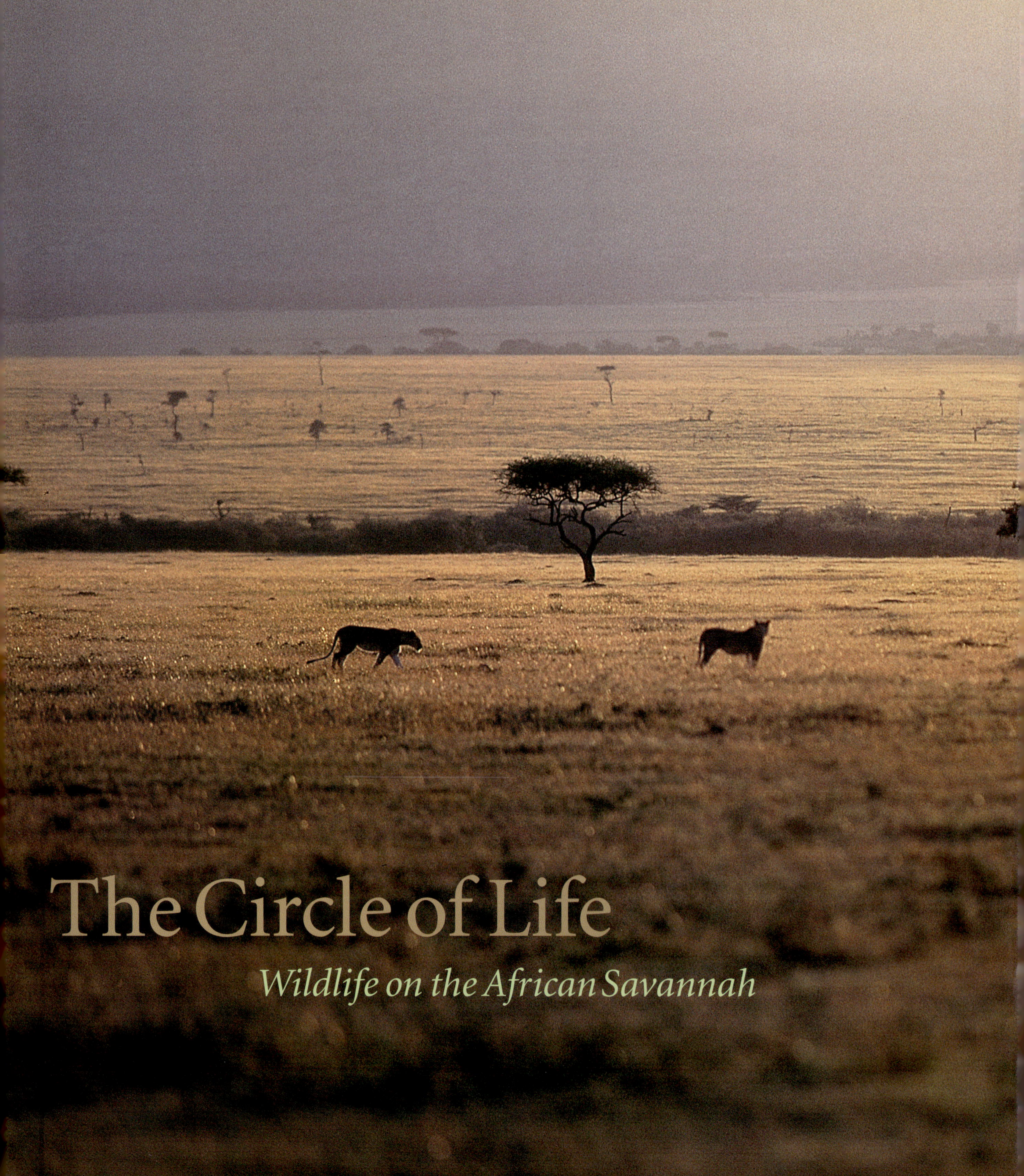

The Circle of Life

Wildlife on the African Savannah

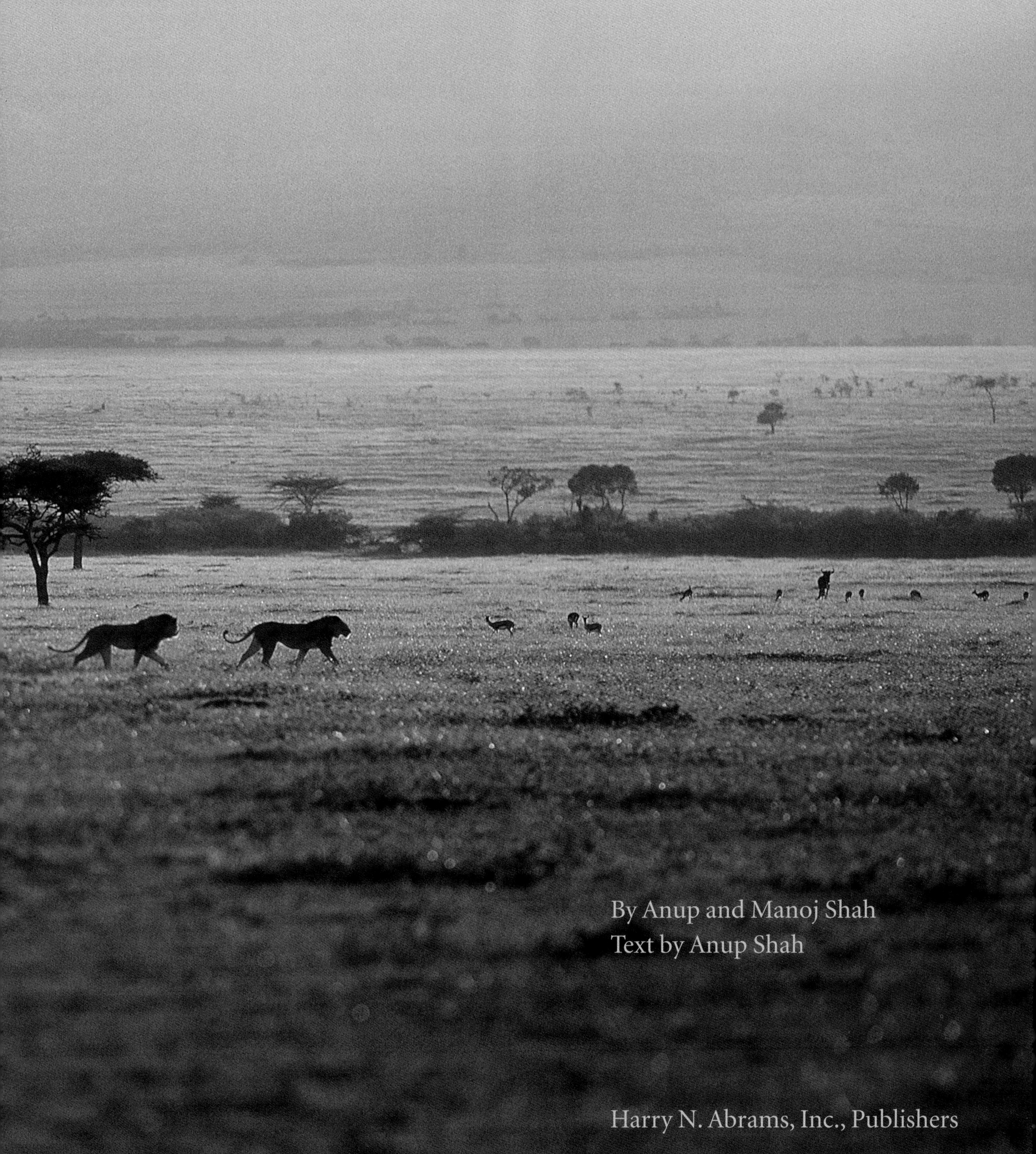

By Anup and Manoj Shah
Text by Anup Shah

Harry N. Abrams, Inc., Publishers

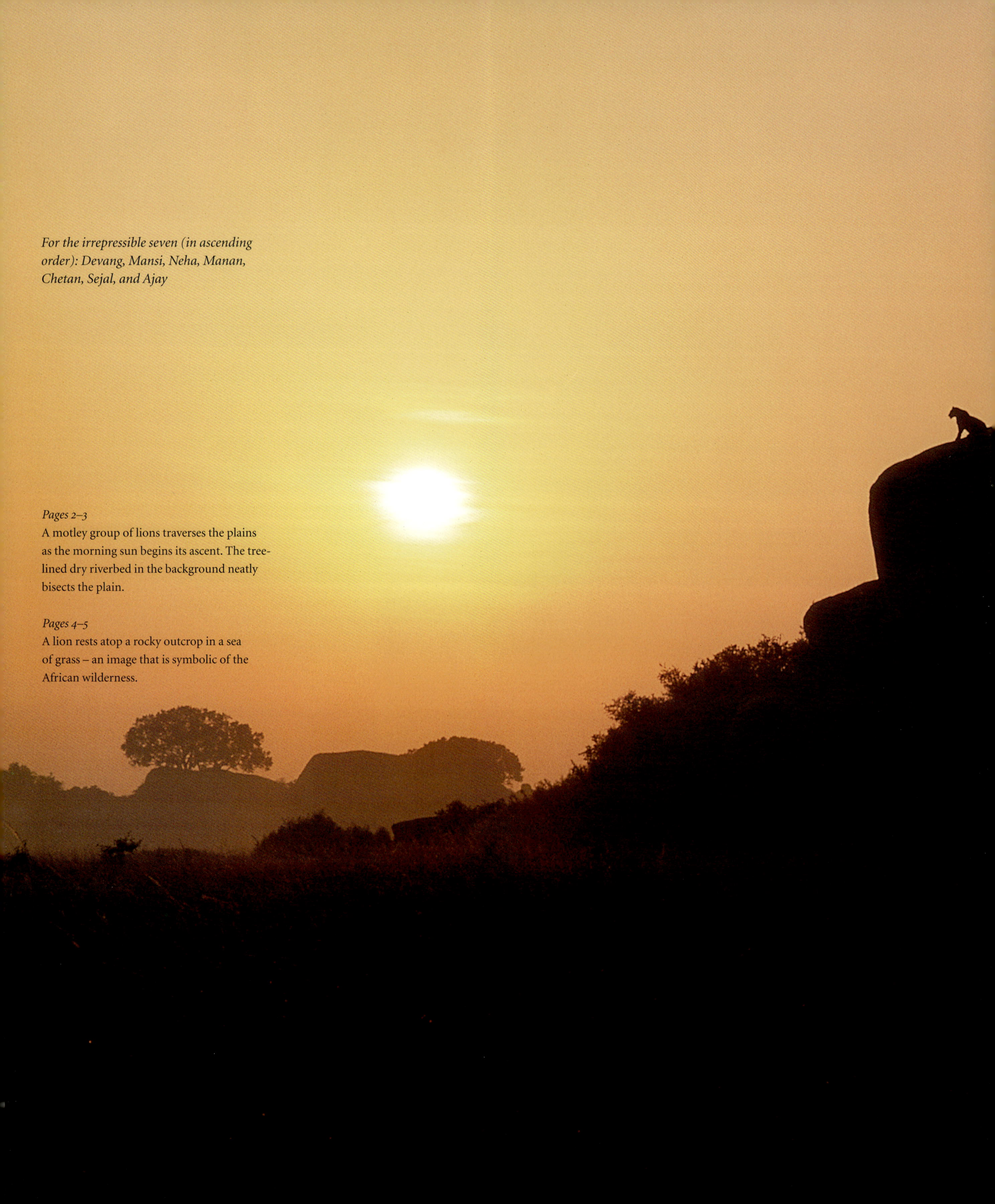

For the irrepressible seven (in ascending order): Devang, Mansi, Neha, Manan, Chetan, Sejal, and Ajay

Pages 2–3
A motley group of lions traverses the plains as the morning sun begins its ascent. The tree-lined dry riverbed in the background neatly bisects the plain.

Pages 4–5
A lion rests atop a rocky outcrop in a sea of grass – an image that is symbolic of the African wilderness.

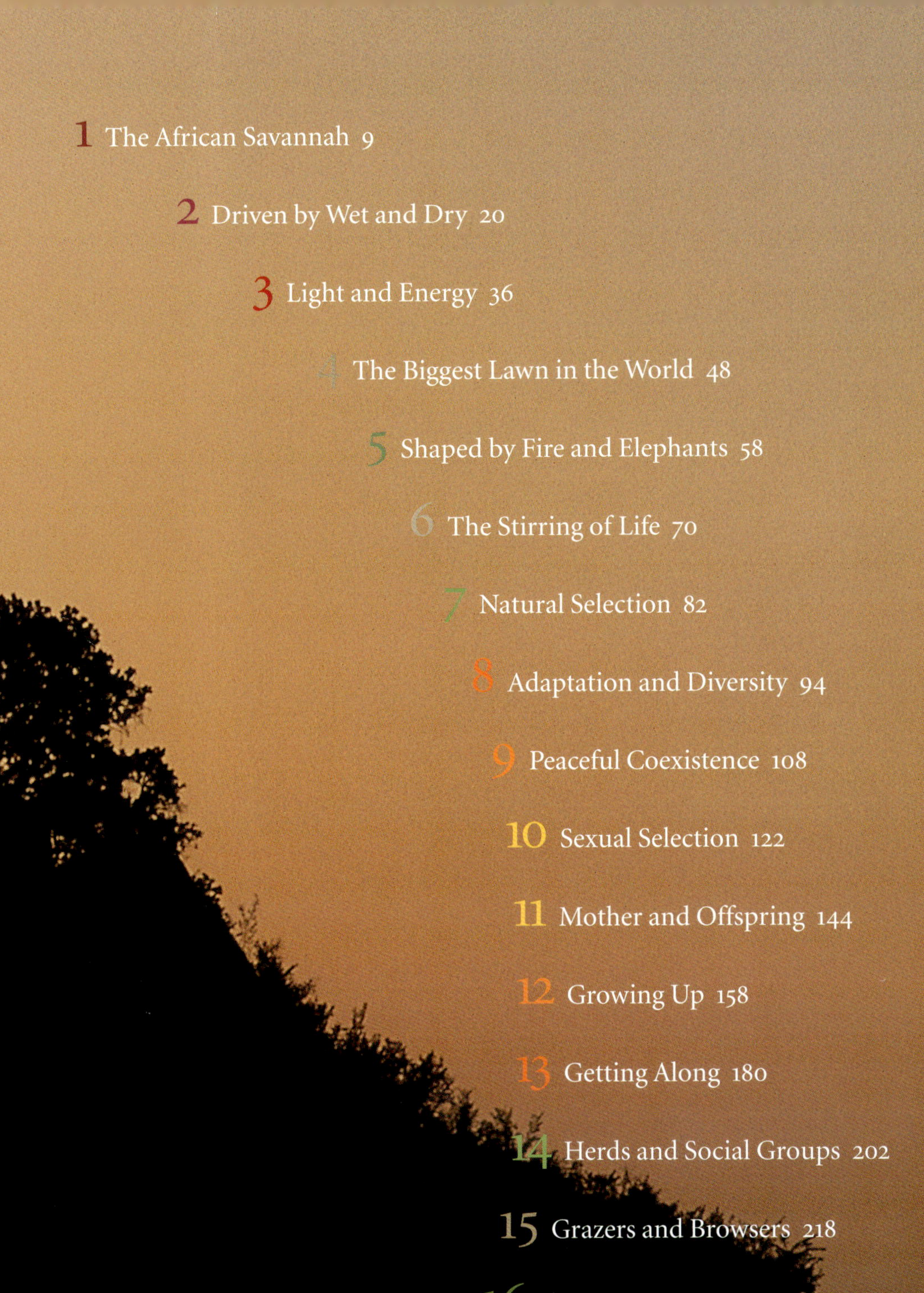

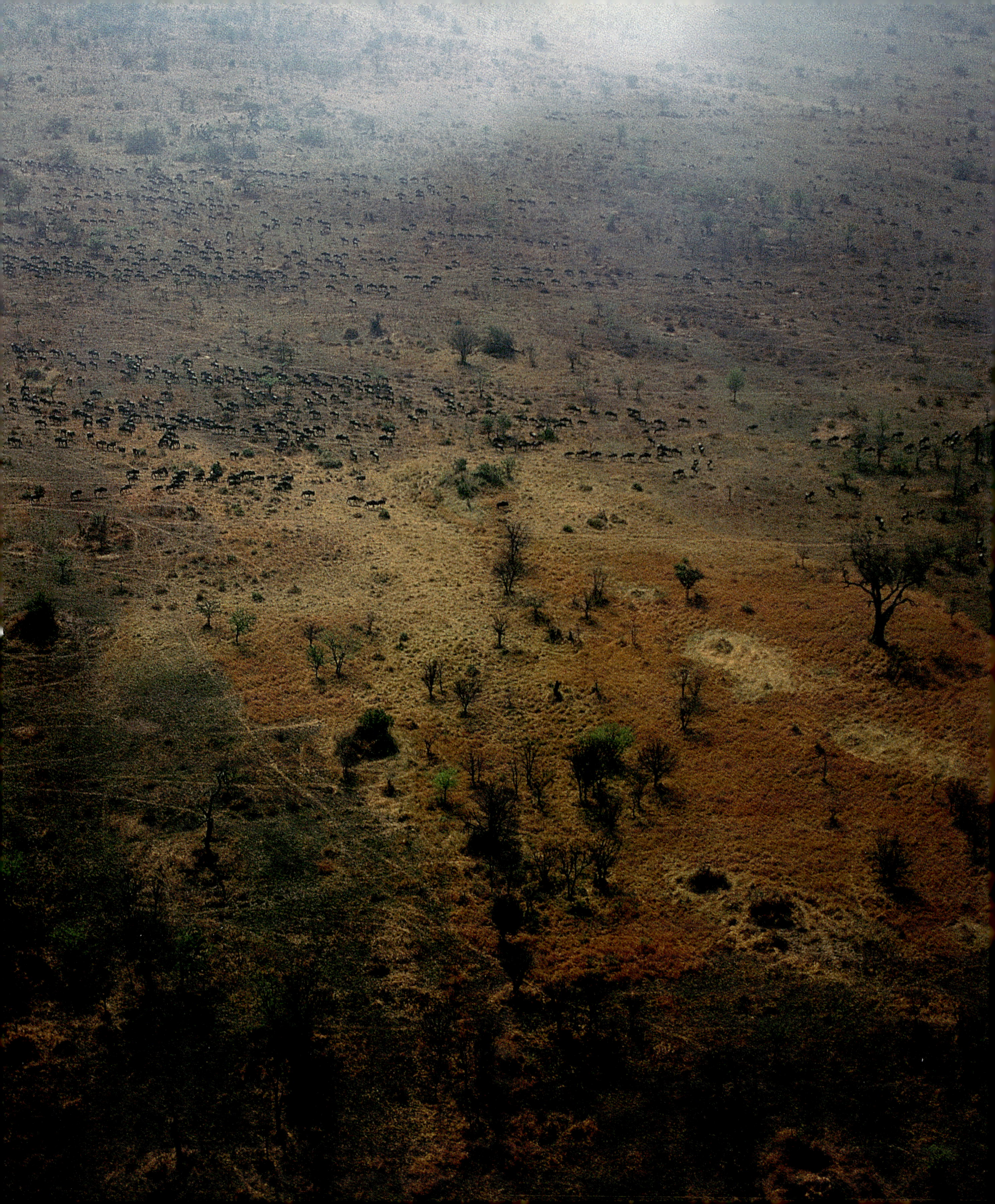

1

The African Savannah

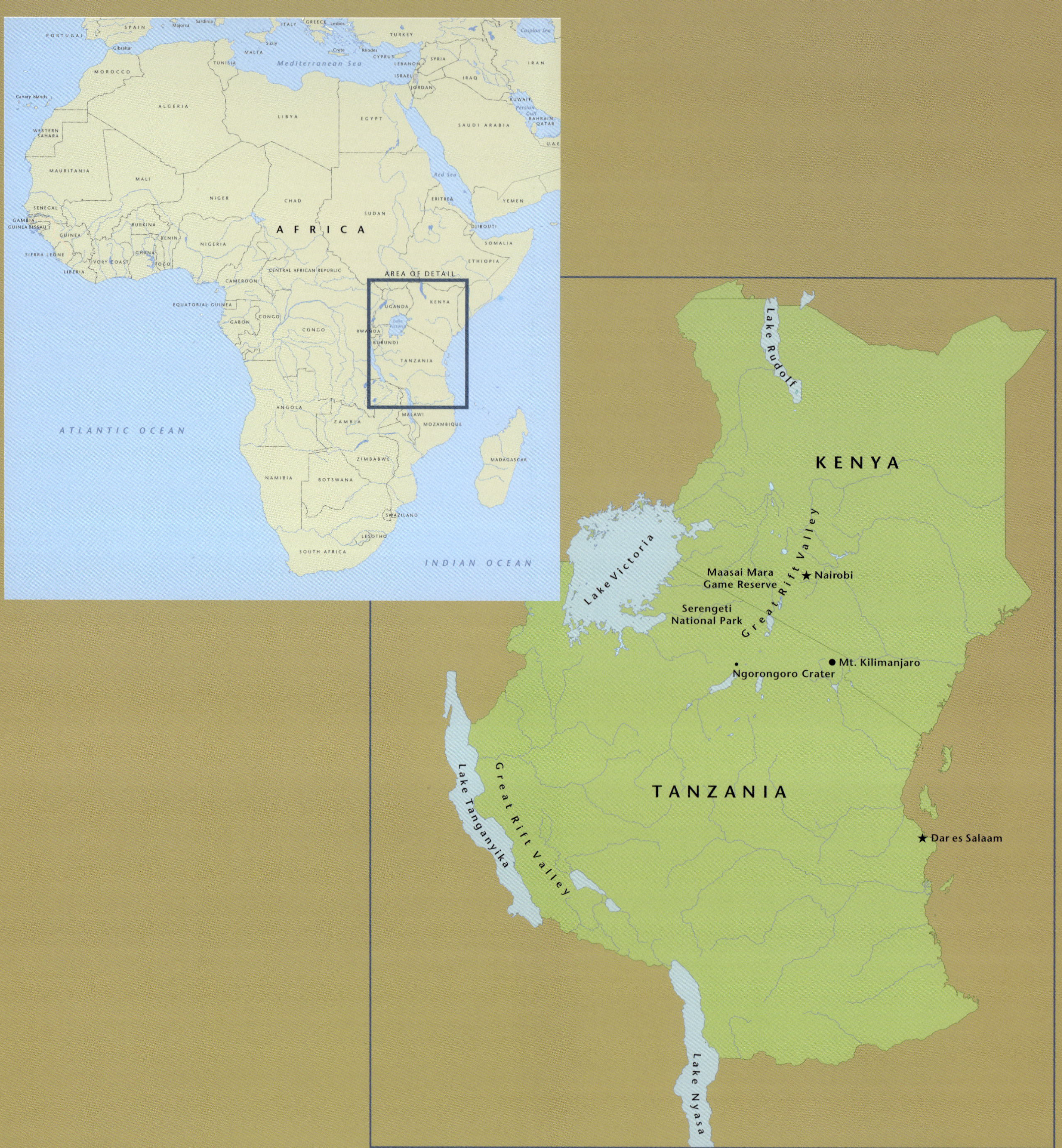

Pages 6–7
A mosaic of grass, bushes, and scattered trees in the dry season.

The African savannah is a relative newcomer to our planet, the latest ecosystem to emerge from the constantly evolving geological and climactic changes that shape the land on which we tread. It is also home to the highest concentration of large mammals on any continent and is an area of land so vast it is easily distinguishable from outer space, covering approximately one-tenth of the entire earth's surface. To better appreciate its unique character, let's take a brief look at how it has evolved.

Until about 50 million years ago, Africa had no extensive open plains or mountains. Instead, the continent consisted of a gentle, undulating landscape covered with vast tropical forests. The temperature throughout much of the world at that time was tropical: New York, London, Paris, and Frankfurt had the same climate as Bangkok has today, and dense, humid forests covered the United States and much of Europe.

Then, a couple of dramatic, long-term climate changes occurred. A global cooling trend began, rainfall decreased, and whole forests were wiped out. In many areas of the Northern hemisphere tropical forests were replaced with evergreen forests that were better adapted to the new, cooler temperatures. This set the stage for the entrance of grass, the central constituent of the savannah ecosystem.

Grasses perform two acts: they are virtually indestructible in the face of adverse conditions, and they rapidly multiply when circumstances become favorable. As grasses seized the opportunity to expand, enormous plains opened up in the Americas and Africa, filling the wide open spaces between swathes of forests.

Enter geological change: The birth of the Great Rift Valley, a huge fault in the earth's crust that is a direct result of the drifting apart of the continents. When the Rift Valley came into being, it spawned numerous volcanoes, and whenever they belched forth lava and ash, they not only modified the effect of rifting by massive infilling but also caused extensive fires, which devastated the forests. Once again, grasses moved in to fill the void.

Most of the Rift Valley activity occurred about 25 million years ago, and a trend toward drier conditions firmed up 10 to 20 million years ago. Over much of Africa south of the Sahara, wooded savannah, or grassland with open-canopy forests (as opposed to the closed, dense canopy of a rain forest), dominated the scene. During this period, ground-dwelling plant-eating mammals that feed on the leaves of trees and bushes, also known as browsers, greatly increased in number and variety, and bovids, defined by the presence of a four-chambered stomach and horns in males, a group which includes antelopes, gazelles, and buffaloes, were slowly evolving into what would later become the major component of the savannah fauna.

About ten million years ago there was an acceleration toward both drier conditions and seasonality. Tropical forests and wooded savannah shrank, and grasslands – both with and without scattered trees – expanded. When the first bovids ventured out to graze on the plains, they never strayed far from their forested safe havens. Increasingly, however, they went further and further out on the plains in search of food, making it more and more difficult to seek cover in their familiar forests. In fact, as predators were still most likely to be found in forests where the cover was thickest, they actually started to run further out onto the plains for safety. It was inevitable that the predators would follow them into the open country, and their prey, unable to take cover, began to rely on speed for escape, and developed longer legs. At the same time, keener eyesight, the better to spot danger from a distance, evolved. The exciting evolution of the savannah as we now know it had begun in earnest.

Today, the African savannah is a complex mosaic of grasses, trees, and bushes, with two predominating characteristics: oceans of grass and distinct wet and dry seasons. It is the stronghold of one of the greatest wildlife spectacles in the world.

Opposite
Vervet monkeys live in the woodlands along the banks of the rivers that cut through the grasslands. It is believed they successfully invaded this habitat from their ancestral forest home.

Pages 12–13
As the Mara River meanders its way through the plains, segments of it are lined with what are called gallery forests, or mini ecosystems within the savannah.

Pages 14–15
A lioness roaring on a *kopje,* a granite outcropping situated in a vast stretch of shortgrass plains.

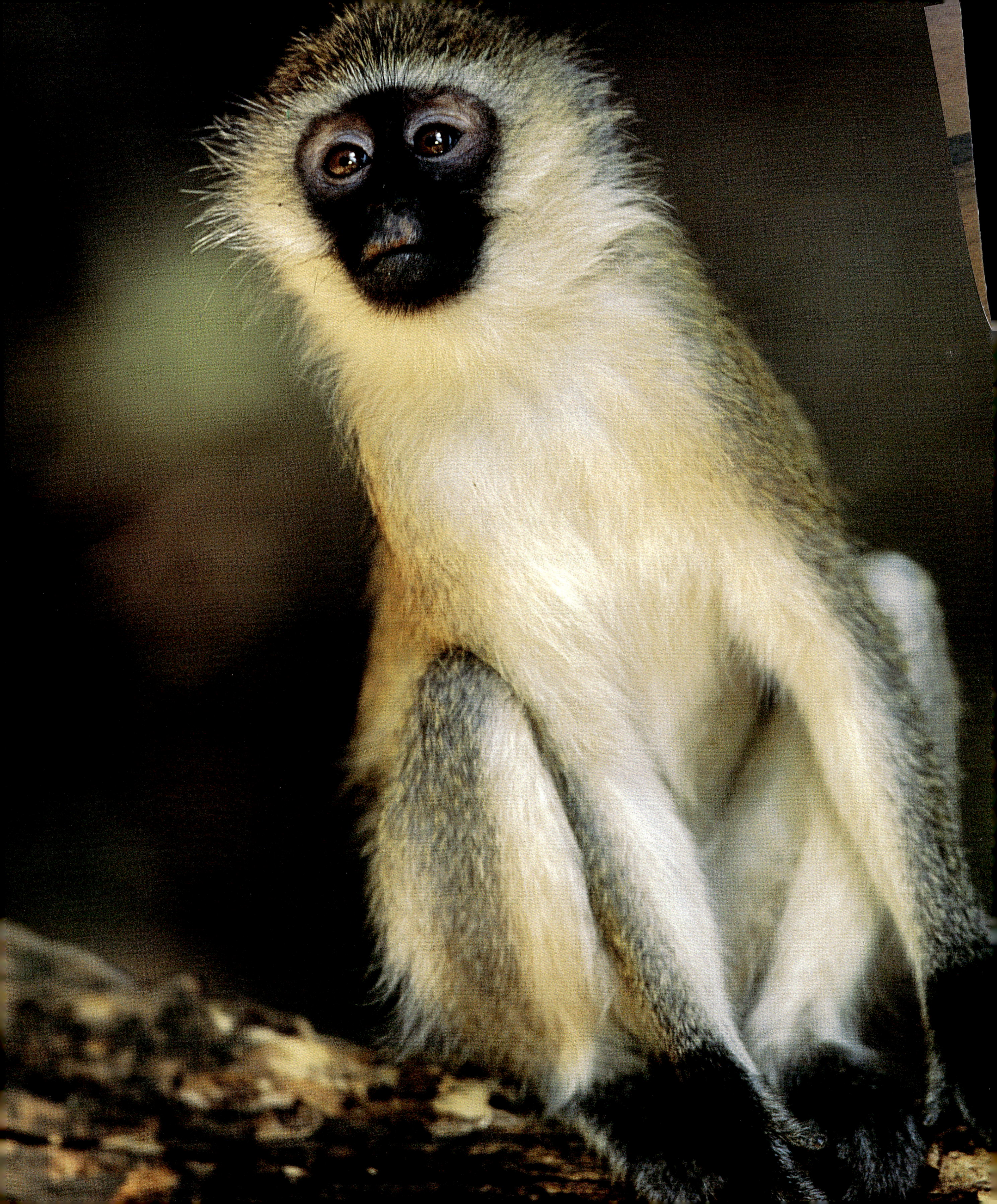

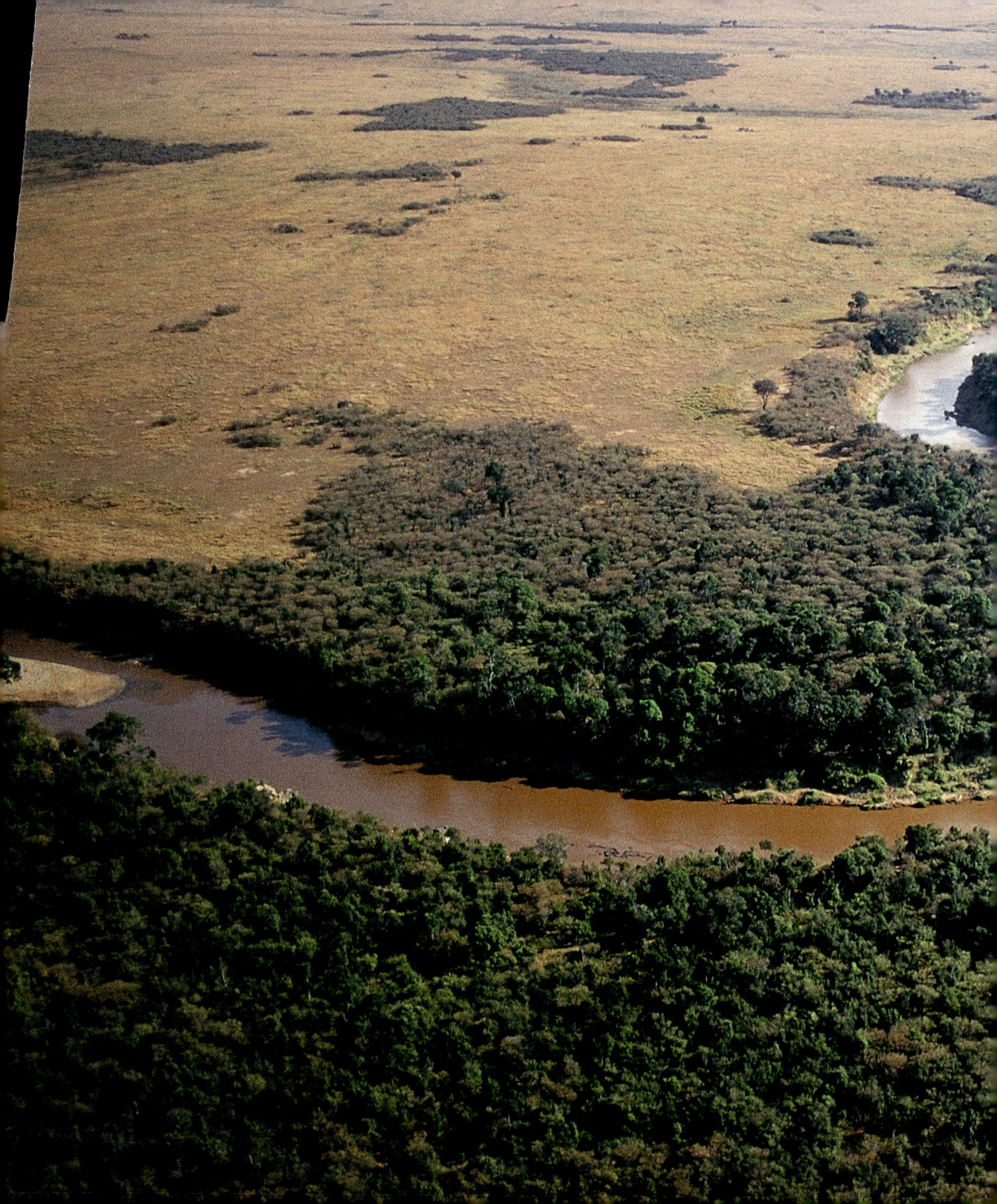

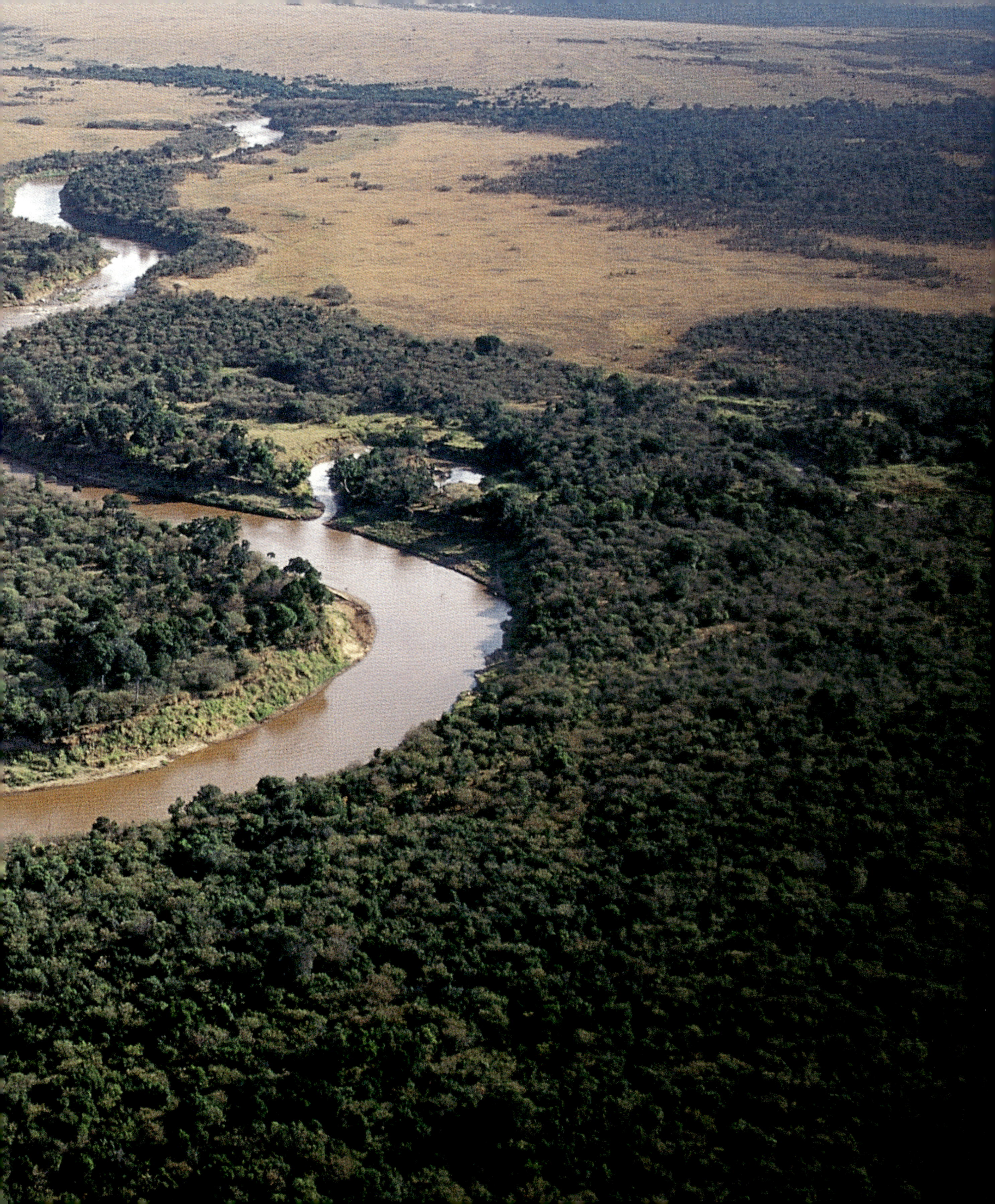

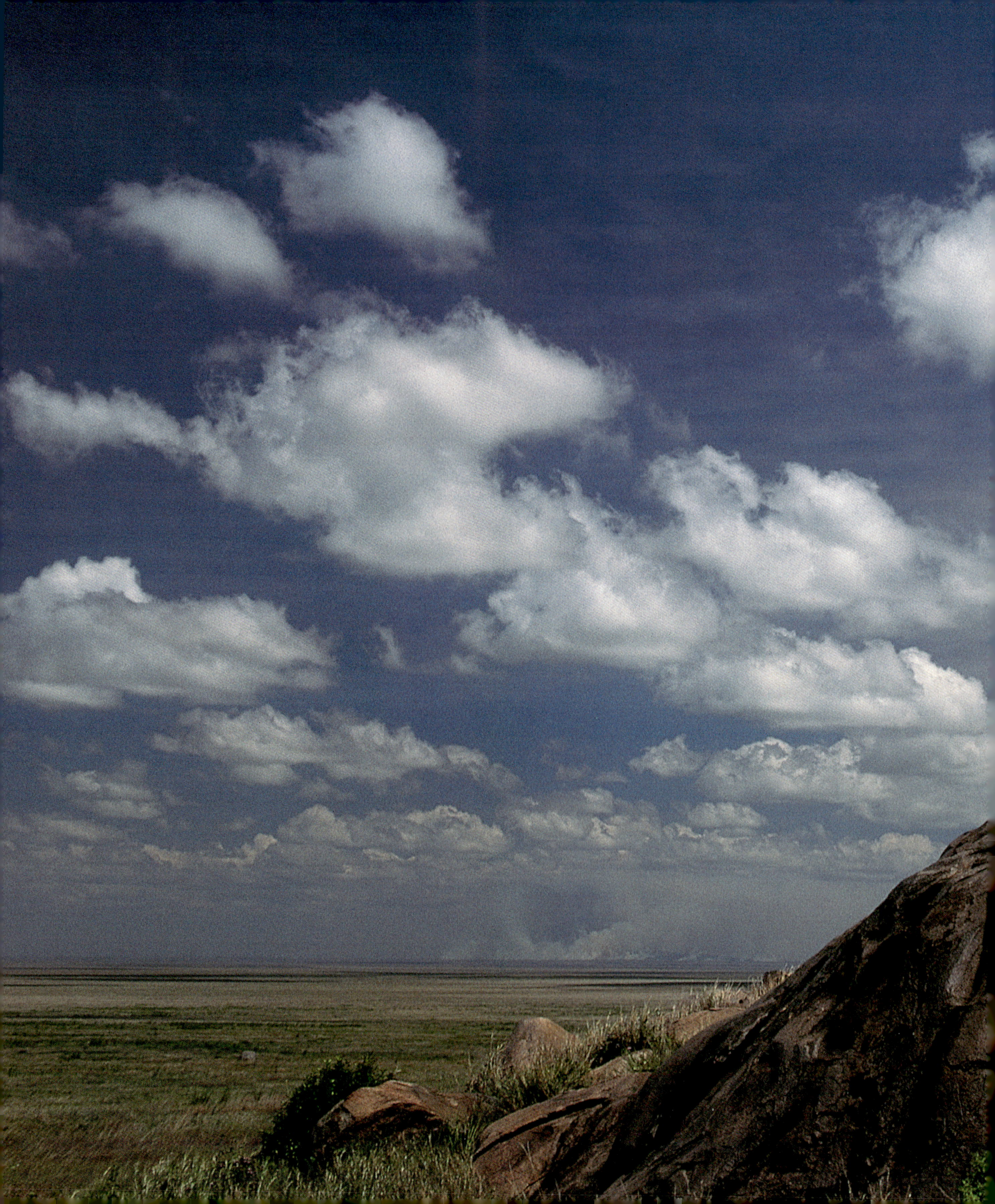

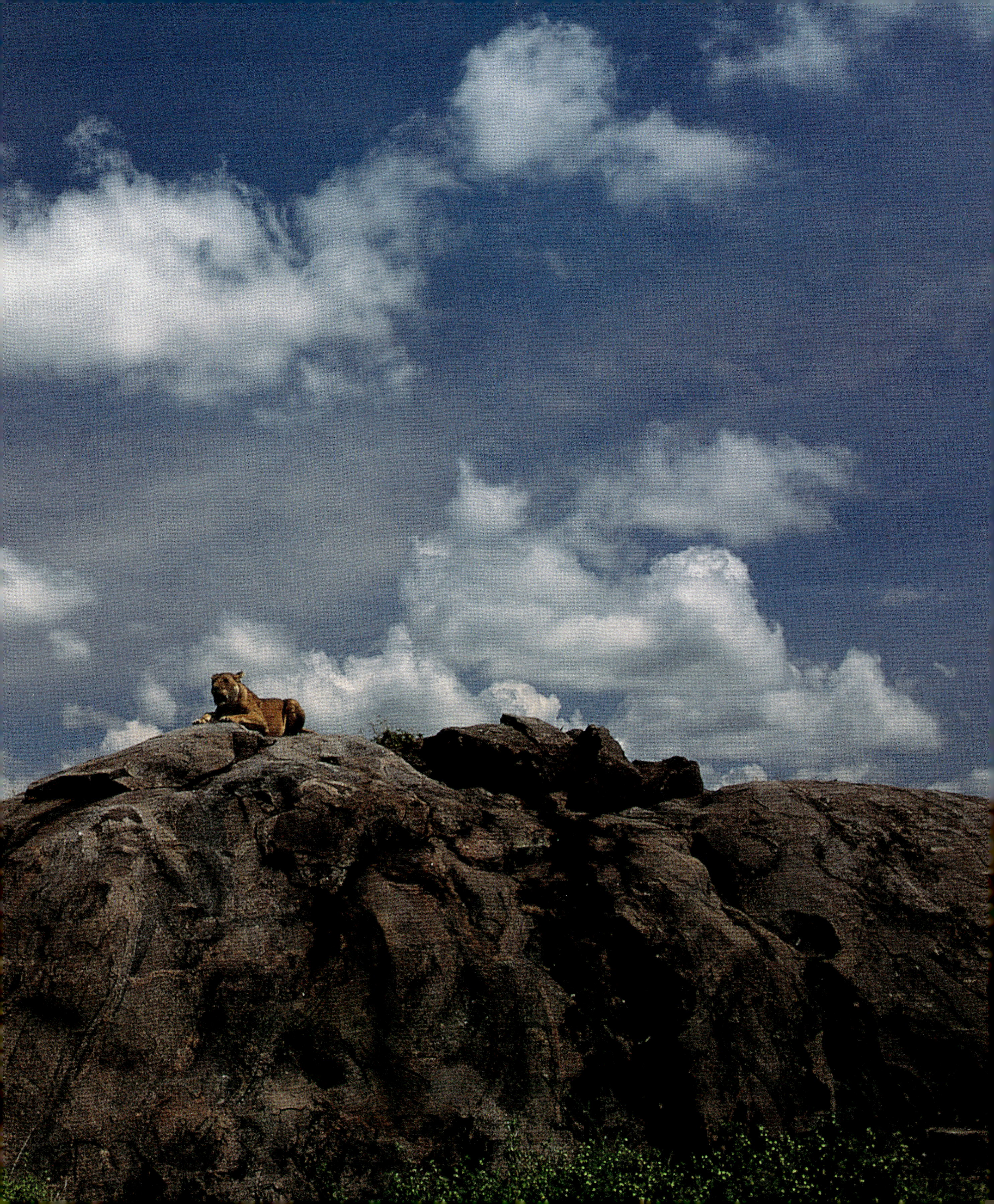

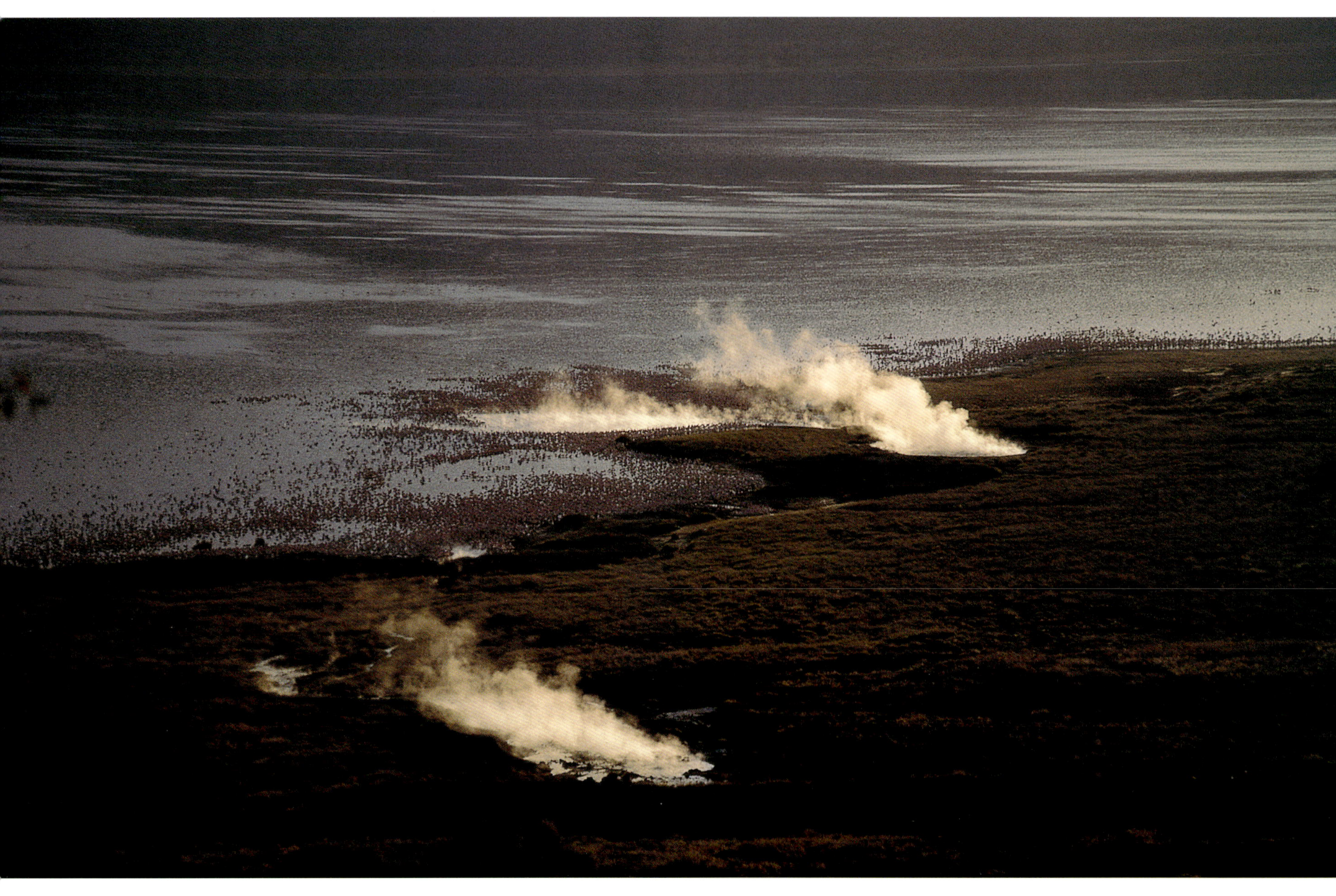

About four million flamingoes are found on the alkaline lakes, such as Lake Bogoria seen here, of the East African segment of the Great Rift Valley.

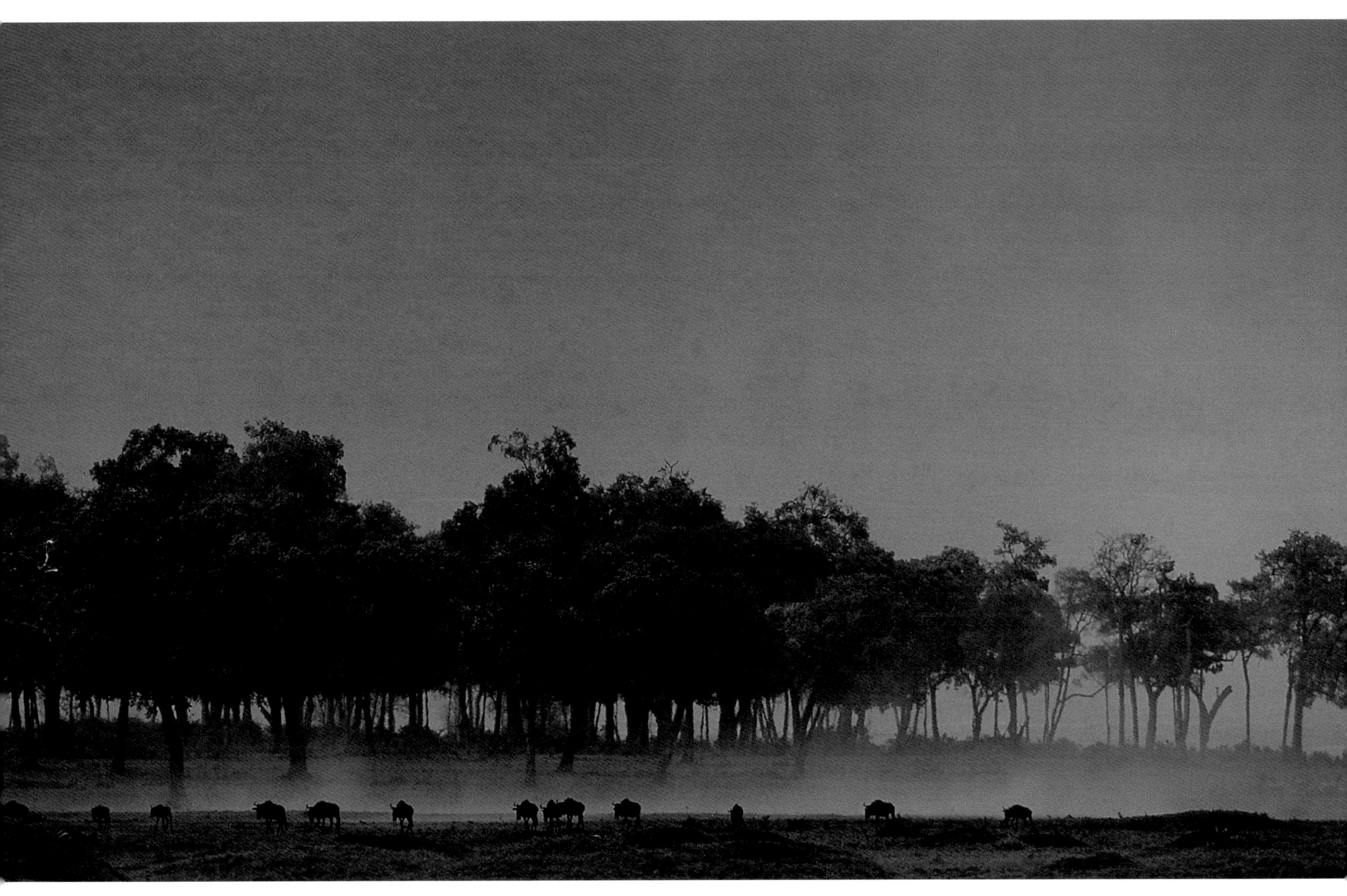

A wildebeest herd marches in a line formation, steering clear of the riverine forest in the background, which might conceal predators.

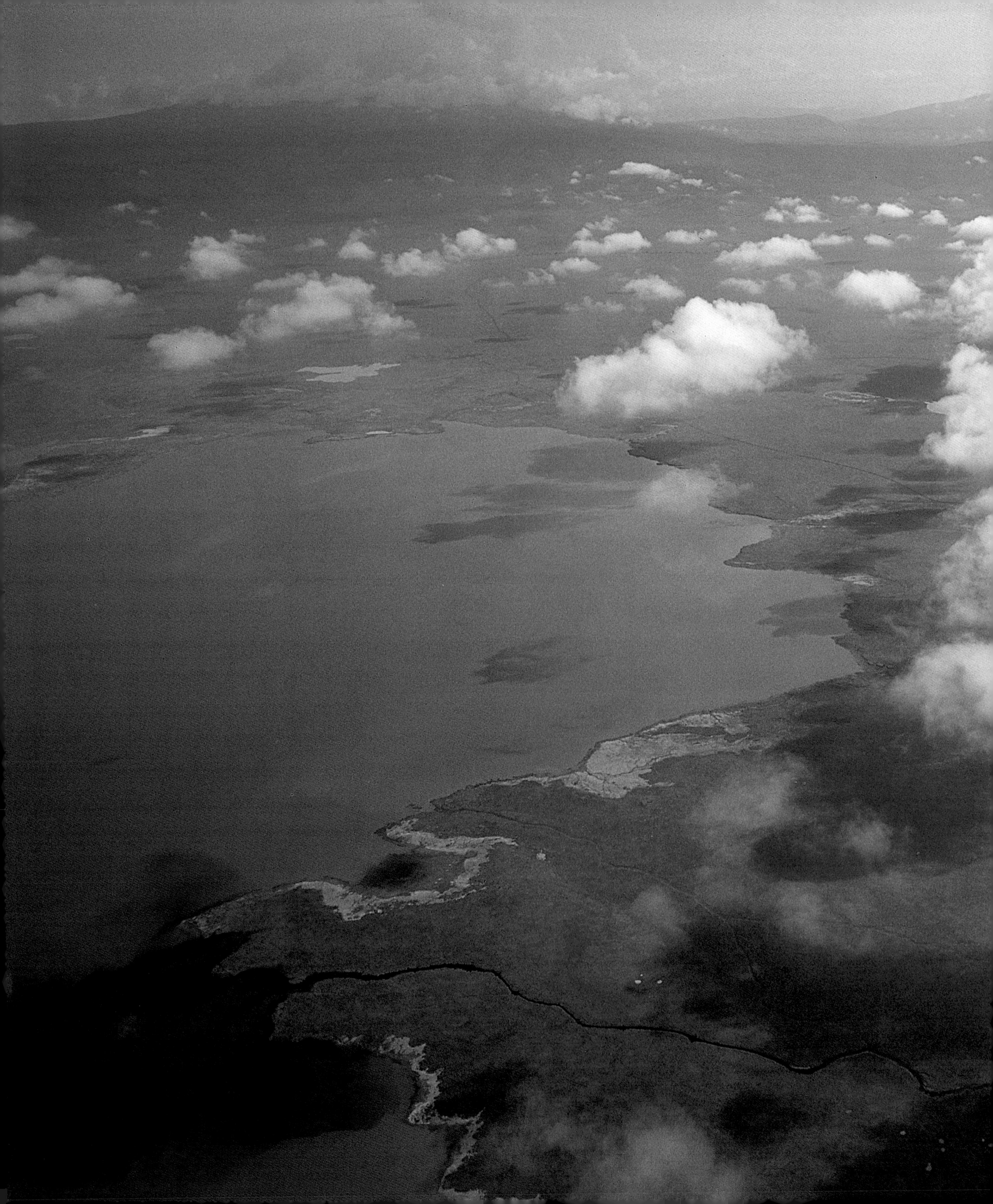

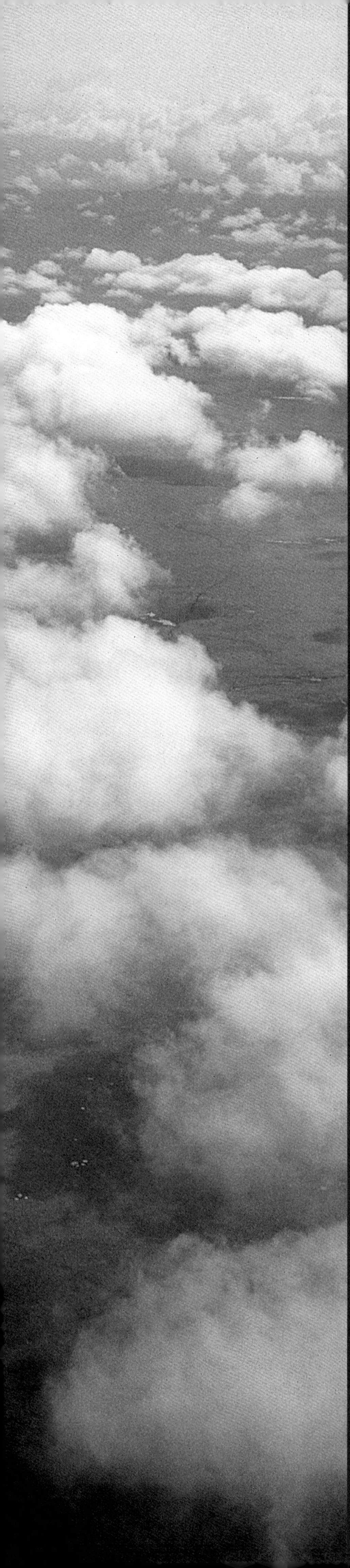

2

Driven by Wet and Dry

Unlike the predictable four seasons that exist in much of the world, savannah has only two – dry and wet – and they are anything but predictable. The concept of normal annual rainfall simply does not exist: In some years the dry season drags on endlessly, in other years it is brief. The year 1992–1993 was so wet that four-wheel-drive vehicles were grounded for weeks; 1994–1995 was so dry that Cape buffaloes looked ready to collapse; 1997–1998 was the season of El Niño rains during which the Ngorongoro crater resembled a rice-paddy field. When it does rain, most of the annual rainfall is concentrated in a two-month period during which torrential downpours dump enormous amounts of water onto parched soil. Most of the rain ends up running off – wasted as far as the plants are concerned.

One June, at the beginning of the dry season in Serengeti-Maasai Mara, I was standing on a granite outcrop, listening to the warm wind howling across the plains, the grass already turning yellow. No doubt, the wind would suck out what little moisture remained. The desecrated and scorched land was bereft of animal life – they had all moved toward the wooded savannah. One by one, the temporary waterholes had choked and no longer provided sustenance.

As the dry season intensifies, the warm wind continues to hiss like a death rattle. The trees look withered, their leaves hanging listless. By August the wind has dropped and very little moves. It is eerily quiet. The dry season moves into September, the hot, shimmering air runs along the horizon like molten glass and distant Grant's gazelles appear to walk on water. The few resident animals try to conserve energy, moving little, and bracing themselves against the occasional dust devils whipped up by sudden bursts of wind.

As the dry season nears its end, the days remain hot, but the air grows heavy. Thunder now rumbles and rolls across the sky, animals jumping at its unexpected bellows. They seem anxious, sniffing the air, waiting for the rain. The thirsting land, too, seems to plead for rain. Finally, heralded by flashes of lightning, the skies break open, and the rain comes.

To survive the extremes of the season, grass and other plants have evolved into extraordinarily resilient life forms. They lie dormant for months, waiting for rebirth. When the first drops of rain, bigger than a dime, finally hit the earth there first arises the sweet smell of wet soil, and of the land reviving and coming back to life. Then, as the rains pick up, grass grows an inch every 24 hours, transforming the barren, shrivelled land into a huge network of oases that expand at a rapid rate. Color changes from brown to green overnight. Acacias explode with white or yellow blossoms. Everywhere there is the rich smell of new grass. Promise of life is in the air.

Then life springs into action. There is a frenzy of activity among the birds. Millions of termites awake and their mounds erupt. Every day, new hordes of insects hatch. Mammals exuberantly shake off the excess water and are injected with a new energy. The savannah shines with freshness and, for once, you don't mind muddy clothes or getting stuck in the muck. After all, life is bursting all over.

Pages 18–19
The flooded Ngorongoro Crater in Tanzania, during the El Niño rains. Driving in the crater at this time was difficult, and large areas were inaccessible even to four-wheel-drive vehicles.

Early on in the dry season, an adolescent elephant relishes in a thorough dusting. Patches of dust have started appearing where the grass cover is thinnest.

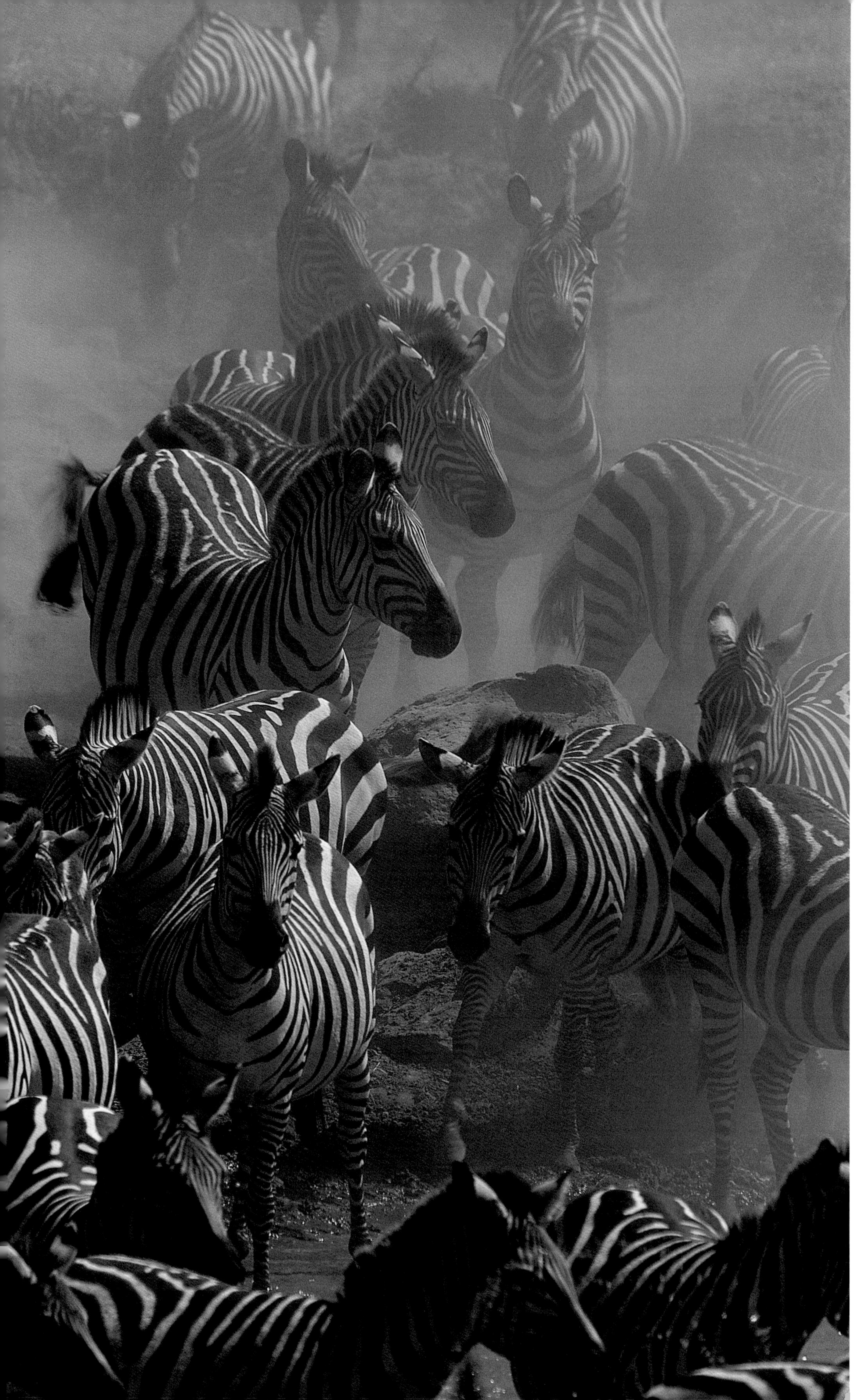

The final leg of the long dry season is signalled by a herd of zebras gathered together on a dusty river bank. Herds will often hesitate at the edge, as if waiting for some sign or signal that it is safe, or some force of momentum to get them into the water and across the river.

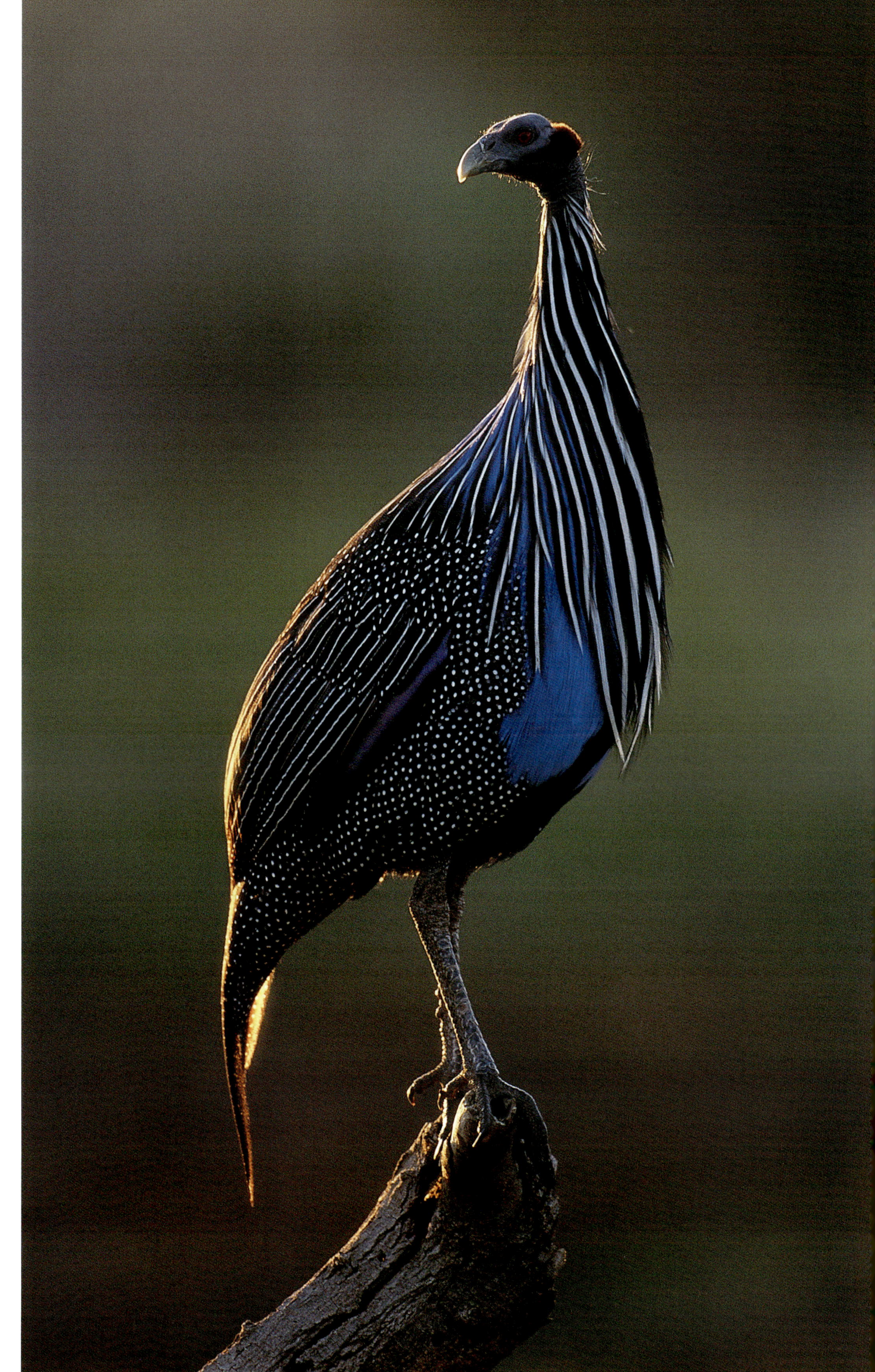

The upper neck, bare of feathers, and the relatively small head of this vulturine guinea fowl give it a vulture-like appearance, hence its name. When these birds start to breed, you know the dry season is soon to end: They can detect infrasound of very low frequency and can hear thunder many hundreds of miles away, enabling them to anticipate the rains long before they arrive.

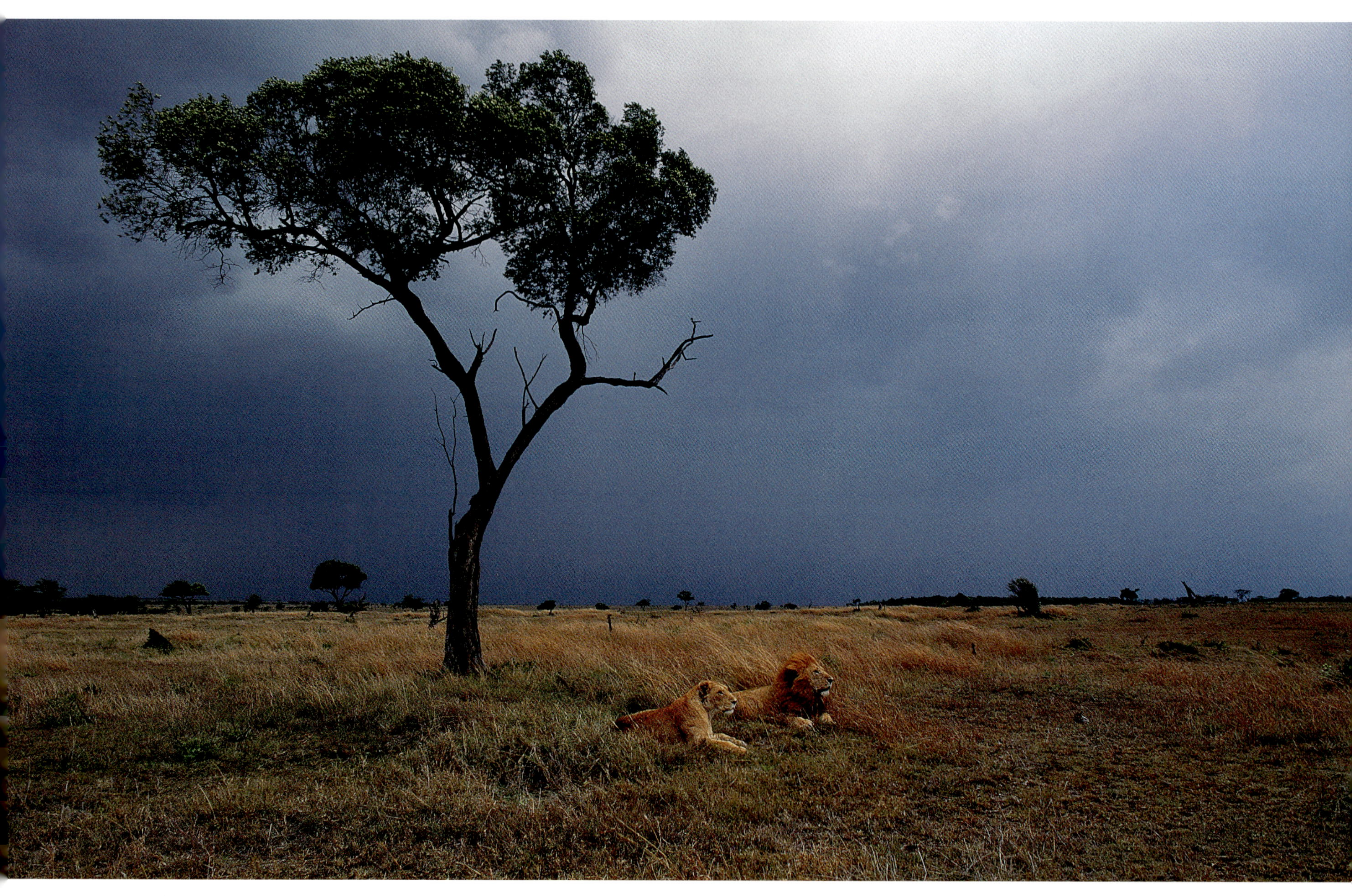

A cool breeze has awakened a pair of courting lions from their afternoon siesta. Storm clouds are gathering as well, heralding an end to the dry spell.

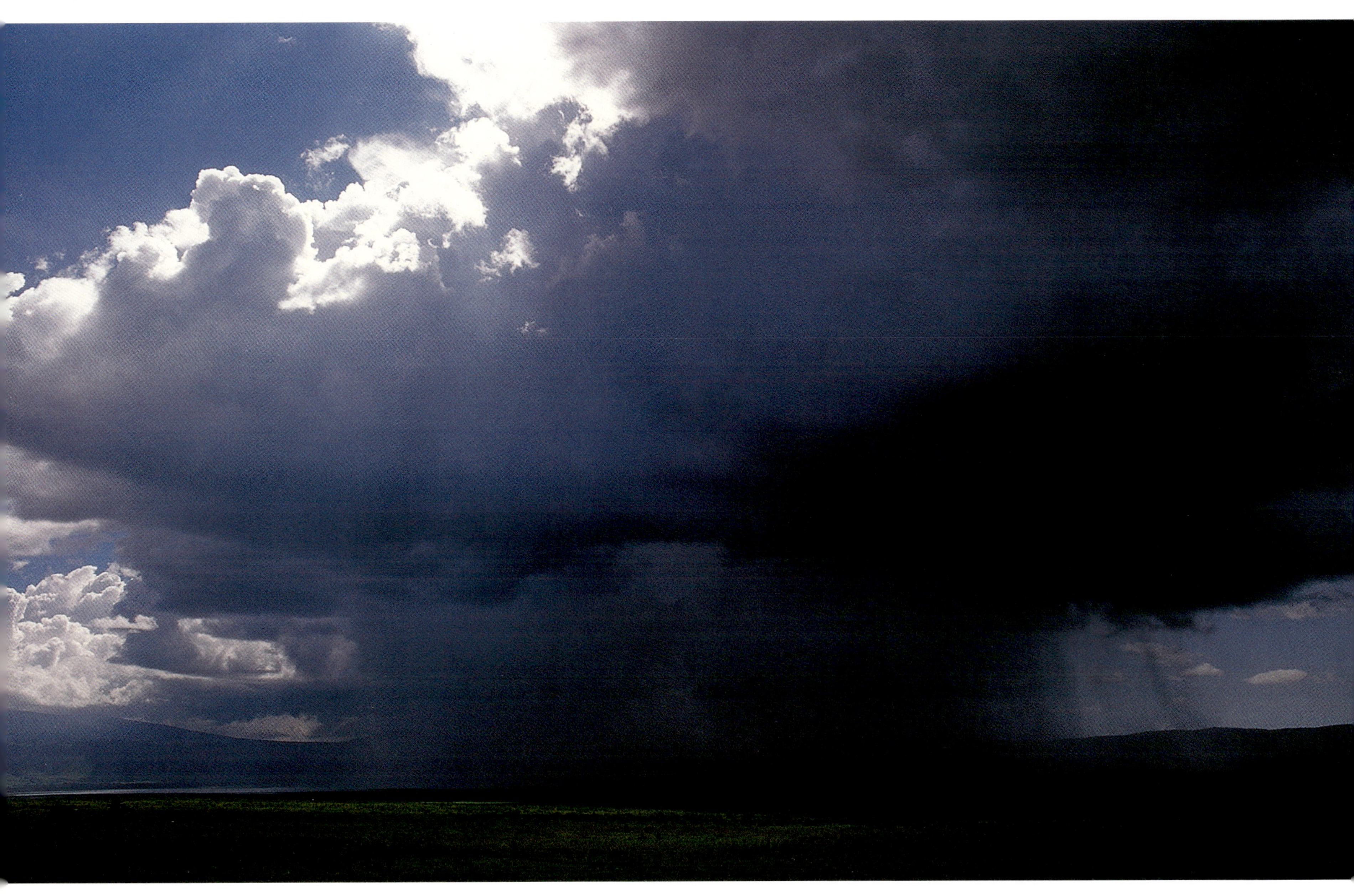

The darkening clouds, gathering winds, and flashes of lightning followed by ominous rolls of thunder signal an approaching thunderstorm.

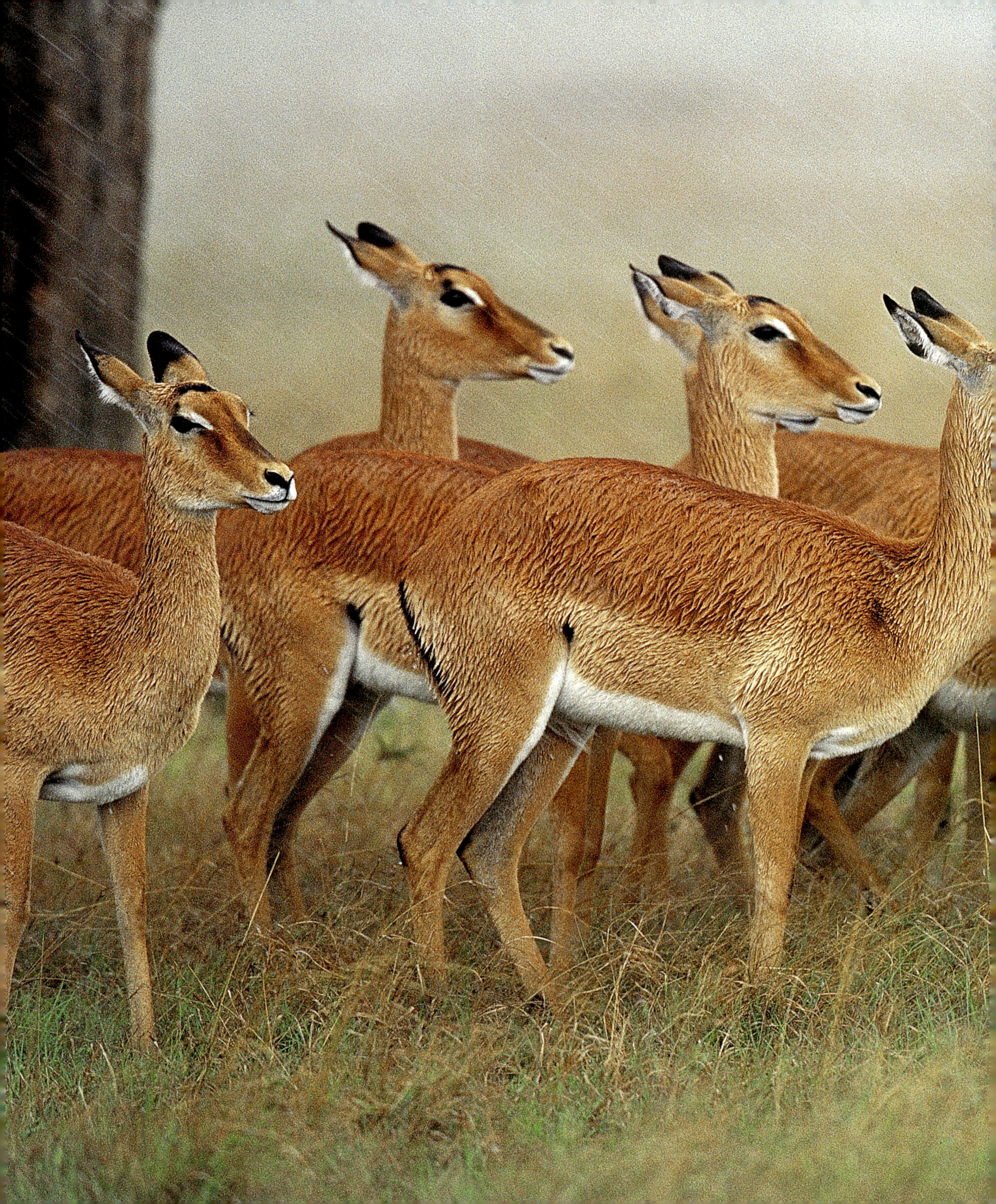

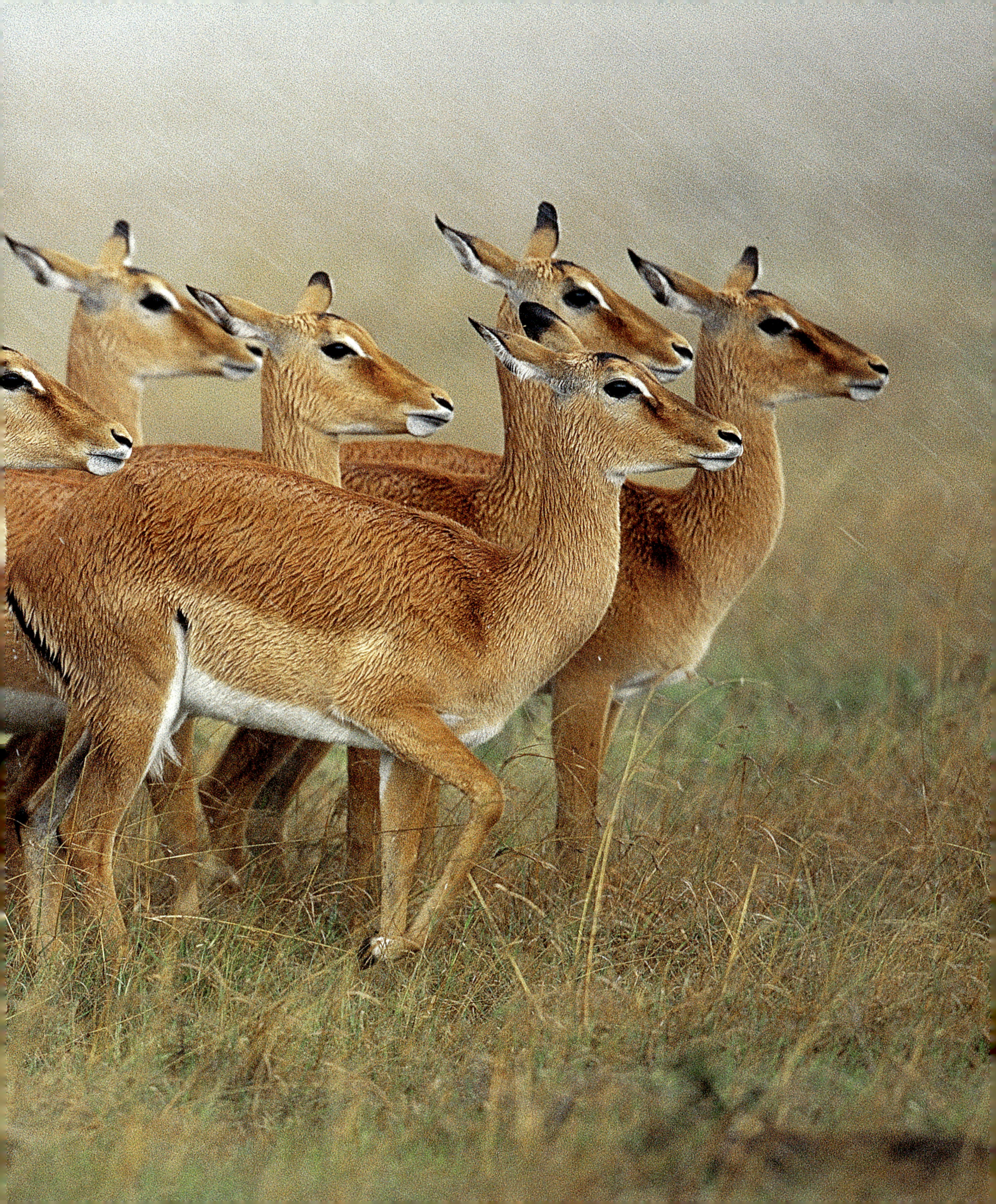

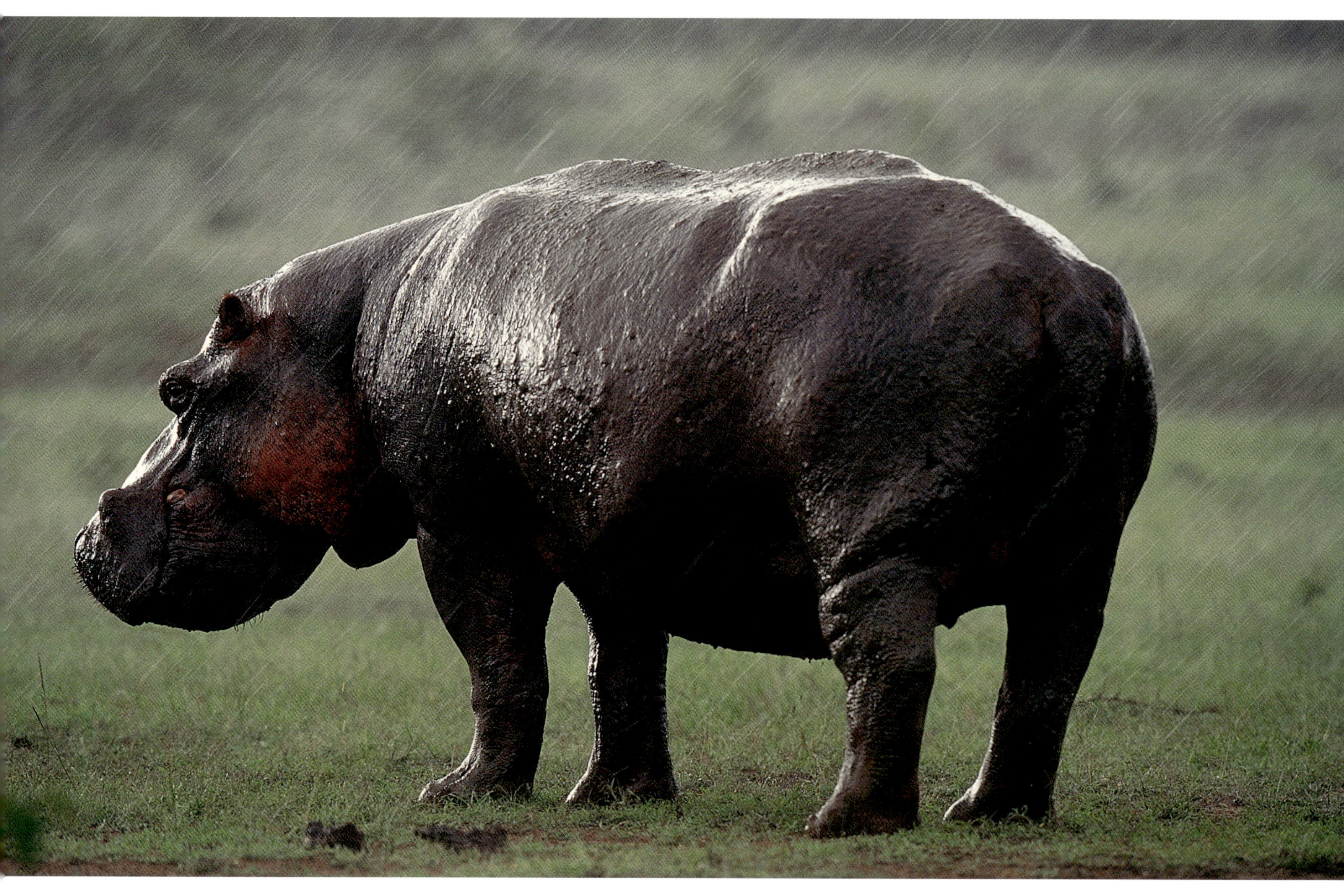

This optimistic hippo bull had started to graze on land, a rare event during daylight hours, when the skies opened up. As the rain intensified, the hippo decided to postpone his meal and returned to the river.

Pages 26–27
The rain had been threatening for some time, and when it finally came down, it caught this impala harem in an area that offered little cover. Patiently, they braved the lashing rains, changing formation now and then in response to the vagaries of the downpour. Once, at the sound of a particularly loud thunderclap, they panicked and bolted, but they quickly regained their composure and resigned themselves to a thorough drenching.

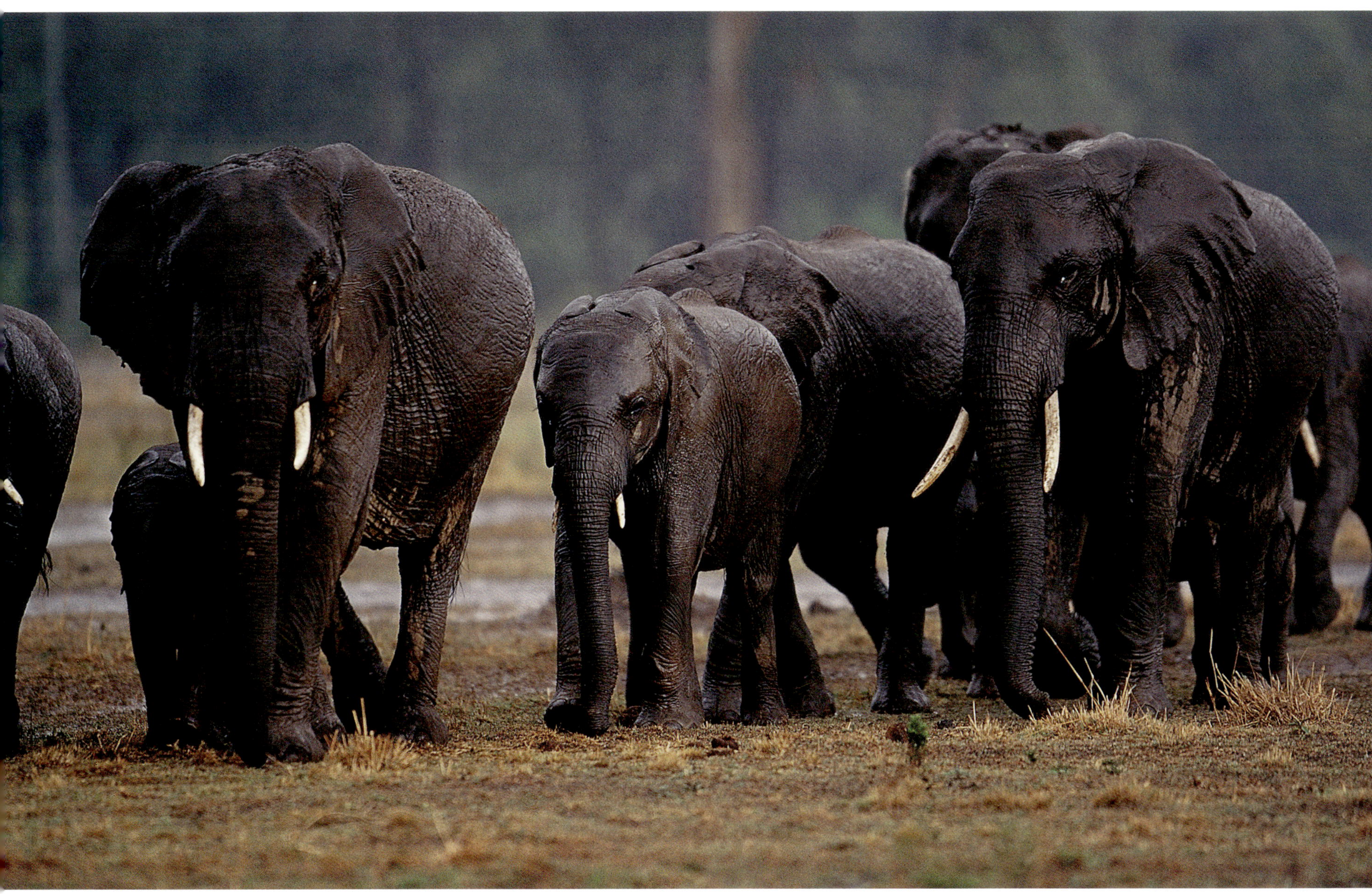

As soon as the heavy afternoon downpour began to die out, this elephant group emerged from the riverine forest to resume feeding.

Pages 30–31
A carpet of flowers adds a splash of color to the landscape as the wet season begins.

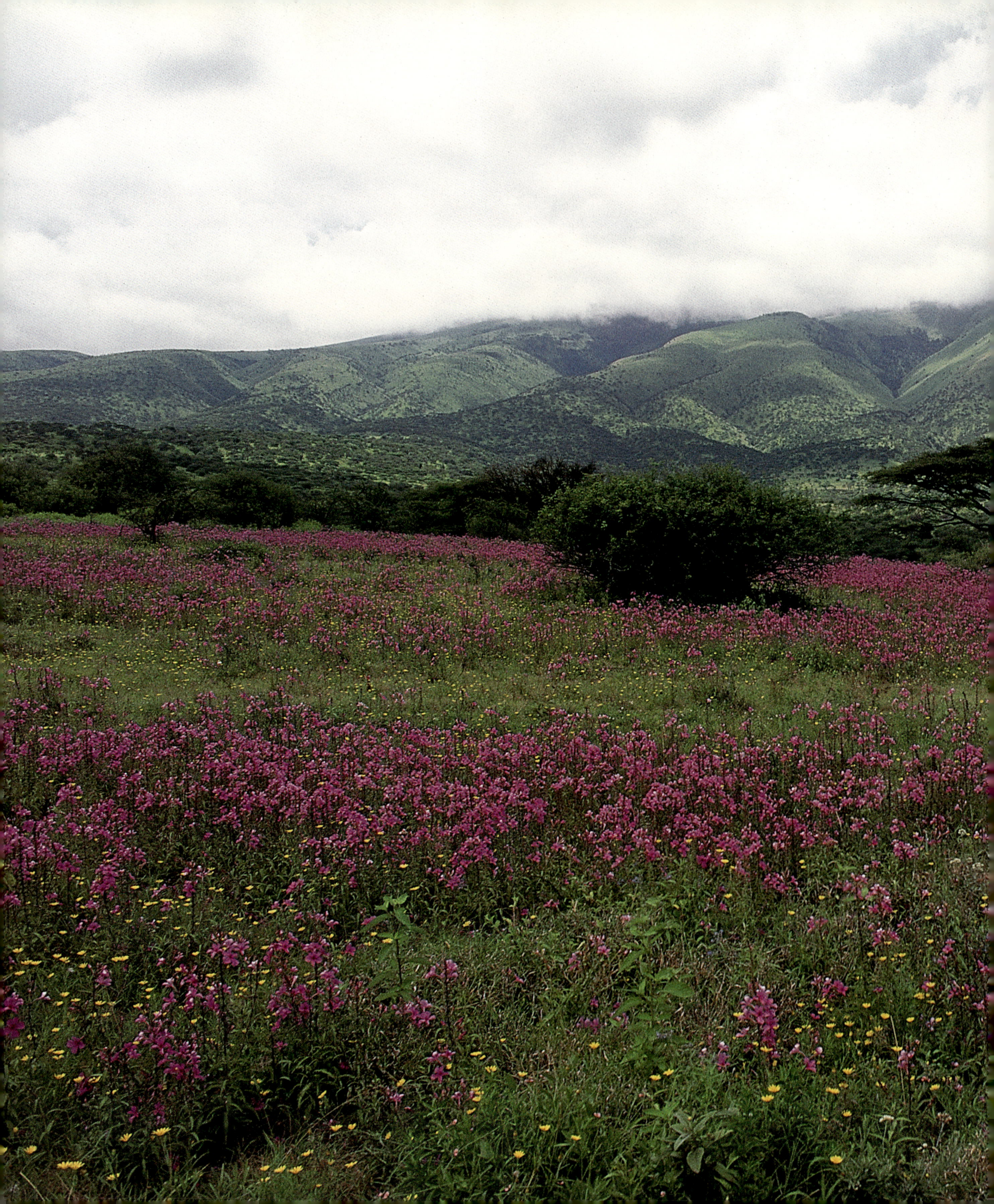

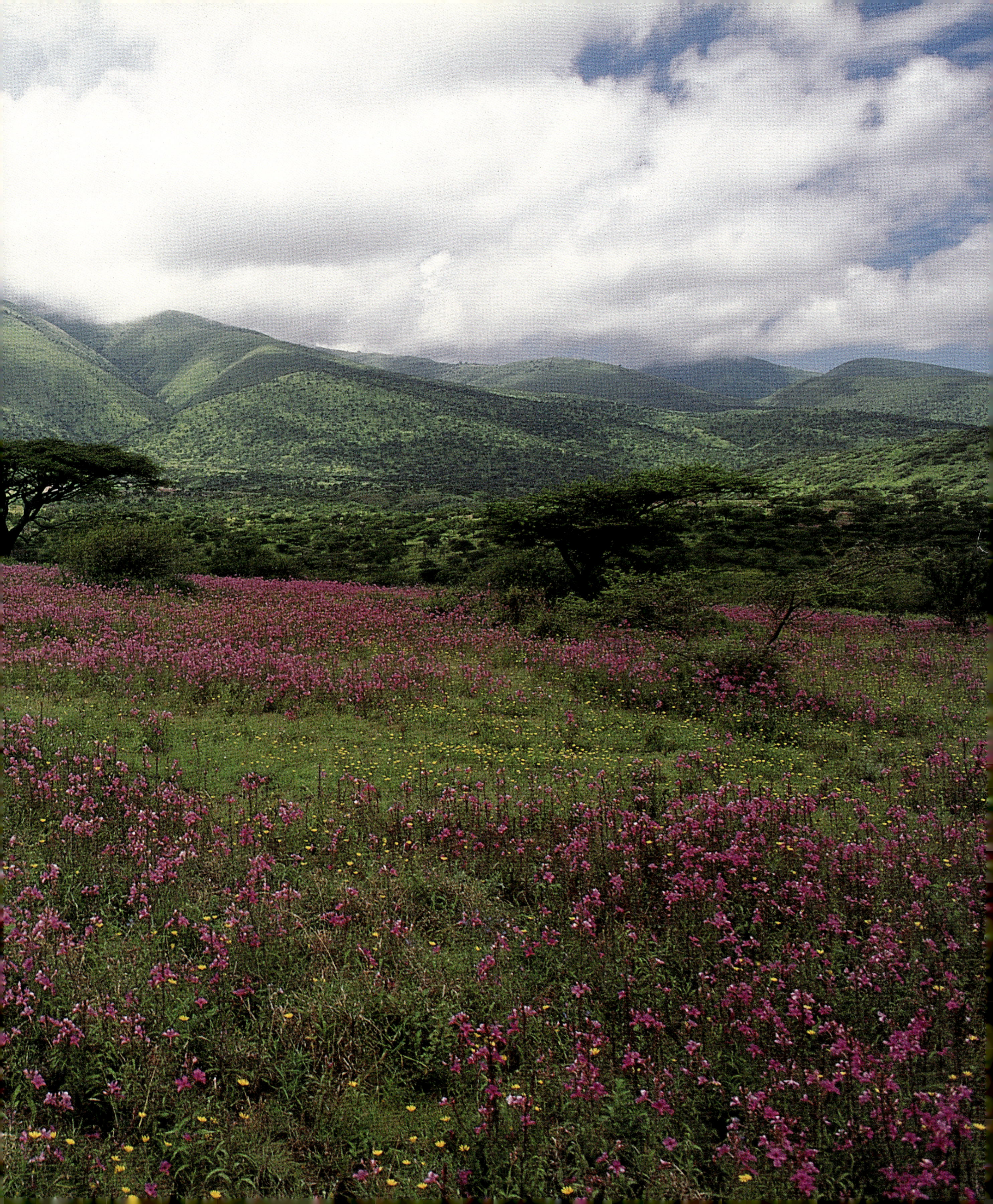

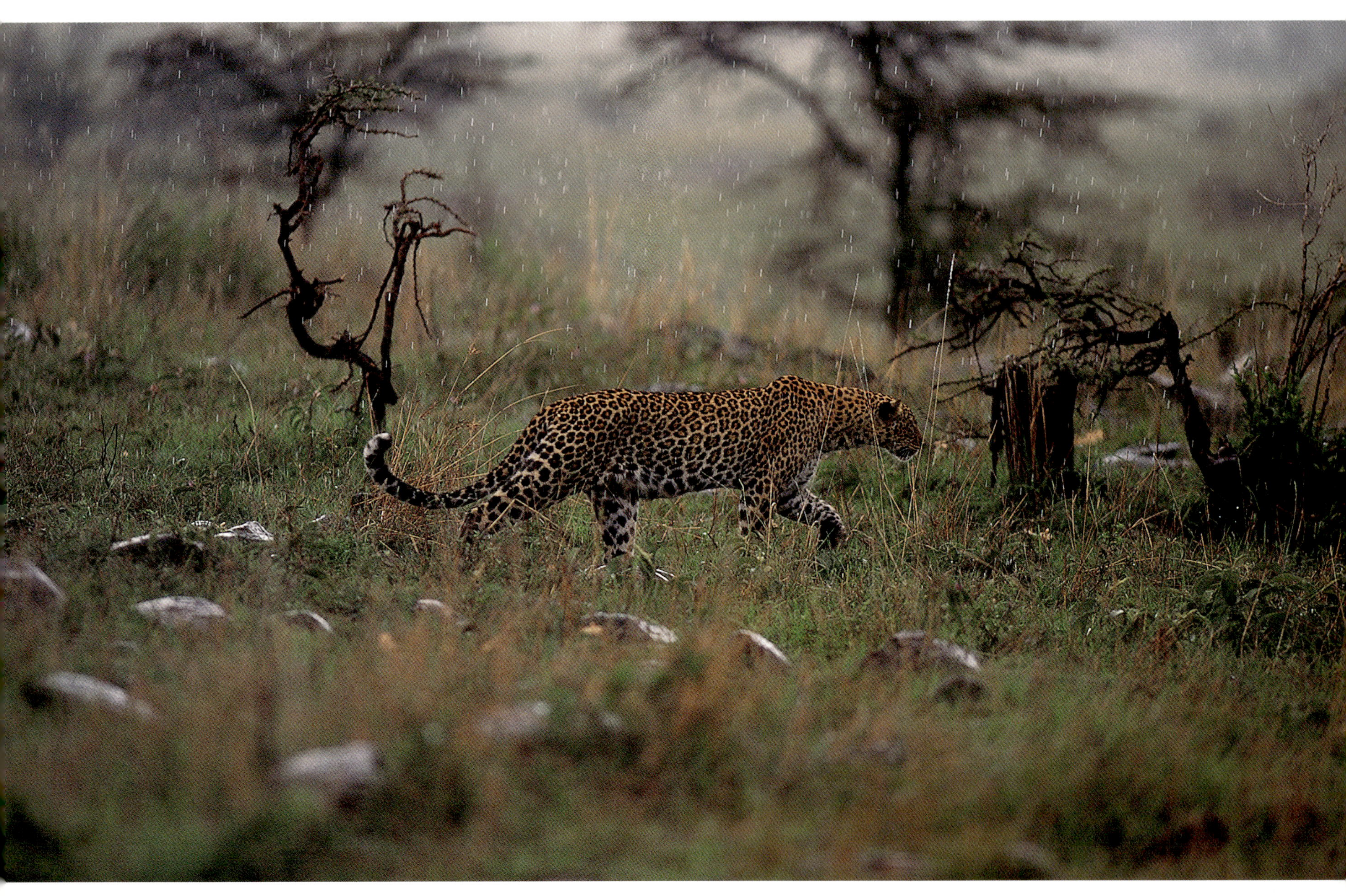

As soon as it started to rain, this leopard went on a hunting prowl. The sound of the falling rain works to the cat's advantage as it makes it difficult for prey animals to hear its approach.

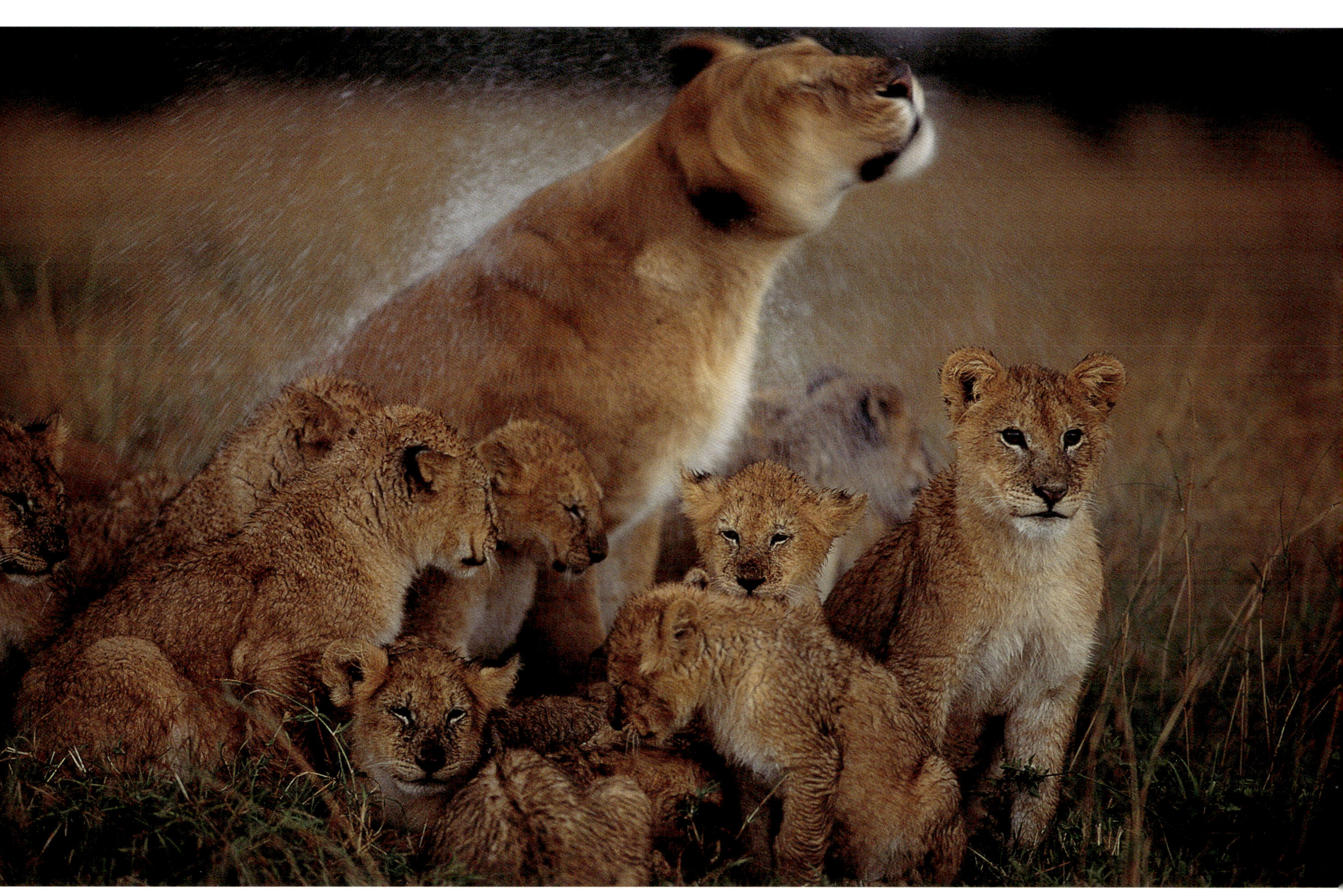

After sitting out a heavy downpour, a lioness left in charge of the pride's cubs shakes off the excess water in preparation for a move. All the cubs except one have emerged from their naps and are engaged in observing life stirring up around them. Lions spend about 18 hours of each day sleeping.

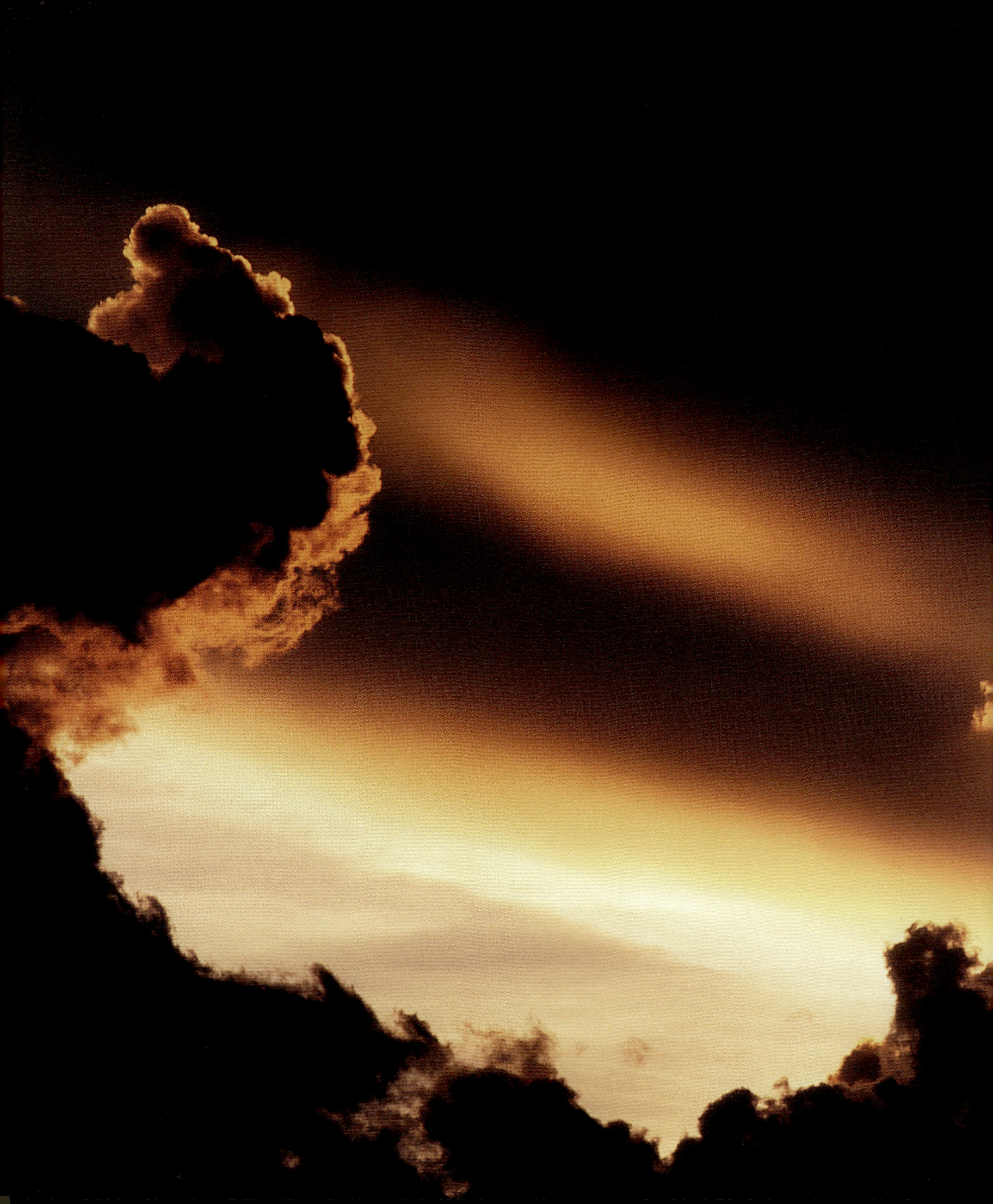

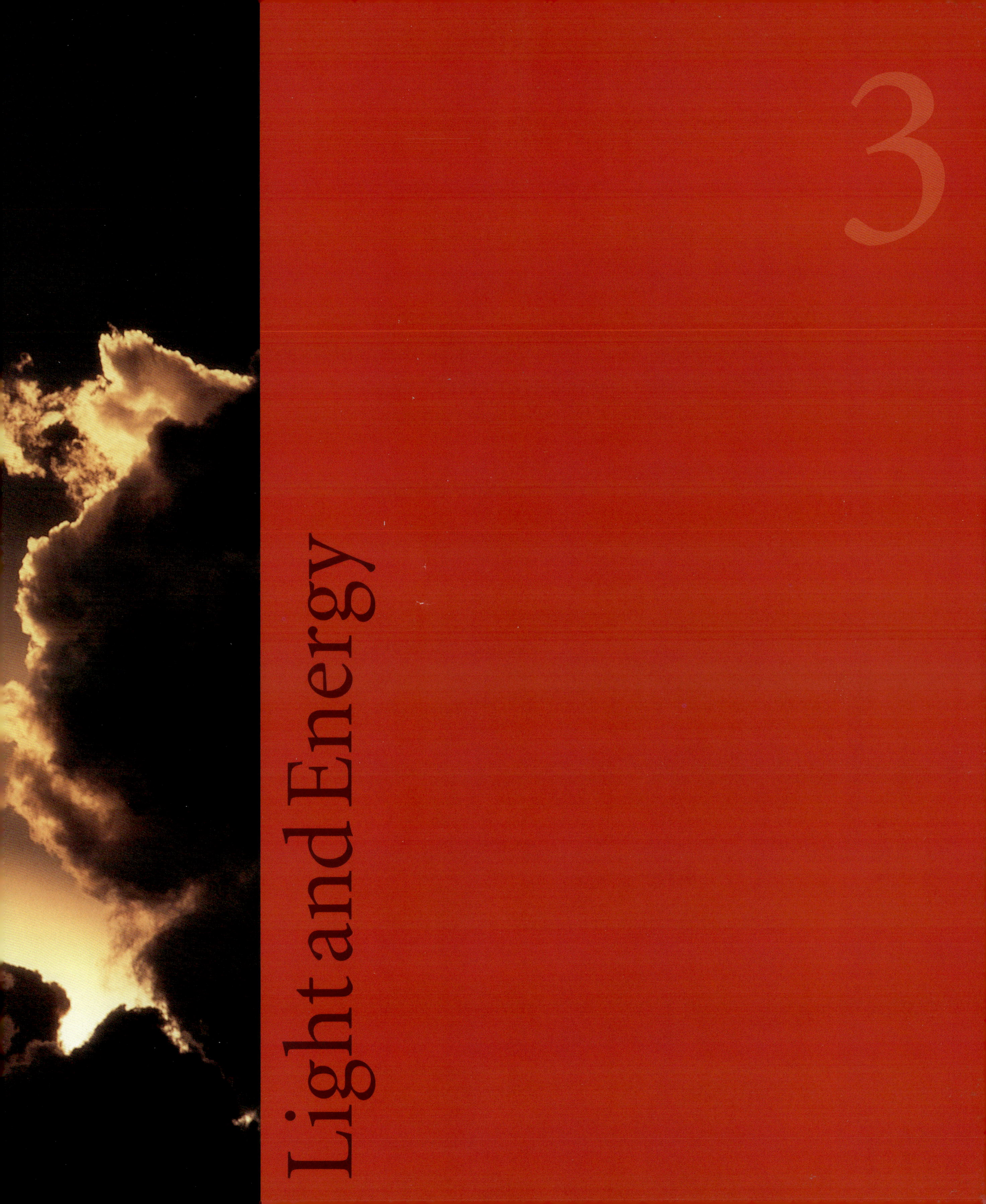
3
Light and Energy

Out on the savannah, the sun plays upon your sensibilities. At sunrise, as the magical light floods over the plains, I feel joyous, but by midday the unbearable heat takes its toll. Resting under the shade of a tree, I take the opportunity to reflect about light and heat and the fact that without the sun there would be no life. A third of the sun's energy is used up in the layer of atmosphere above us, driving the cycles of weather, but the rest filters through to power life. How? After all, no one can eat sunlight.

Enter stomatolites, algae-like microorganisms, today found living in only two locations in the world: Australia and the Bahamas. Three-and-a-half billion years ago this primitive form of life managed the trick of capturing a tiny bit of the sun's energy, a molecule of carbon dioxide, and combining them to create the fuel of its own existence. The by-product of this simple process was a minuscule amount of oxygen. Over the next two billion years, the stomatolites raised the oxygen level in the atmosphere to 20 percent, enough to allow the development of other, more complex life forms.

Today the green plants of the savannah do what the stomatolites did (and do), but they're rather more sophisticated about it. It's called photosynthesis, or "making with light." With solar energy from the sun, carbon dioxide from the air, nutrients from the soil, and chlorophyll from their own cells, the plants produce simple sugars, starch, and protein – the building blocks of the food chain. From here on, the sun's energy percolates through the entire pyramid of life. Plants form the base of that pyramid, and the plant eaters such as elephants, buffaloes, zebras, antelopes, and primates, are on the next level up. Animals that feed on the plant-eaters – the big cats, eagles, snakes – are the third step up the pyramid. And since the savannah has a great quantity and a large variety of plants, particularly grasses, there is plenty of food available for all.

This simple image of the pyramid is not quite so linear in reality. Some large predators feed not only on plant-eaters but also on small carnivores. Leopards will kill and eat impalas as well as jackals. Hyenas will feed on wildebeest as well as cubs of the big cats. An eagle will catch a snake, which feeds on lizards, which feed on grasshoppers, which feed on plants. And so it goes.

All plants and animals that die are food for the scavengers. Termites and earthworms clean up dead vegetation while vultures, marabou storks, tawny eagles, hyenas, and jackals take carrion. Animal waste is carried off by dung beetles and maggots. Finally, the decomposers – bacteria and fungi – get to work on the leftovers.

Solar energy is central in this food chain as material in the savannah passes from plants to grazers and browsers, and thence to carnivores, and from there to the scavengers and decomposers. But the sun exacts a price. Once rain has fallen, the amount ultimately available to plants is largely dictated by the sun, for its intense heat evaporates nearly 80 percent of the rainfall. What a delicate balance exists between sun

Pages 34–35
Solar energy filters through layers of atmosphere before reaching the earth where it drives the cycle of life.

and savannah! And here's one more thought to ponder: If the temperature in the sun's furnace were to be turned up slightly, by no more than 0.1 percent, the savannah would become a barren and bleak desert within a mere few hundred years.

It is with these sobering thoughts about our precarious hold on earth and a sense of vulnerability that I watch the sun descend. The evening light is diamond bright and so clear as it kisses the plains that I feel heady with its beauty. As the light starts to fade, and the shadows lengthen, I gun the engine and head for camp in a thoughtful frame of mind.

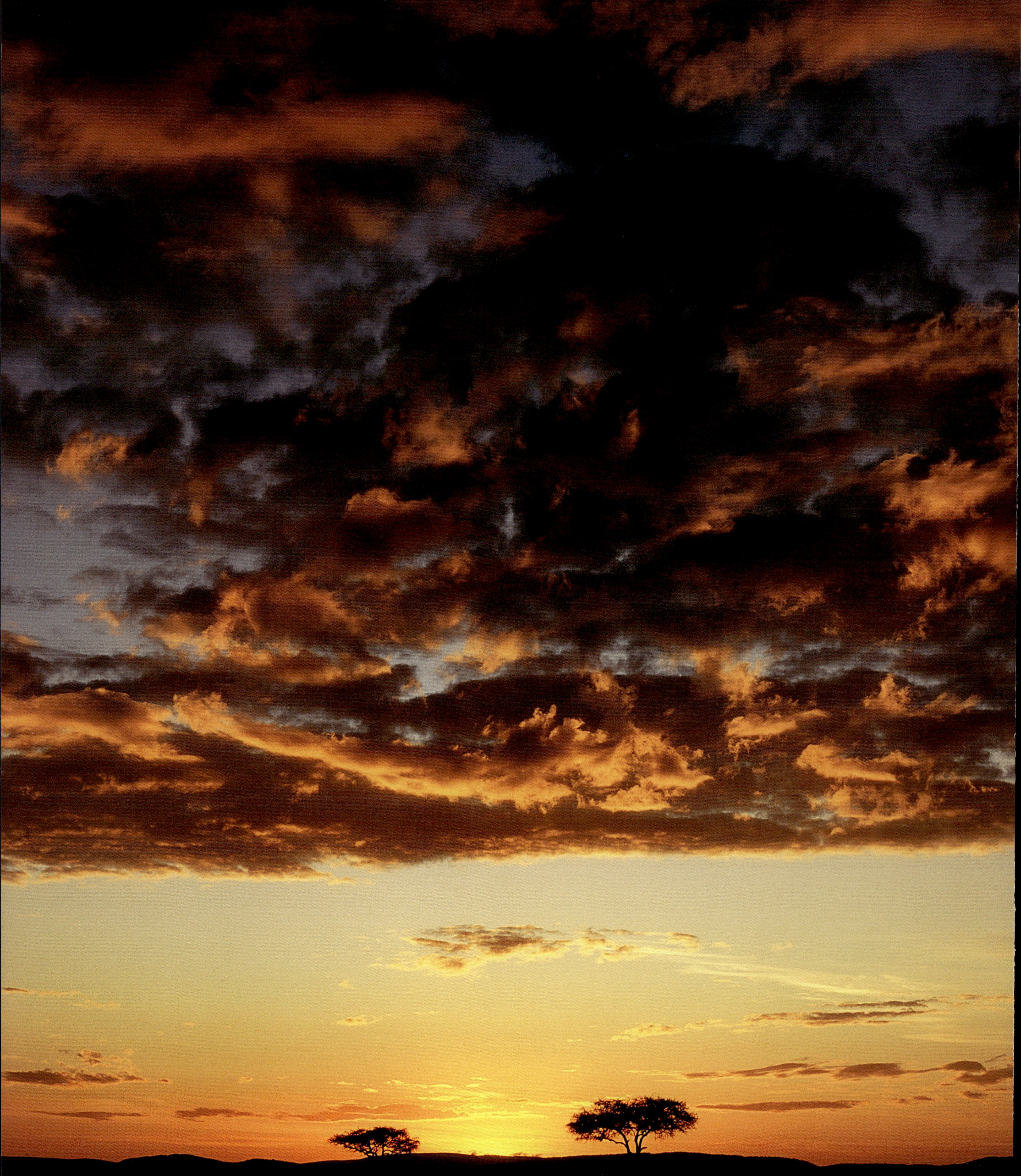

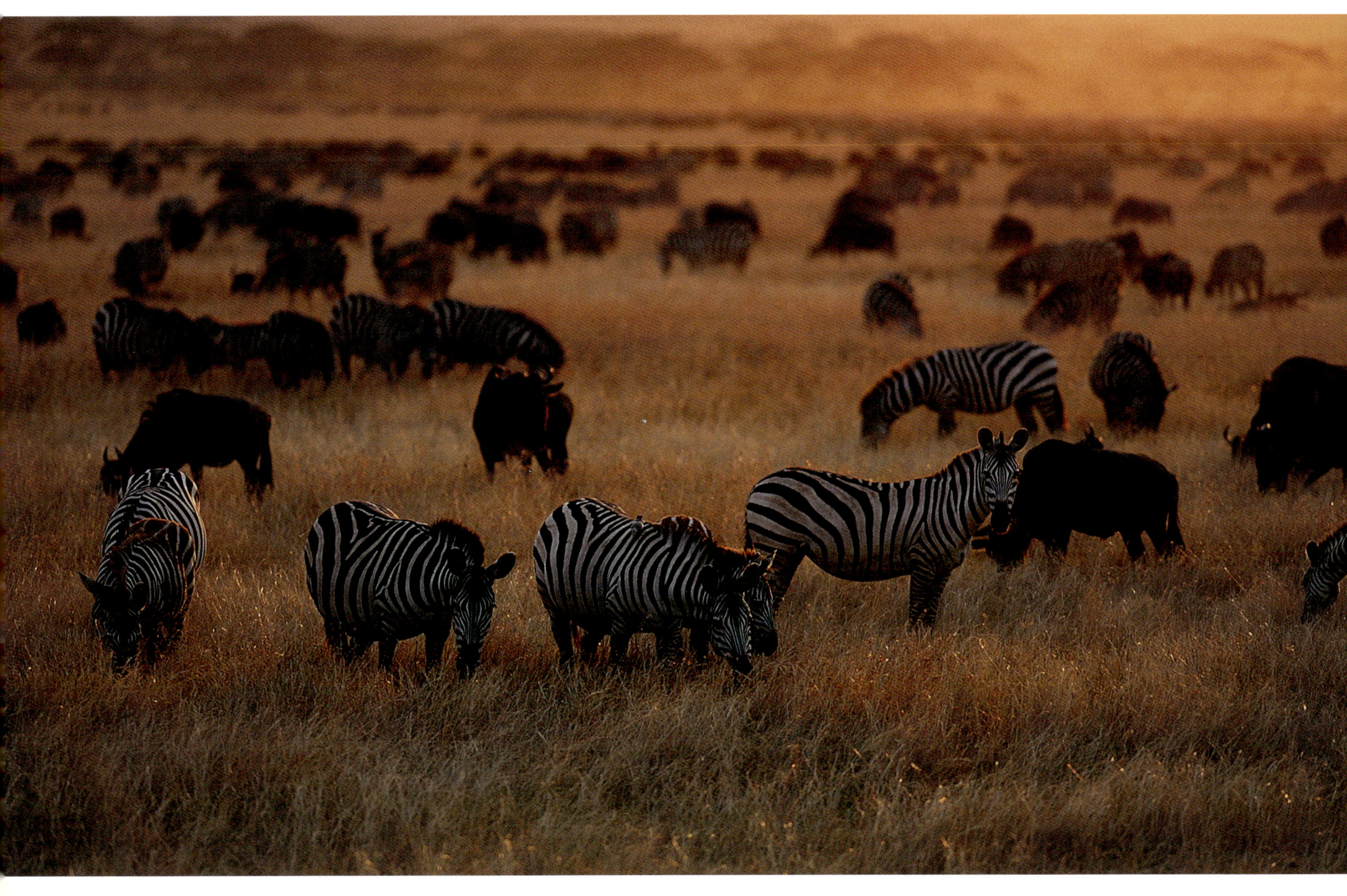

Entirely dependent on grass for survival, a mixed herd of zebras and wildebeests tuck in during the twilight hours.

Pages 40–41
A Maasai giraffe bull browses on leaves that, through photosynthesis, convert solar energy into the building blocks of life.

Opposite
The sunlight at dawn is particularly appealing as it adds a glowing orange halo to everything caught in its rays.

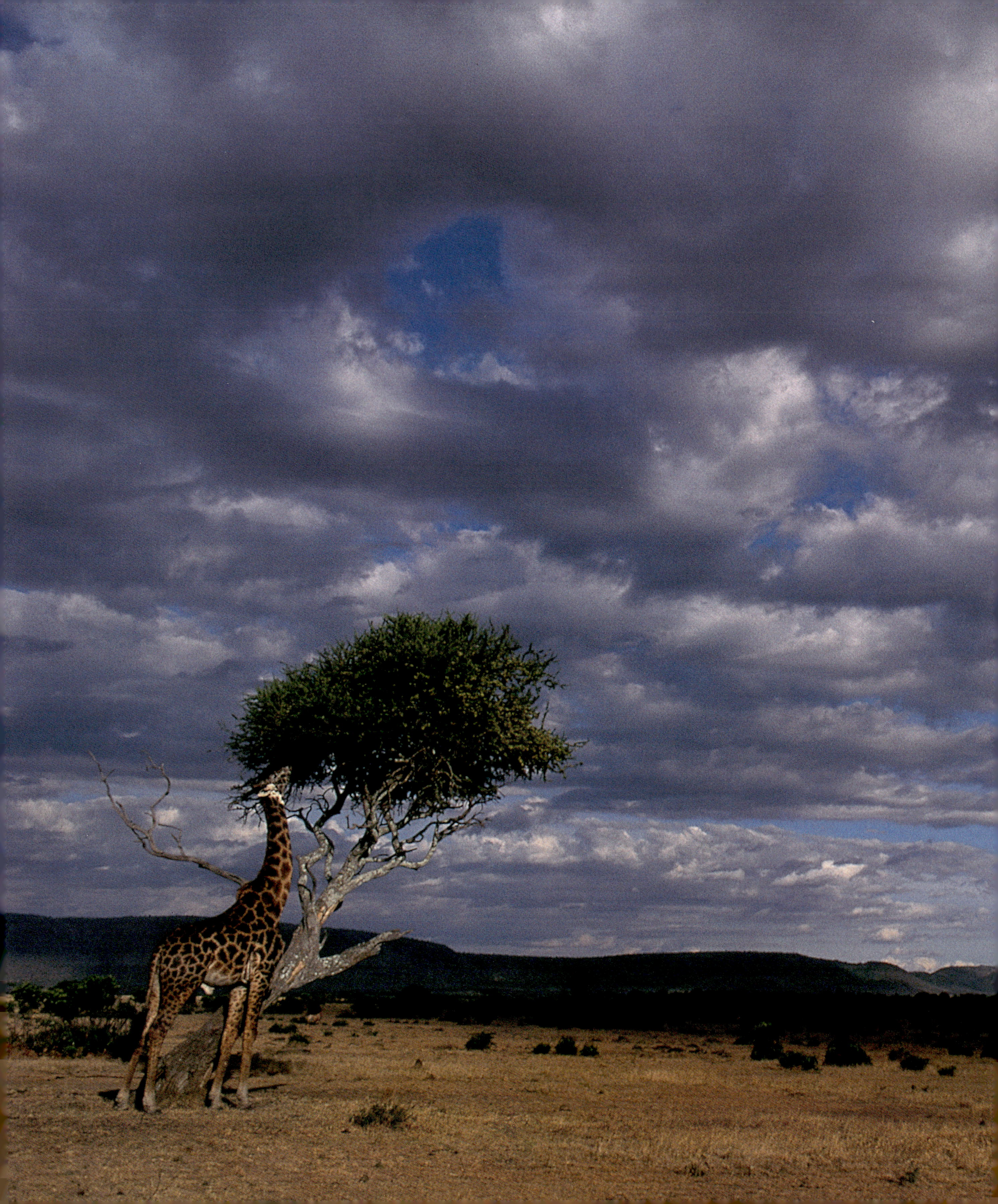

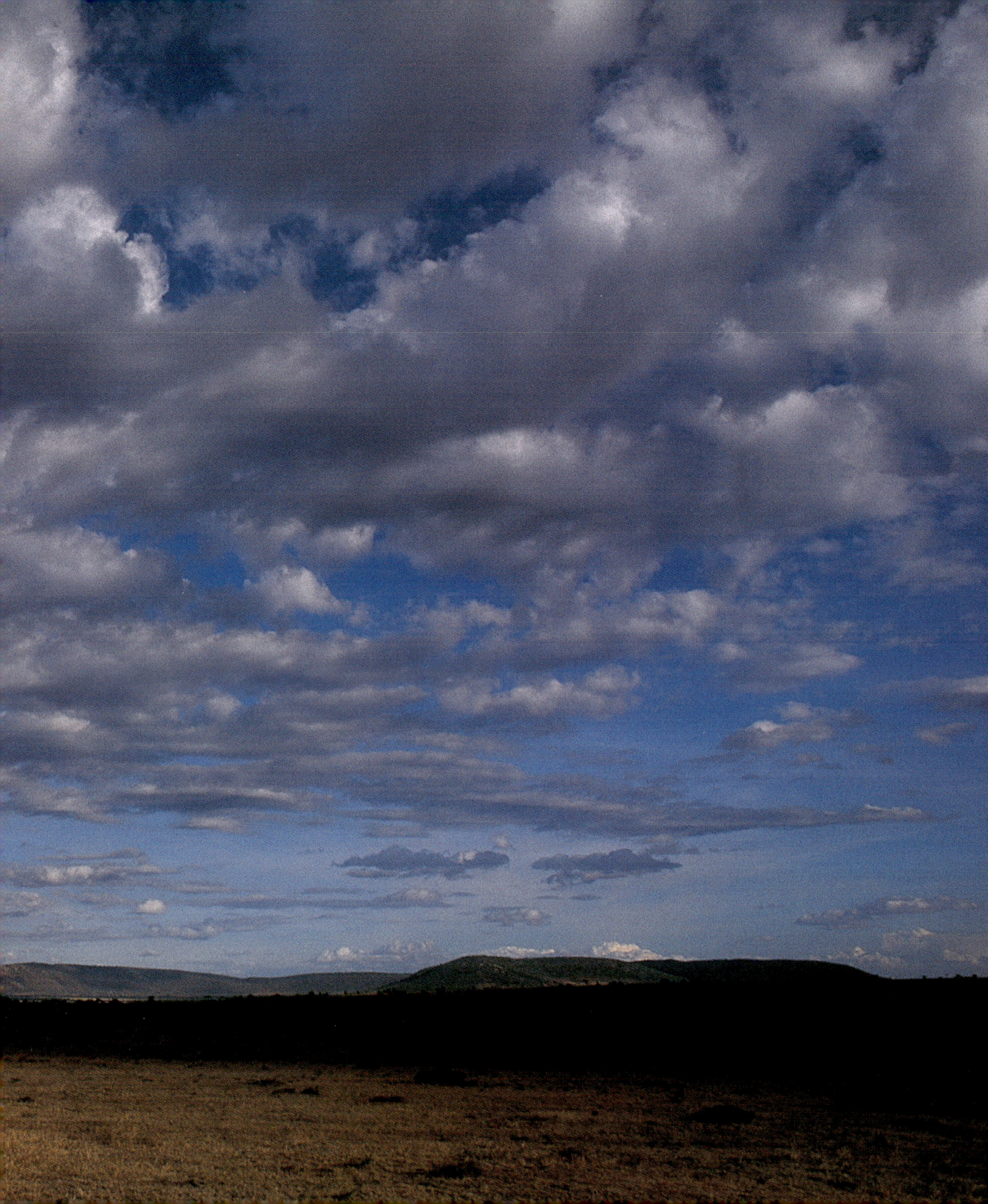

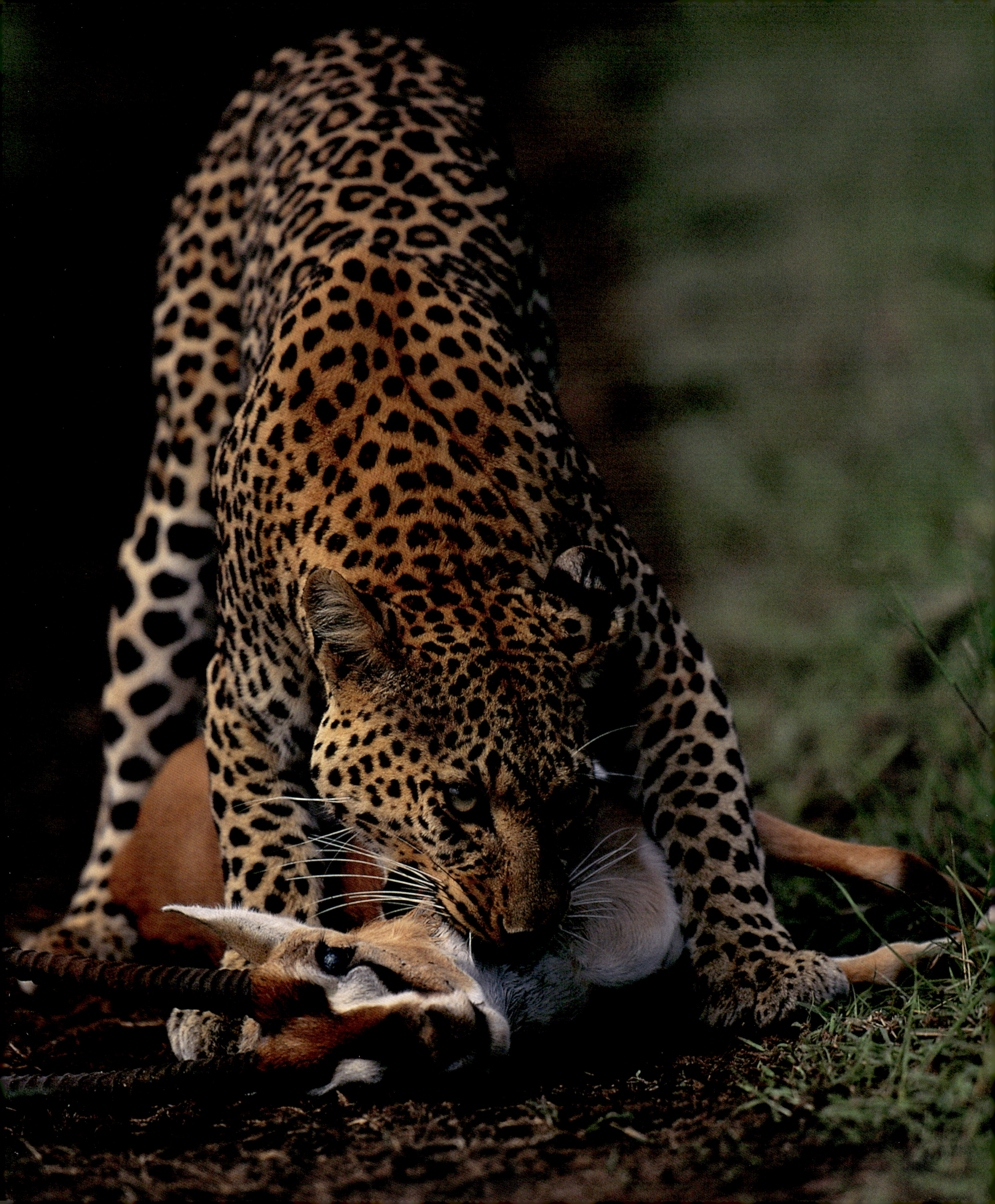

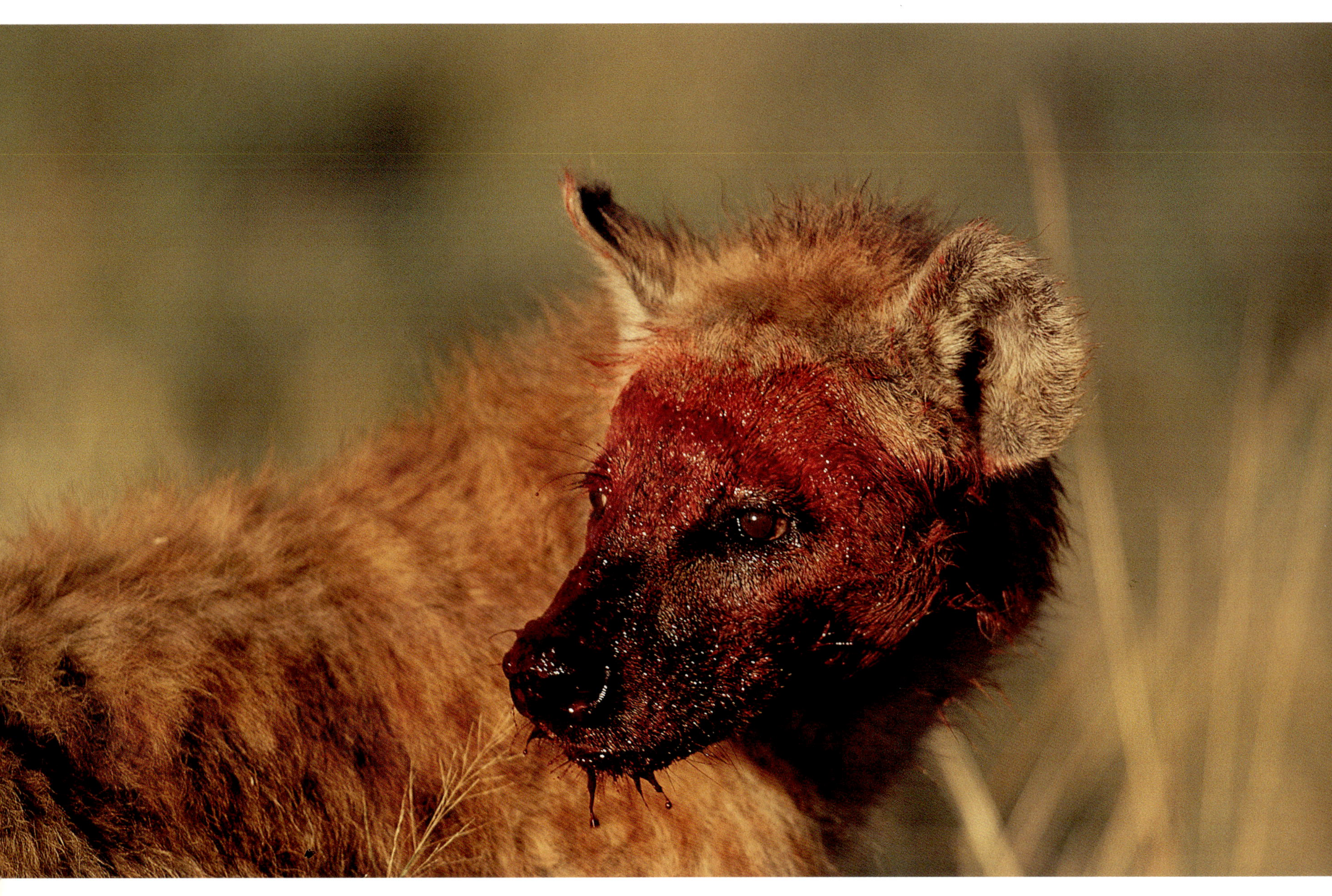

Purely out of habit, a spotted hyena interrupts its meal of wildebeest flesh to quickly scan its surroundings for possible danger. This versatile carnivore can digest all parts of a herbivore carcass except the horns, hooves, and teeth.

Opposite
A female leopard pauses while dragging a heavy male Thomson's gazelle kill to a secluded location. She will benefit from the rich concentration of protein that has developed in the flesh of the gazelle as a result of its diet of low-protein grass.

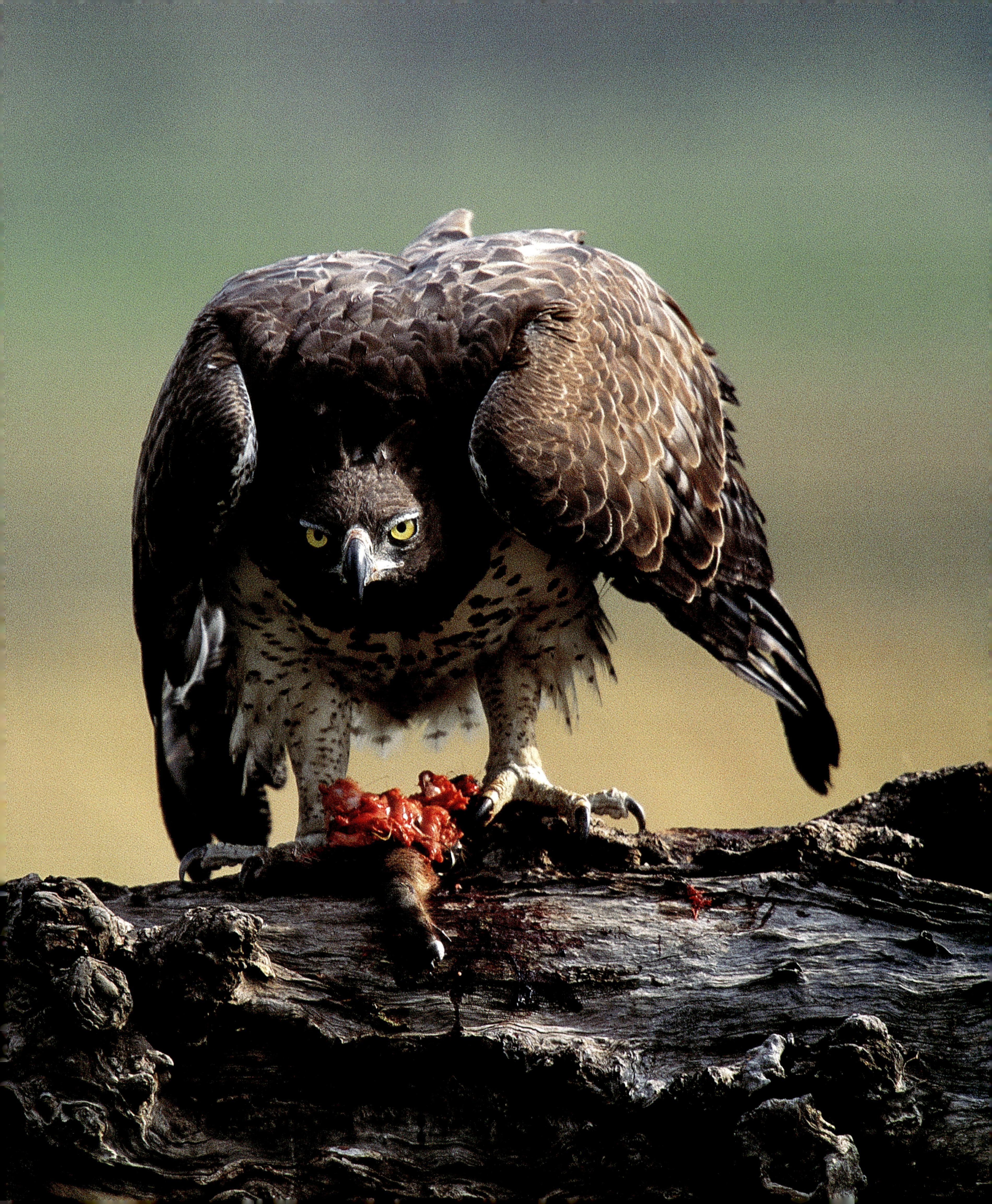

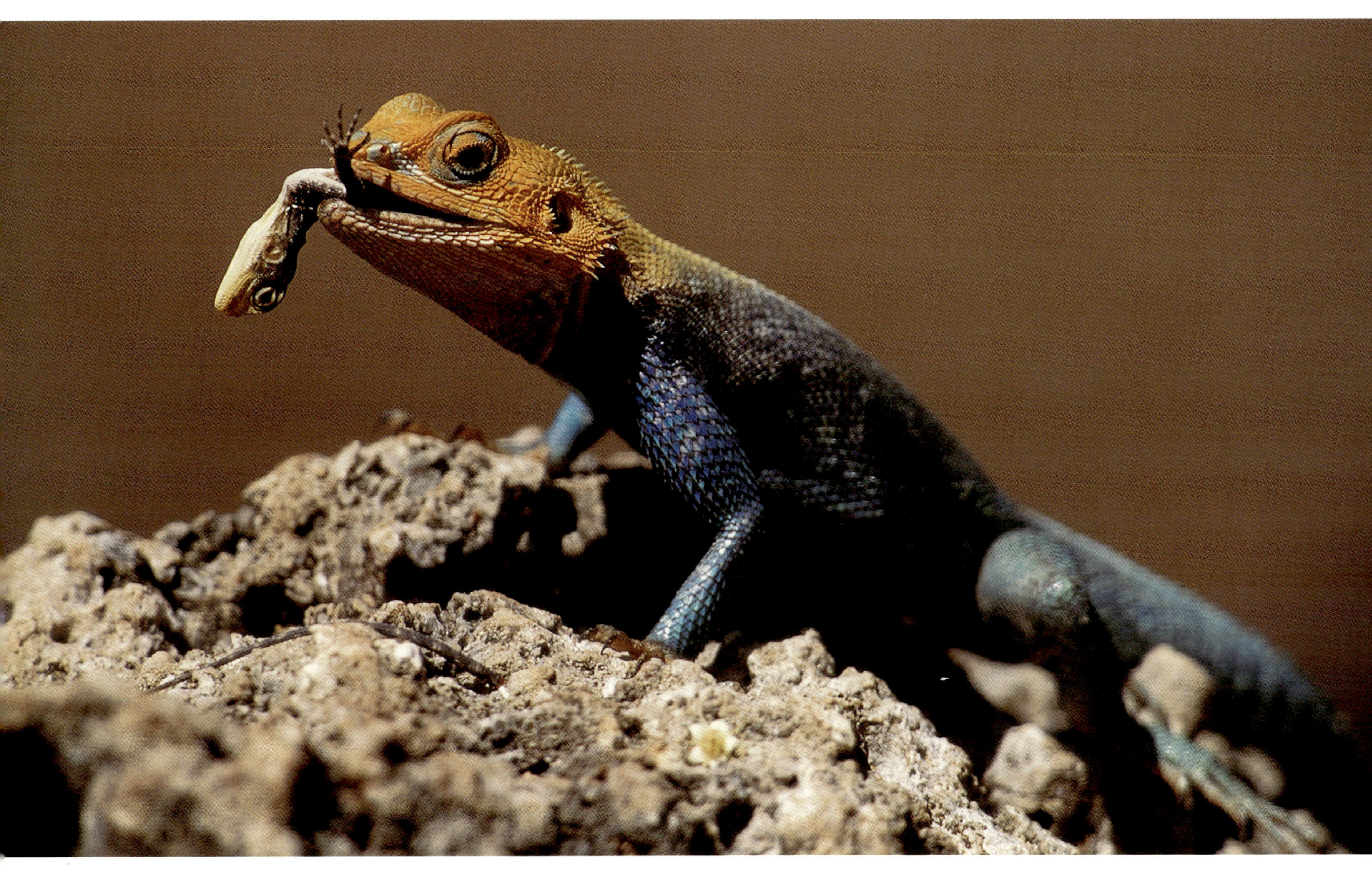

A male agama lizard devours the baby of another agama.

Opposite
This martial eagle managed to catch a gazelle fawn. After feeding on it for a while on the ground, the eagle carried the carcass up onto a fallen tree trunk to resume feeding. Perhaps it had sensed that there would be competition for the meat.

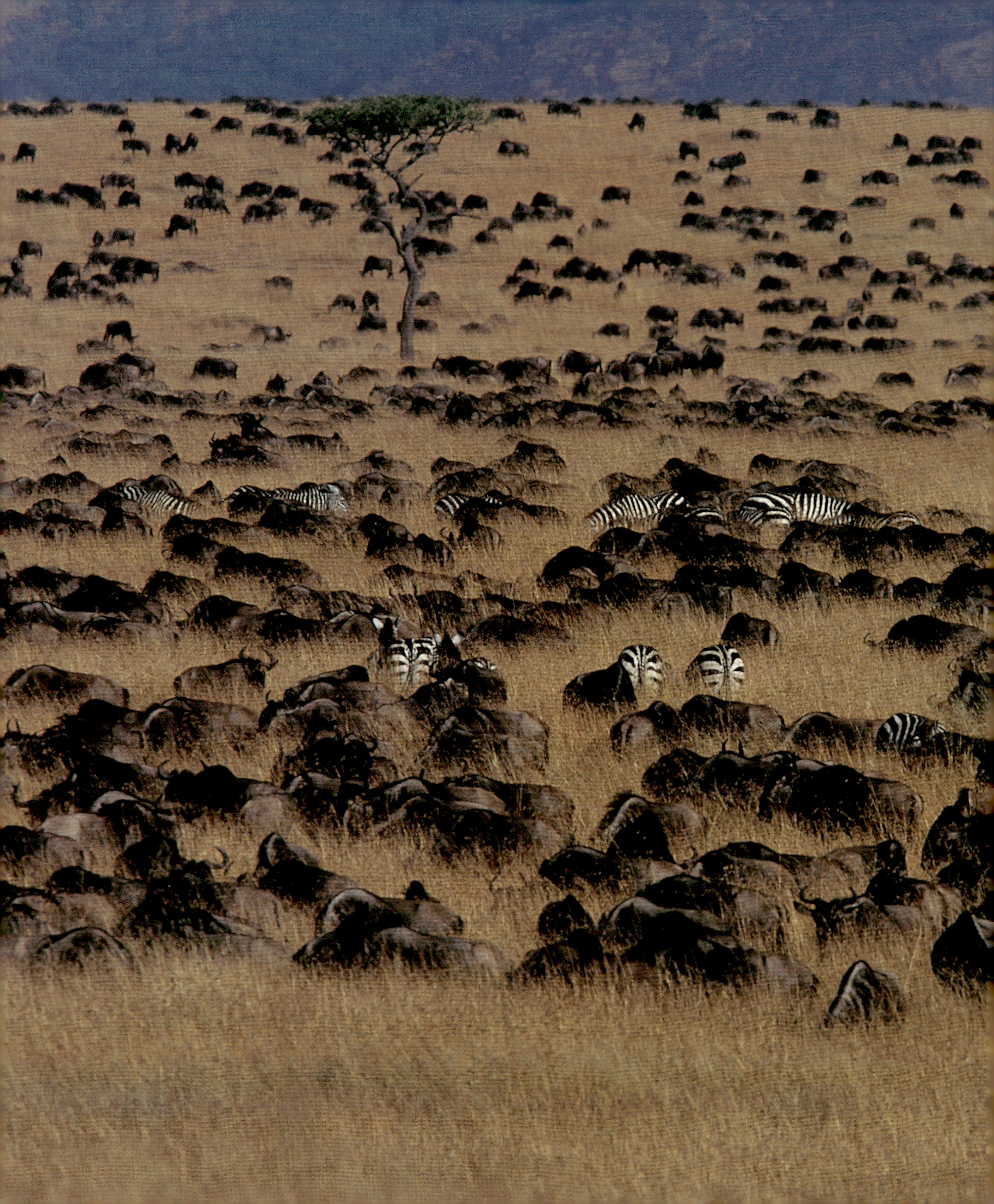

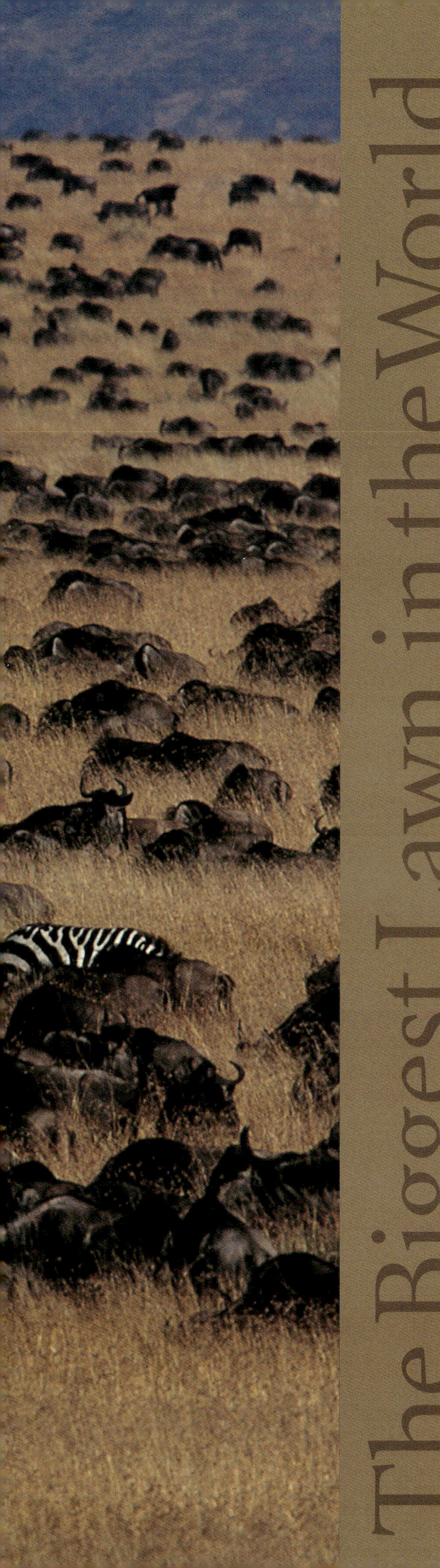

4

The Biggest Lawn in the World

It is an eerie experience as you drive through the short grass plains of the Serengeti and slowly come to the realization that the world is a mighty big place. Initially, the sense of space and the feeling that you could drive on and on and never come to the end of this landscape is utterly intoxicating. It's like being at sea, except for the smell of grass in the wind. But there comes a point in your journey when you have to get out of the car and place your feet on the earth. The ground feels reassuringly solid. Turn yourself in a 360-degree circle and you see only grass meeting the sky at the edge of the world. It makes you feel small and insignificant, like a drop in the ocean.

However, the African savannah is not all short grass plains. The savannah comes in different shapes and sizes, and its character varies greatly according to the presence and distribution of bushes and trees. It helps conceptually to distinguish three types of savannah, although in reality they tend to merge into one another. First, there are the nearly treeless short-grass plains, where you can drive for miles and hardly see a single tree. Then there is the wooded savannah where trees, particularly flat-topped acacias, relieve the monotony of the rolling plains; this is the image of the savannah that most people are familiar with. Last, there is the bush savannah where more bushes than trees grow, but where grasses still continue to dominate. Superimposed on these various landscapes are the meandering rivers, the banks of which are often lined with yellow-barked acacias, bush, or even forest.

Once out of the car, you want to see and feel everything, to explore, and to contemplate. And grass is everywhere. There's no end to it. Grass is actually a newcomer to planet earth, first appearing about 25 million years ago, roughly the same time when monkeys became distinct from apes. Grass can thrive in a climate of pronounced wet and dry seasons as long as rainfall in the wet season is at least 20 to 30 inches in most years. Occasional thunder showers during the dry season are an added bonus. Although there are many different species of grass in the savannah, it is convenient to group them into two primary categories: annuals, which grow fast, form abundant seeds, and die in one short season; and perennials, which have ways of surviving the long dry season, such as fibrous roots that can penetrate deep if soil conditions permit, and some even have runners, a special type of root on the stem, in which "food" can be stored.

Grasses are extremely hardy plants. Fires, both natural and man-made, occur often in the dry season, but grasses manage to survive even when all surface growth has been burned away. Their underground portions, protected from the fire, lie ready to sprout when the rains return. Grasses can also cope with the constant trampling and grazing of large herbivores or plant-eating animals. The short grass plain of the Serengeti is a lawn really, grazed, trampled and cut by thousands of hooves. But unlike many other plants, growth occurs mainly at the base so that even when most of the leaf above ground is eaten or

Pages 46–47
The landscape of the Serengeti–Maasai Mara plains is a study in contrasts over time: when the grazing is good, the mixed herds break up the monotony of grass; when the grazing is done, the land appears barren.

destroyed, the part that is left behind continues to grow. What is more, saliva deposited by the grazing animals contains a substance that actually stimulates growth.

Now, as you drive along, you're bound to spot a *kopje,* a granite island in a sea of grass. It is tempting to get out of your tin box on wheels and climb this intrusion poking through the surface of the plain, yet these intrusions dot the landscape at fairly regular intervals. Sun, wind, and rain have sculpted each of these ancient remnants into an intricate network of slopes, cracks, and crevices. These isolated islands have ecosystems and climates that are totally independent from the surrounding plains. There are even species that live among the rocks of kopjes and nowhere else.

It is impossible to resist climbing to the highest point, savoring the immense views as you go, searching for an inviting place to sit. And wonder. Was the wilderness always like this? Why has it hardly changed during the course of human history, some two million years? How is it possible for so many species of plants and animals to live side by side? According to ecologists, the answer has to do with the wide diversity of life forms living in mixed neighborhoods. It's amazing to think that far from leading to confusion, this very diversity may be the reason for community stability.

Slowly and somewhat reluctantly you bring yourself back from your reverie and find yourself perched atop this kopje in the middle of a vast open space. Then the African night descends rather suddenly and your destination is many miles away, just over the horizon. It is time to head back.

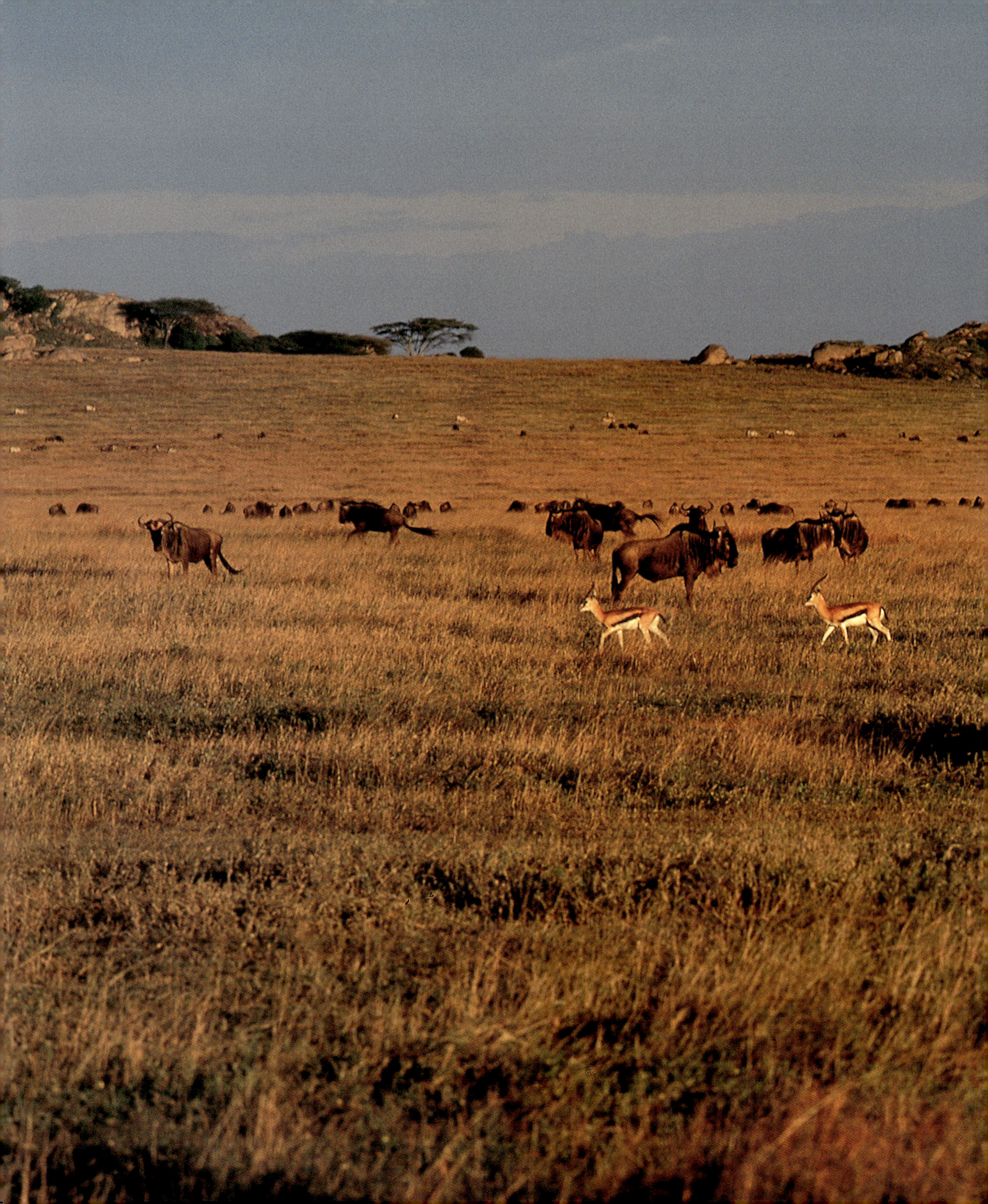

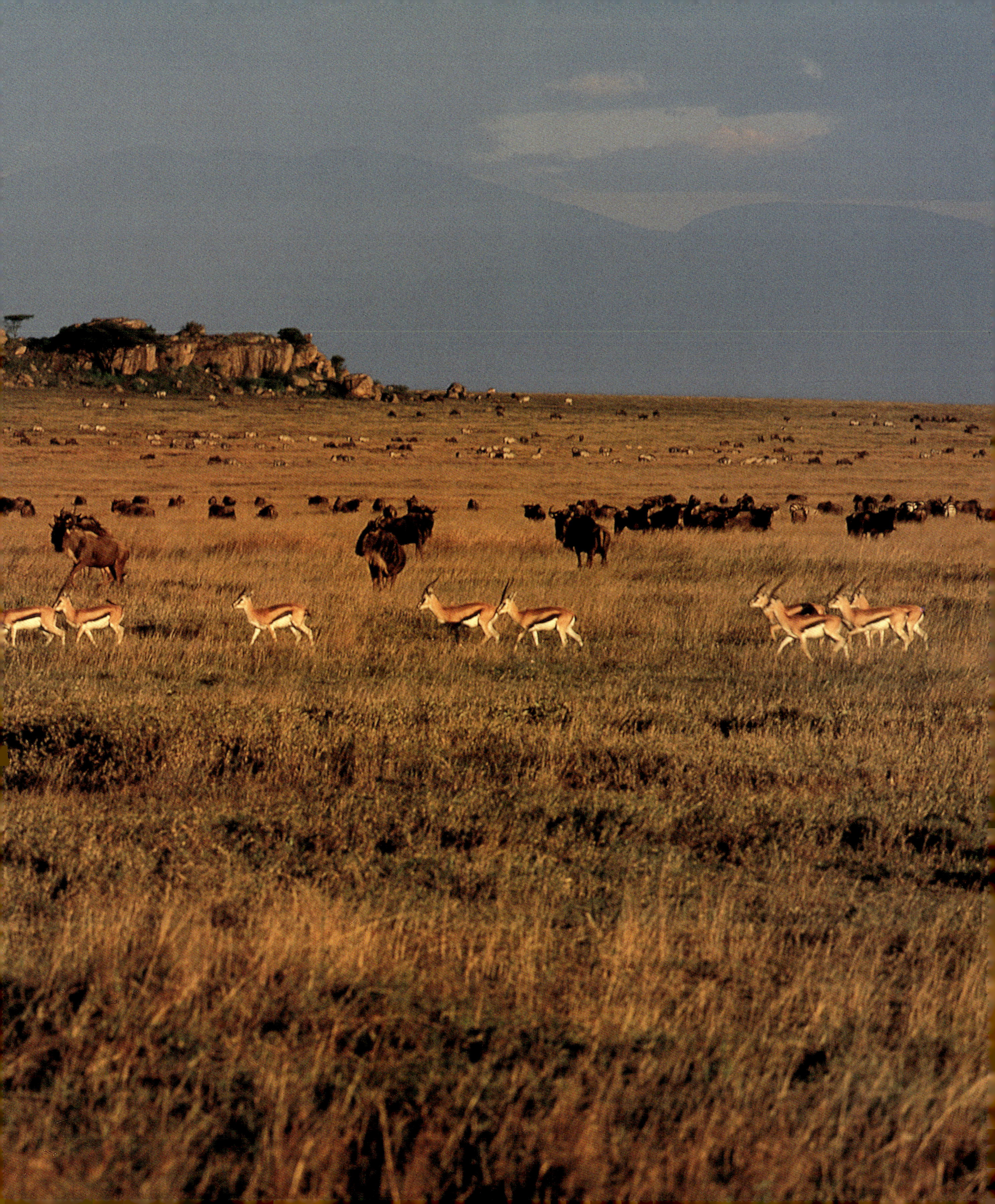

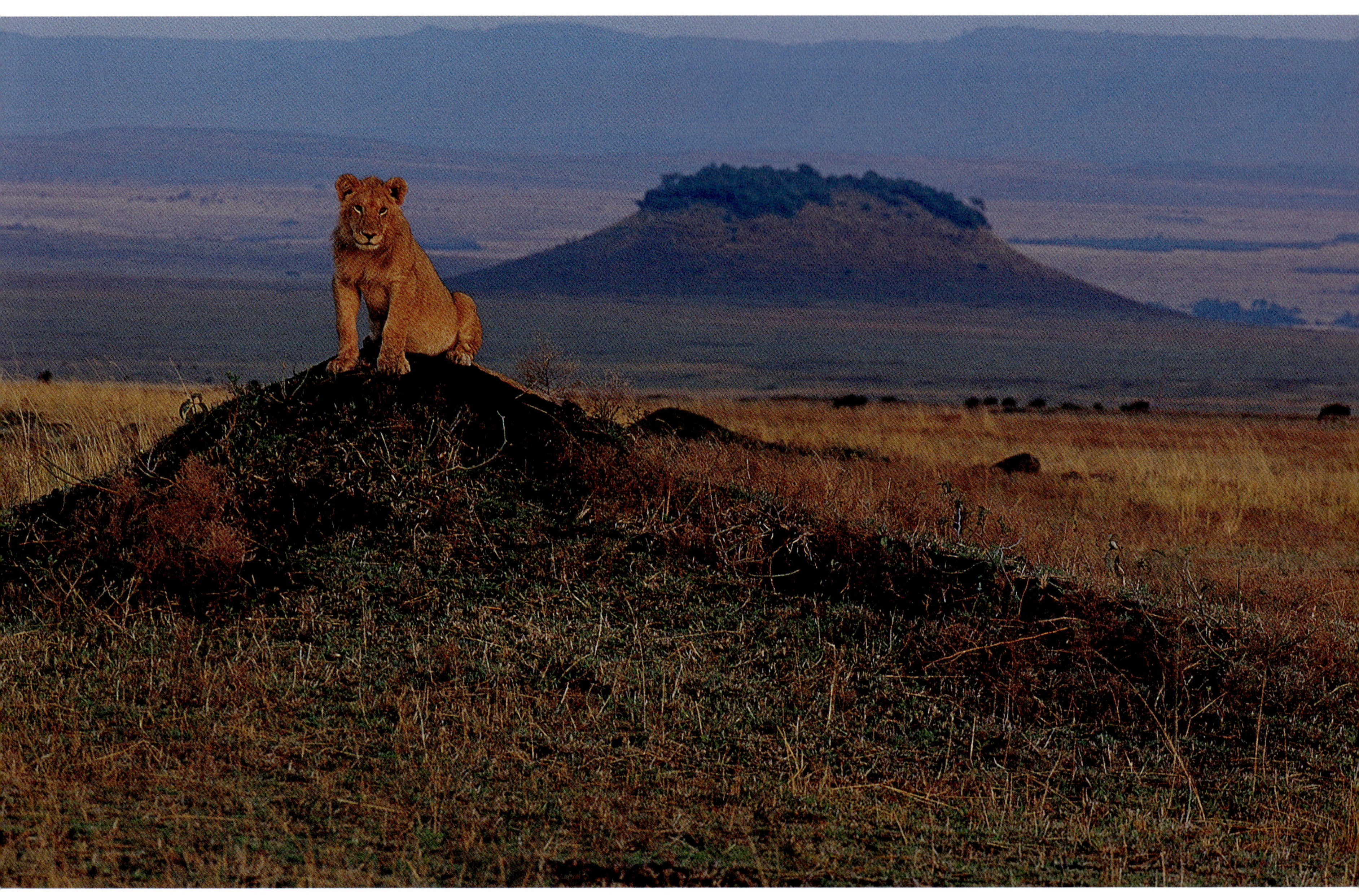

A lion cub surveys the land from a mound in Maasai Mara. Here you often come across open grasslands punctuated by small hills rising and falling like waves.

Pages 50–51
A typical scene as evening approaches in the Serengeti: Against the backdrop of a kopje, a variety of grazing animals feed on the grass at their hooves while others walk to greener pastures.

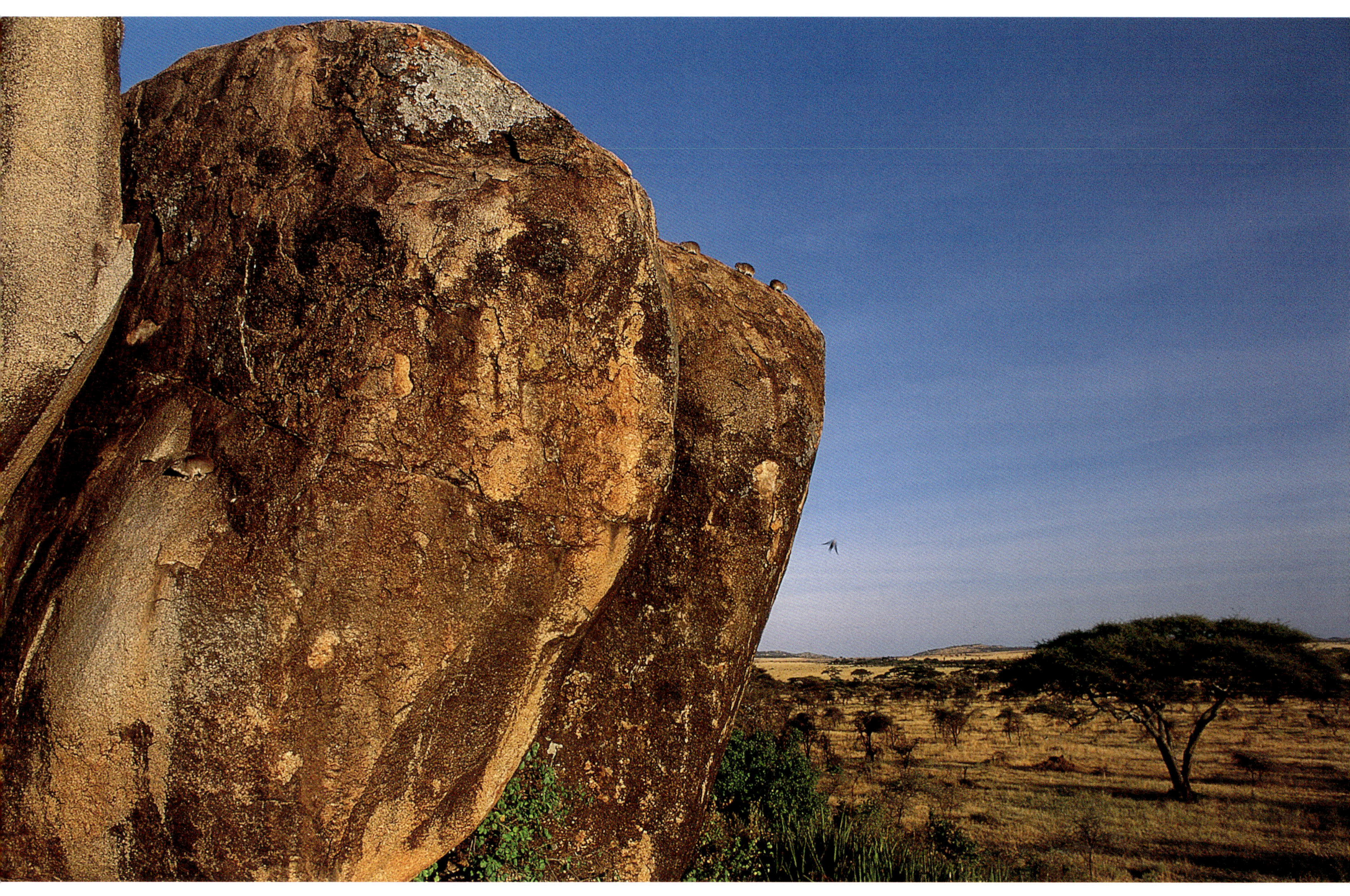

Rock hyraxes look out onto the grasslands from their kopje, where they will live out their entire lives.

Pages 54–55
Driving in the Serengeti short-grass plains, the vastness of the savannah is almost overwhelming, but it becomes even more encompassing when you climb atop a kopje and gaze out to the farthest horizon.

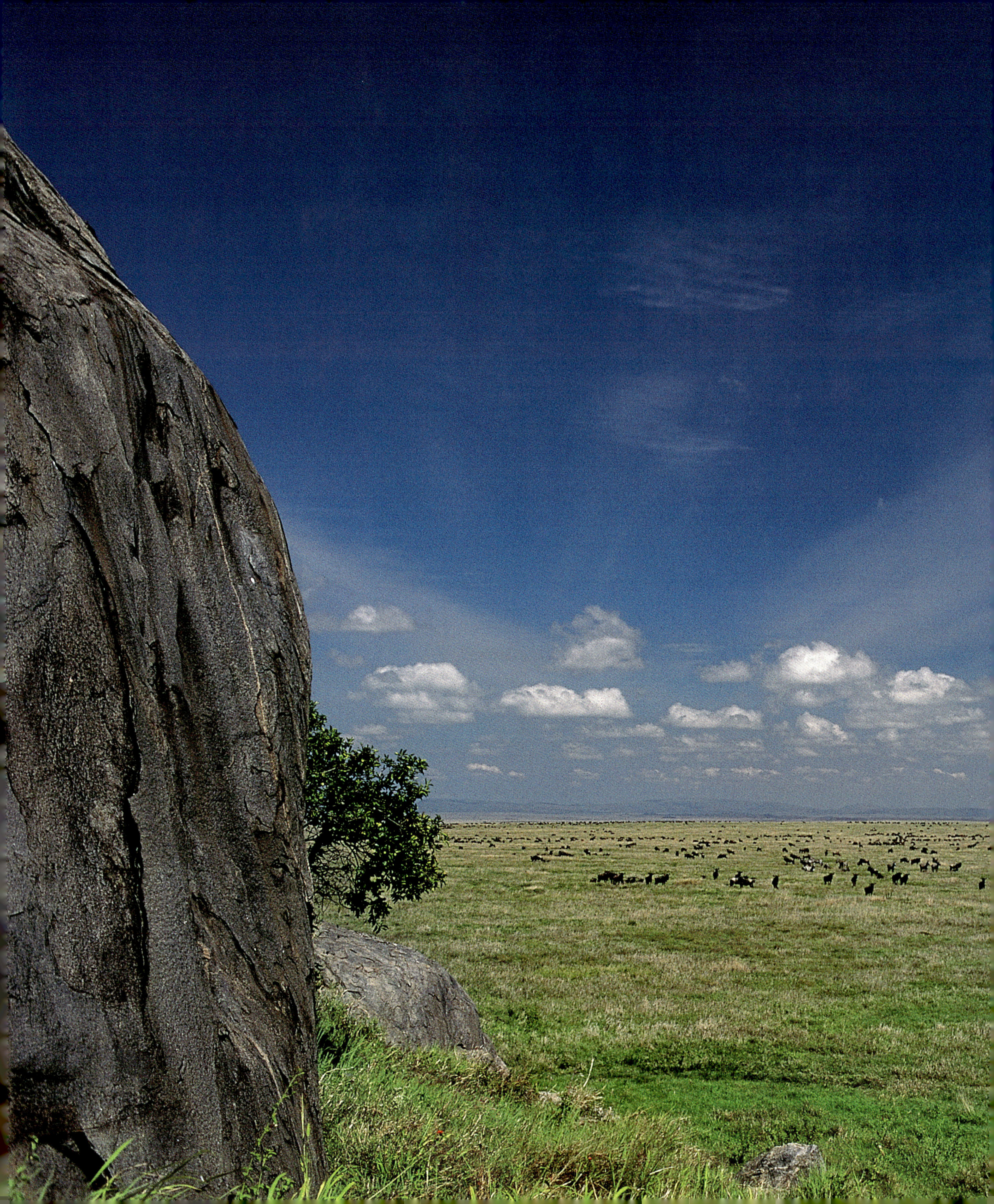

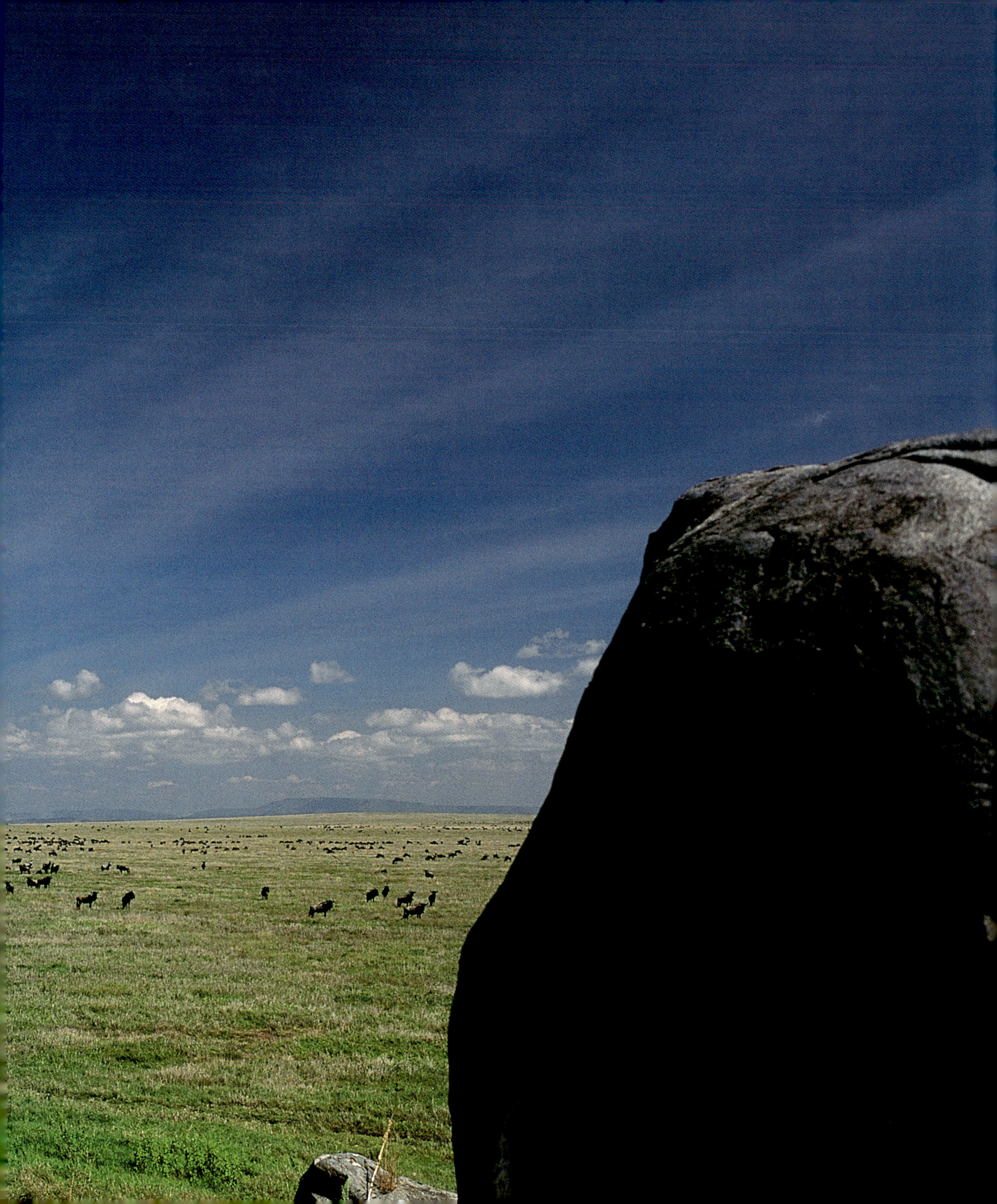

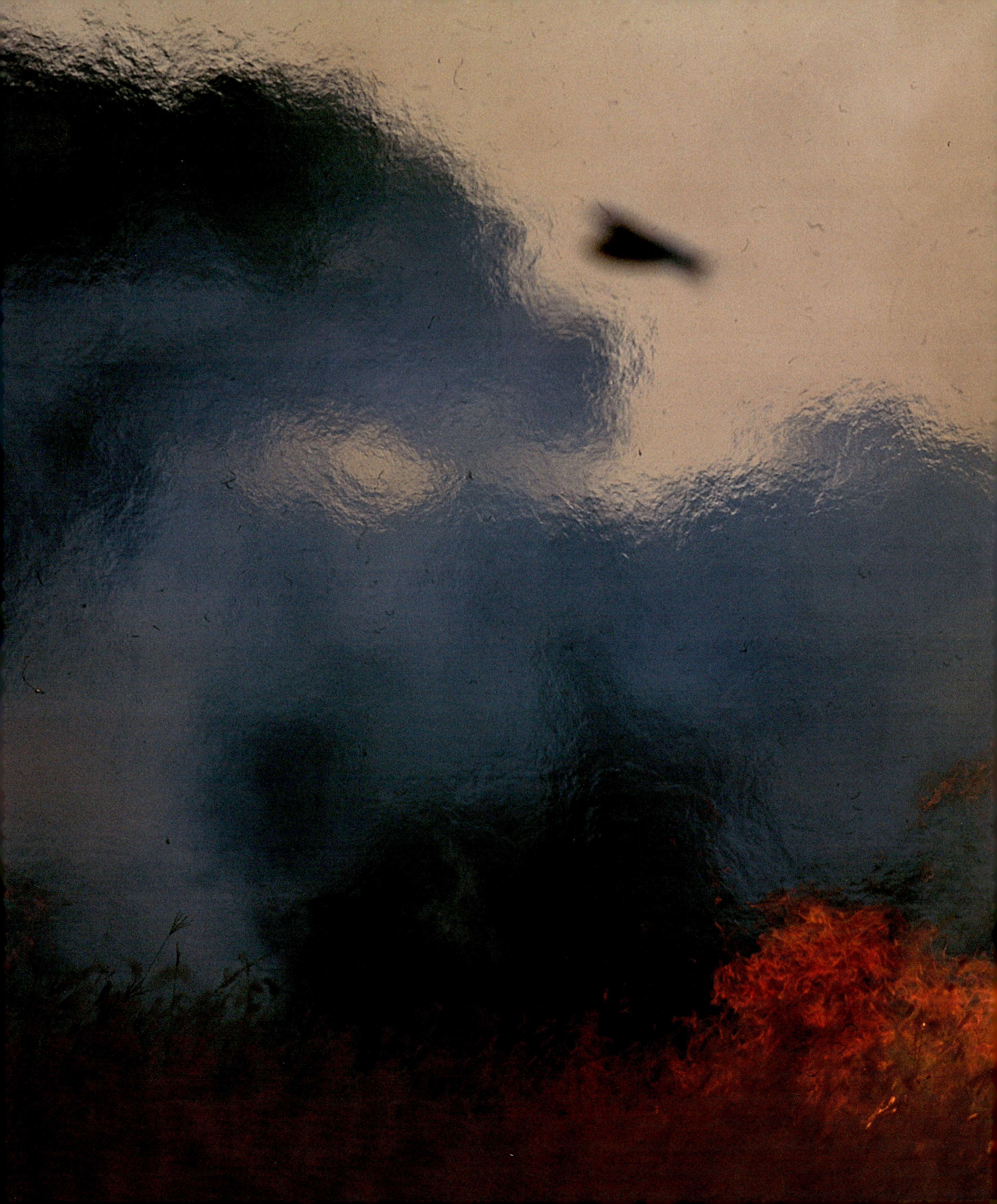

5

Shaped by Fire and Elephants

Driving back to camp one cloudless evening, we were expecting a spectacular sunset – we were not disappointed. It was July, the month of dry, or hot, burns as the fires that occur then are called, and the smoke trailing up to the skies helped make for a dazzlingly colorful sunset. Besides sunset extravaganzas, fires have an important modifying effect on the savannah, as very large chunks of it go up in smoke every year. A large hot burn can kill mature trees over a wide area and also suppress the growth of tree seedlings. But like grass, a few tree species have adapted to withstand burning by acquiring a thick bark that's virtually fireproof, and, in the case of some acacia species, the roots have also thickened.

While it can be said that grasslands are maintained by fires – they allow new growth, soil becomes more fertile – some have shrunk as shrubs that have adapted to resist fire have crept in. Therefore, the overall net effect of fires, good or bad, is difficult to assign. One thing is certain: when fires sweep across the plains, they can be lethal for the animals.

The feeding behavior of elephants is another significant landscape modifier. They break branches, rip off the bark of trees, push whole trees over, and pull out saplings, roots, and tufts of grass, among other things. A big bull can consume up to 60 pounds of vegetation daily. A large number of elephants is quite capable of turning a woodland into a semi-woodland in a relatively short span of time. Sounds careless and destructive, right?

But wait a minute. There are many positive effects of feeding elephants. When they trample coarse vegetation into the ground, they enrich the soil and reduce the evaporation of moisture from it. This also allows some grasses to sprout tender shoots. When elephants knock down trees, they favor the growth of grasses, which benefits grazers. By making trails through otherwise impenetrable scrub, they open the door to new food sources for other species. Being messy eaters, they provide plenty of leftovers for small antelopes such as duikers and dikdiks, and in periods of drought they save lives by digging new wells in river beds. When they roll and wade in puddles, they seal up holes in the ground beneath, making the bottom solid as a bowl and more impervious to drying elements. A single bull excretes 40 tons of droppings per year which fertilizes the soil and provides food for dung feeders. The dung also contains the undigested seeds of plants which are widely dispersed in this way. Elephants are the only mammalian agents capable of releasing the energy locked up in wood and, via their droppings, redistributing it back into the system.

Elephants lead serene, majestic lives. When elephants are allowed to roam freely they tend to remain in balance with their environment. They do not over-graze or over-browse because they are constantly on the move looking for alternative food sources, and although they make a mess when feeding, they are efficient feeders: A two-ton elephant consumes less vegetation per day than a two-ton herd of topi. Even when elephant numbers increase, thereby reducing their food supply, their population will soon natu-

Pages 56–57
As a raging fire sweeps through brittle grass, very little can be heard above the roar of the flames. Clouds of acrid smoke pour high into the sky and scenes viewed through the immense heat waves become distorted.

rally decrease through disease, malnutrition, and starvation. Birth rates will fall, and a new equilibrium is reached between elephant numbers and their food supply. There seems little doubt that when elephants are totally free-ranging, as they had been for millions of years, they have many beneficial effects on the savannah.

Today, elephants are largely confined to national parks and national reserves. They cannot easily journey to the alternative food sources that their ancestors once freely exploited, so their numbers increase, and precious vegetation disappears. Whether this situation will correct itself remains to be seen. Wildlife management is a highly flawed science and extremely complicated, with many lives – animal, plant, and human – at stake. The next steps must be considered with extreme care. But I must admit I have my doubts about seeing this experiment through, because of the seemingly uncontrollable urge of humans to practice active wildlife management.

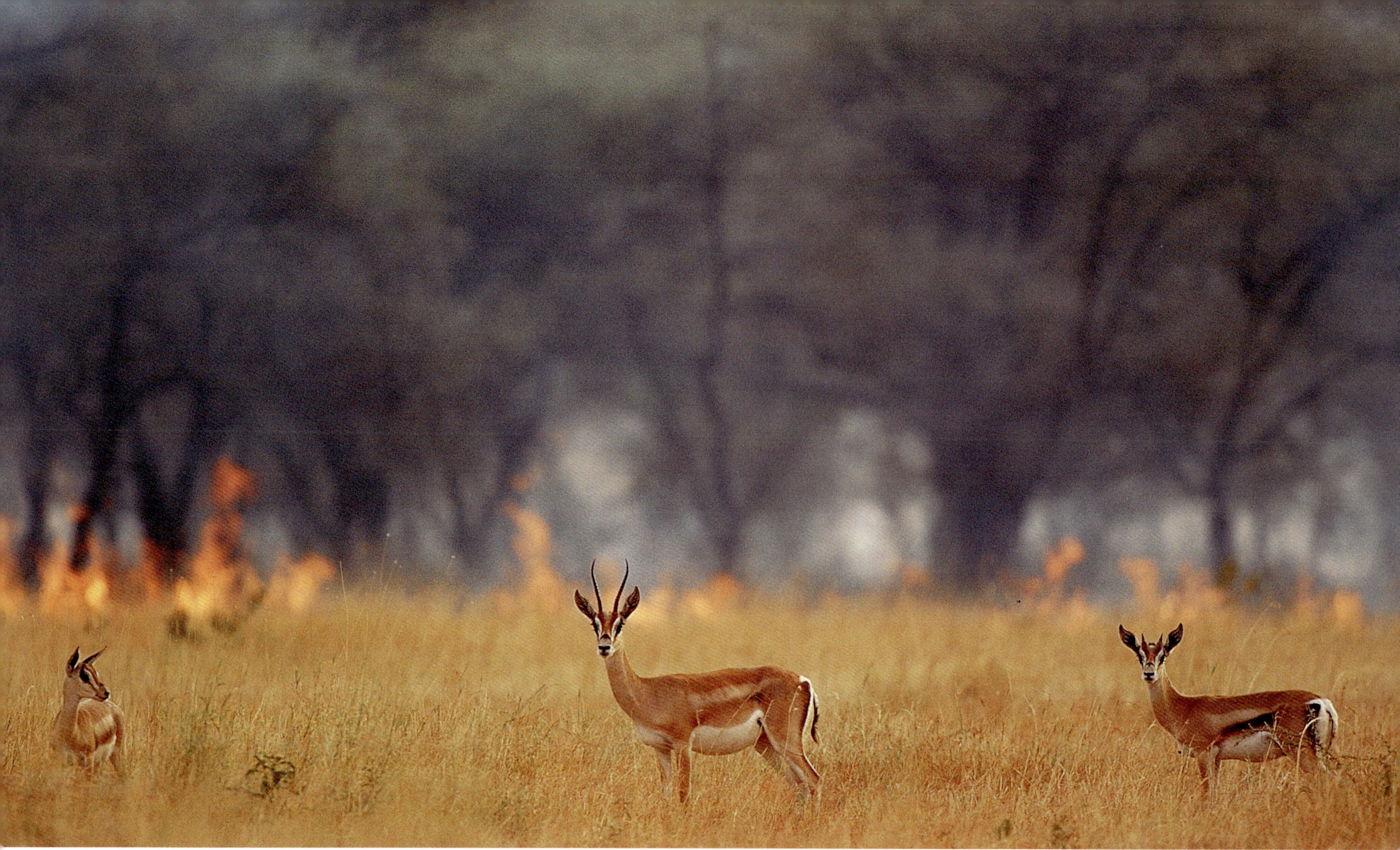

This is what's known as a hot burn. It started in the morning and spread during the day, fueled by the dry grass and unchecked in the absence of fire breaks. Herbivores like Grant's gazelles can easily escape fires due to their swiftness.

Opposite, above
Fire encourages certain grasses and suppresses woodland regeneration by destroying tree seedlings. Some tree species are fire resistant and will resume growth after a fire.

Opposite, below
Birds like this white stork, attracted by the prospect of an easy, hot meal, move slowly along in the fire's wake, jabbing at fleeing beetles and the like.

Pages 62–63
Smoke from a large grass fire rises thousands of yards, and the ash drifts half-way around the world. This is one way in which tons of material is exported from the savannah.

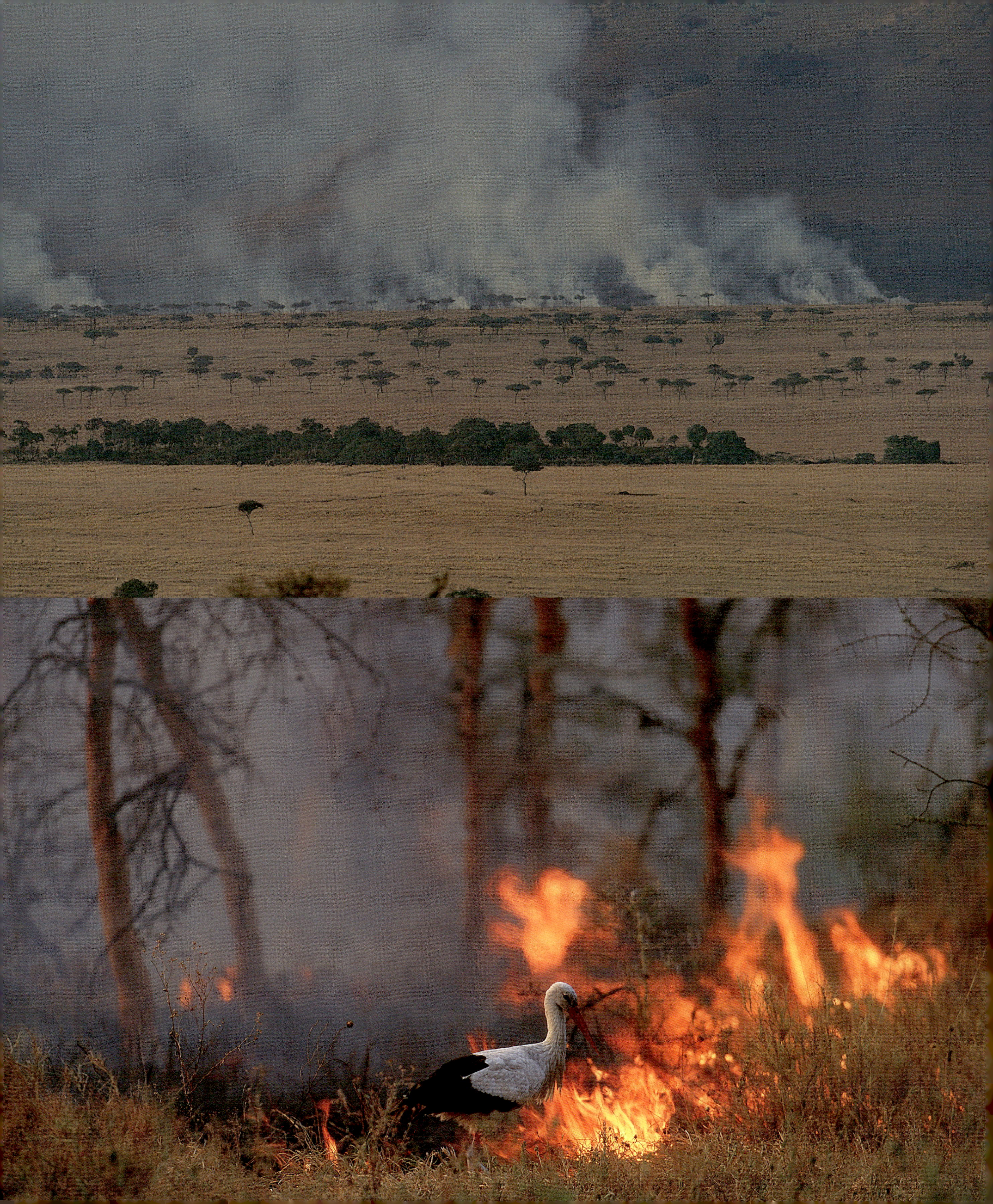

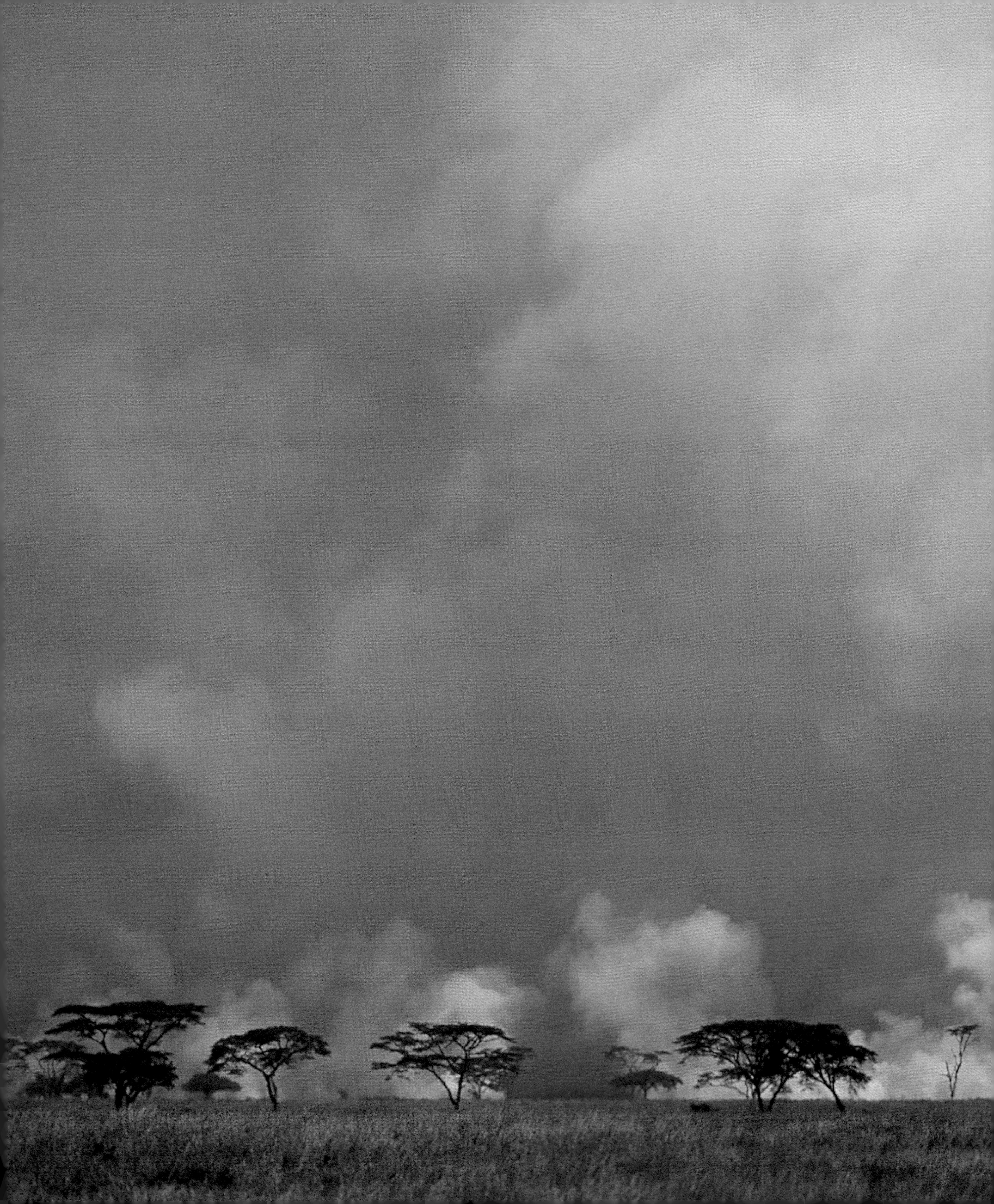

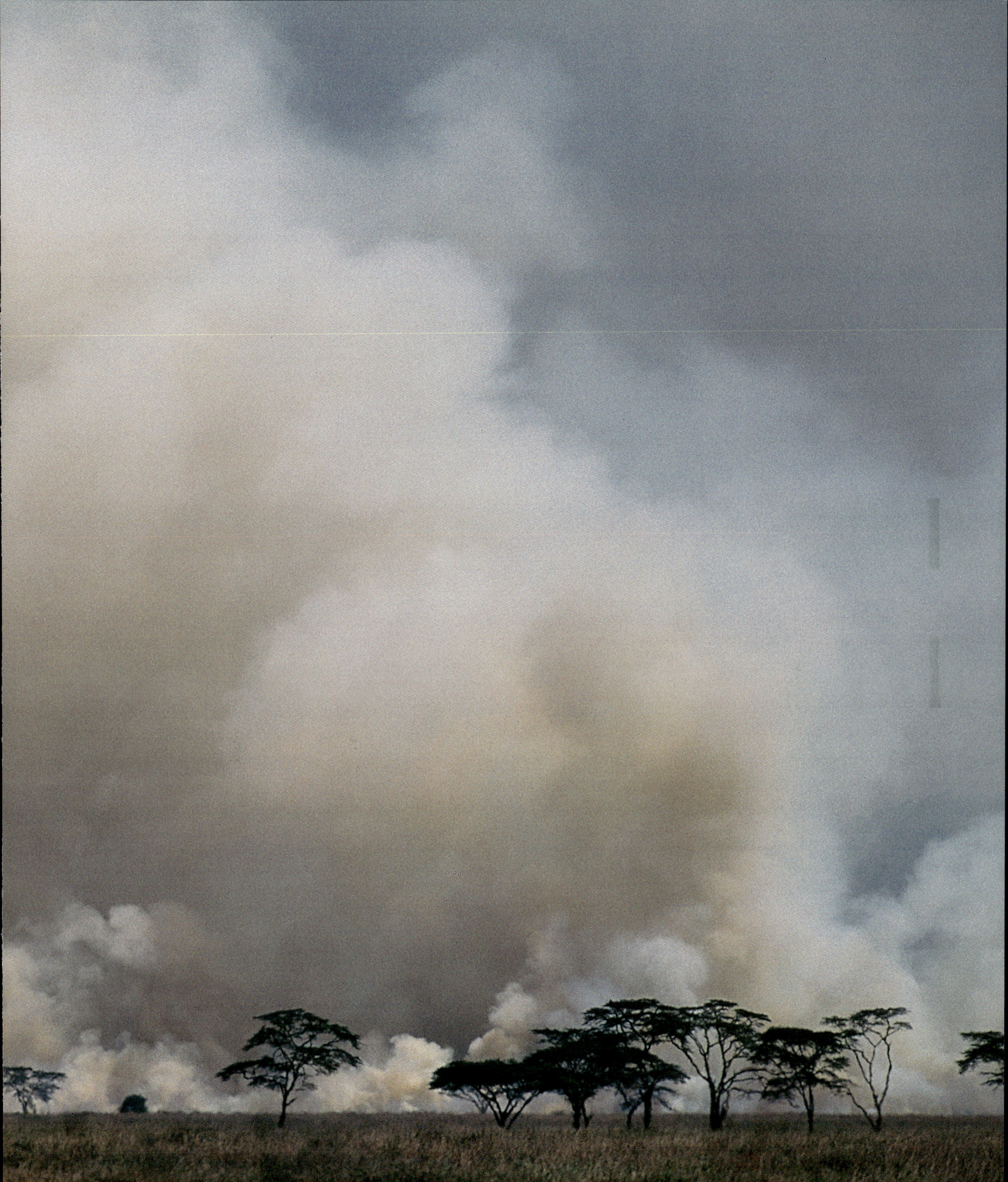

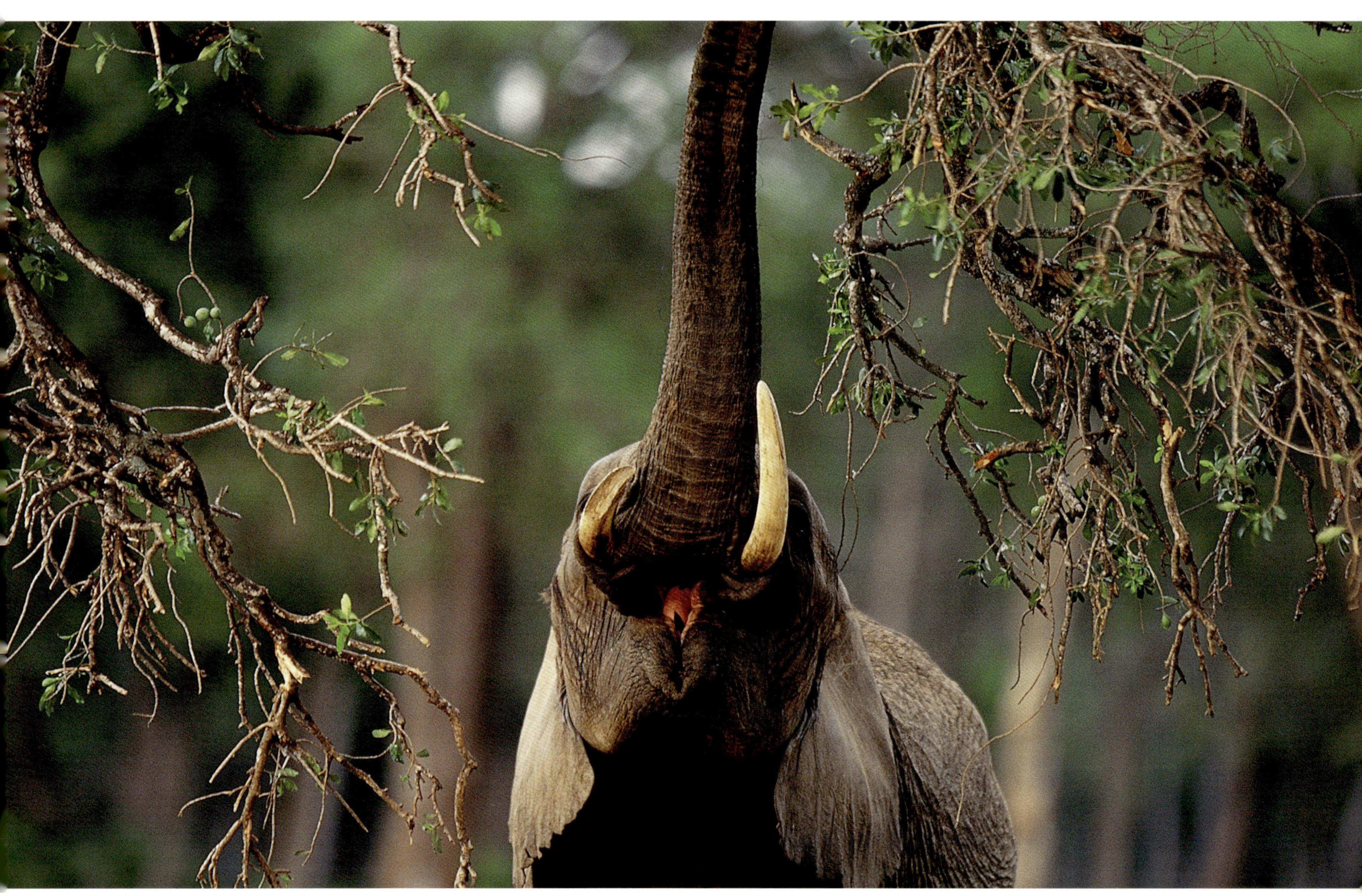

An adult elephant uses its trunk, a remarkable evolutionary fusion of nose and upper lip, to advantage. The elephant can pull the branch down to its level and even break it, if necessary.

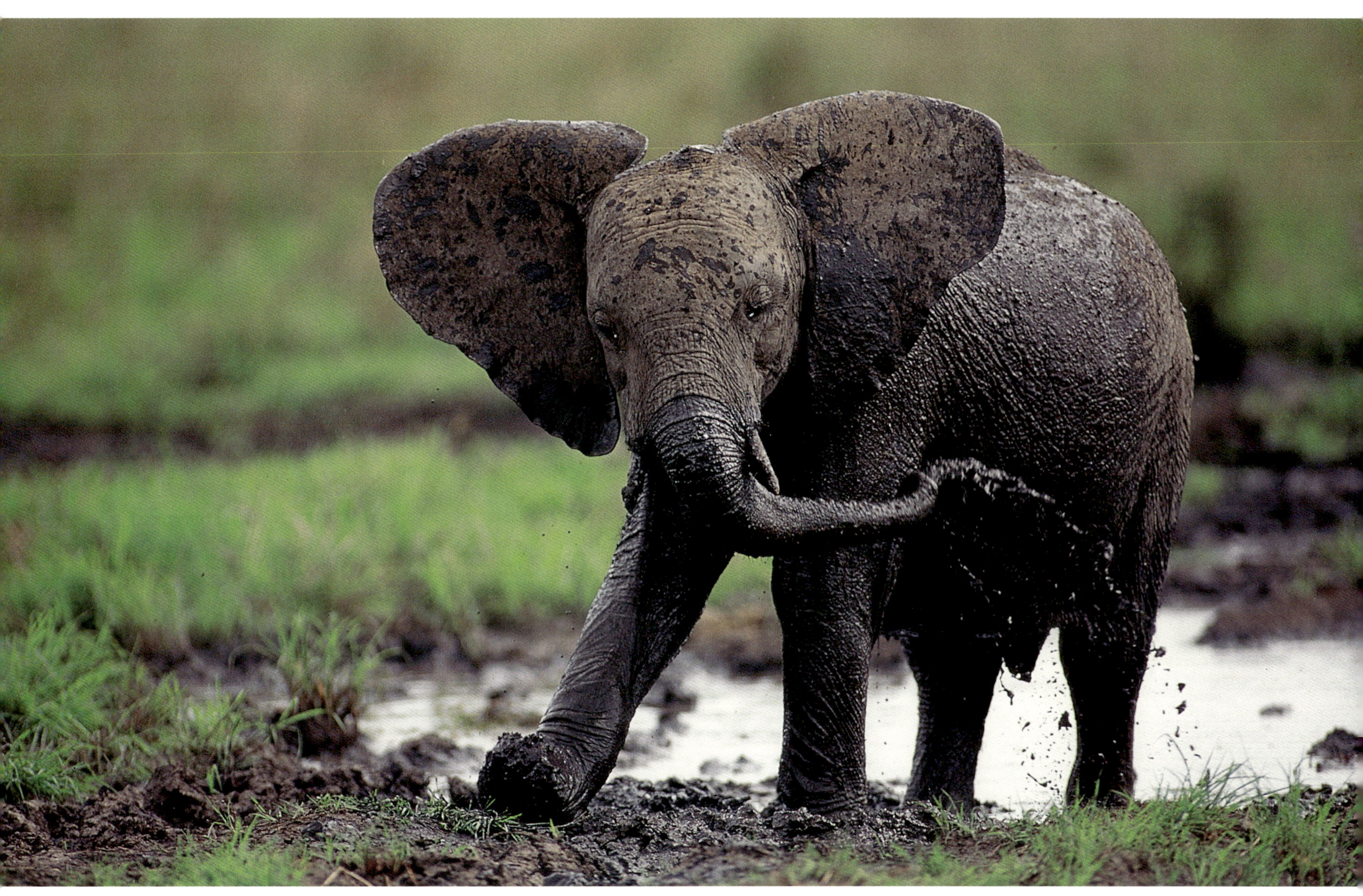

A young elephant enjoys a mud bath. In the process of bathing, elephants slightly modify their habitat. This small pool could easily become a large watering hole over the course of hundreds of years if elephants decided to make it their regular bathing place.

Pages 66–67
An elephant family group is busy foraging as dawn breaks. In open areas, a group like this spends much of the time feeding while on the move.

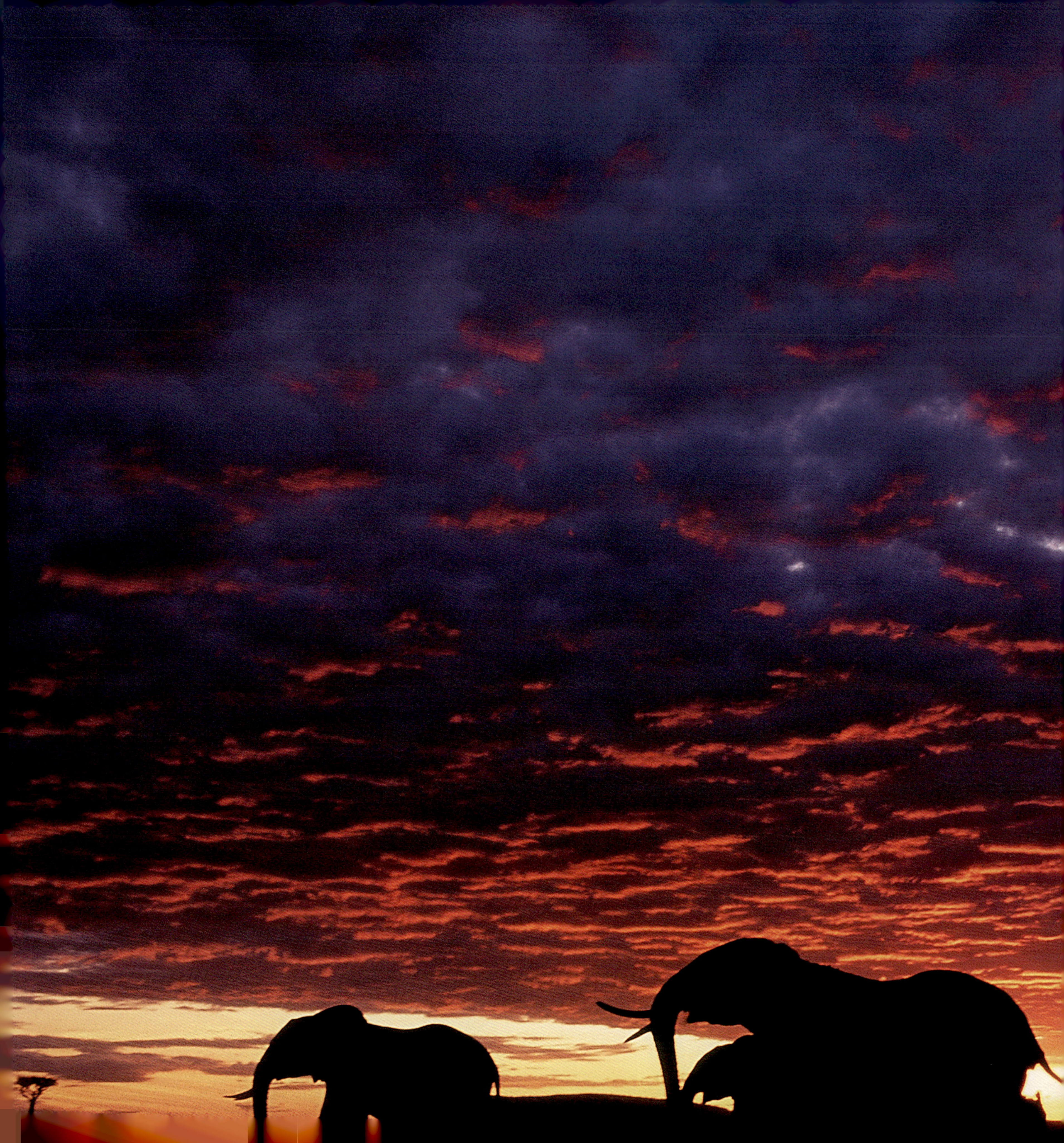

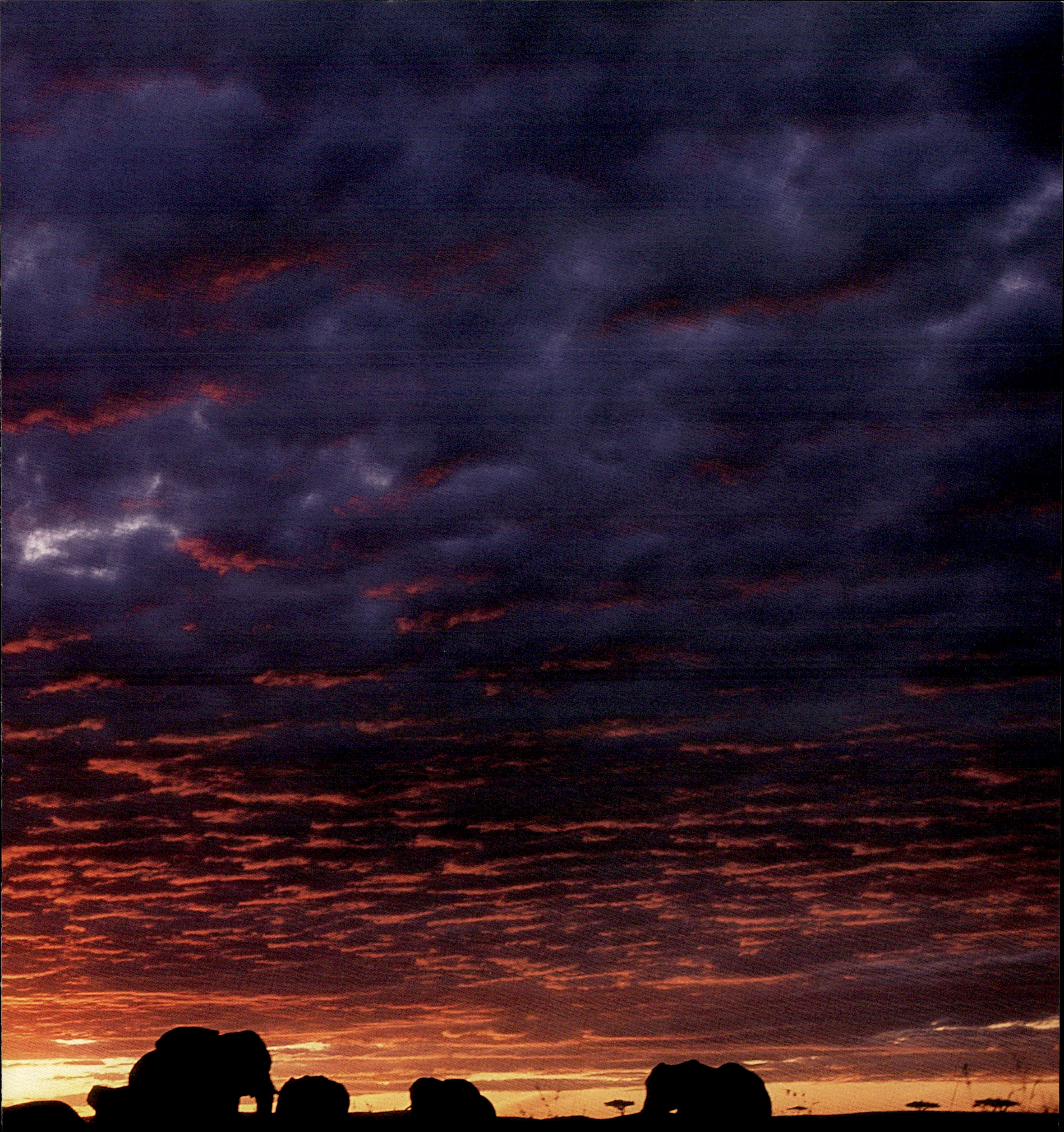

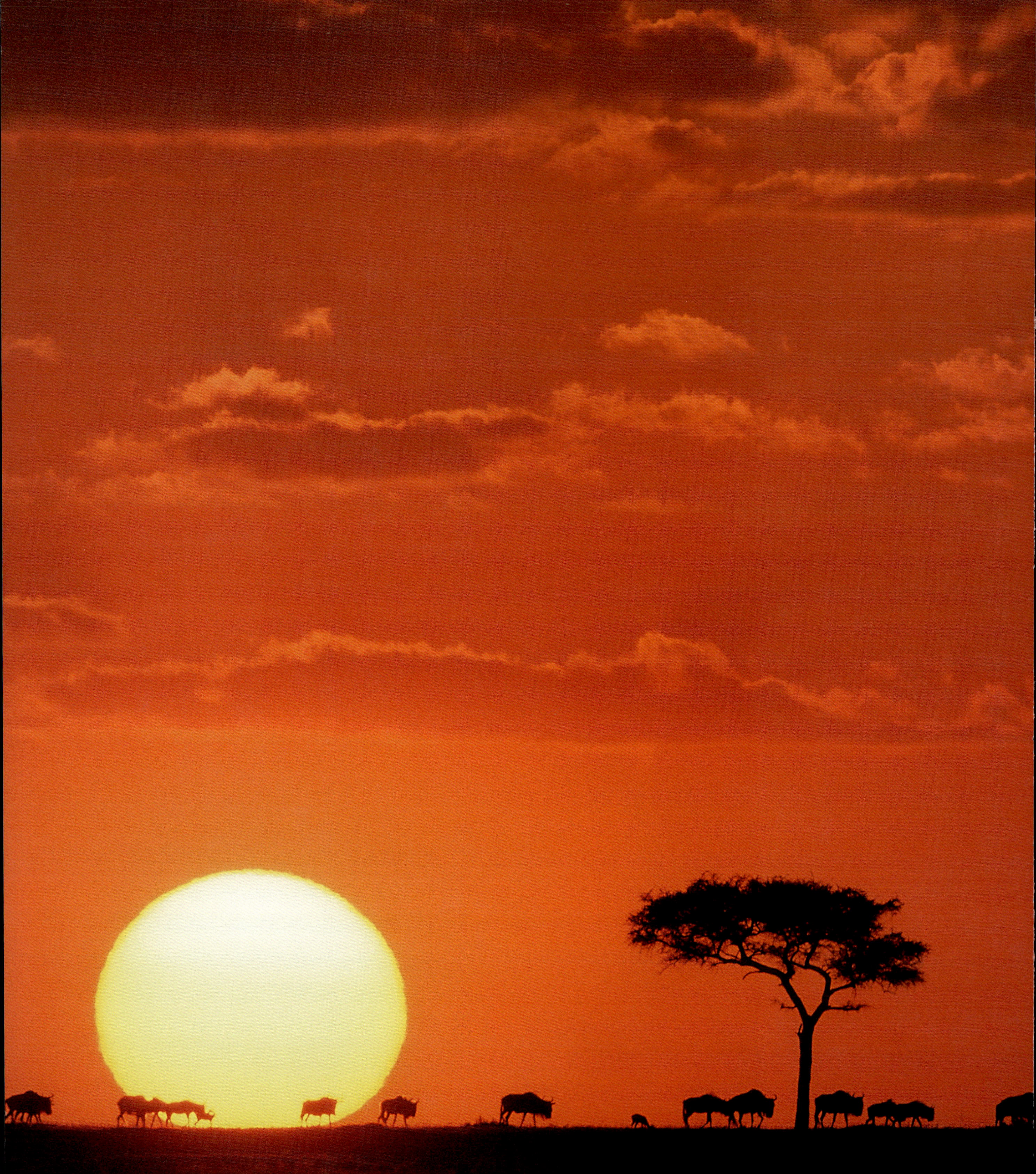

6

The Stirring of Life

In the early 1970s you could drive from southern Serengeti in Tanzania all the way to northern Maasai Mara in Kenya. I was only a wide-eyed kid in shorts back then, but I still have vivid impressions of an exhilarating journey my family took along this route. There was the changing landscape of grasses, bushes, and trees, and at the time I was not yet aware of the hundreds of species of insects, amphibians, and reptiles. I entertained a casual interest in birds and noticed a few of those, but it was the mammals – big and small, herbivores and carnivores – that captivated me. It was a whirlwind trip broken up by family picnics along the way, but I still remember the snapshots of life: lions mating, cheetahs streaking past, rhino mothers feeding with their young, giraffes necking, leopards resting with one eye open, buffaloes stampeding for no apparent reason, vultures circling the skies, hyenas cackling, wildebeest herds moving in abstract graphic formations, wild dogs loping across the plains. I sensed then, as I still do now, that I was witnessing glimpses of lives secretly led. What were these lives? And what governed the behavior of animals? My mind buzzed with a million questions.

The Serengeti–Maasai Mara, two national parks adjoining one another across the Kenya-Tanzania border, is a special place for watching animals. The best time is early morning, before the sun rises. Upon leaving camp, you will be greeted by a cacophony of sounds in the morning darkness: hyenas whooping, lions roaring, a wildebeest grunting, zebras yelping, a fish eagle calling. Notice how these sounds carry far in the clear air. It feels cold, but the dawn arrives quickly, heralded by light and color seeping over the eastern horizon. The sun appears, reluctantly at first, but then rises fast, a huge red disk, catching trees and animals in silhouette as they move along the edge of the world. The low sun generously floods the plains with a delicate light tinged with gold, casting long shadows across the glistening grass. The vast space and subtle mix of colors suffuses your senses. The air is crisp, and you can feel and hear and smell the herds. They are on the move. A new day has begun in the unfolding pageant of life.

There is a jackal striding effortlessy yet urgently – where to? A hyena running with a large bone in its jaw – is it a subordinate that has snatched a piece from a kill and is making good its escape? The wildebeests are filing past in a long, long line – only they know where they are going. Two zebra stallions in a bachelor's group are locked in combat – ritual or with intent to injure? An eager male gazelle, tail wagging furiously, is following an indifferent female – is she leading him on or is she in heat? The impalas in a harem of thirty or so are alert but all looking in different directions – is it a false alarm? A cheetah with three cubs is stepping down a mound – has she spotted breakfast? A pride of lionesses are heading for shelter, muzzles streaked red – where is the kill?... there it is – where the vultures are circling and descending not too far away.

Pages 68–69
Migrating wildebeests often start out before dawn, moving sedately in single file.

To the casual observer, the savannah appears quite peaceful from mid-morning to mid-afternoon, when the heat is at its height. The tempo of life seems rather slow, but those endless vistas, outwardly so benign, are deceptive. What is not immediately evident are the violent images: half-eaten carcasses, bloated vultures, scattered skulls and bones. This land where predators thrive is full of drama and there is always tension, a feeling of suspense, of something about to happen.

In the cool of the evening, life stirs again, and the illusion of quiet is dispelled as leisurely movement, less frantic than at dawn, starts up again. The animals are relaxed: zebras reluctantly give way to approaching vehicles full of tourists; baboons saunter to their roosting trees; lions lying on a mound are yawning, grooming, and watching the parade of animals; and not far away a leopard is stretching on a thick tree limb in preparation for a nocturnal assassination.

Why do animals do the things they do? One explanation for their behavior claims to get at the very nature of life. This theory is also capable of answering the big-picture questions, such as why are big carnivores – big cats, hyenas, wild dogs – relatively rare in the savannah while huge numbers of their prey roam freely? Why is there so much diversity of species? How do the different species live in such harmony? Why is it a pyramid of life, rather than a square or a rectangle? There is always the risk that over-analysis will tarnish our sense of the wonder of nature. But the right kind of analysis can yield an understanding that not only educates, but actually enhances that sense of wonder. I say, let's take the risk.

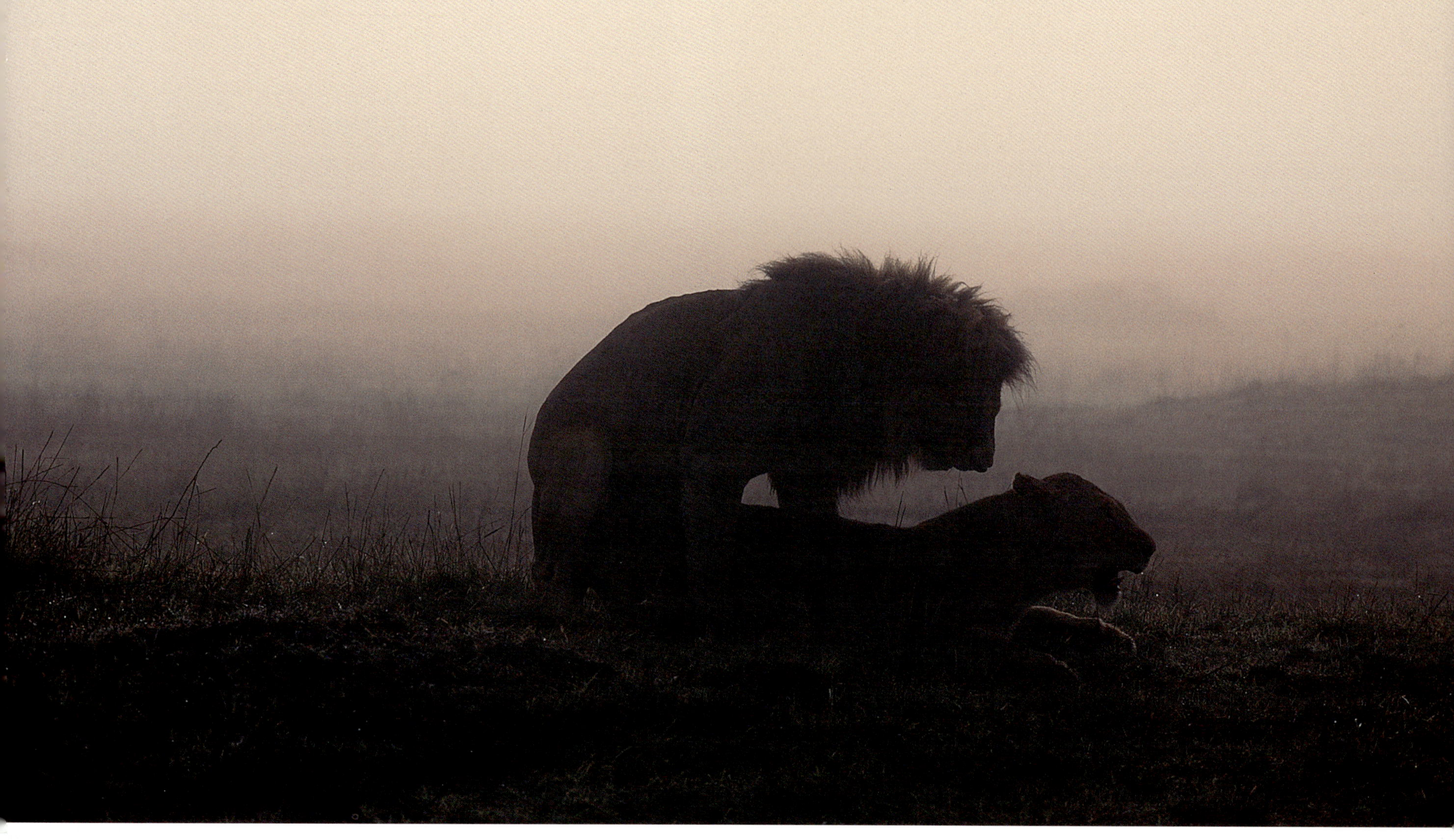

Against a backdrop of early morning mist, a pair of lions on the Serengeti is ensuring that their genes continue into the next generation.

Opposite, above
A cheetah, the lead in a pair of males, sprinting at a wildebeest group in a bid to separate a young calf from its mother. The mother was not intimidated and kept the cheetahs successfully at bay.

Opposite, below
These giraffe bulls are neck-wrestling and attempting to hit each other with their stumpy horns. Although such combats are ritualistic, there was a rare instance in which one giraffe was knocked out for about 15 minutes.

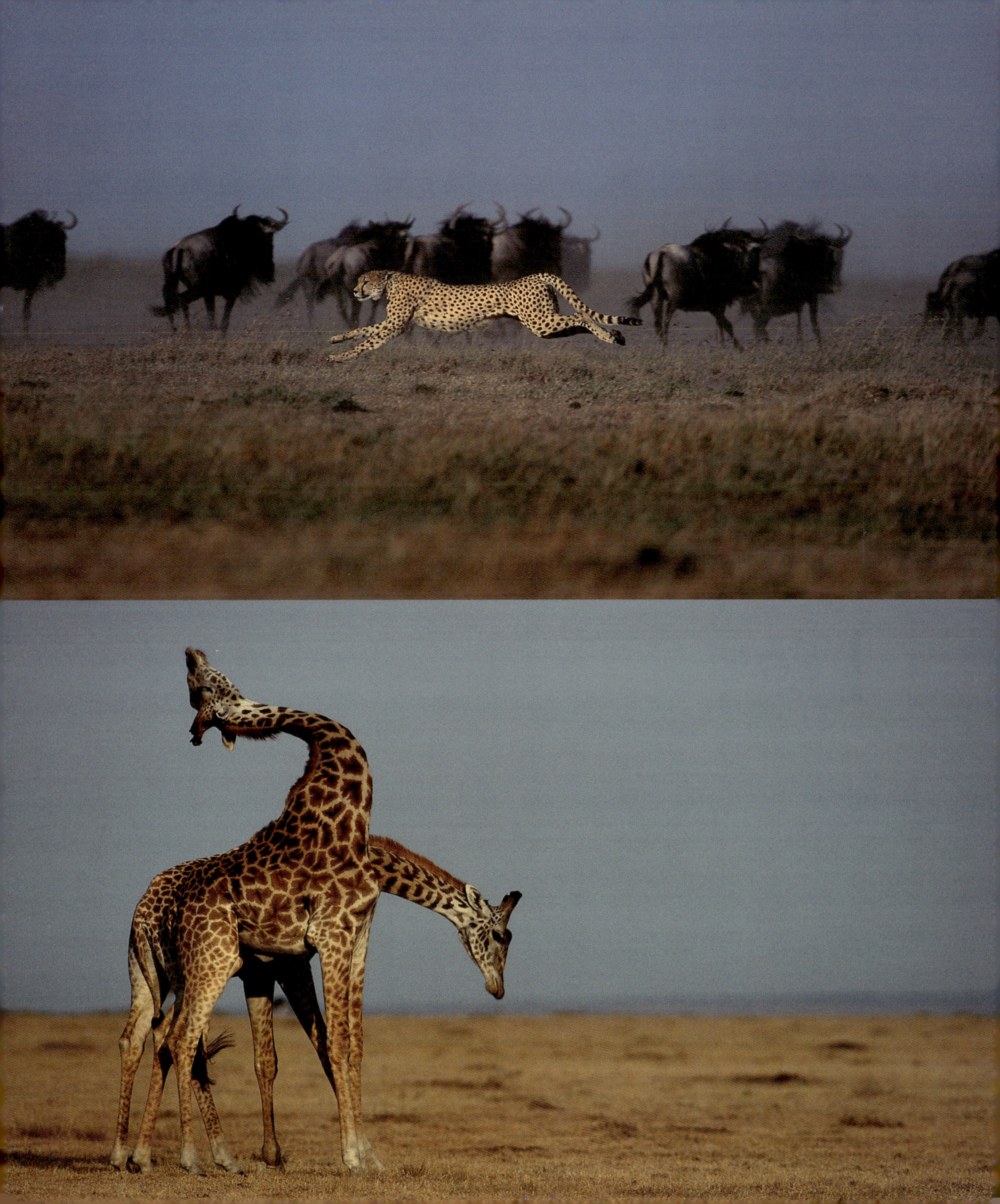

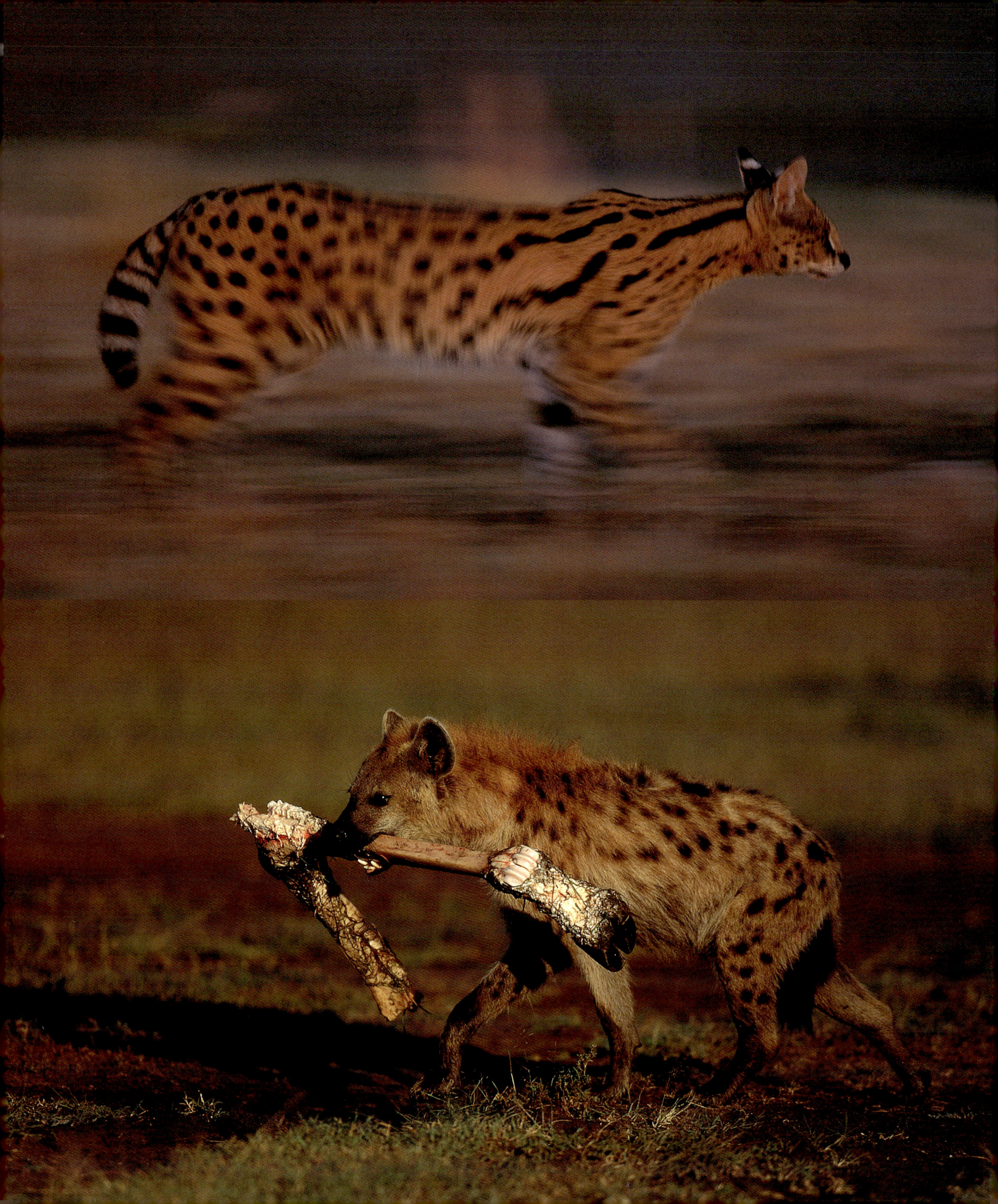

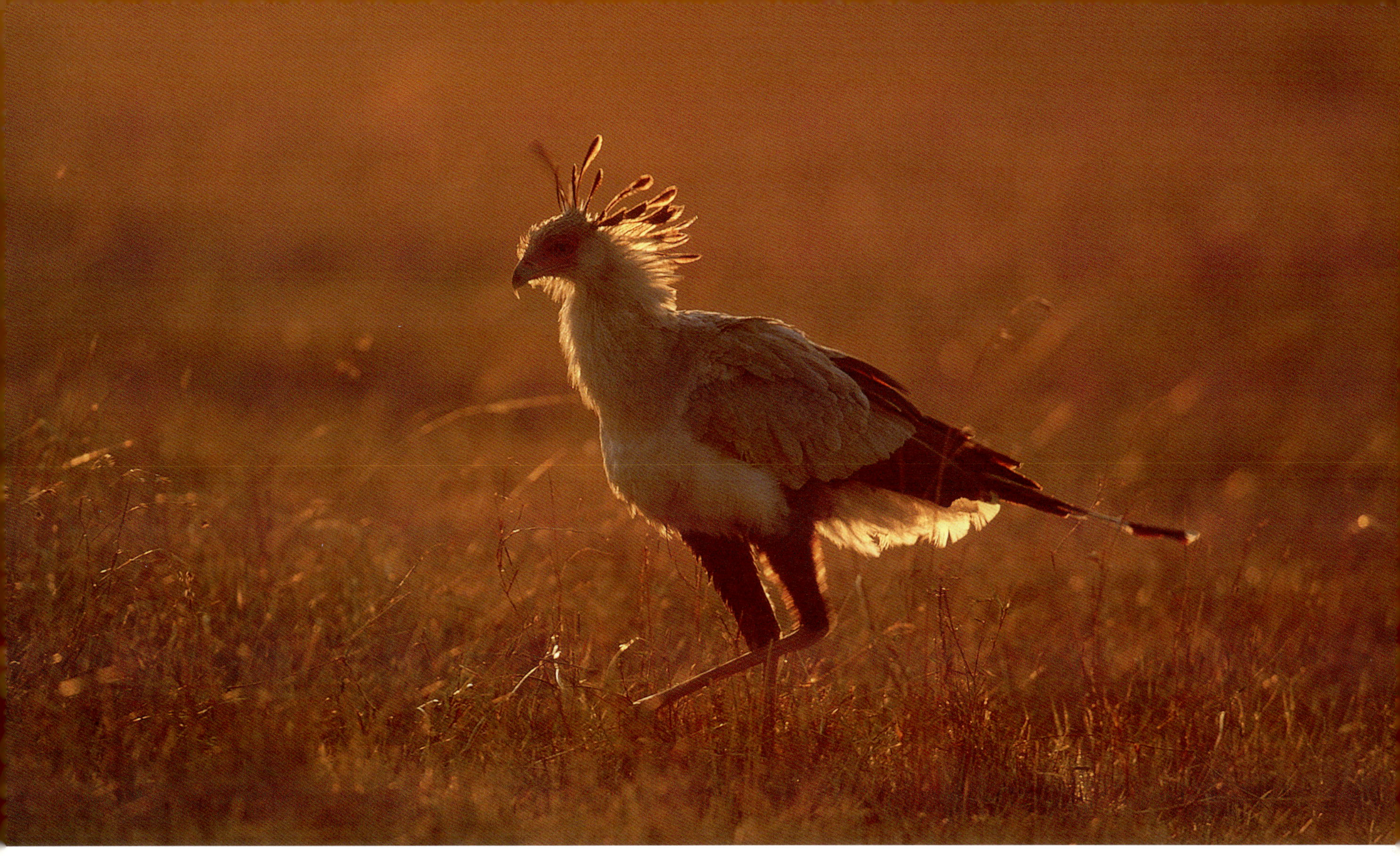

Out on the plains, a long-legged secretary bird treads purposefully through the grass like an eagle on stilts, searching for eggs and insects such as locusts, lizards, and snakes. It kills reptiles by striking them with repeated blows of its powerful feet.

Opposite, above
Daybreak finds a busy serval cat on the prowl. The cat occasionally stops to mark a prominent cluster of grass, a sign that he is a territorial male.

Opposite, below
This young spotted hyena is carrying off a giraffe bone, which it will eat in a secluded spot away from competing clan members. The spotted hyena packs tremendous jaw power and is capable of breaking open bones to get at the bone-marrow.

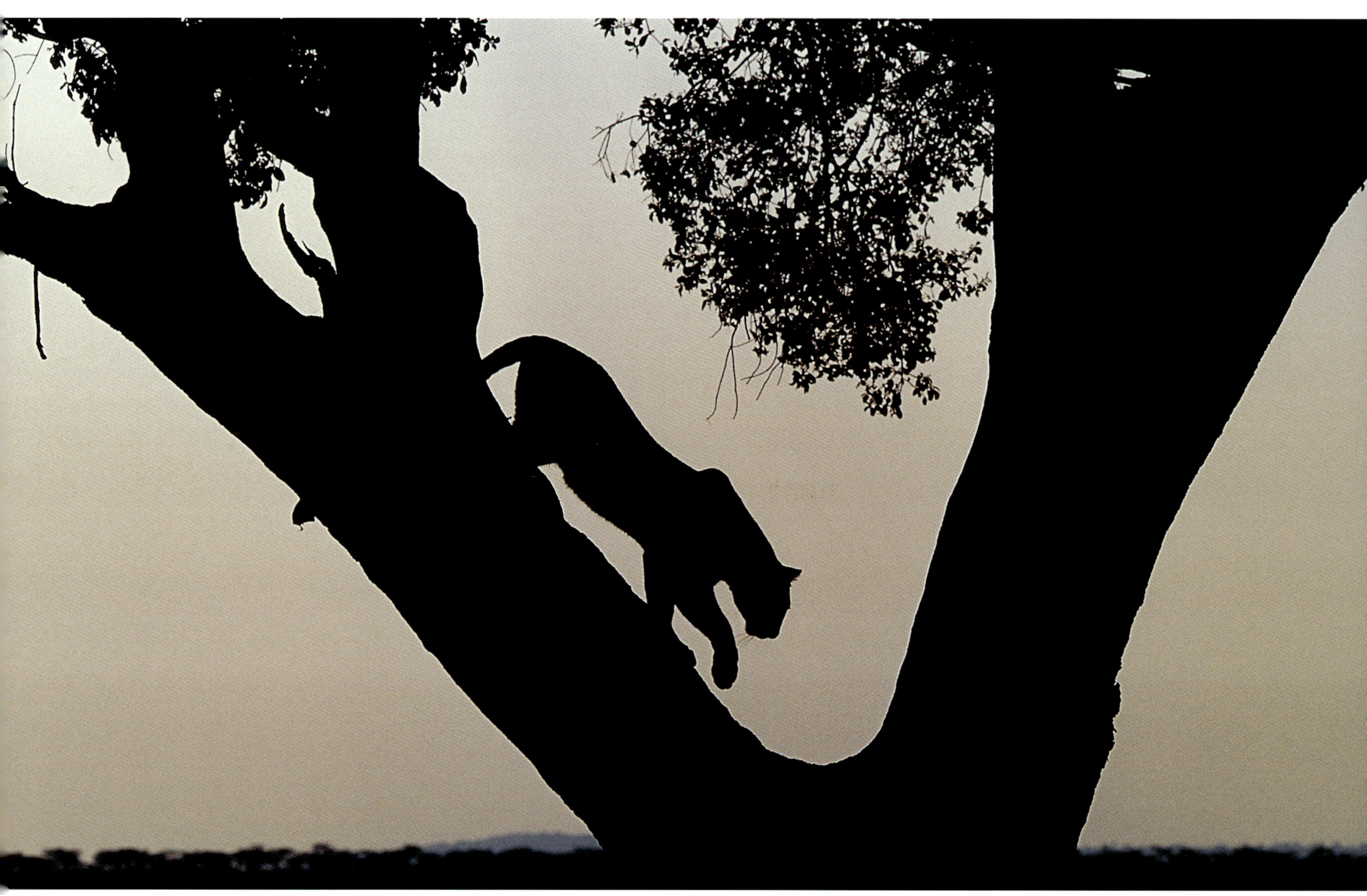

In the last hour of daylight, when the red-necked spurfowl begin to call, a leopard wakes from its siesta, stretches, and descends from its tree to begin a foray in the dark.

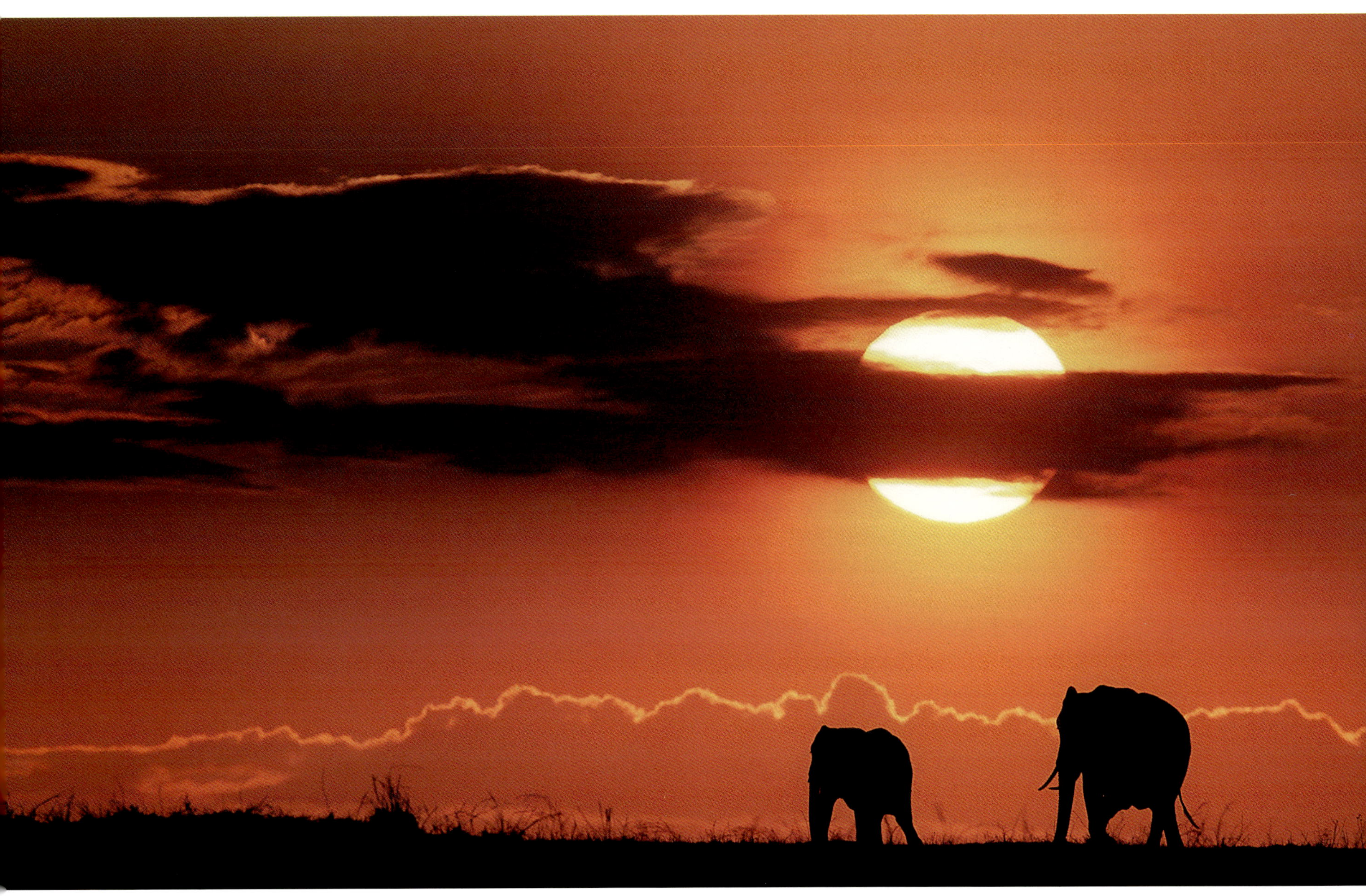

After a night spent foraging in the open vistas, an elephant group, the first members coming into view here, traverses the undulating plains as it heads back to the cool of the riverine forest.

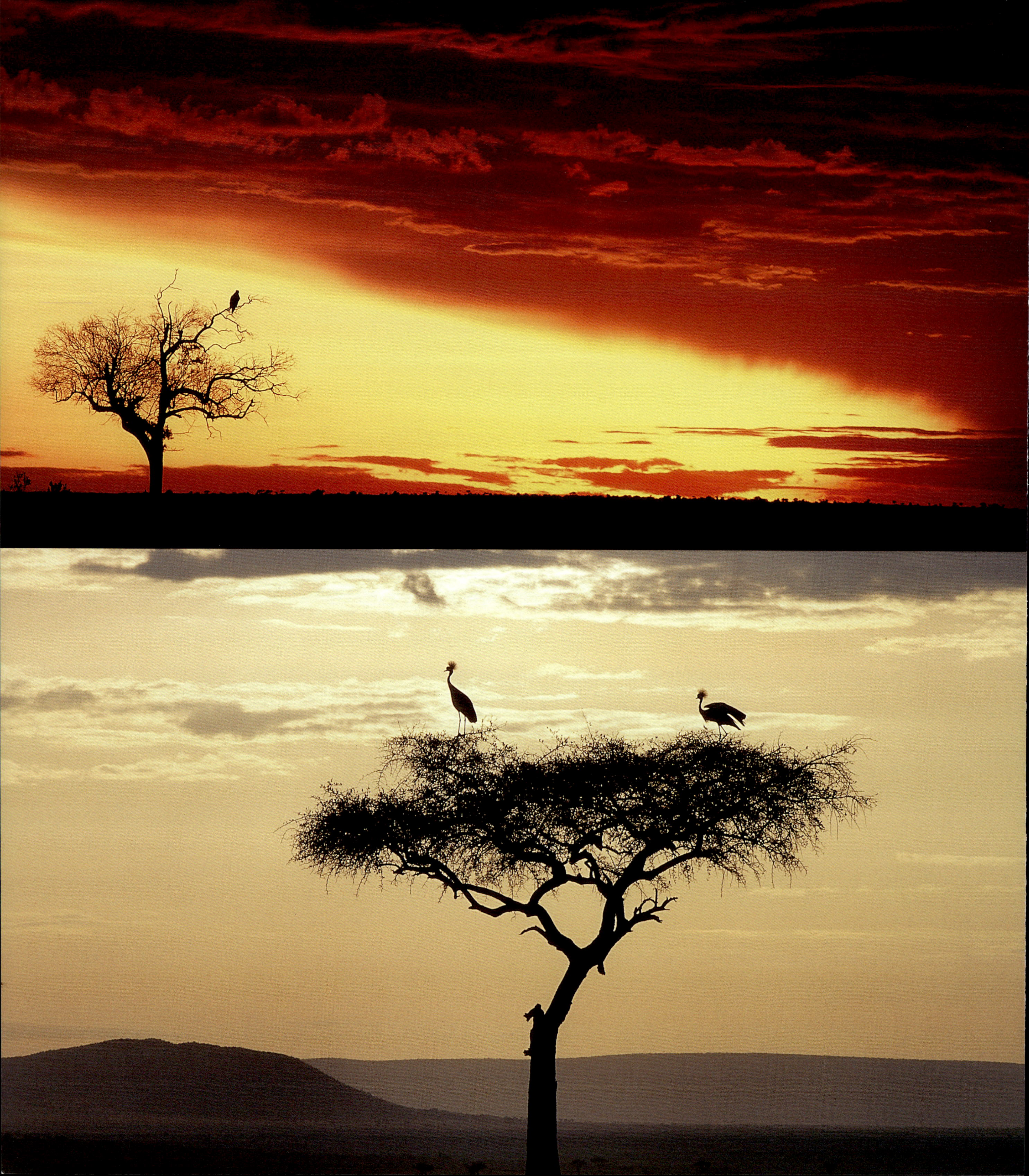

Olive baboons gather as the day ends to roost in trees. They will stick close together throughout the night and return repeatedly to this sleeping site.

Opposite, above
Dusk descends over the savannah as an eagle perches on a withered, leafless tree.

Opposite, below
A pair of crowned cranes atop an acacia tree, preparing to settle down for the night.

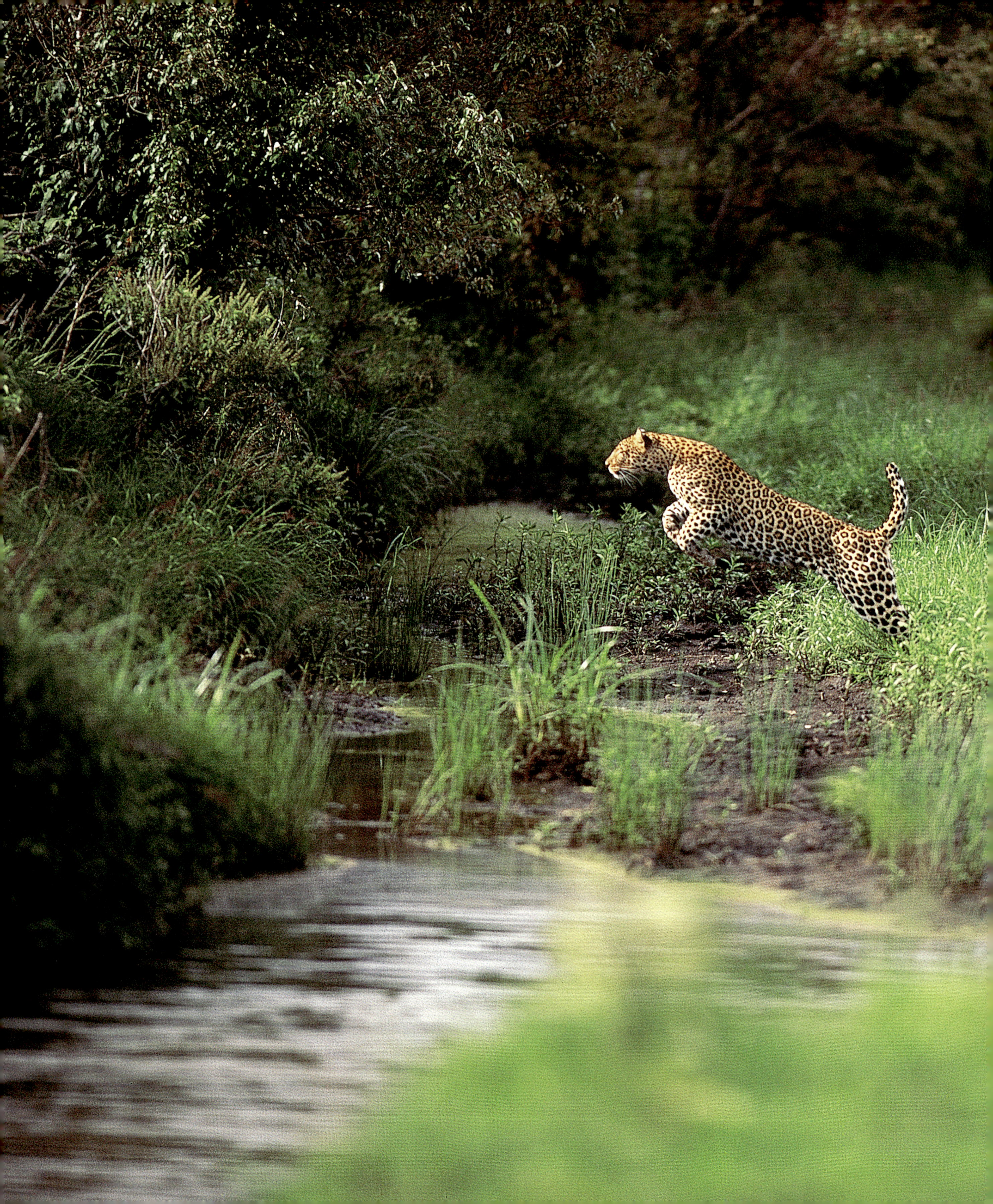

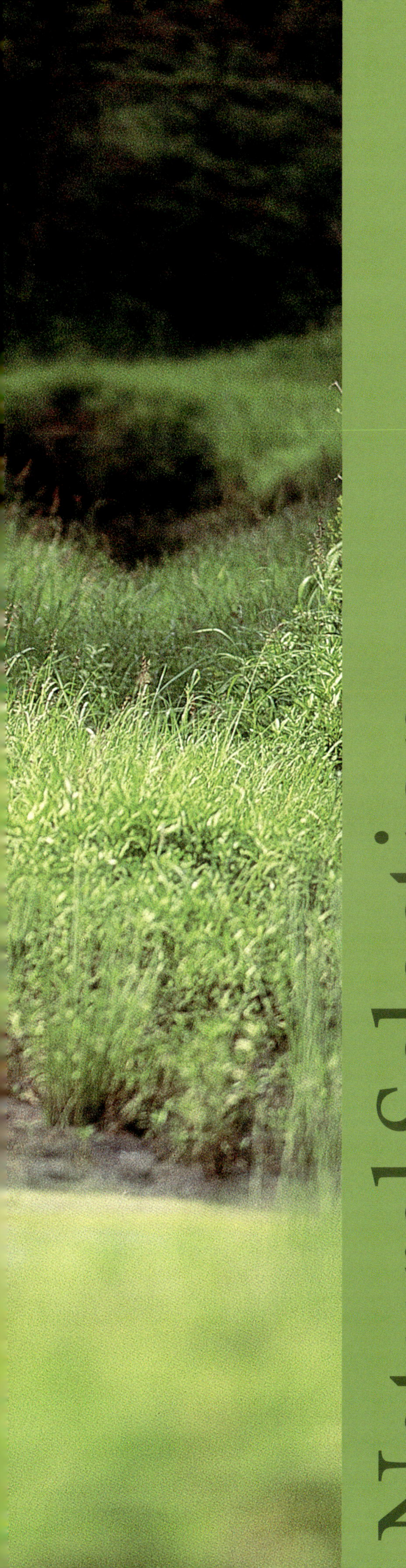

7

Natural Selection

The African savannah is a nation of millions upon millions of animal inhabitants and a staggering amount of other biomass, and yet there is no army to defend the nation's borders, no government to prescribe top-down solutions to problems, no police or law court to enforce acceptable behavior. There is no need. The fact is, everything works rather well when left to its own devices.

But what is the organizing principle, the "invisible hand"? The only credible principle that we know of is the theory of evolution by natural selection. A well-balanced ecosystem like the savannah works as long as natural selection is allowed to take place without interruption and has been in operation for millions of years.

Since it was originally advanced by Darwin, researchers have built on the theory of natural selection with many new discoveries, most notably in the area of genetics. The modern version suggests that selection takes place at the most basic level of all: the gene. Every living entity on the planet has a unique combination of genes, which can be viewed, in the simplest of terms, as a set of instructions for how to make a body and influence behavior. It is these instructions that have been assembled by natural selection.

For natural selection to occur, four conditions must be met. The first of these is that living entities must have the ability to reproduce; with no reproduction, life ceases. Second, there must be some mode of inheritance; genes of the parents must be passed on to the next generation. If there is no inheritance, then the advantageous features of a parent would simply be lost. Third, there must be variation within the population. If each individual in the population is identical, natural selection cannot operate properly. For example, some jackals are more agile than others. Generally speaking, the more agile jackals will outsurvive the less agile ones, and those genes will be passed on. Finally, there must be competition between individuals of the same species. For competition to occur, resources have to be in short supply. If resources are insufficient to support a community, not all individuals will survive and reproduce, or they will reproduce at differing rates of success. Those individuals who are better adapted to acquire resources will leave more offspring who will inherit the competitive edge of their parents.

However, the instructions encoded in the genes are often not perfectly replicated every time an individual reproduces. Copying errors (or genetic mutations) can occur, and these produce new variations, such as improved hearing or sharper teeth. If such "mistakes," or new features, make the individuals stronger and help them survive longer by enabling them to adapt better to their environment, they will be passed on. Those features that do not, will be weeded out over time because those individuals will not survive long enough to reproduce and pass on their genes, or they will be unattractive to the opposite sex and less

Pages 80–81
The powerful muscles in leopards' limbs enable them to climb tall trees in a few bounds; subdue large, struggling prey animals; and leap across rivulets from a standing jump, as this female is doing.

likely to reproduce. Thus, cheetahs have genes that make them the fastest mammals on earth (slow cheetahs having died out), and serval cats have genes that give them a keen sense of hearing (serval cats with weak hearing having failed to survive).

Natural selection is a device for change, and evolution and adaptation are its consequences. Those ancestors that adapted well, benefiting from a sequence of favorable mutations of genes, passed them on to build the bodies and minds of today's savannah residents.

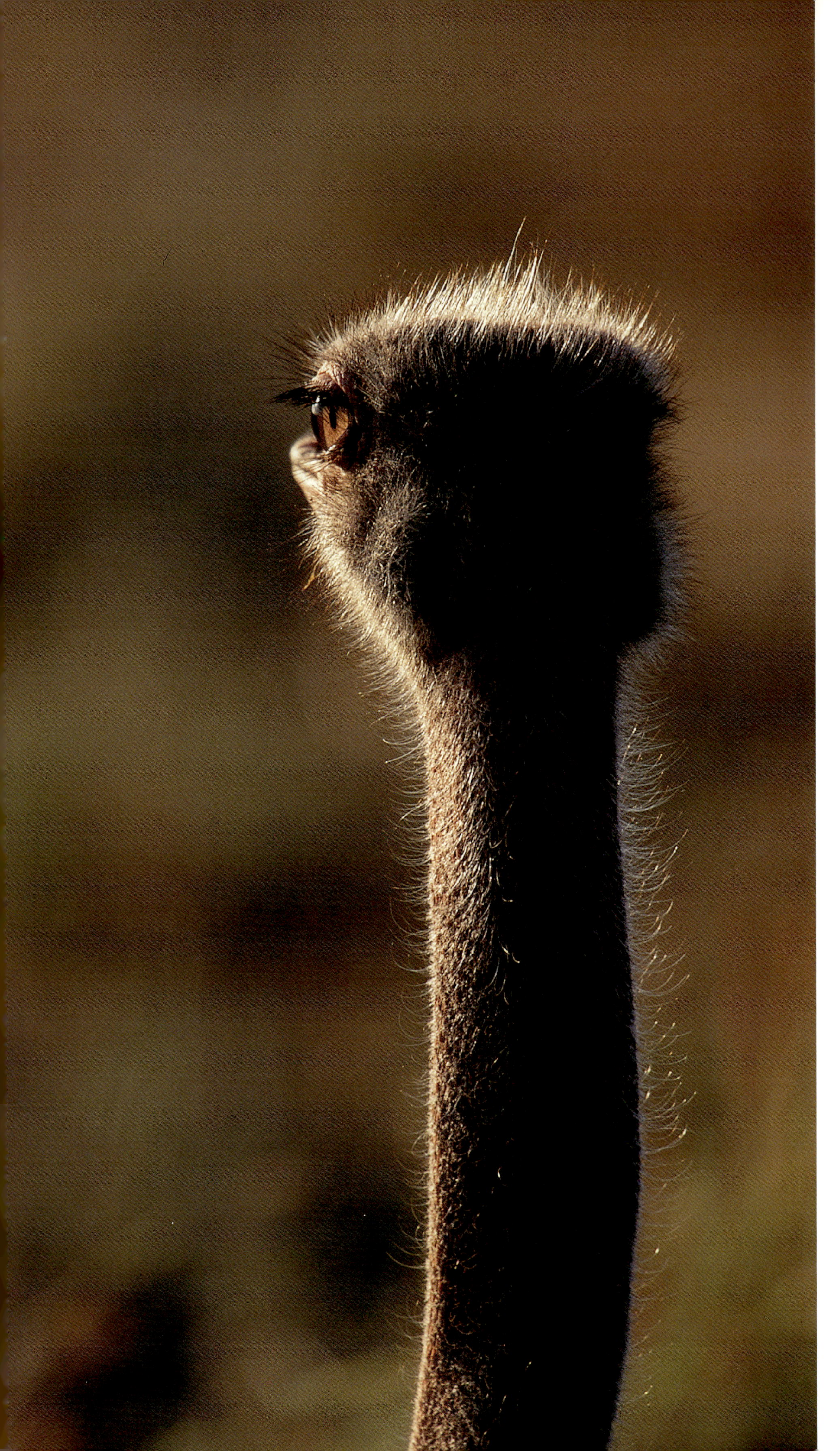

Ostriches' long, thick eyelashes act as a protectant, and their huge eyes, along with their height and long necks, enable them to scan far distances across the grasslands.

Opposite
A Maasai giraffe reaches up to feed on succulent leaves growing high on a tree. The tall, long-necked giraffes have established a special niche for themselves in the wooded savannah.

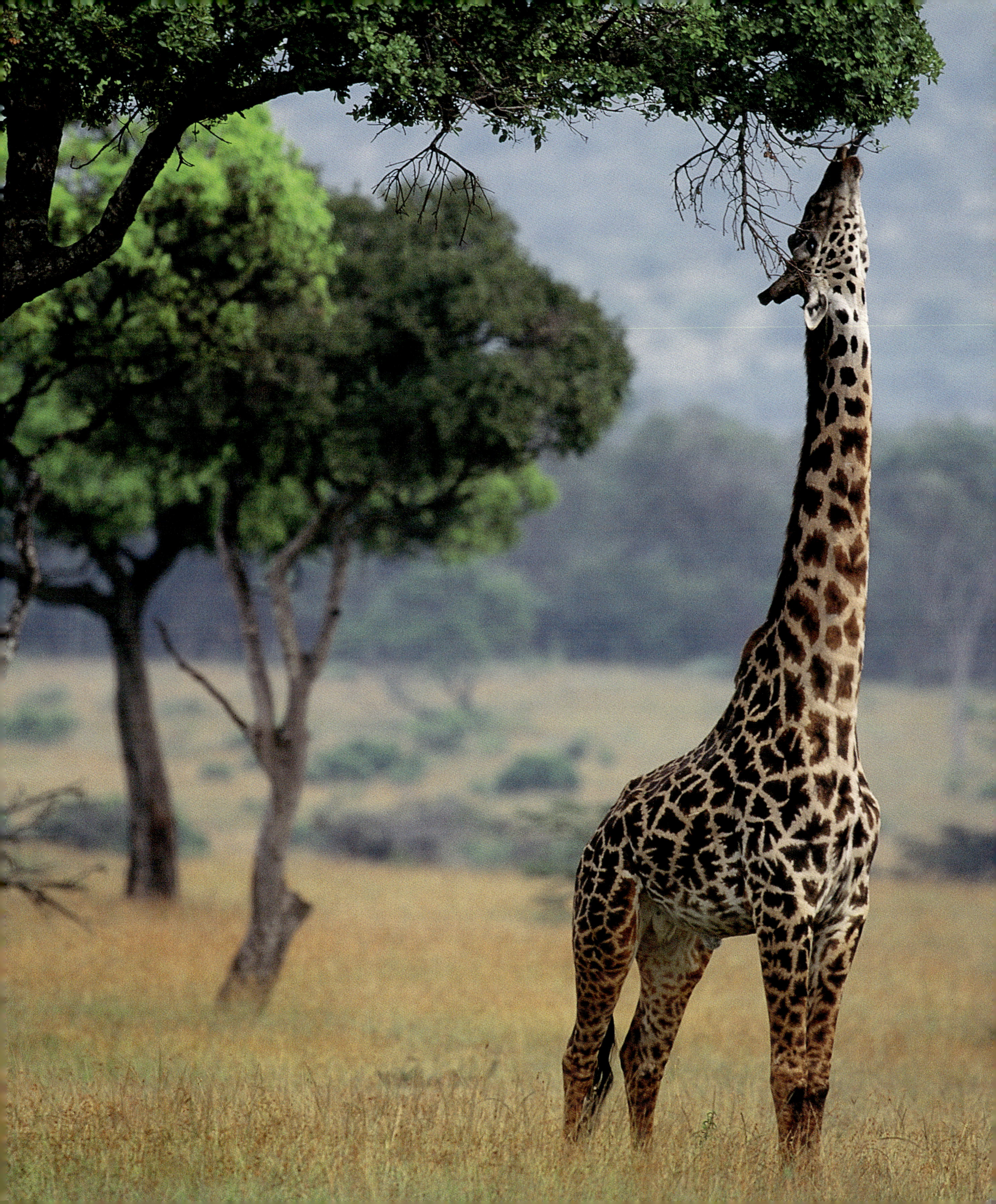

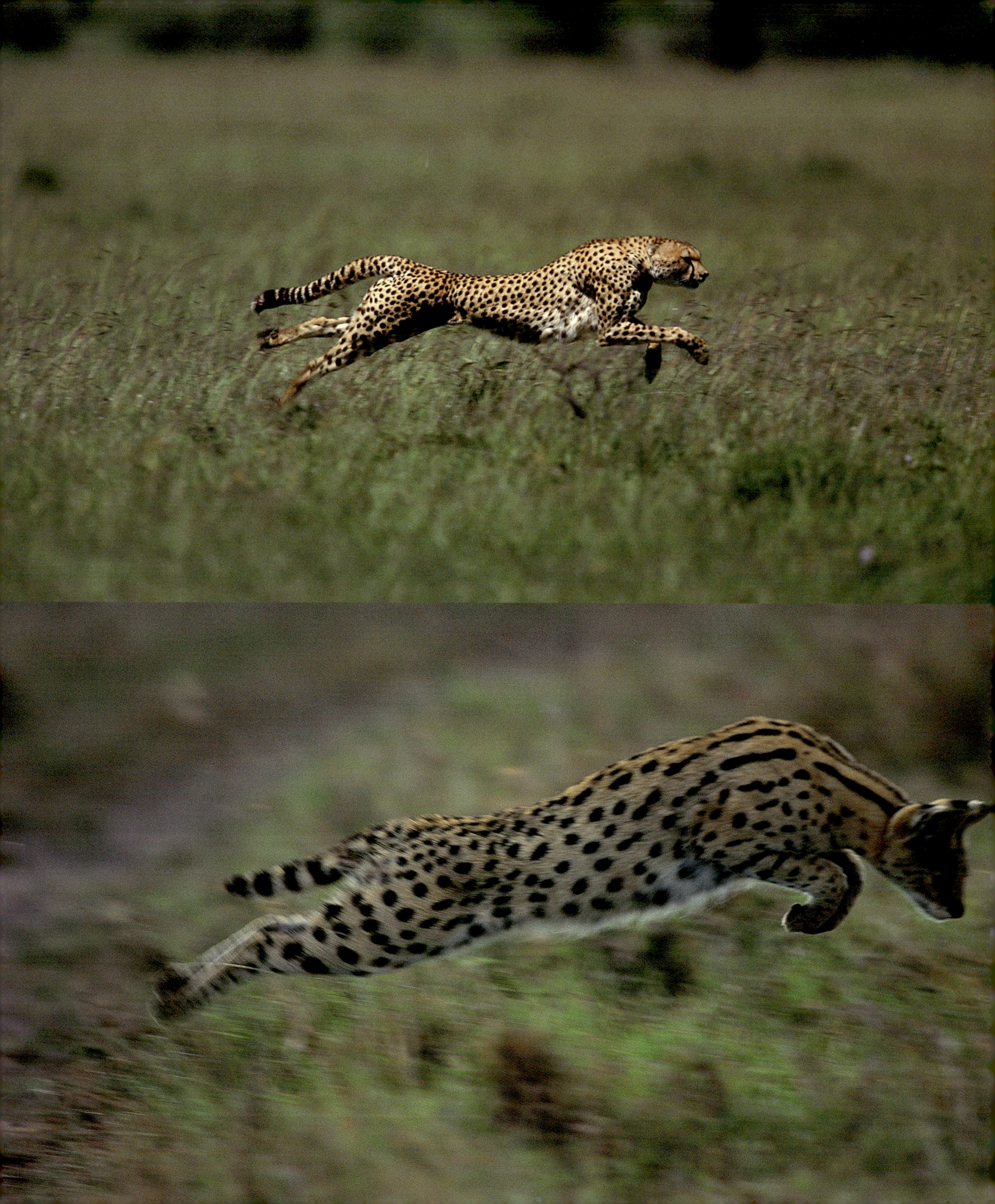

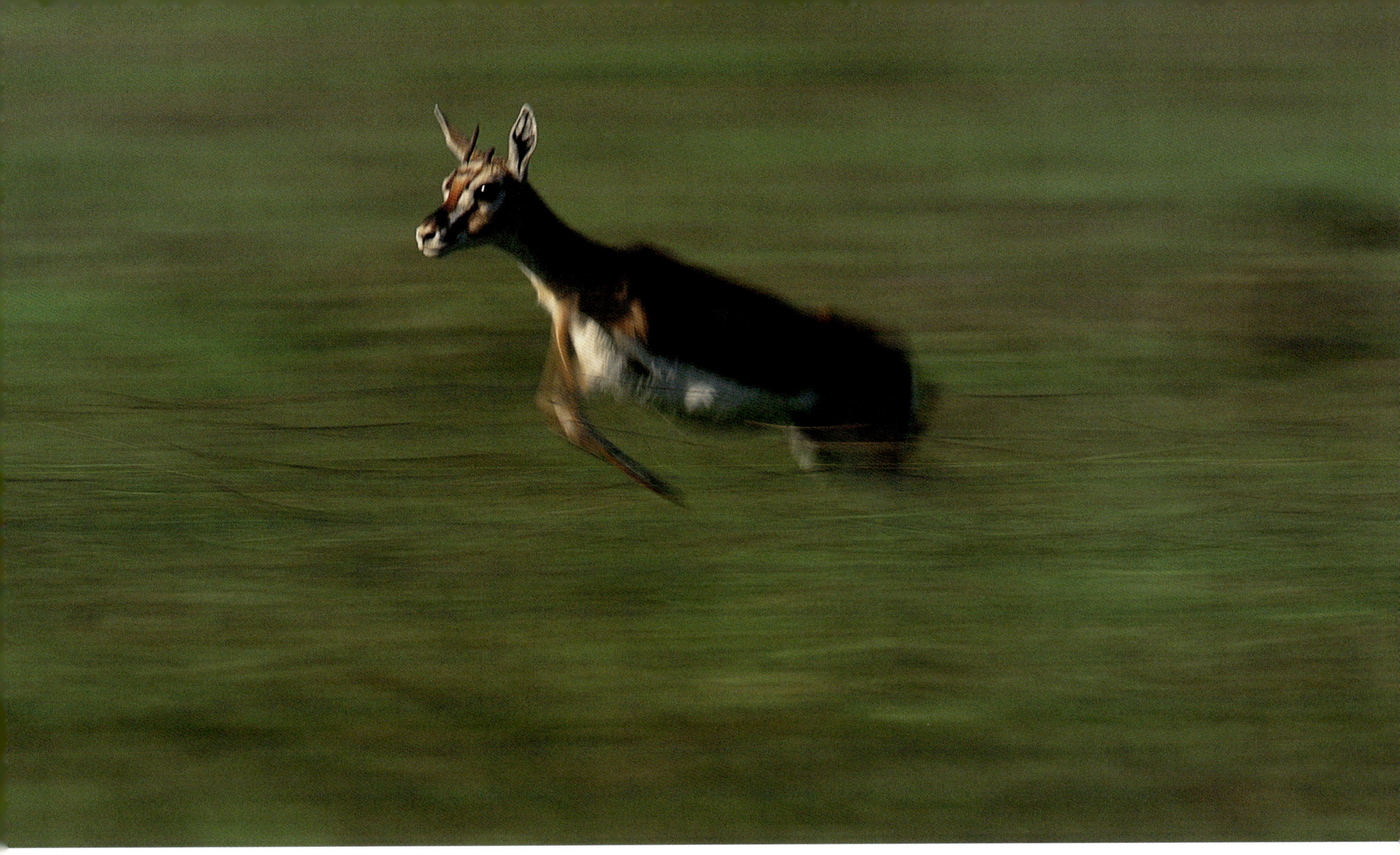

Alerted to a cheetah on the hunt, a Thomson's gazelle bounds through tall grass. In order to escape the cheetah, the gazelle will swerve and zigzag while running at a speed that almost matches the cheetah's. Cheetahs cannot run at the same speed in zigzag formation, only in straight-ahead bursts.

Opposite, above
The body of a cheetah on the hunt is stretched full out as it runs at top speed. During this phase of its sprint, the big cat is virtually sailing over the grassy plains. Its flexible spine, small head, and large nasal passages have been fine tuned for swift movement and astonishing bursts of speed. The cheetah is the fastest land mammal with sprints up to 55 to 60 mph.

Opposite, below
This male serval cat was prowling, ears cocked, when he picked up a rustling sound in the grass. He swiveled his ears toward the sound, and, having pinpointed the location of a foraging rat, he steadied himself then pounced.

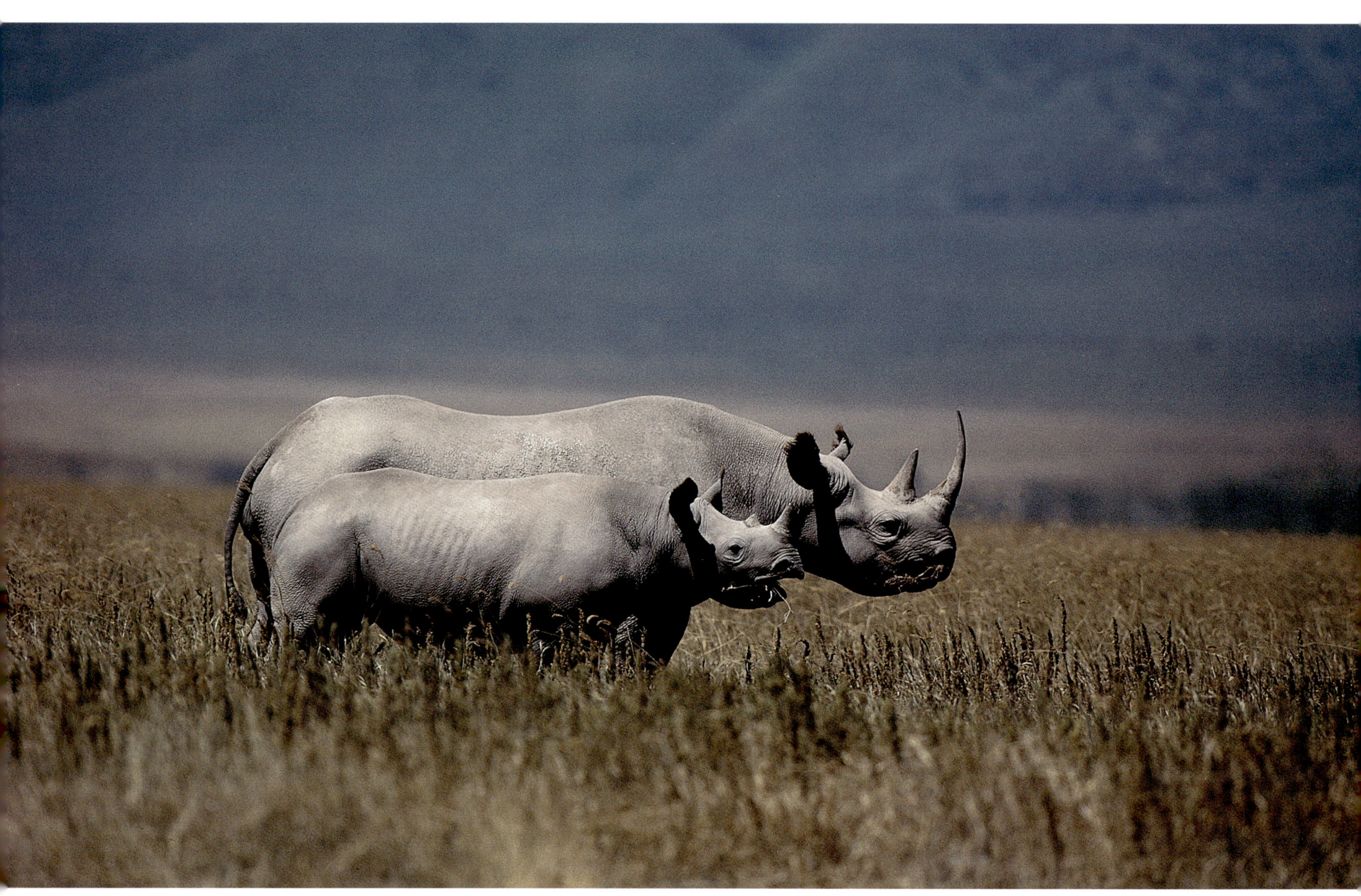

A black rhino calf stands alongside its mother in the Ngorongoro Crater. Baby rhinos are born almost perfect miniatures of their parents.

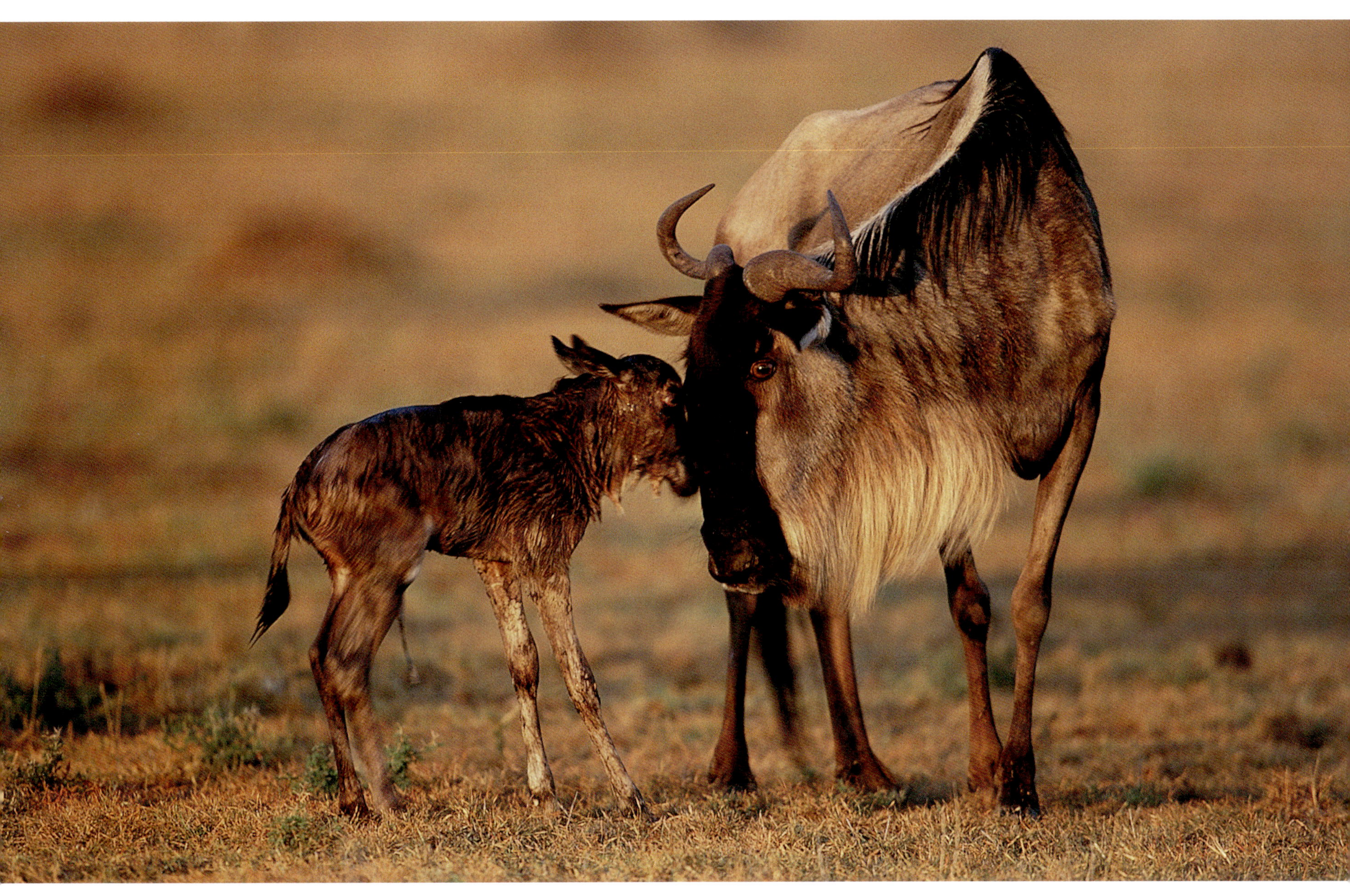

Having licked the afterbirth remains from her newborn's fur, a wildebeest mother exchanges smells with it. After this process of imprinting, most of the energy spent by the mother on looking after the calf will consist of suckling and protection.

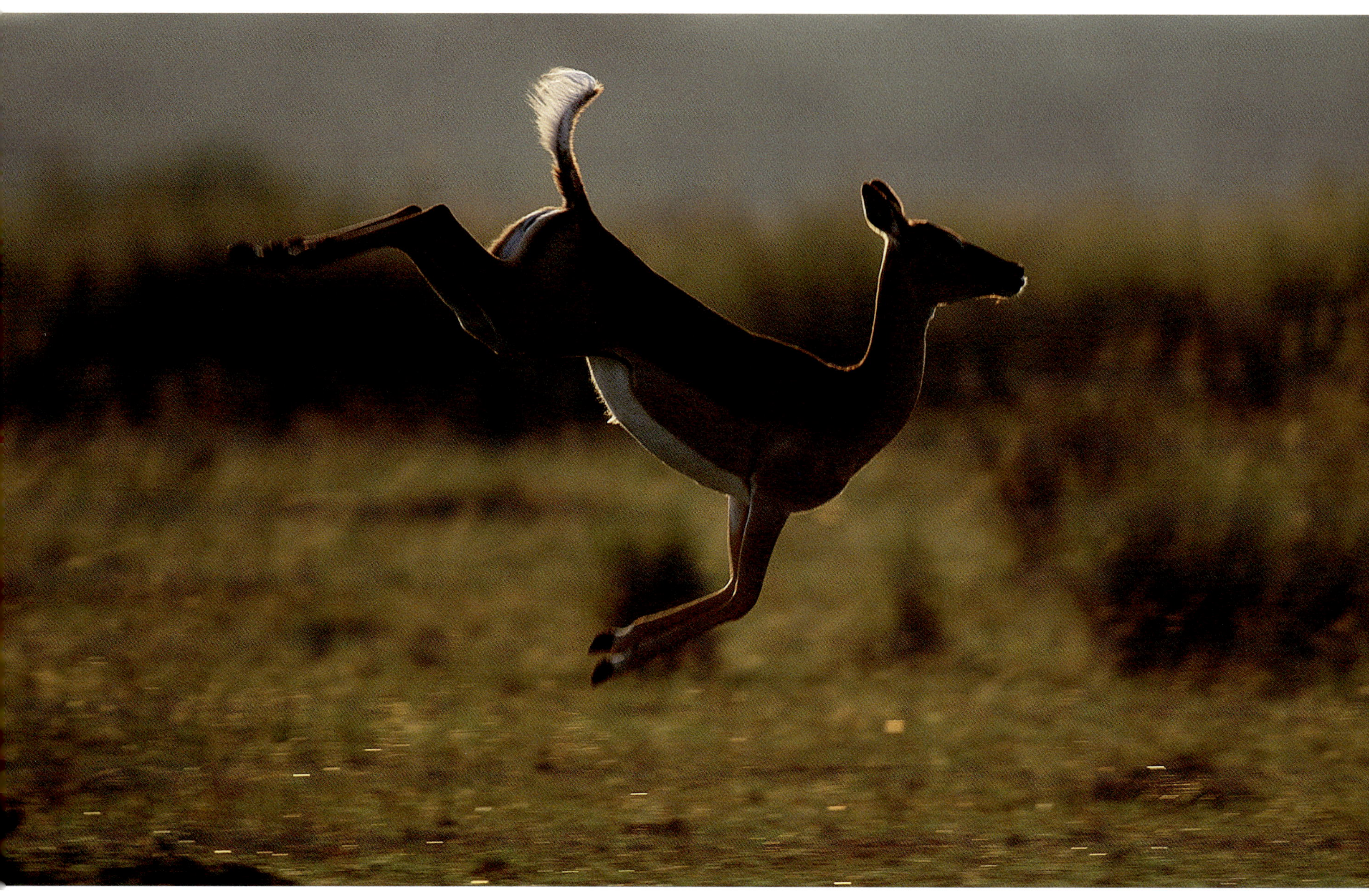

About the size of a white-tailed deer, the impala is the epitomy of lithe gracefulness as it smoothly transitions from running to leaps and bounds.

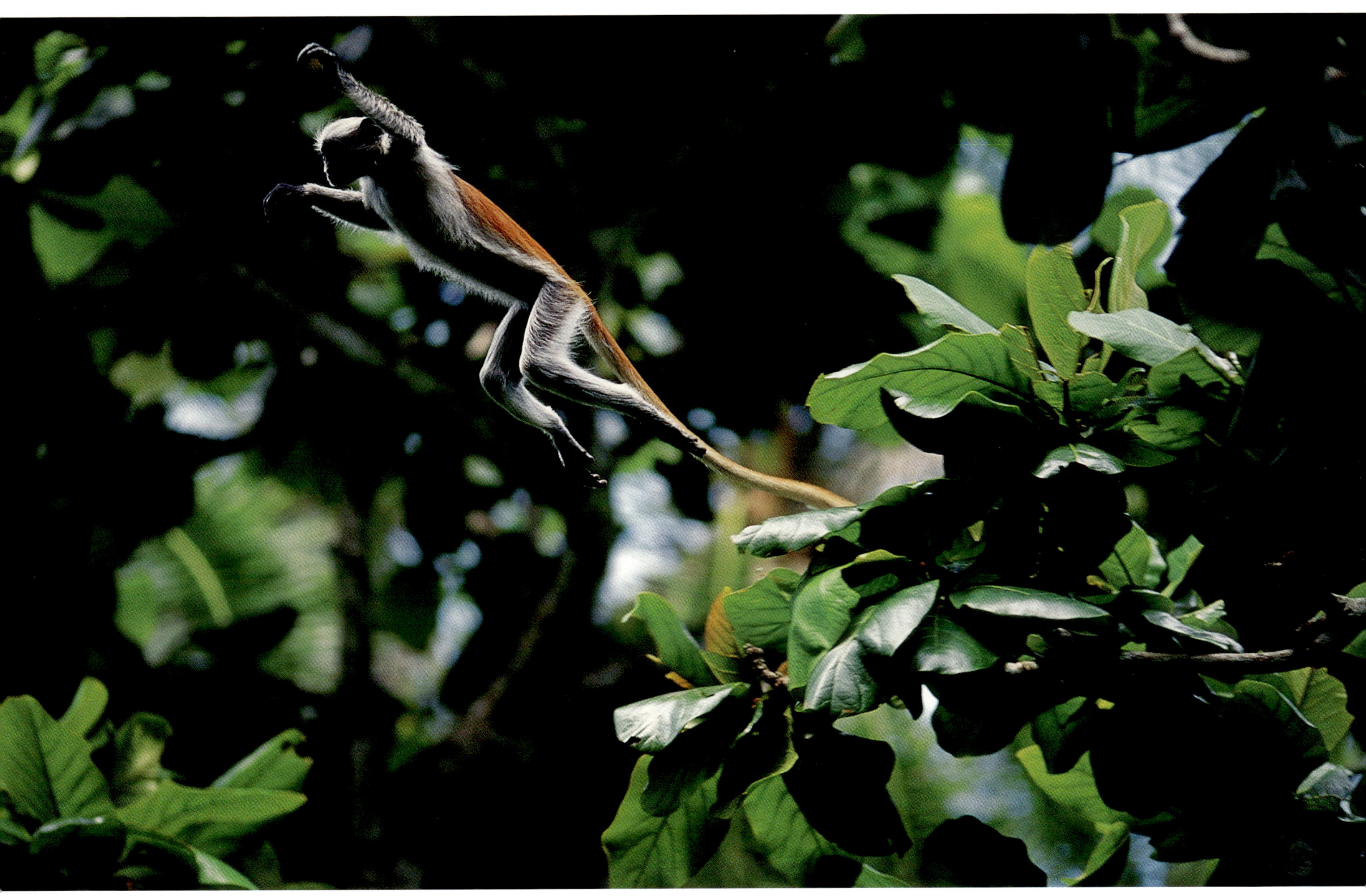

Colobus monkeys are superbly adapted to life in the trees, in part due to a feature they do *not* have – usable thumbs. Without this appendage, the monkey can curl its four elongated fingers into hooks that neatly wrap around branches. They also have feet that are half the length of their legs, which helps as the monkey swings upward from one branch and lands, feet first, on another branch. Treetop-to-treetop leaps of 25 feet are routine.

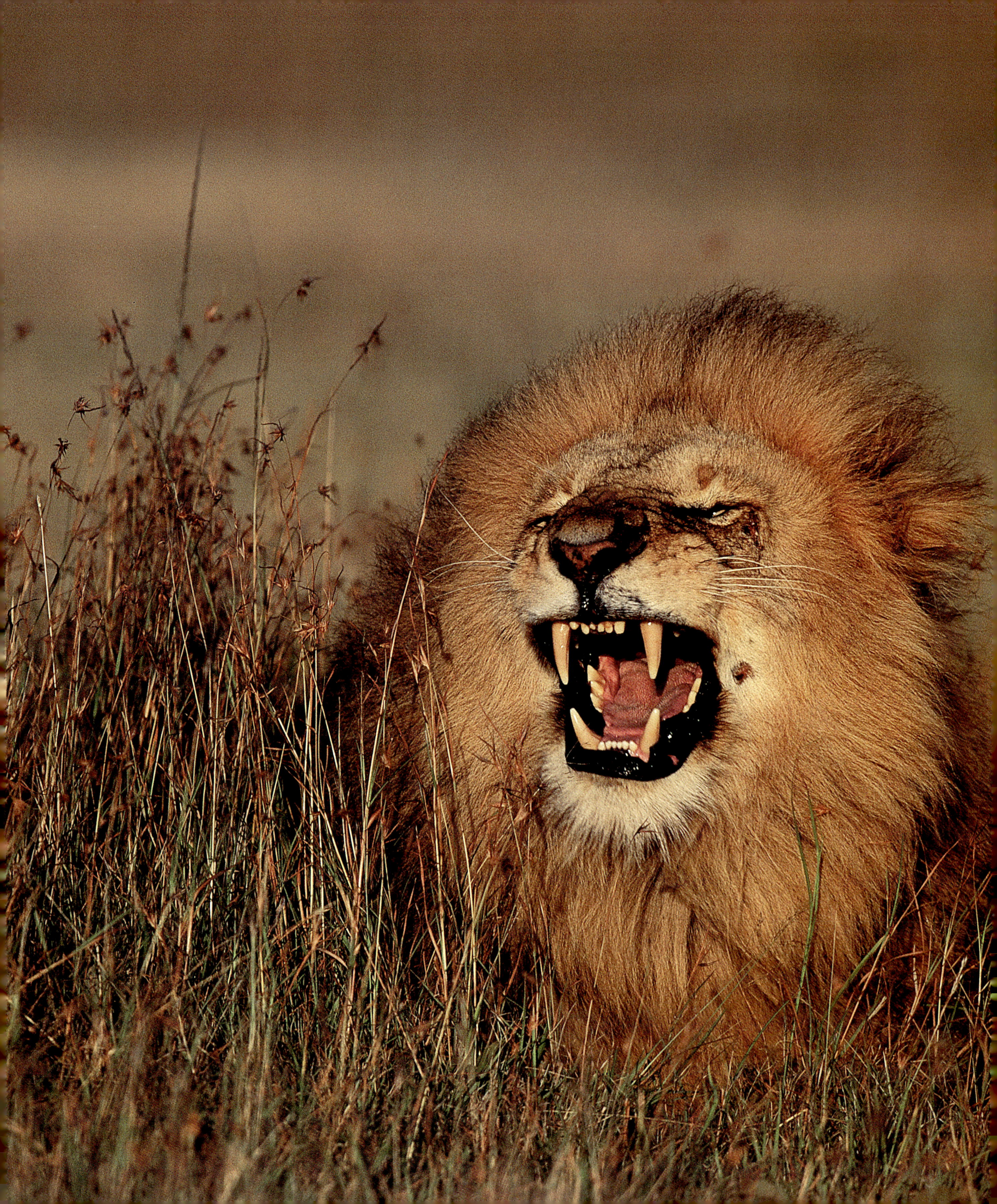

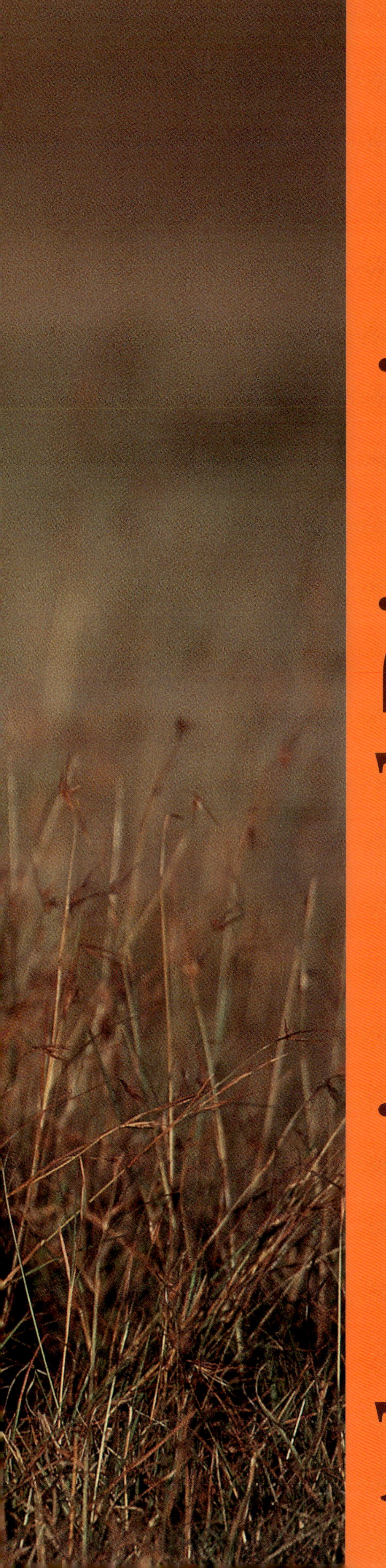

8

Adaptation and Diversity

There is a joke around the savannah that a wildebeest is designed by a committee using the spare parts of other savannah animals. While it may look ungainly, the wildebeest is no chimera. Every part suits the needs of the whole, which is that of a medium-sized herbivore superbly adapted to life in the tough and unpredictable savannah habitat. A wildebeest can move fast and economically over vast distances in search of food and water, but it expends no more energy to run a particular distance than to walk it. Thus, it is enabled to take advantage of the widely scattered distribution of grass, yet remain within easy striking distance of water no matter where it is.

The wildebeest today is a legacy of its ancestors, designed from genes that have survived the eons. Yet a large percentage of its plumbing, wiring, and architecture has been unchanged for thousands of years. And if you go much further back in time, you will learn that with thousands of generations – and hence many, many mutations – to work with, the mammalian body plan accommodates an enormously wide diversity of species.

A good illustration of evolution is not so much a ladder, as it is a bush. Consider the group of animals known as bovids, which include antelopes, buffaloes, wildebeests, and even the domestic cow. A striking feature of this large group is that it consists of an extremely wide range of species, from the tiny dikdik to the massive Cape buffalo. The buffalo is a large unselective grazer, whereas the eland feeds selectively in light woodland, a large chunk of its diet consisting of the leaves of small wild flowers. The Grant's gazelle is a specialist, capable of living in very dry and hot environments. The waterbuck is a specialist too, but as its name implies, ranges around water sources, feeding on lush, green grass. Each species has adapted to its own niche in the environment, but all are linked by a number of common characteristics (such as horns and a four-chambered stomach), and all share the same ancestor.

The example of the bovids illustrates the typical way in which lineages evolve, by radiating out into different ecological niches (known as adaptive radiation). Cats are an even better example. All cats have a common ancestor from whom they have all inherited the ability to stalk and ambush prey. The stalk-ambush strategy, with its suite of anatomical and behavioral adaptations, links all cats and has been the basis of a massive radiation over five continents.

Yet why are there so many species of, say, bovids in the savannah? Why not fewer? The short answer is this: The habitat of the savannah is extremely diverse, and natural selection has enabled bovids to adapt to this diversity. One major reason for such diversity is variability in soils, which drives plants to specialize. One grass species will evolve to tolerate soils containing high concentrations of a mineral that other grasses find distasteful. Yet another will have found a way to cope with prolonged drought. And so it goes, and after a few million years, a wildly diverse landscape has developed. The result is a wonderfully varied ecosystem in which specialized plants lead to specialized plant-eaters and so on up the pyramid of life.

Pages 92–93
A tawny-colored male lion, who would otherwise blend into the yellow-brown grass, reveals himself when he raises his head to better decipher a scent he has picked up.

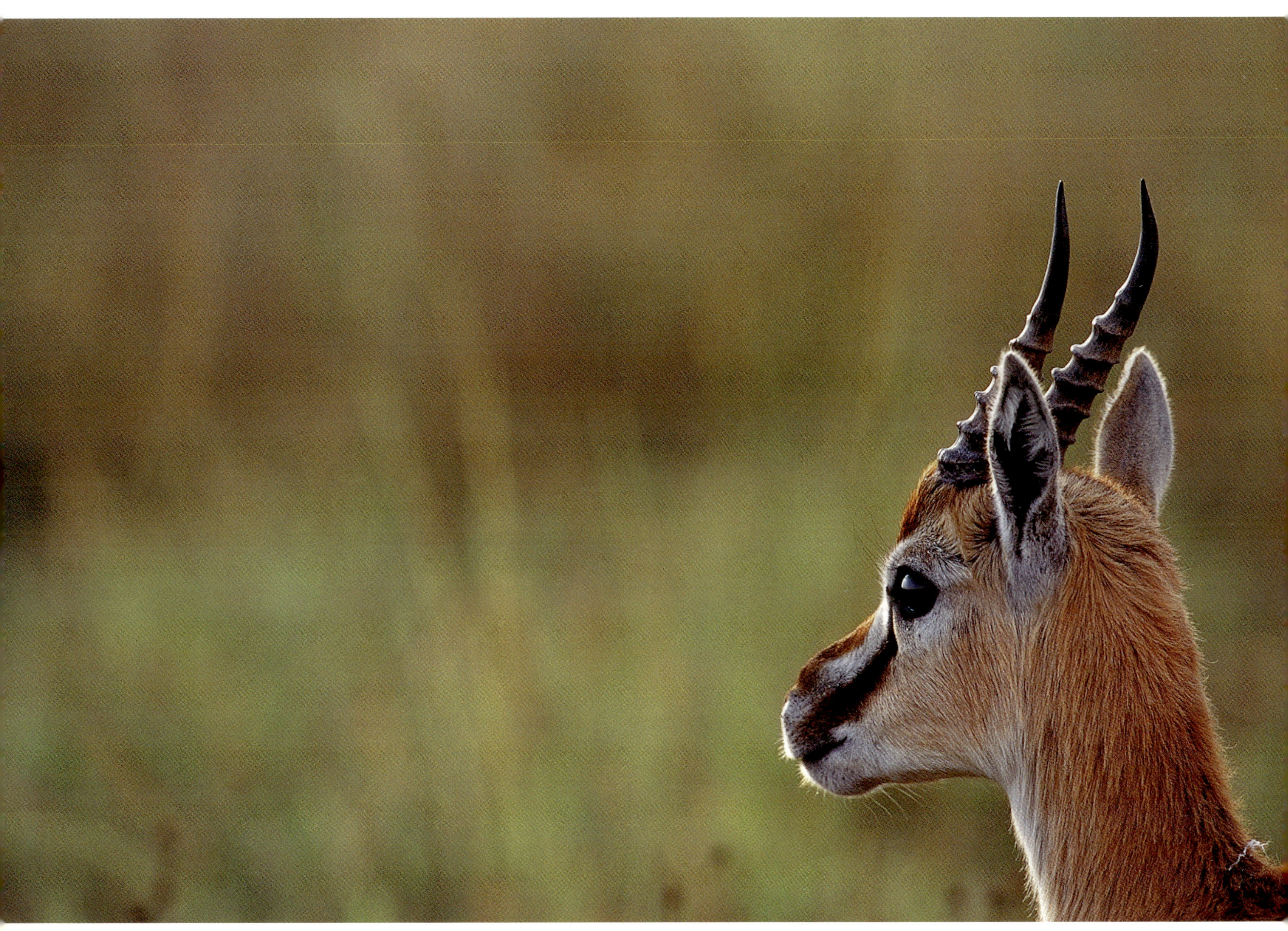

This Thomson's gazelle's horns grow fairly close together and are ringed. In the female, the horns are more slender, smoother, and shorter than the male's.

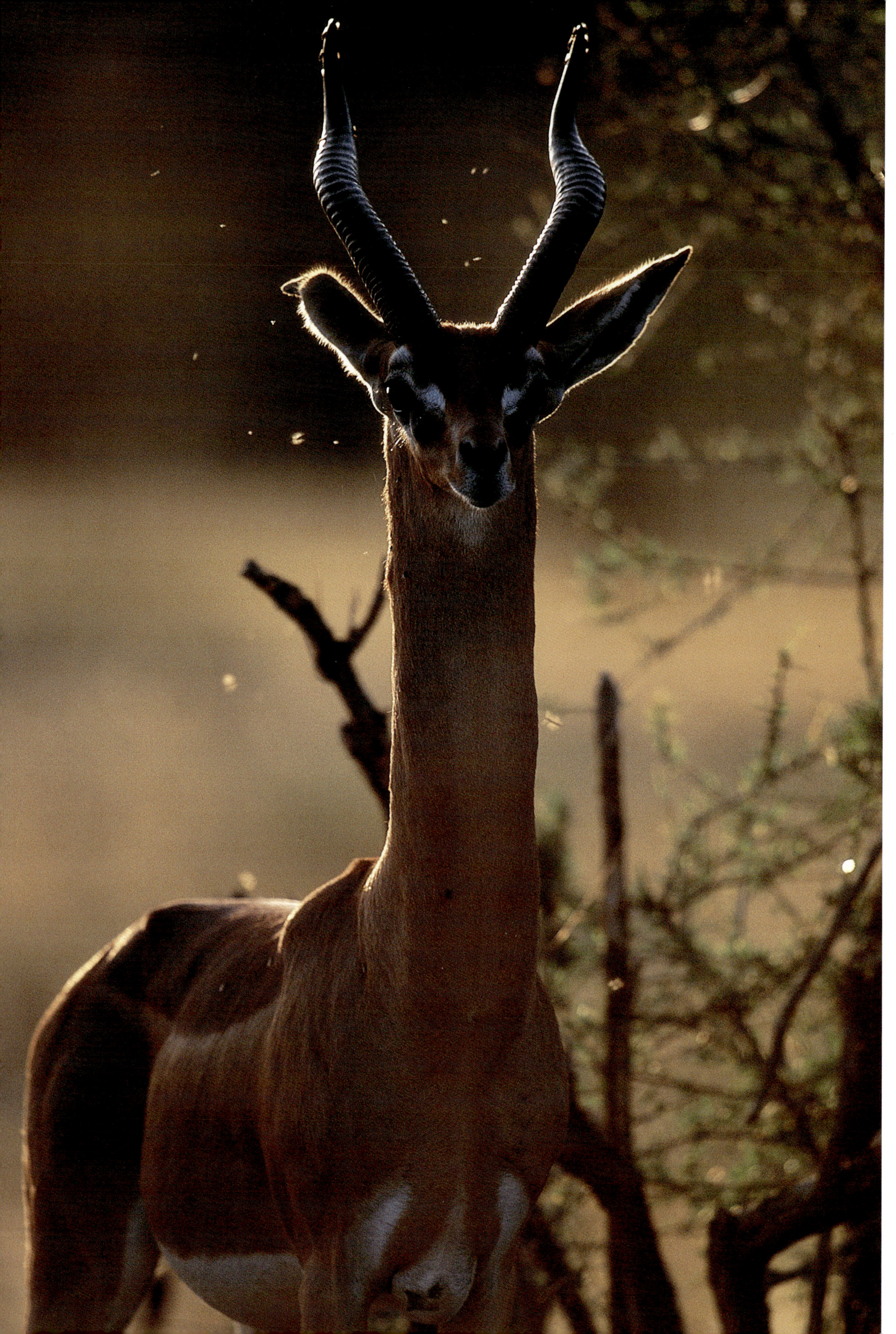

Opposite
In gerenuks, only the males carry horns, which are short and heavily ringed. The gerenuk inhabits arid savannah in which there is a good supply of thorn scrub.

Elands are Africa's largest antelope and similar to the American elk in body size. They wander in grasslands and light brush country, feeding on nutritious leguminous and other broad-leaved plants, a diet which helps account for their large size.

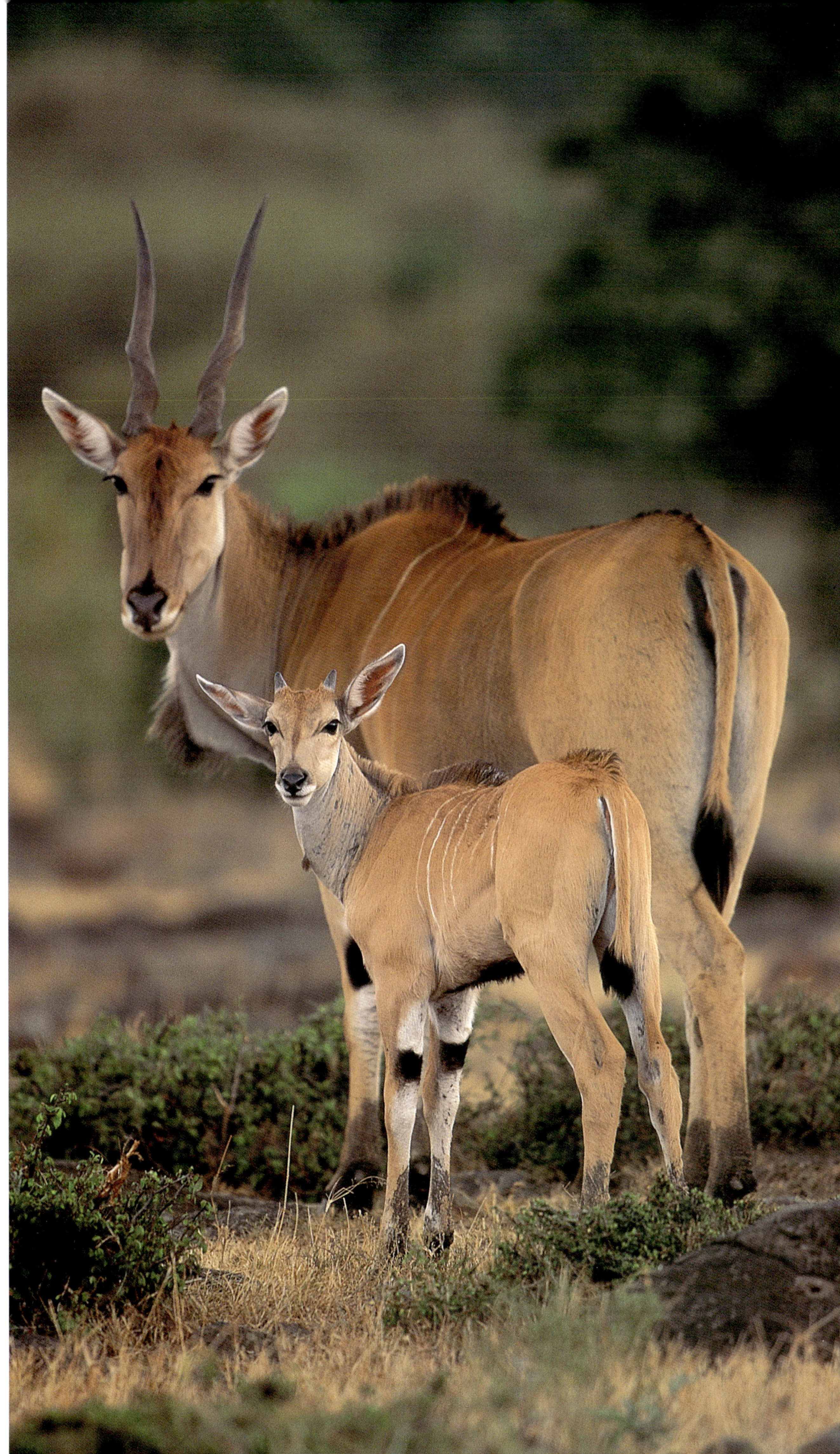

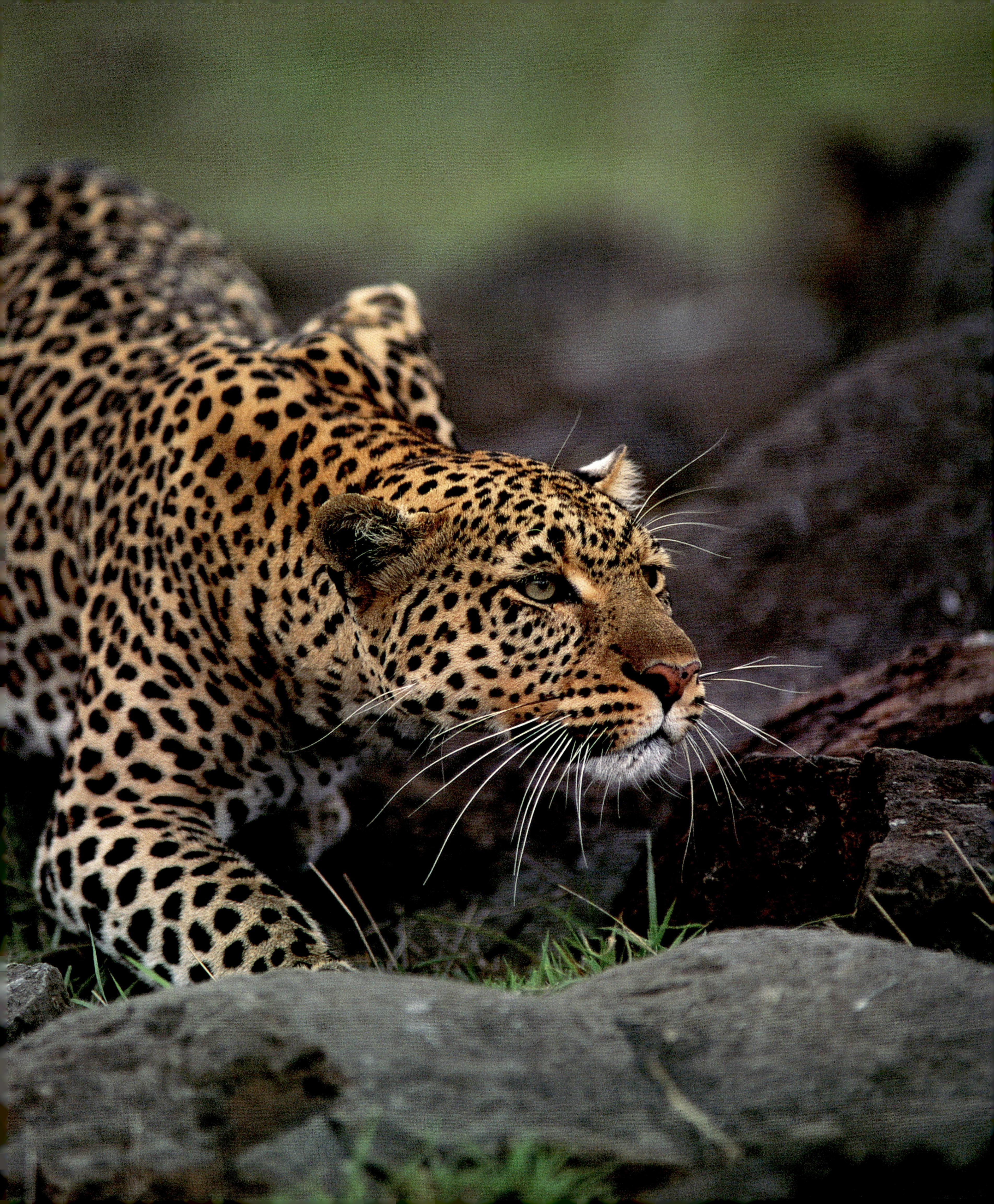

Opposite
All senses on the alert, this female leopard stalks an unwary impala. Stalking prey is a characteristic of all big cats.

A topi's lyrate horns are thick and deeply ringed, and its face is typical of a savannah antelope with its large, sensitive nose, well-developed ears capable of swiveling, and eyes located high up on the sides of its head. All together, its features make a great danger-detection apparatus. Topis inhabit open savannah grasslands and woodlands.

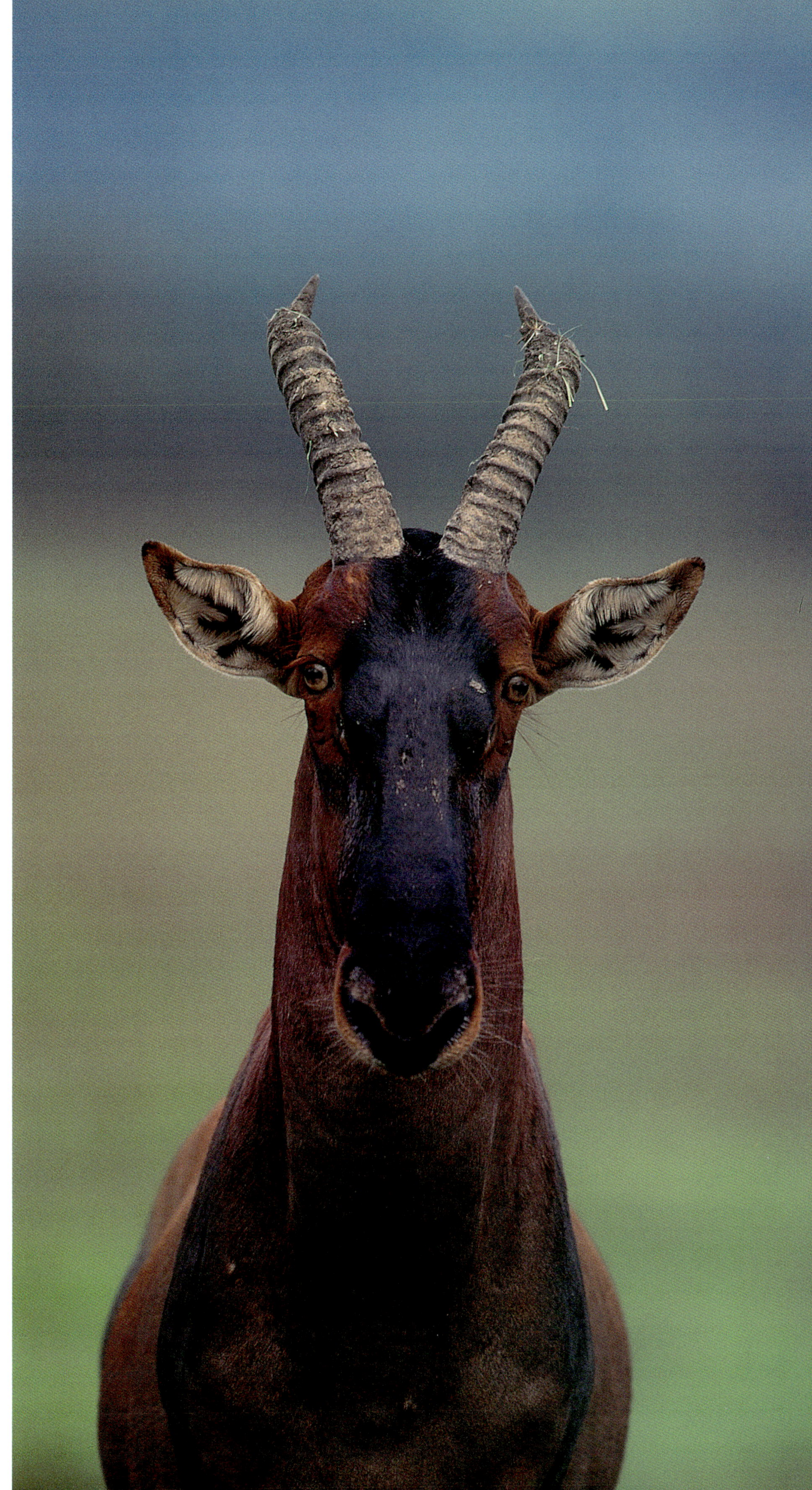

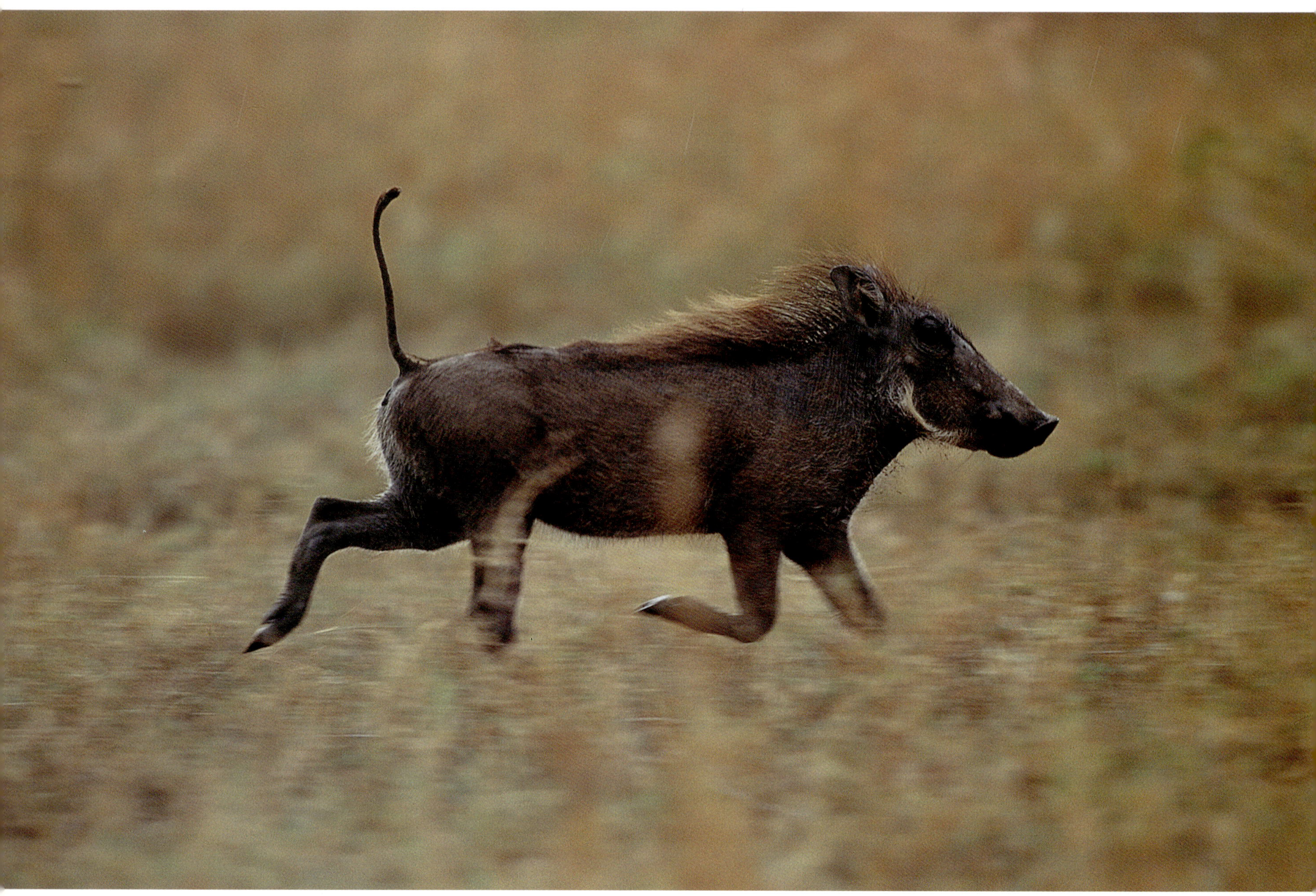

Tail raised like an antenna, a warthog canters to safety. Warthogs are quite aggressive in temperament, and if cornered by a lion, they will charge at the cat with every intention of causing injury.

Opposite
A male patas monkey keeps an eye on his harem from a distance. Patas monkeys live in semi-arid savannah with a liberal supply of acacia trees, which make up a large portion of this monkey's diet. The patas is also known as the hussar monkey because of its rather flamboyant appearance with its white mustache and its red, black, and white coat.

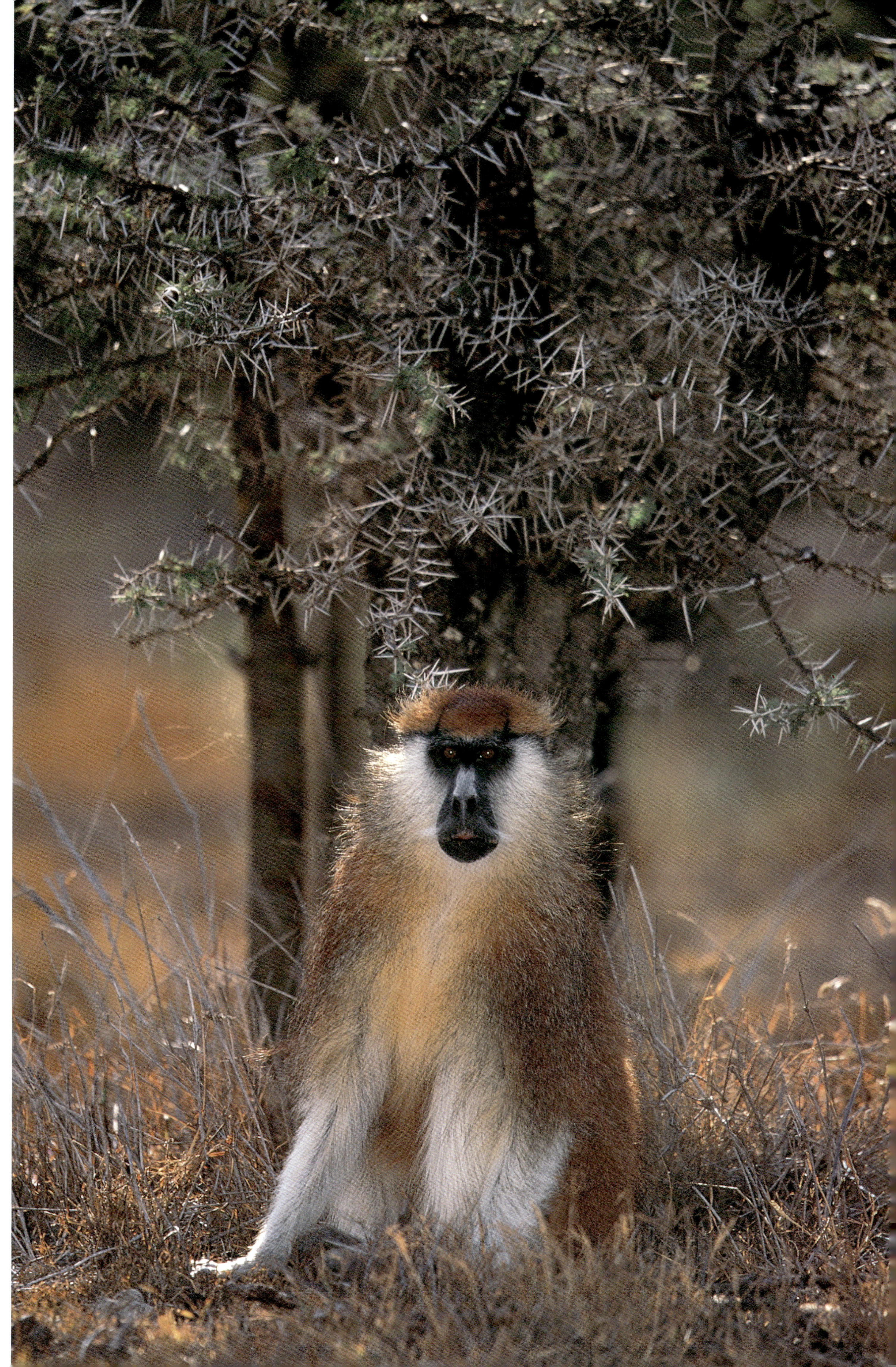

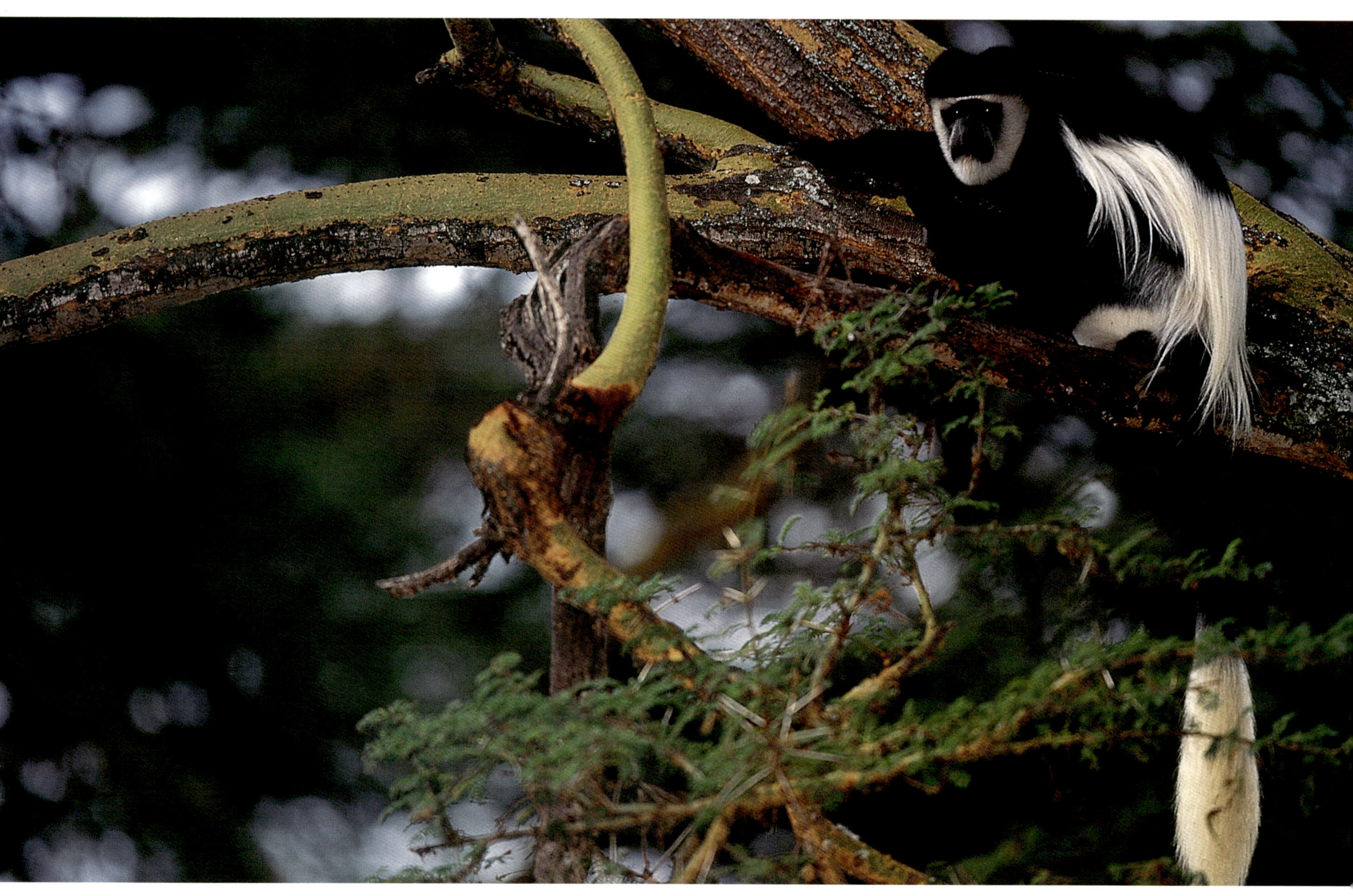

These colobus monkeys are able to survive on a small number of tree species in a very limited area. To supplement their diet, they will often descend to the ground to eat soil and clay.

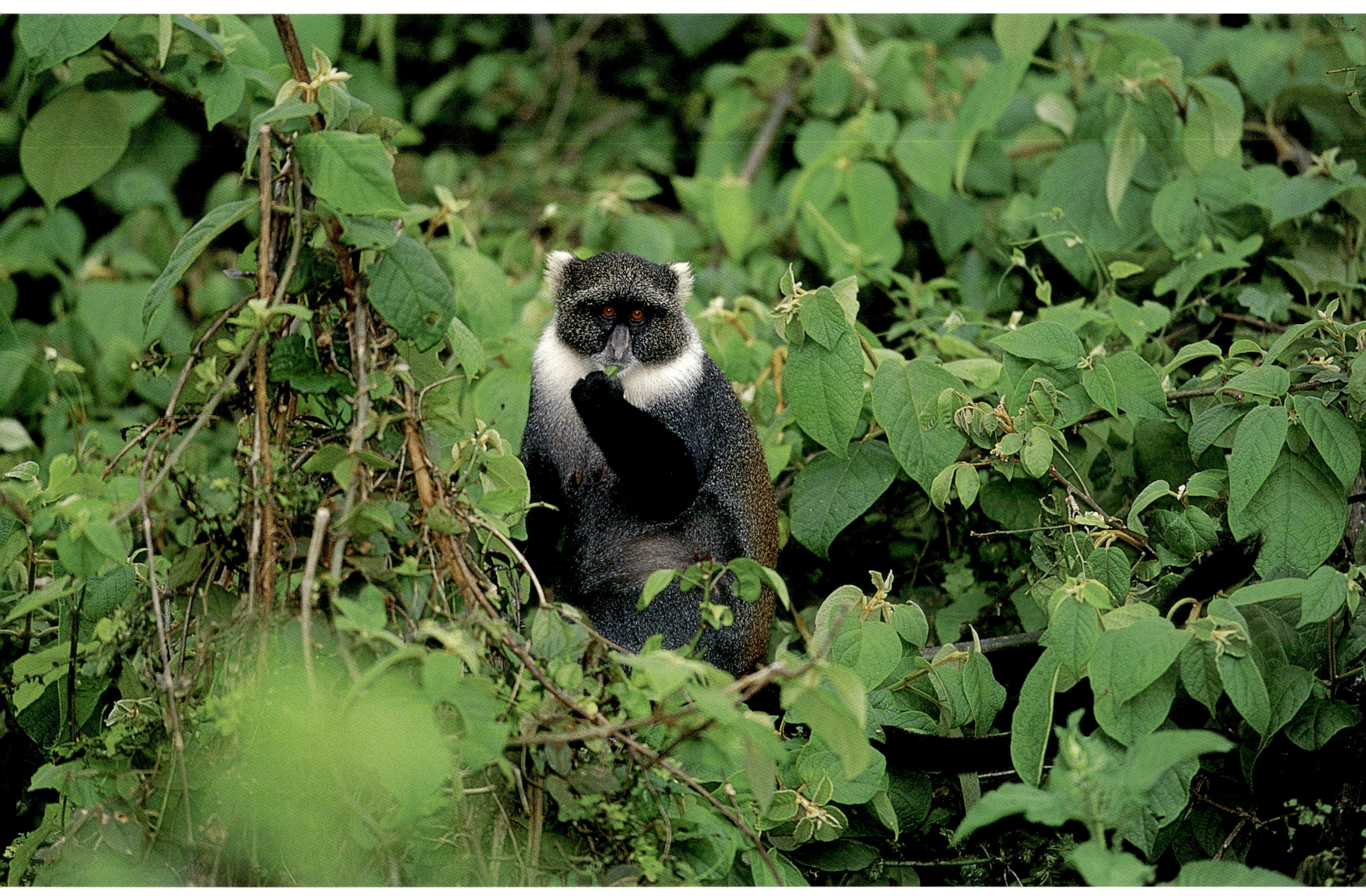

Sykes monkeys like this one rely heavily on leaves and fruit for their diet, unlike smaller guenons such as red-tailed monkeys, which feed largely on insects.

Pages 104–105
Flamingoes often congregate in the tens of thousands on Lake Bogoria in Kenya. Although the lake has a high concentration of sodium carbonate, it produces a microscopic algae, which is the mainstay of the flamingo diet. It also influences the color of their feathers.

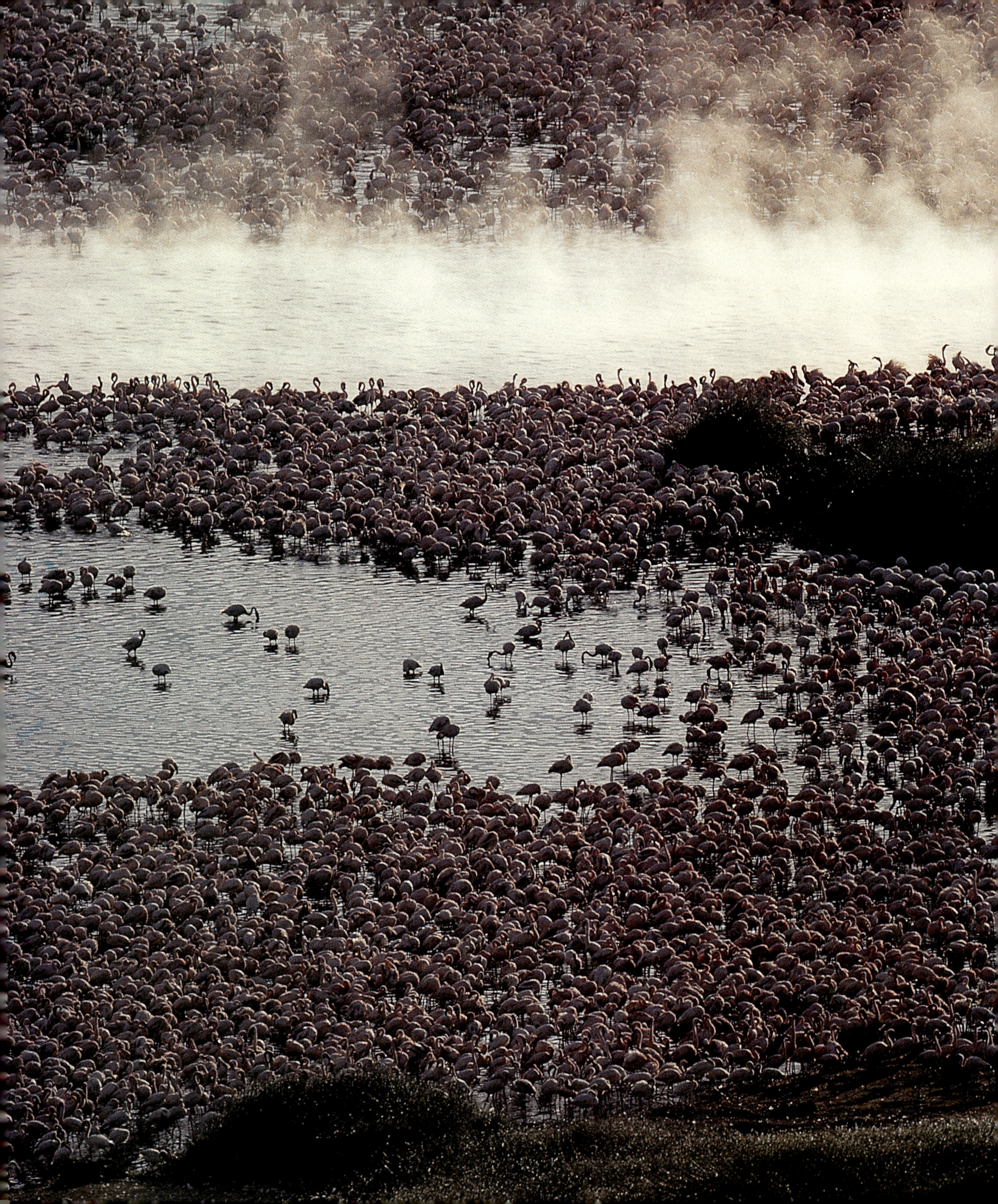

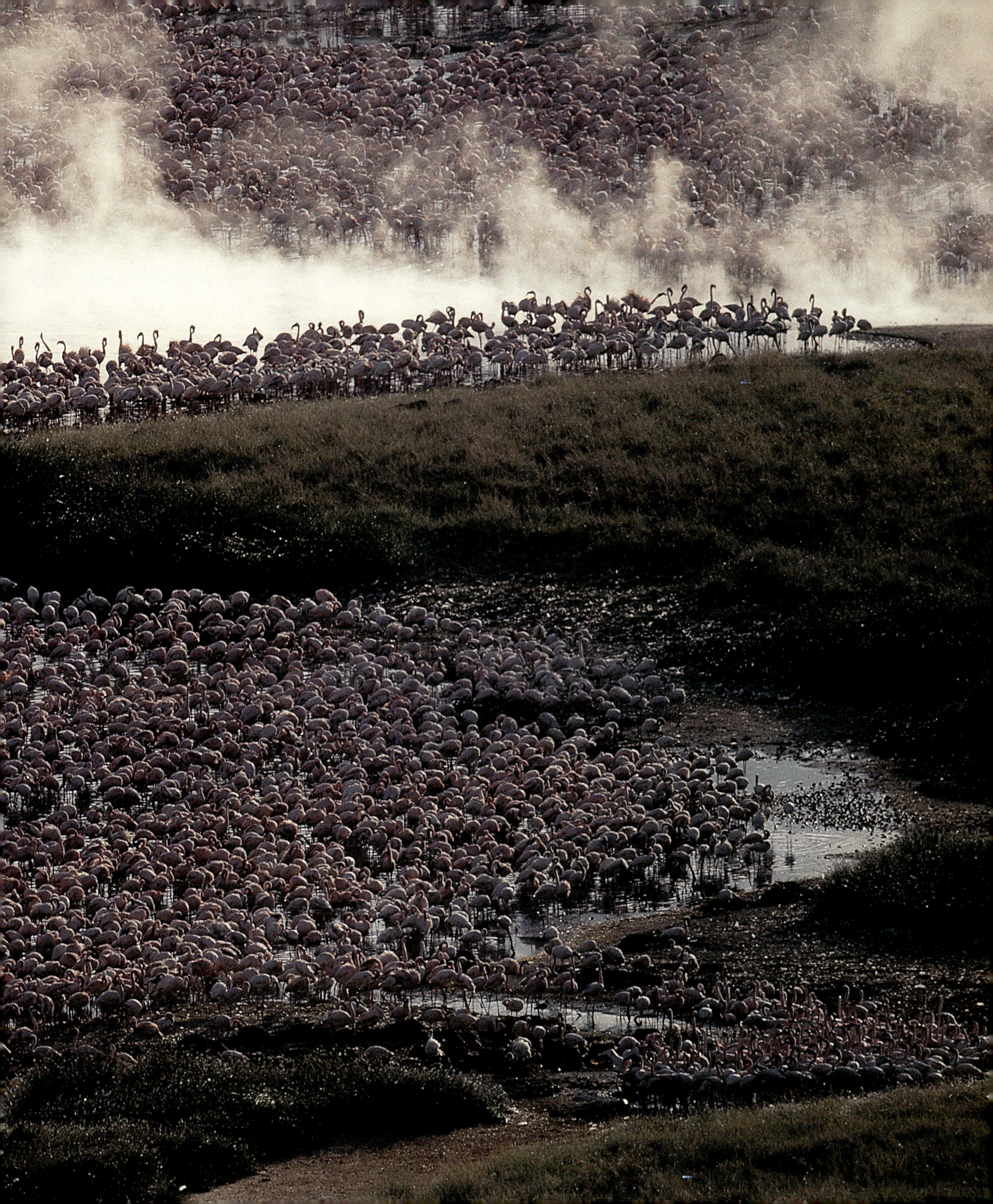

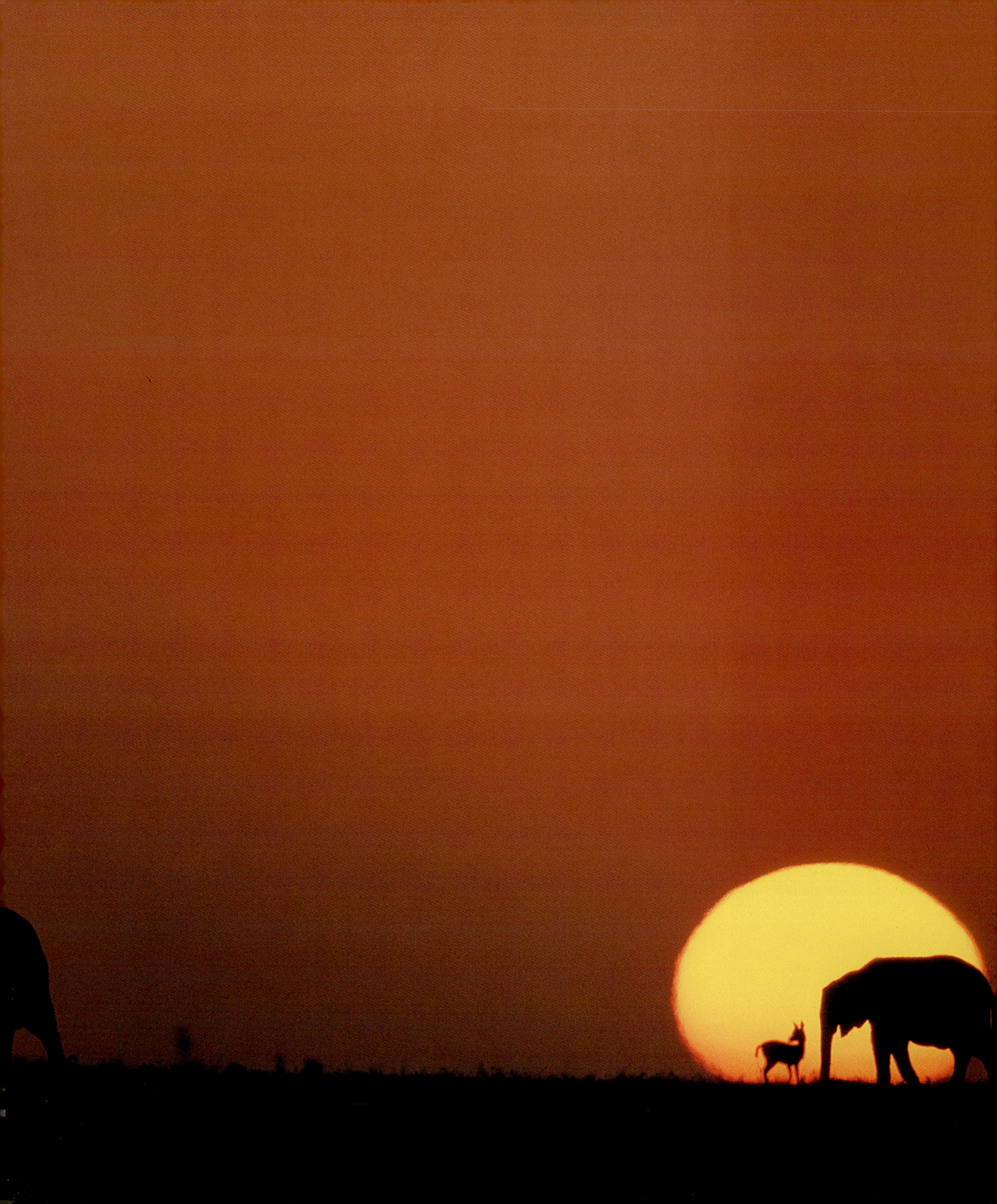

9

Peaceful Coexistence

In the savannah you may come across a puzzling scene: Right before your eyes there are seven species of herbivores – wildebeest, zebra, topi, hartebeest, Thomson's gazelle, Grant's gazelle, and warthog – all feeding together in close proximity to one another. They appear relaxed and tolerant of one another. How can this be? A large part of the answer has to do with the idea of niche separation.

Almost every species in the savannah has its own niche for which it is uniquely adapted. The term *niche* not only refers to the animal's food and water needs, but also its way of life. The niche of the cheetah, for example, is the grassland habitat where it hunts gazelles, drinks, and does everything else to survive and reproduce.

Consider the need for water. Those that need to drink daily, such as waterbuck, reedbuck, and Cape buffalo, live at or very near water sources. Wildebeest and zebra can go without water for two or three days so they can range more widely. Oryx can abstain for weeks at a time and are found in dry habitats. Grant's gazelles can live without drinking altogether, relying only on the water in the vegetation and dew that may form at night.

Another way in which niche separation occurs is the manner in which different species use particular parts of the same habitat – a patch of grass, for example. Tall grass is avoided by small herbivores since they cannot easily find the grass type they prefer, and it may conceal hungry lions. Elephants, having no fear of lions, trample into chest-high grass and feed on the heavy coarse material. Buffaloes often follow elephants, trampling the grass further. If conditions are damp enough, the trampled grass will sprout new shoots, which attracts zebras. Zebras prefer the stem part of the grass over the leaves, for which purpose they have incisor teeth in both jaws, allowing them to easily nip off the tough stems. The wildebeests that follow have broader mouths to gather up their preference for more leaf and less stem. The pastures refined by the wildebeests are then quickly occupied by gazelles and hartebeests who have more delicate mouths with pointed muzzles. They selectively nip off the leafy parts of the grass, close to the ground. Egyptian geese then graze on the shortest swards, termites clean up the debris, and insect-eating birds take continual advantage of the insects stirred up by the feet of the grazing herbivores.

Although this example of niche separation, known as the grazing sequence, appears neat and tidy, there are complications. While some species such as giraffes, elands, and woodpeckers are specialists, being dependent on a few kinds of foods which they exploit using highly specialized structures and techniques, others, such as elephants, leopards, and baboons are generalists, having the ability to feed on a greater variety of food and therefore able to adapt to more than one habitat. Inevitably, competition can result, especially in times of scarcity. And there is sometimes competition for resources among herbivores:

Pages 106–107
The sun appears on the horizon, swelling as it rises, until it becomes an enormous golden orb silhouetting a grazing elephant and a Thomson's gazelle.

African elephants occasionally kill rhinos; zebras have on rare occasions been known to maim and kill the young of gazelles and wildebeests.

Cheetahs share the grasslands with lions and hyenas and feed on prey animals that lions and hyenas are keen to scavenge, so there is much competition between these overlapping niches. With their superior weaponry and muscle-power, lions and hyenas will rob cheetahs of their kills and even kill their cubs.

There is almost no separation between the niches of lions and hyenas, which results in a great deal of tension. A consequence of this is that the two species have evolved characteristics that allow them to coexist. Lions have evolved into group-living creatures, which allows them to more successfully defend their kills. Time and time again, a pack of hyenas has been observed to drive a single lioness away from her kill, but they wouldn't dare attack a pride of lionesses at their meal.

Fortunately, most species on the savannah have their own niches, thereby reducing conflict and promoting a somewhat harmonious and peaceful coexistence.

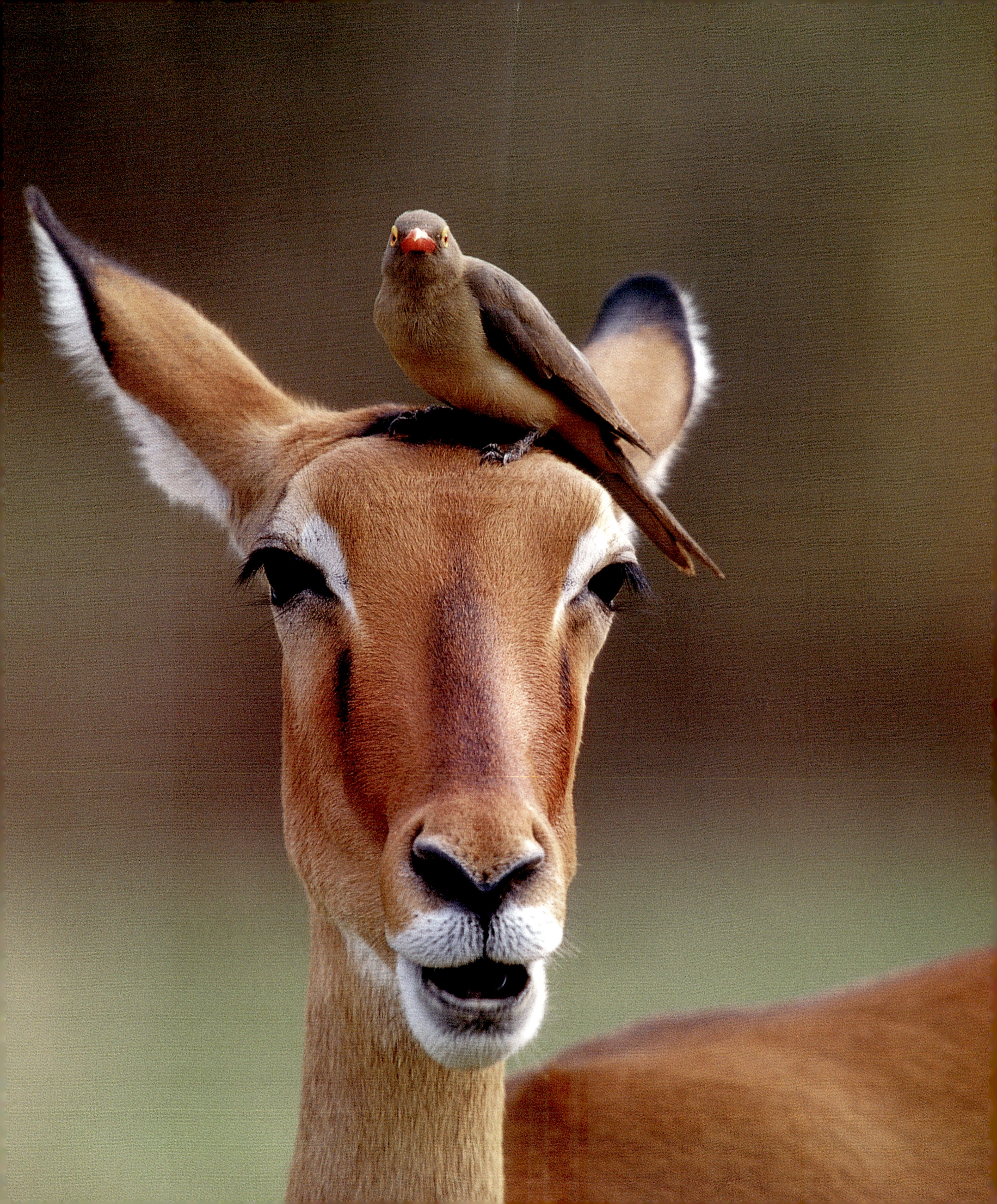

Opposite
In this example of mutualism, a form of symbiosis, red-billed oxpeckers have long been thought to aid mammals like this impala by picking ticks and other pests off their skin. But they may also peck at wounds already existing on the animal, which delays healing time.

The gerenuk often rears up on its hind legs to feed, which more than doubles its vertical reach.

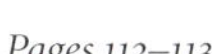

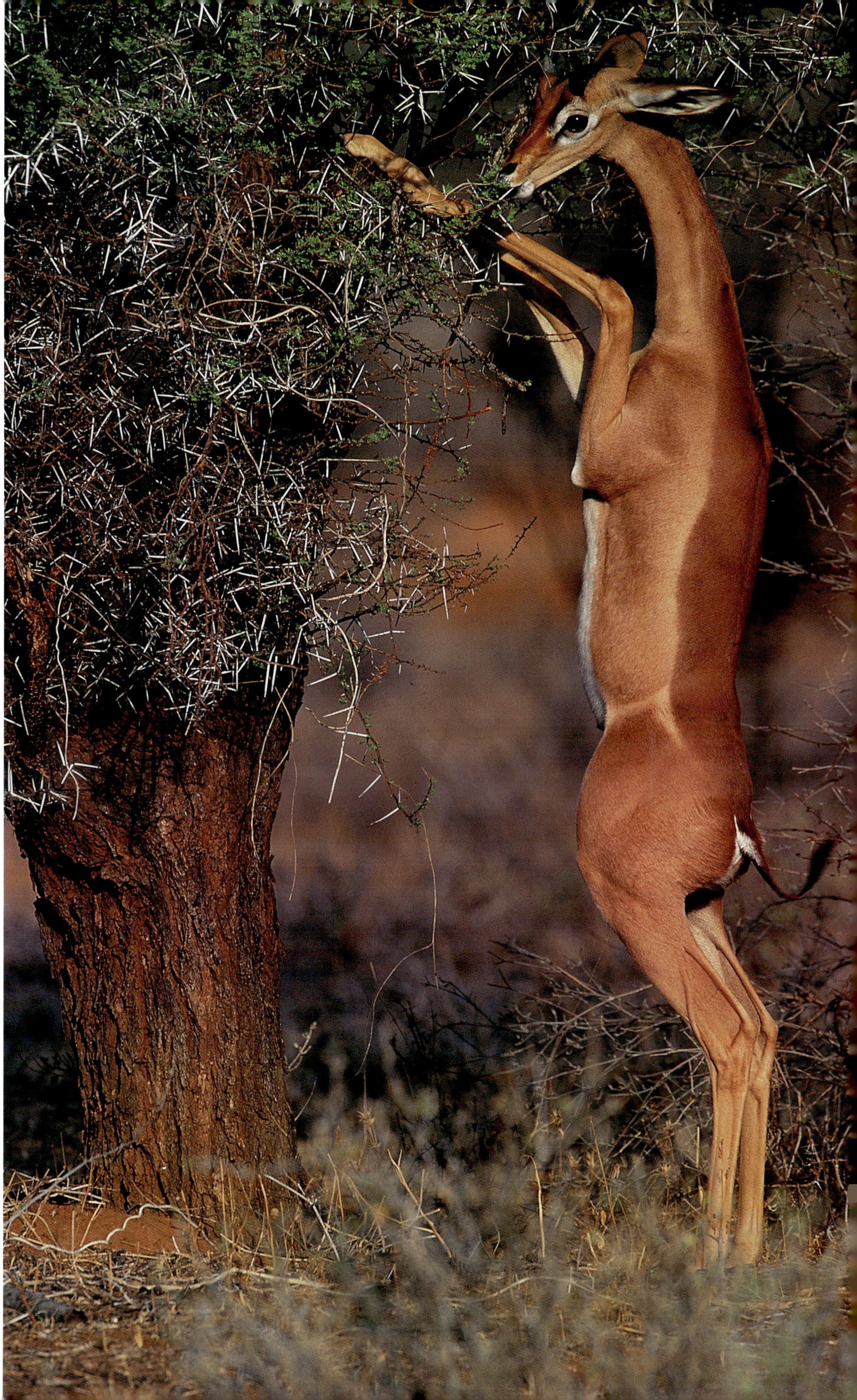

Pages 112–113
A cattle egret is on the lookout for insects and other delicacies stirred up by this grazing white rhino. Since there is no competition for resources between these two, there is no animosity, and in fact they have developed a rather symbiotic relationship. While the rhino releases food for the egret, the egret relieves the rhino of a wide variety of aggravating insects.

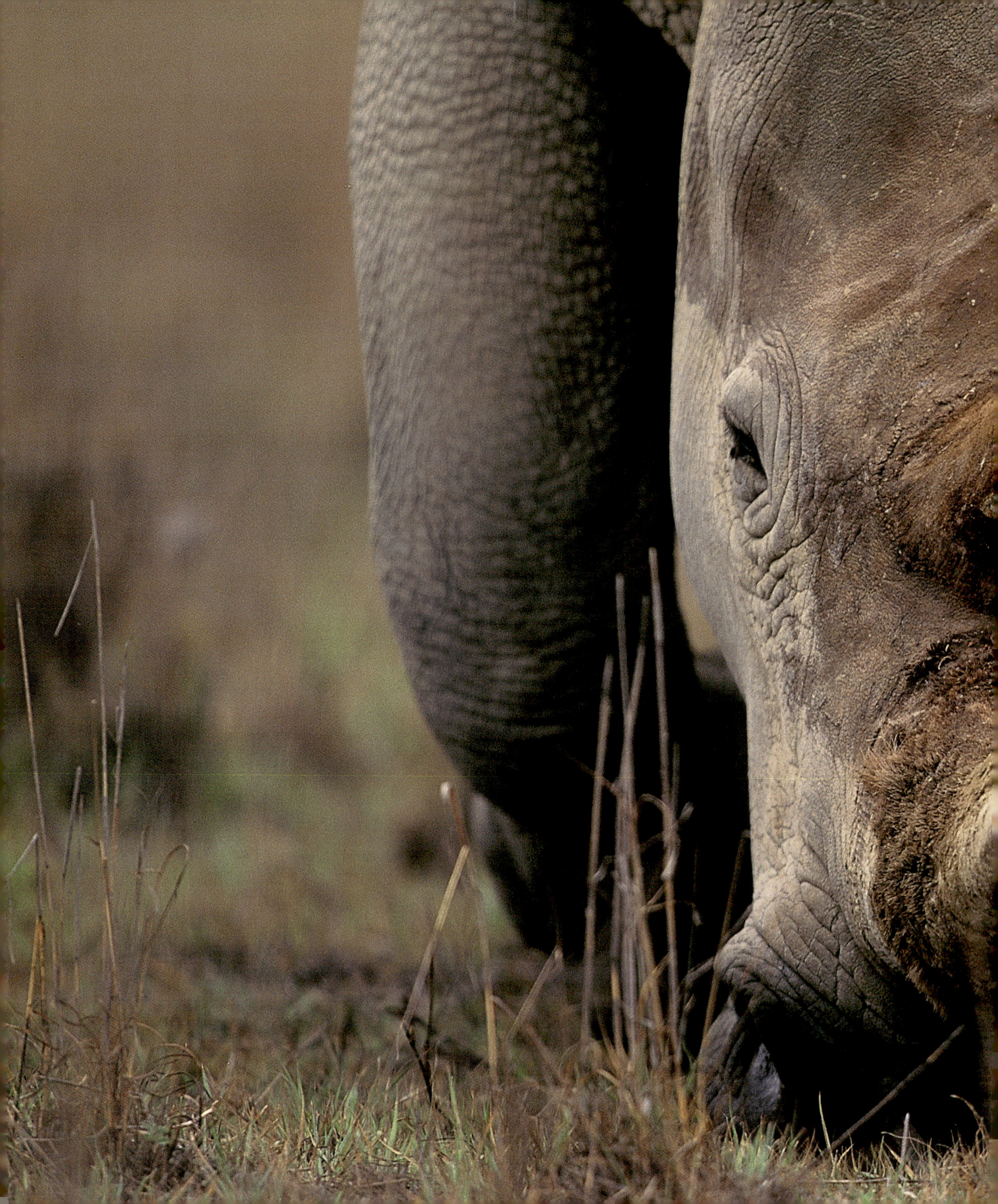

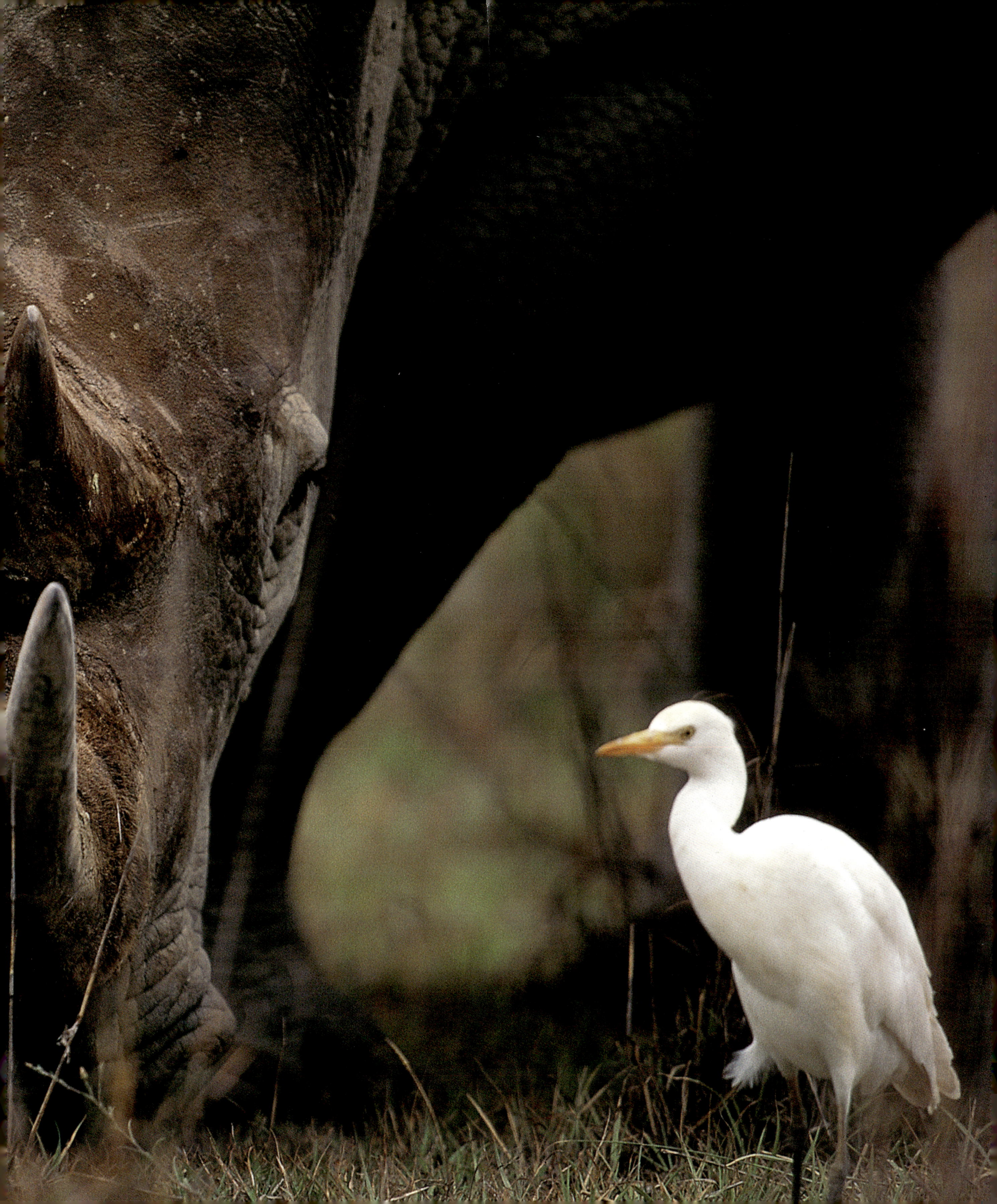

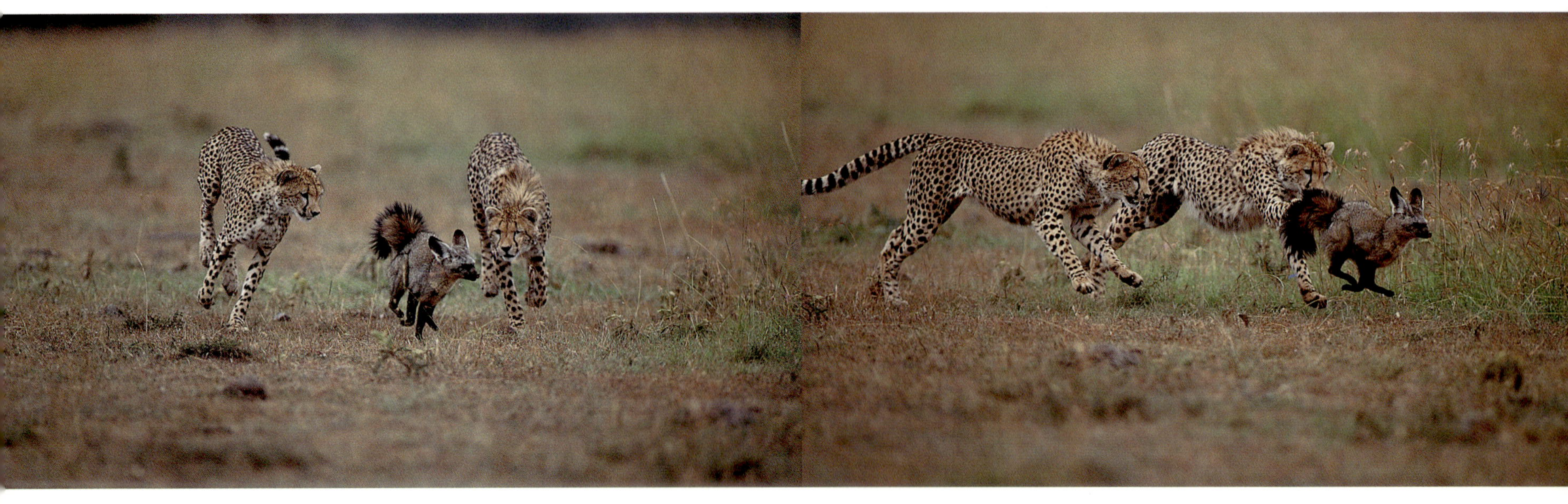

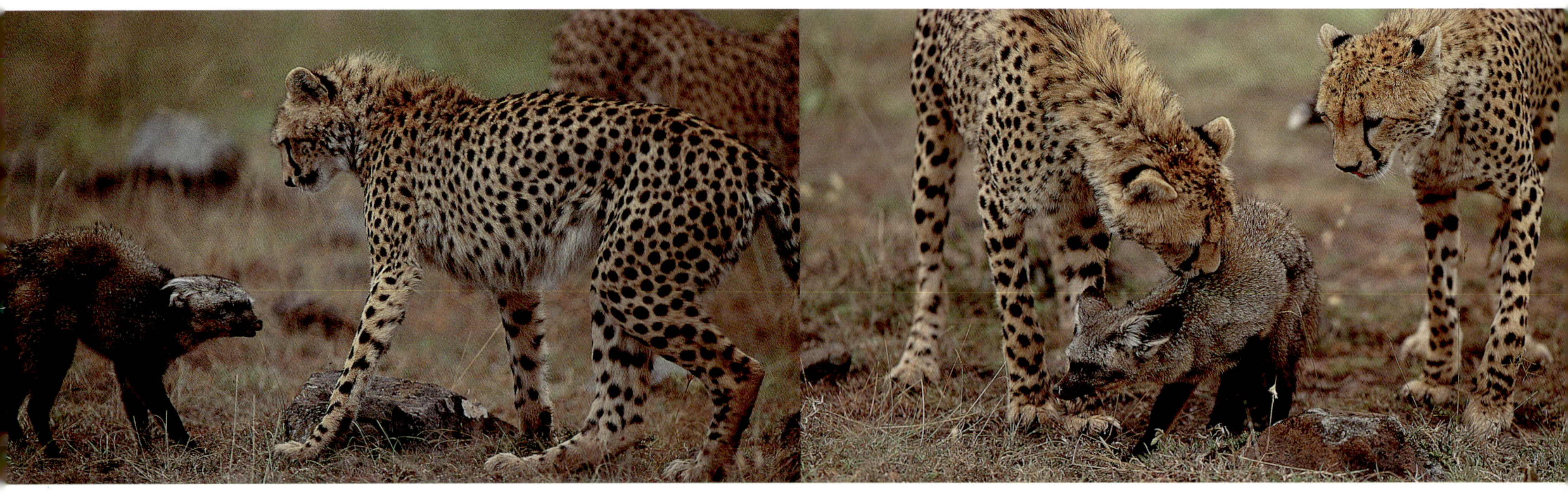

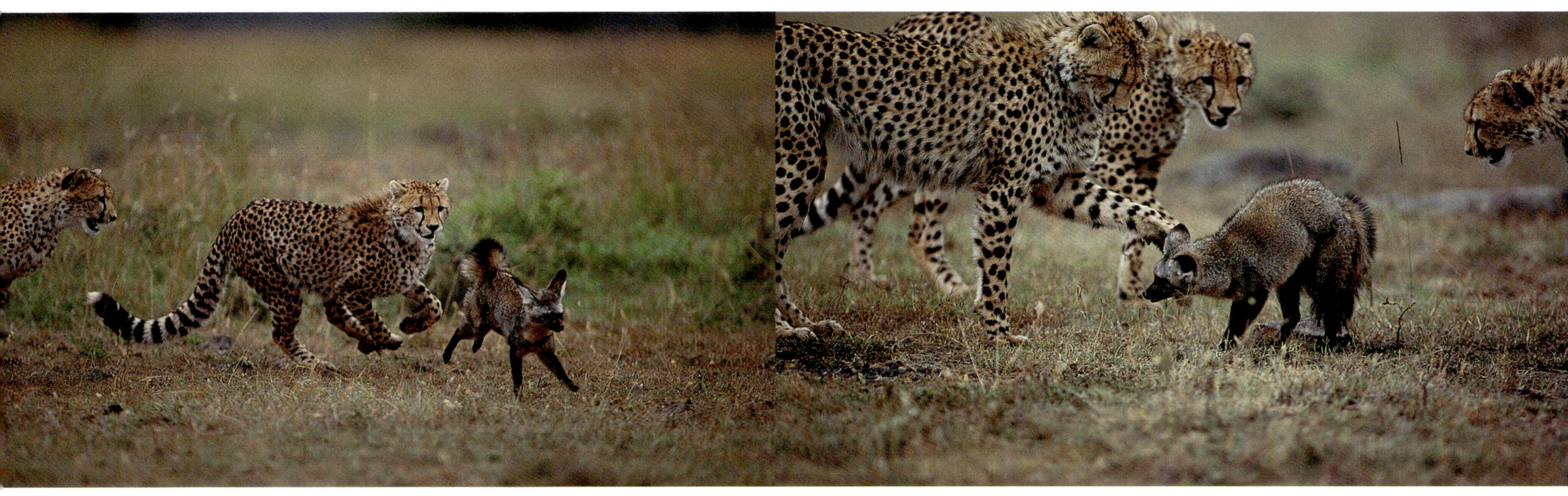

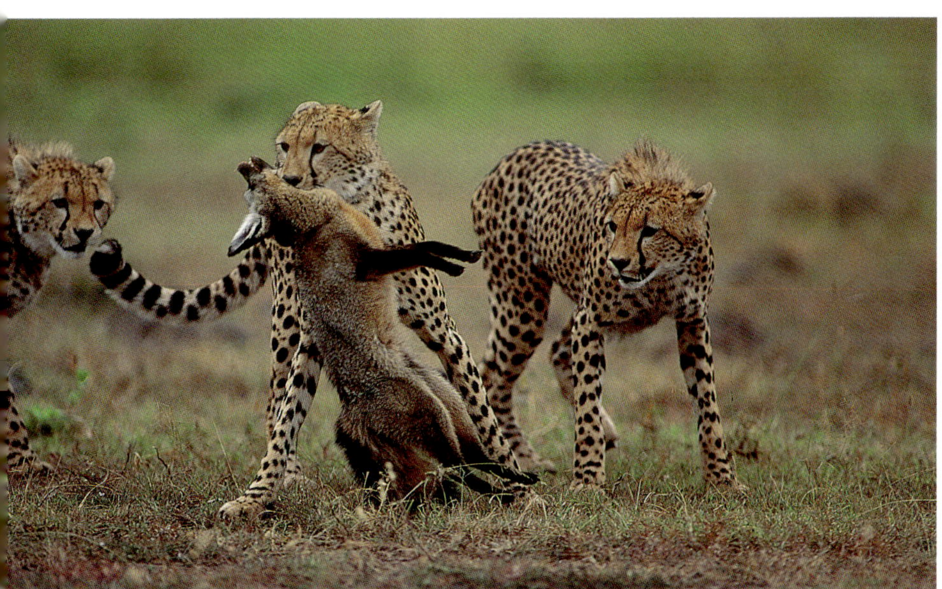

Opposite and above
One cloudy morning, a cheetah mother with three adolescent cubs chanced upon a bat-eared fox foraging on the open plains. While the mother showed no interest, the teenagers went into chase mode. There was nowhere for the bat-eared fox to hide, and the speedy cheetahs easily caught up with the terrified animal. The cheetahs were momentarily taken aback as the fox turned on them snarling and growling, but then curiosity got the better of them. They sniffed it, pawed at it, and one cheetah even carried it triumphantly in its jaws.

Meanwhile, the cheetah mother, who had been scanning for likely prey, moved on, and the cubs, noticing her departure, reluctantly left the traumatized, but unhurt, fox behind. The fox sat very still for about 15 minutes, probably regaining its composure, then it got up and resumed business as usual.

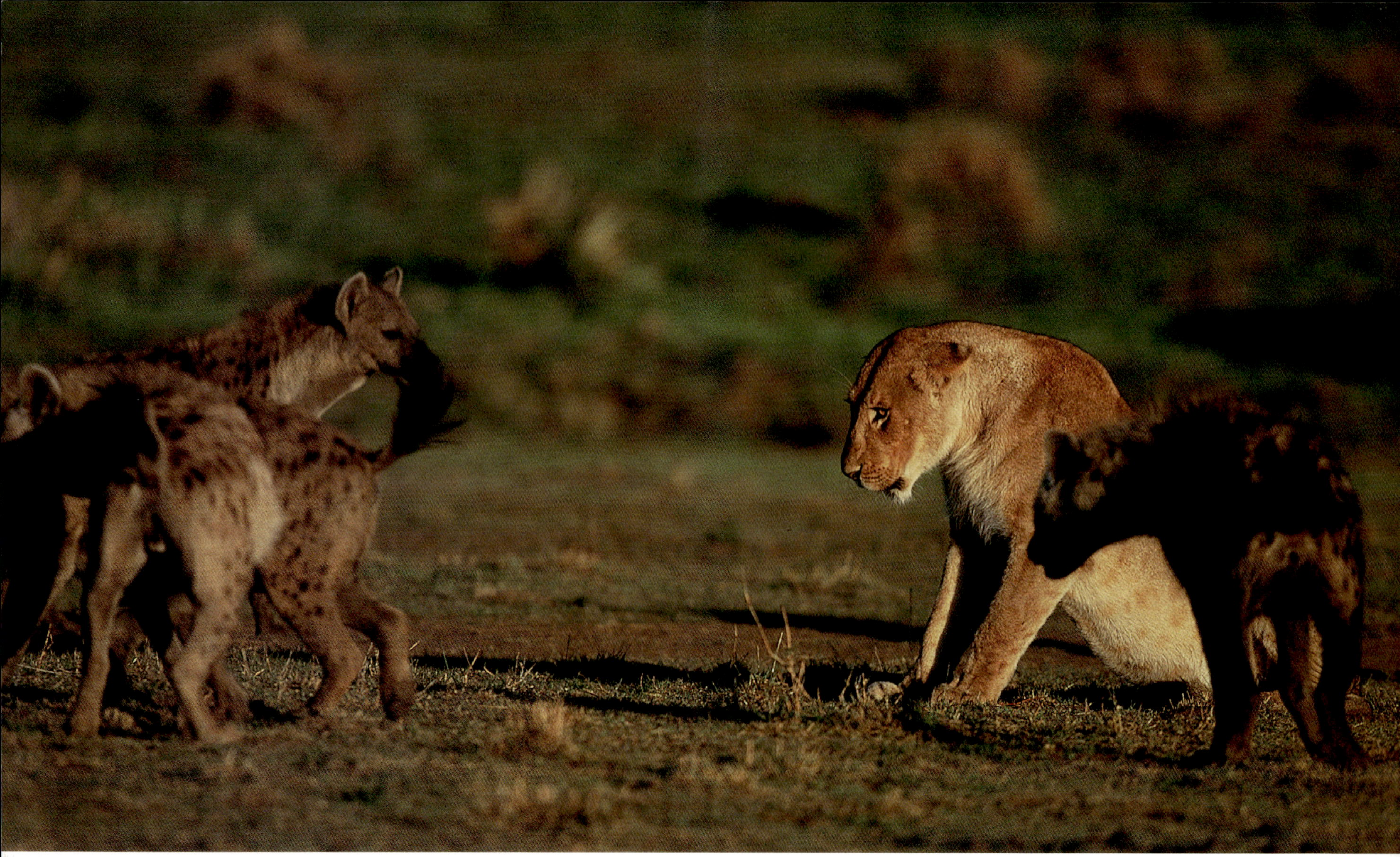

Several spotted hyenas attempt to "psyche out" an adolescent male lion, who seems determined to hold his ground. He did.

Opposite, above
A male serval cat sprays a clump of grass in the first few minutes of a new day. Male serval cats are territorial and will aggressively defend their turf.

Opposite, below
On a misty morning, a male lion investigates a scent that has caught his attention. It is believed that he can detect different kinds of urine spray left by various lions, informing him as to who has been here and when.

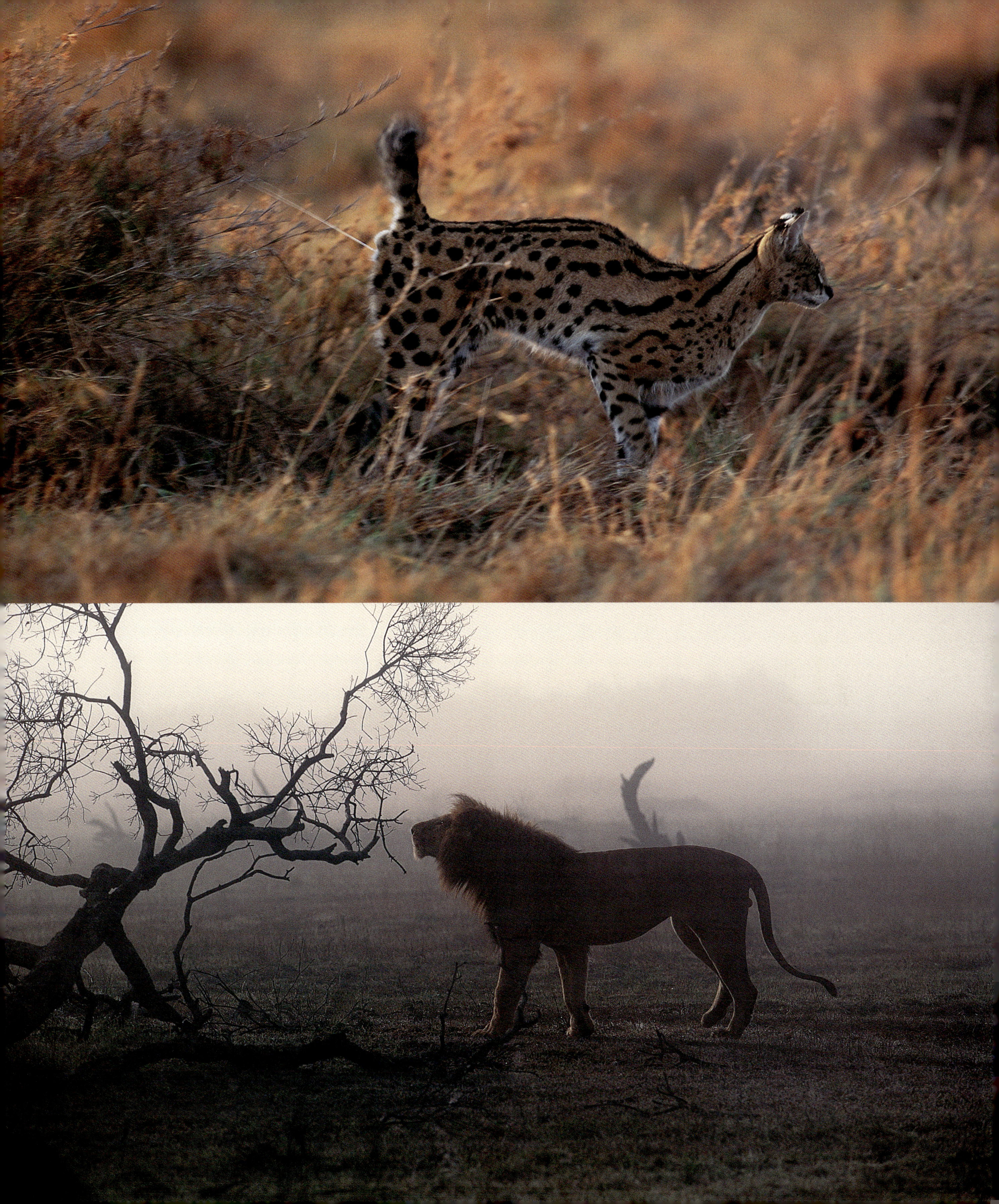

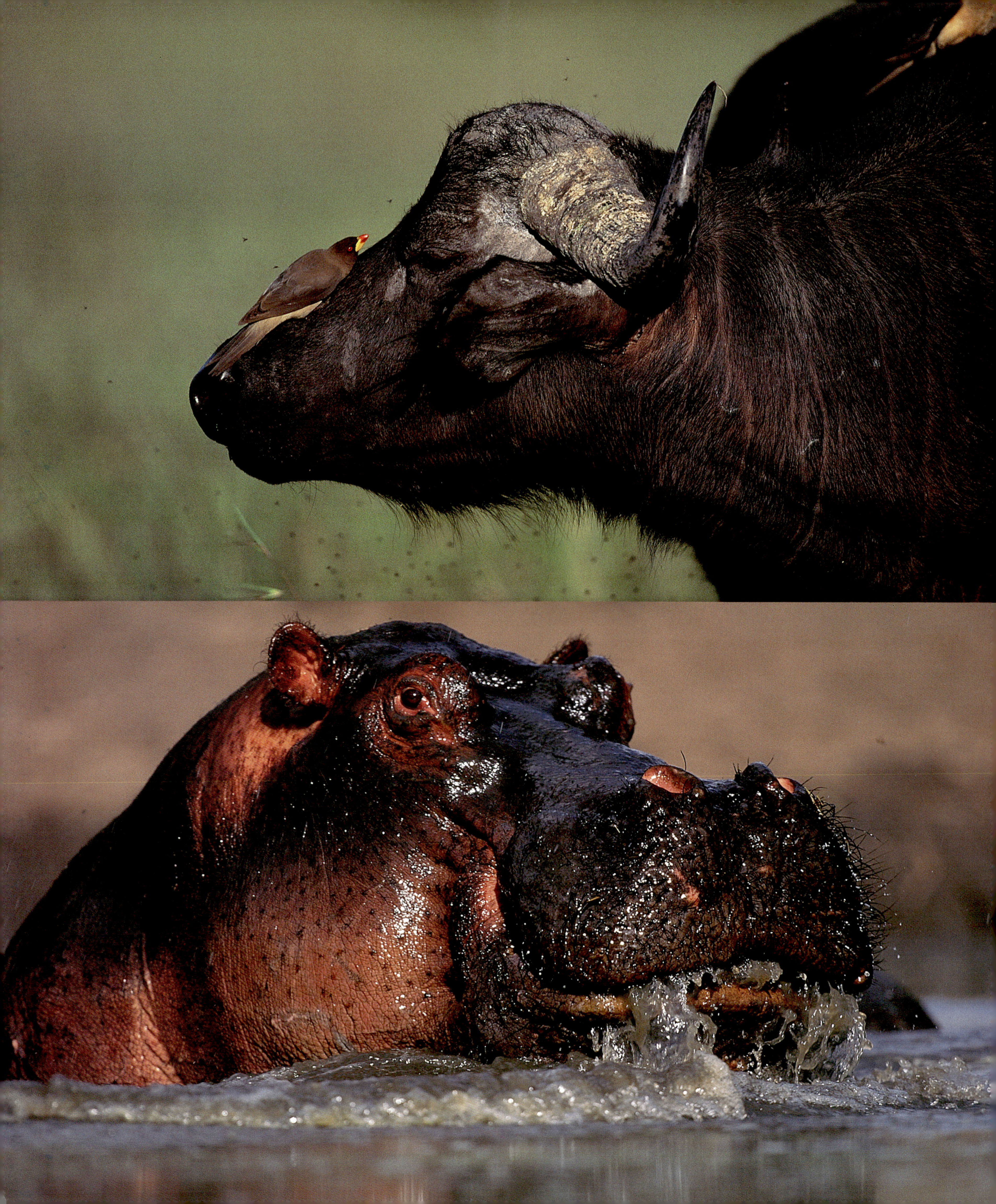

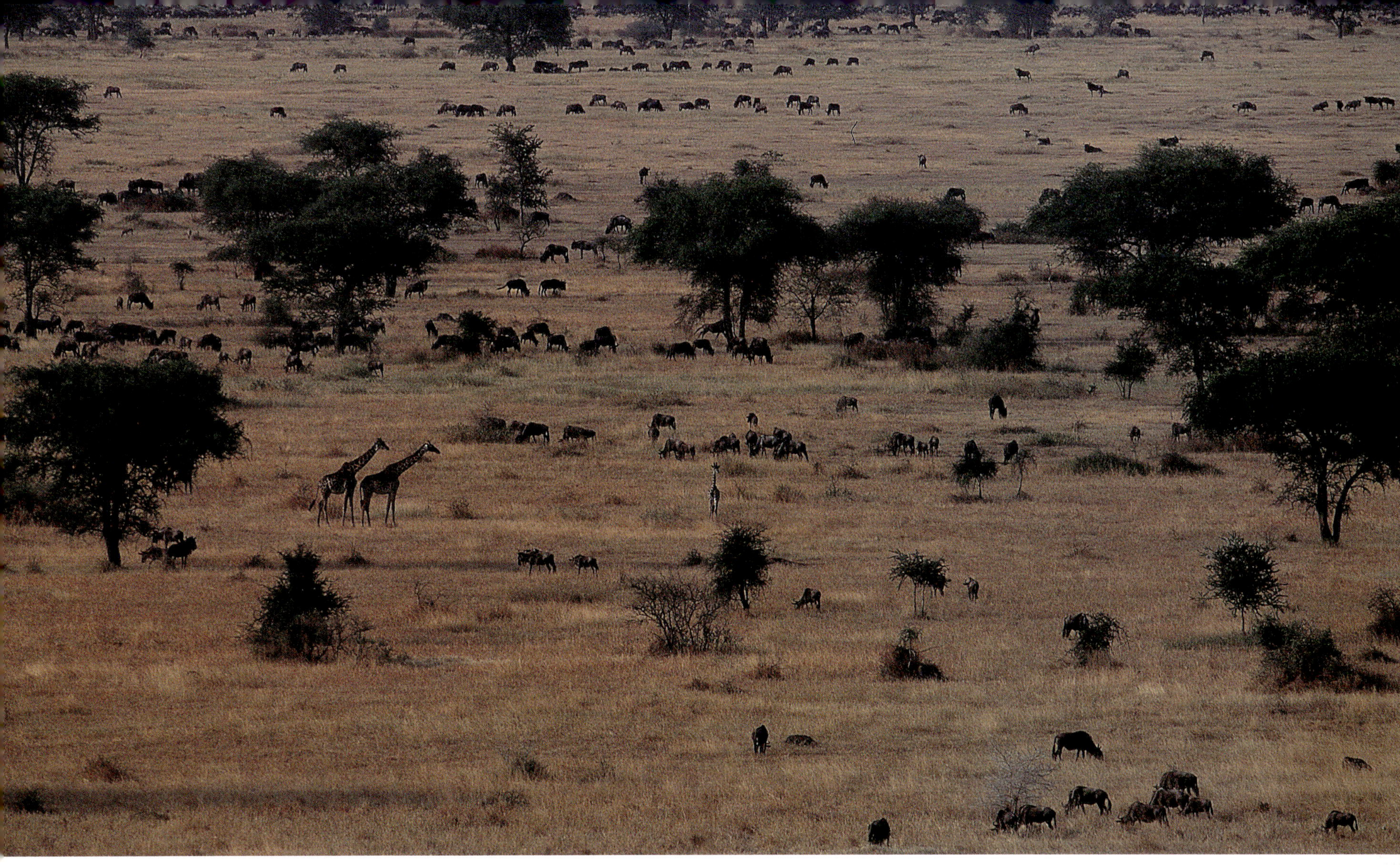

The presence of giraffes among the mixed herds signals the wooded savannah setting, but, as ever, grass dominates.

Opposite, above
An oxpecker searches for insects in a Cape buffalo's hide. The Cape buffalo is a living menagerie of insects, most of which are parasites.

Opposite, below
A male hippo creates ripples in the water by "chomping" on the surface. This is an aggressive signal sent to other males in the vicinity. It is a warning to the others to keep away and stay away.

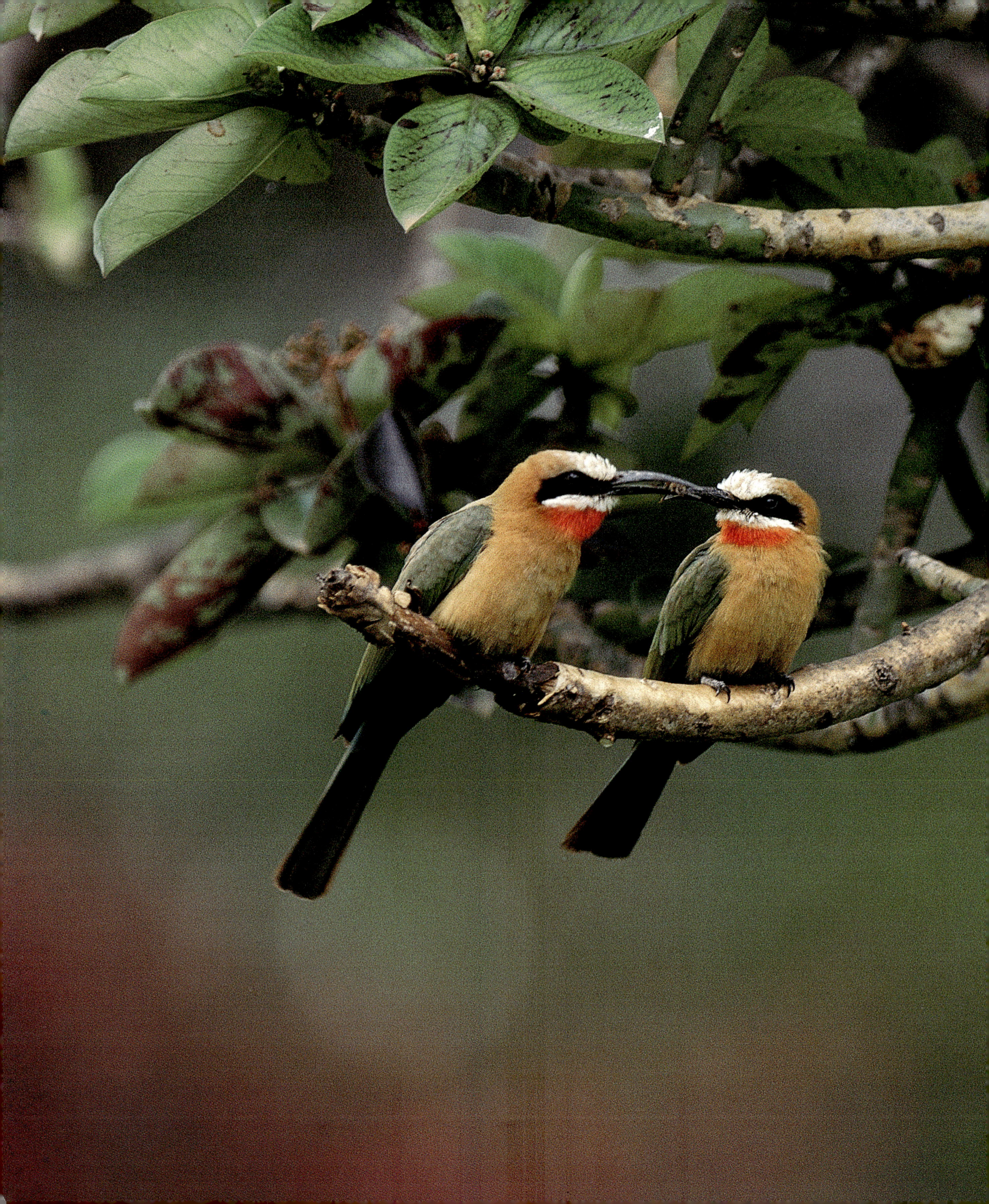

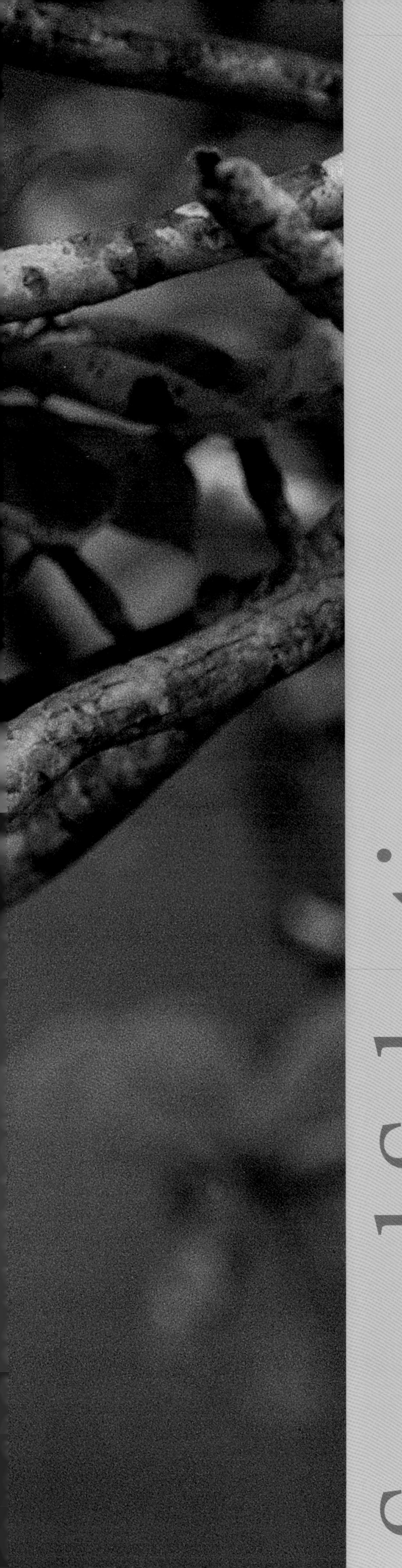

10

Sexual Selection

Watching ostriches courting, lions mating, and other species on the savannah doing more or less the same, I'm struck by the matter-of-fact approach animals take to reproduction. Animals inherit the drive to survive, to use their senses, to avoid danger, but above all, they inherit the drive to reproduce. It is said that evolutionary success means leaving the maximum number of offspring who will survive long enough to have their own offspring. An animal can be brilliant in its means of survival, have an efficient metabolism, resist all diseases, learn faster than its competitors, and live to a ripe old age, but if it is infertile, its excellent genes will not be passed on, and all of its wonderful adaptations will disappear. For this reason, animals are designed for reproduction, and everything else is a means to that end.

For most of their lives animals are preoccupied with the search for a suitable mate and the process of persuading it to part with its DNA. On the savannah, females do the choosing and males do the competing. This is primarily a consequence of the fact that throughout mammalian species, the sex cells of males are much smaller and more numerous than that of females. A sperm is minuscule, biologically "cheap" to produce, and manufactured in the testes in enormous numbers. Eggs, on the other hand, are large, made in much fewer numbers, and "expensive." In other words, eggs are a limited commodity and therefore more precious. Furthermore, from the moment of conception, the mother must care for the baby, which expends an enormous amount of energy, and in most mammalian species on the savannah the mother must resign herself to getting no help from the father after her offspring are born. Throughout the whole process, a great deal more of a mother's energy and resources are invested, so if a baby dies, her losses are far greater than a father's.

However, the female has a strong card in her hand. She can refuse to copulate. Since she has something of high value, she can exercise her power by being selective in her choice of mate and going for quality genes. Some males do carry better genes than others, genes that would enhance the survival prospects of her offspring. So, if a female can somehow detect a male with great genes, perhaps using externally visible clues, she can benefit her unborn.

With an almost unlimited supply of sperm at his disposal, often the male's best strategy is indiscriminate promiscuity. But if one male fertilizes several females, then other males have to go mateless. So, from a male's perspective, females are scarce, and if obtaining a female partner creates competition among males, then so be it. But competition makes female choices easier: She can simply pass over the losers.

Therefore, unsurprisingly, competition for fertile females is a selection pressure bearing on a male's weaponry. Many males, depending on the species, have evolved into impressive warriors. Male lions are heavy, large, and powerful. The horns of male impalas can inflict lethal wounds. Evolution also seems to have selected males more obviously designed for seduction than females in many species. For example,

Pages 120–121
A male white-fronted bee-eater has caught an insect on the wing and offers it to his mate. She has been receiving such gifts ever since he began courting her.

studies in the Serengeti show that lionesses prefer males with large, dark manes. Lavish ornamentation, like a lion's mane, signals quality to a female, perhaps because mediocre males cannot afford the luxury of "expensive" display items. By choosing the flashiest partners, females unwittingly create males that are more and more extravagant and gorgeous over time. Females of many species tend to be dull-looking not only because they need to blend into their environments to better protect their young, but also because they don't need to compete for males – they are the precious commodities on the plains.

Animals have an overwhelming urge to breed, the fulfillment of which determines whether an animal is a success or a failure. The reproductive success of males depends on how many females they mate with, but not vice versa. Females, it seems, are the shoppers, and males are the sellers, hawking their wares to attract female customers.

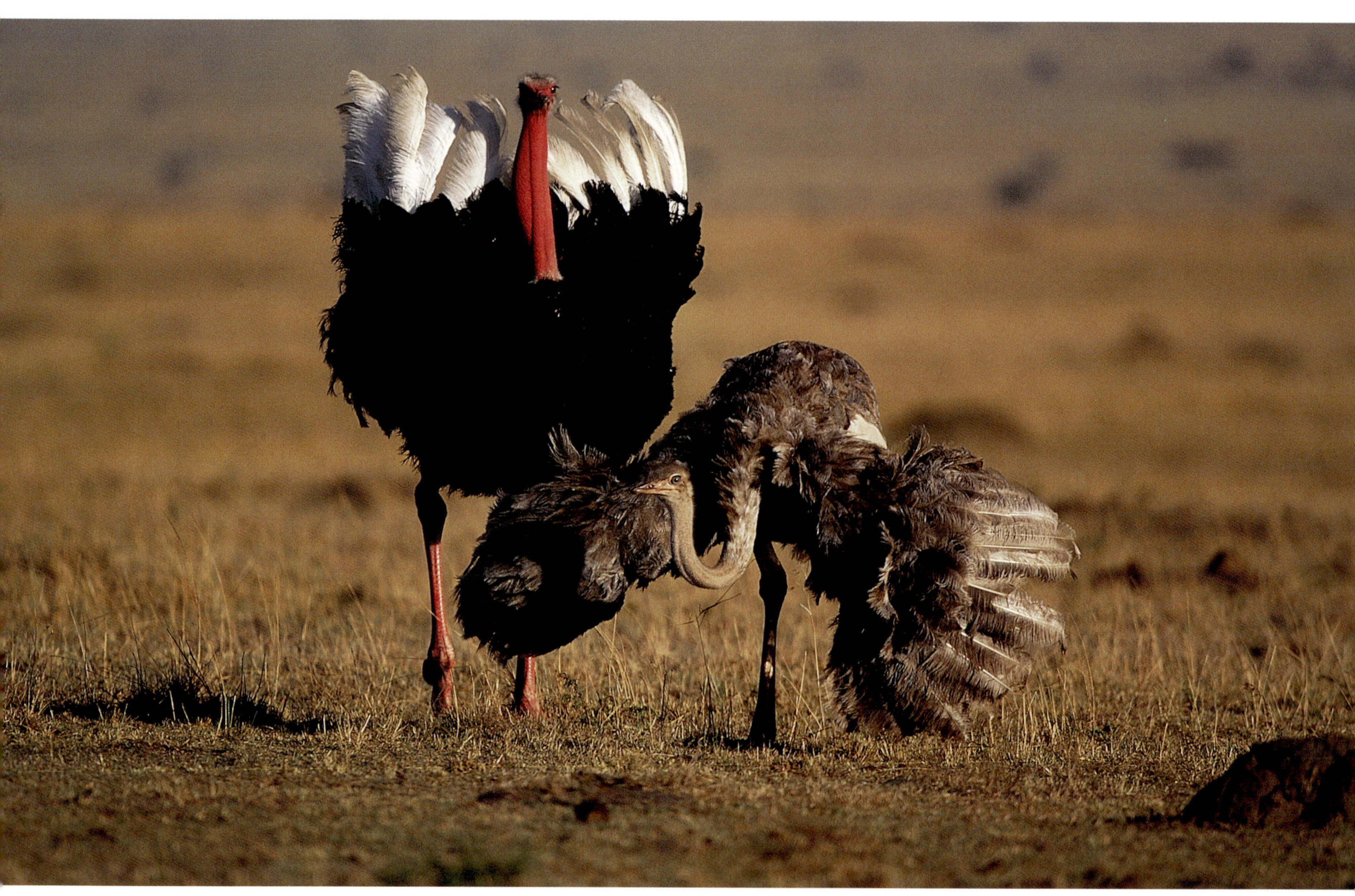

This pair of ostriches was leisurely making their way to the plains, walking some distance apart, when the female went into a kind of a dance routine, wings out-stretched and flapping, running merrily about. Recognizing this call to copulate, the male came over at once, eager to mate.

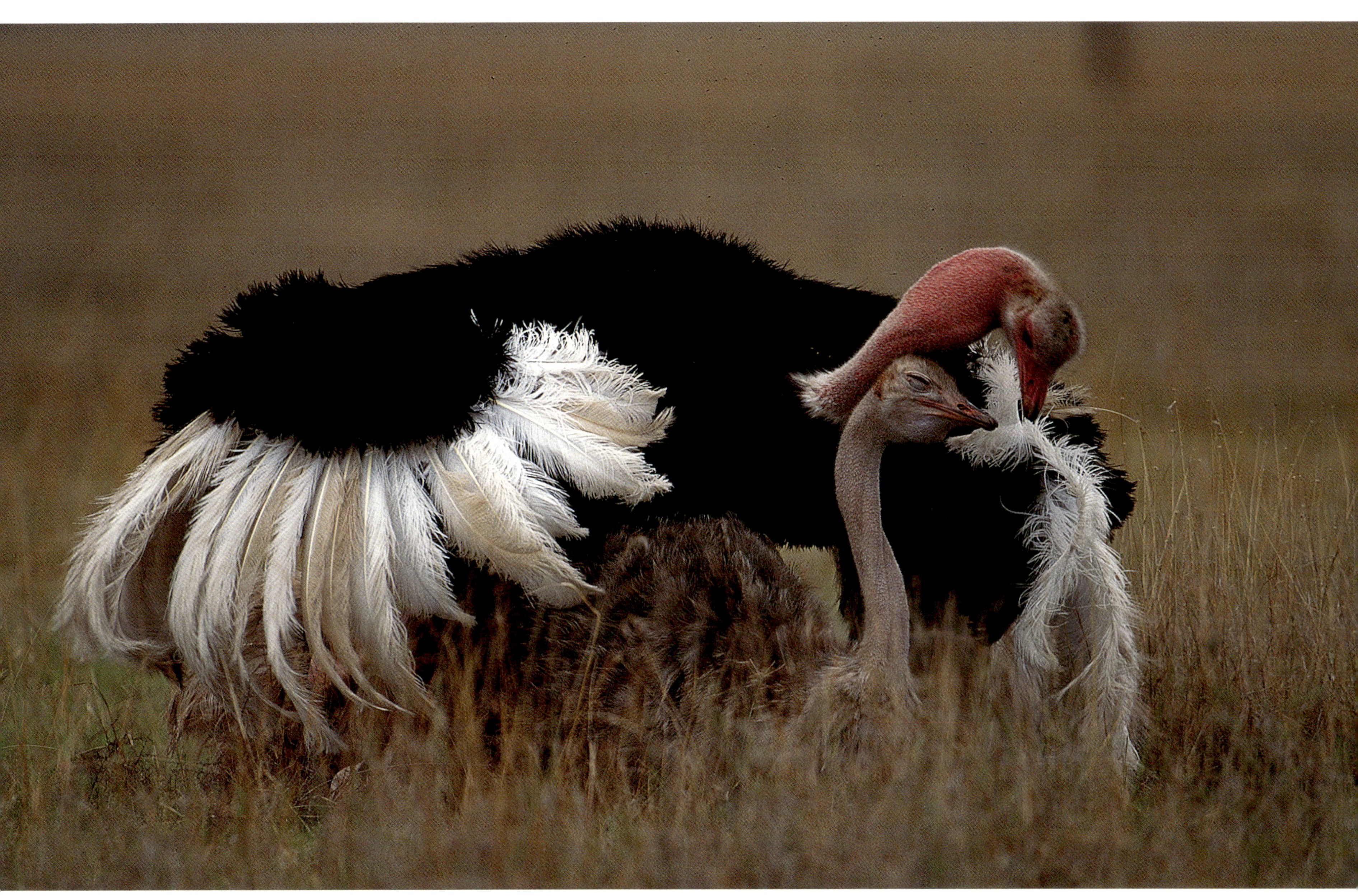

The female had stopped grazing and suddenly began to preen herself. Then she approached the male, ruffled her wings, and danced and bowed around him. Within minutes his pale pink neck had turned crimson. As she began to run away, he chased after her. As soon as he caught up, she dropped to the ground. Very gently, he crouched over her, making a parasol with his wings. As they mated, they seemed to fall into a trance, their eyes sometimes open, sometimes shut, necks swaying dreamily from side to side.

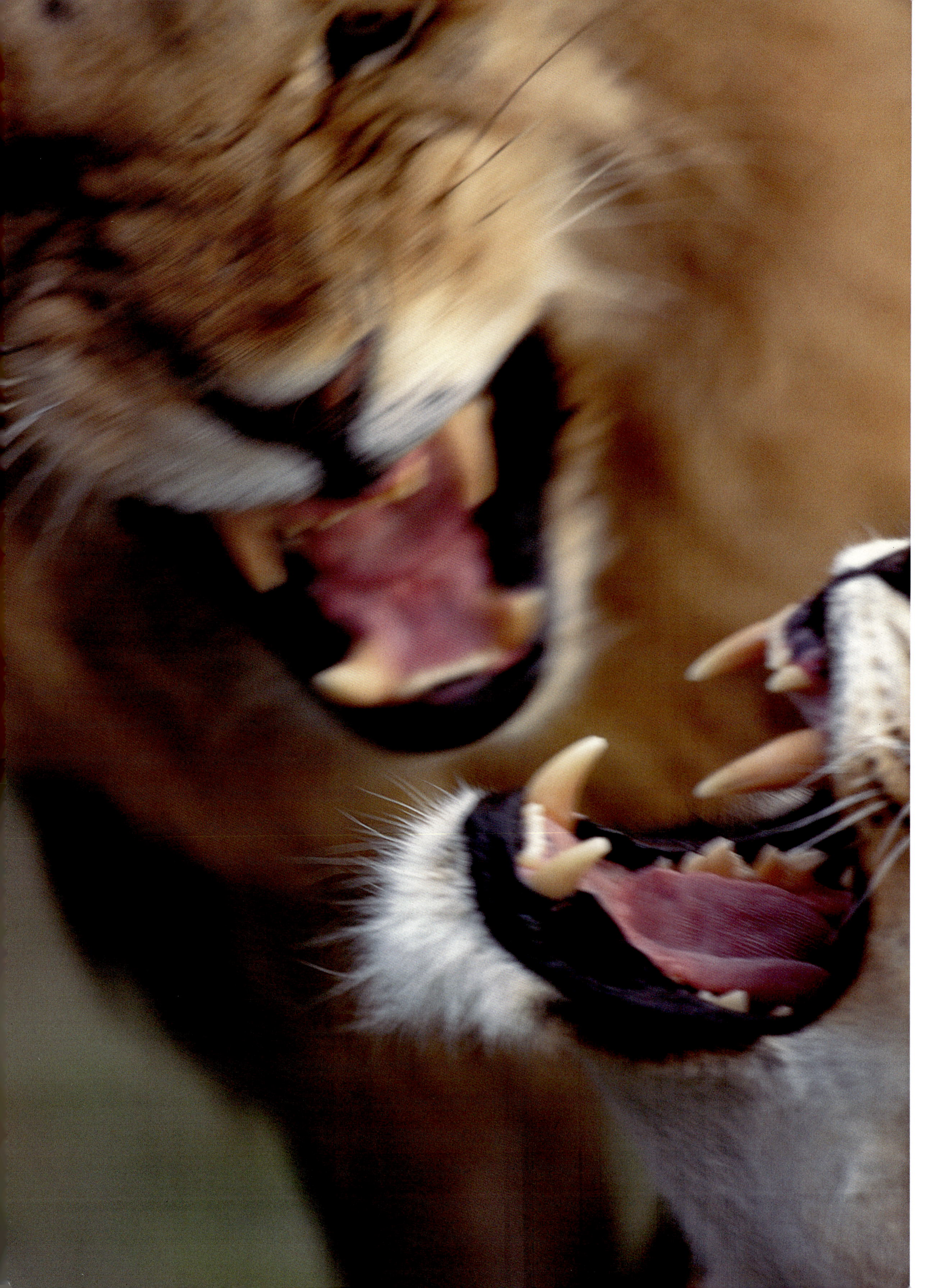

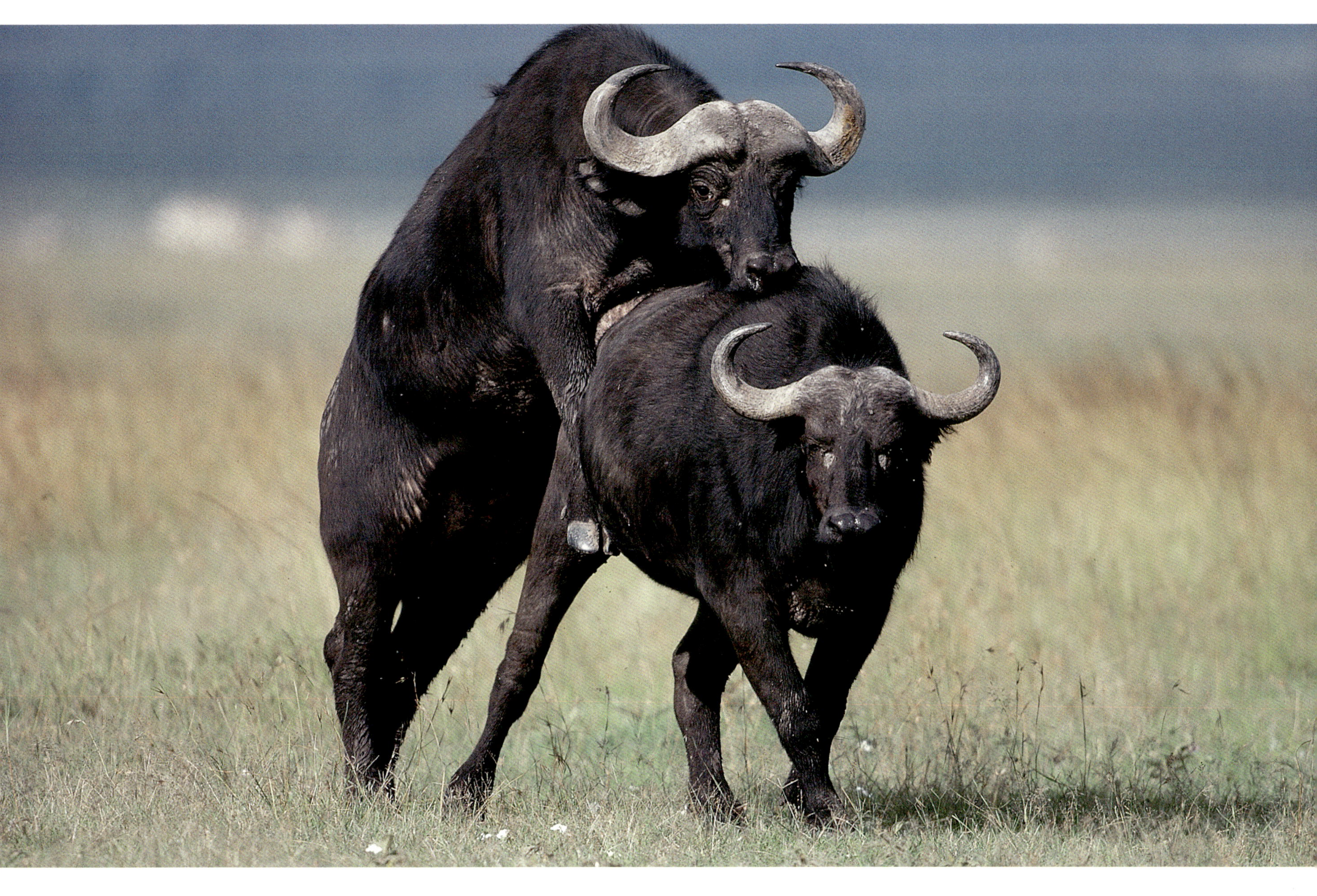

This Cape buffalo pair are members of a large herd, but they have separated themselves from the herd to carry on the mating rituals. The male initiates the ritual by rubbing his face on his mate's back. She is in a receptive mood, so he heaves his huge body up to mount her. The mating couple rotate in a semicircle before the male dismounts.

Opposite
A lion pair grimaces as it nears the end of copulation. At the very end, the lioness swiped a paw at the male who dodged it expertly. She then rolled over, seemingly savoring the act.

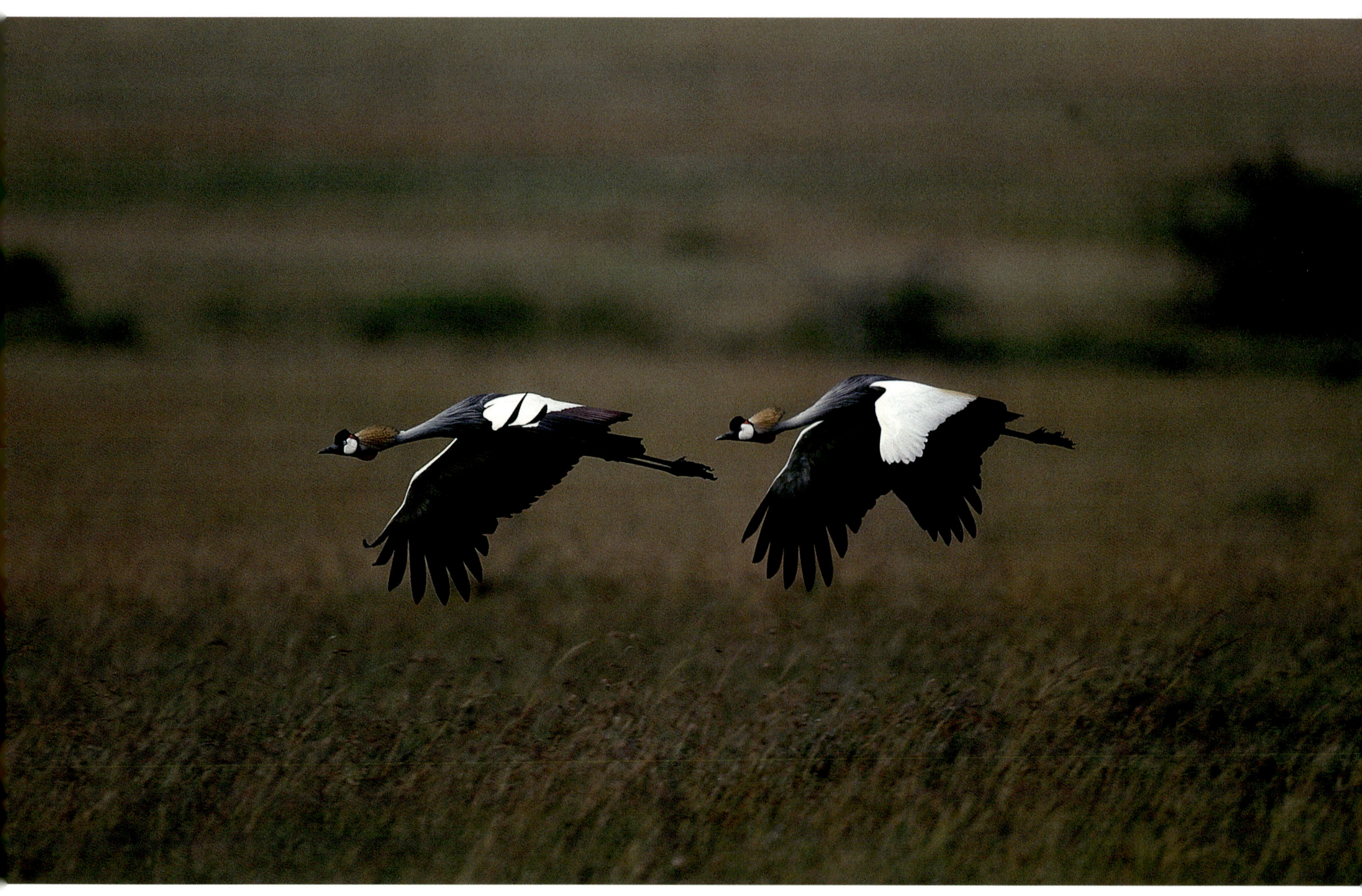

The crowned-crane breeding season has begun, and an unusually large flock of thirty has assembled. This couple have separated from the flock to carry out an elaborate courtship routine but will return to the others once it is over.

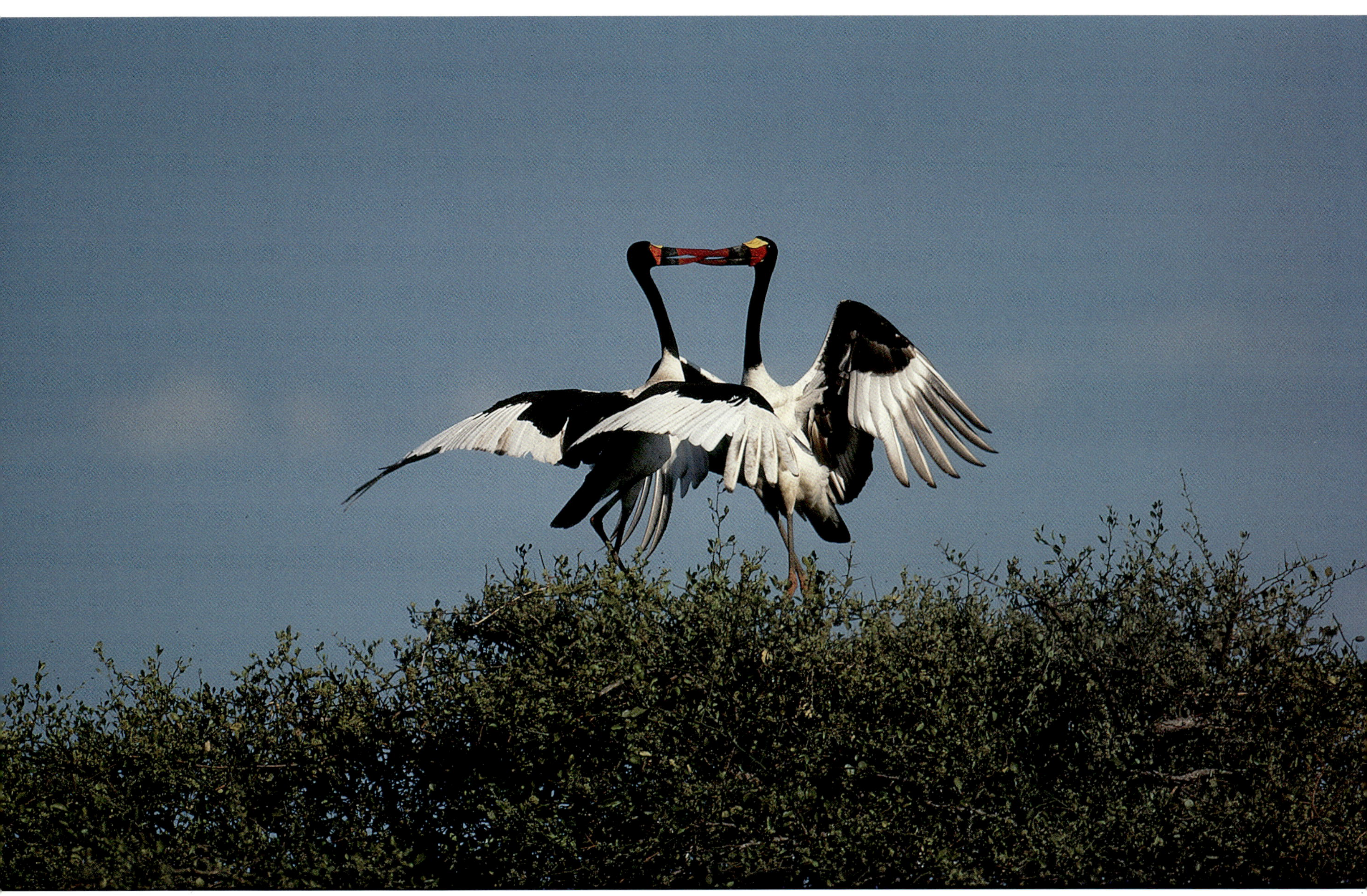

Two saddle-billed storks atop an acacia tree are engrossed in courtship. First, they face each other, the male with his wings spread, one leg raised. Their beaks touch and both spread their wings and move slowly in a circle. The male then takes to the air and lands gently on his mate. At the climax, both, half-sitting, spread their wings out fully. Then, mating over, the male returns to his position next to his partner.

Pages 130–131
Two warthogs competing for a mate size each other up, then butt heads in what is more a highly formalized ritual than an angry battle. After a few knocks, one turns and runs. There are no injuries and no spilled blood.

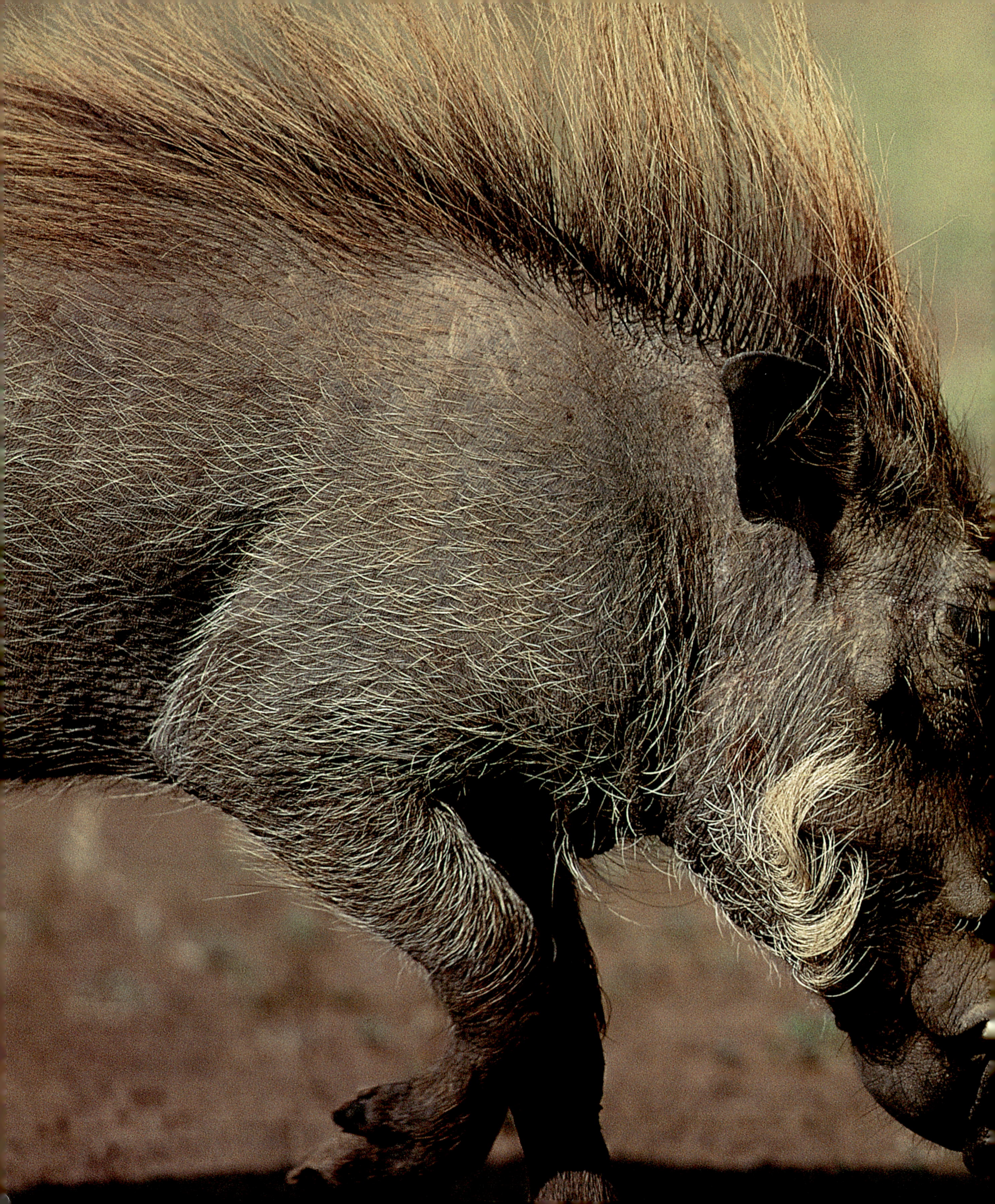

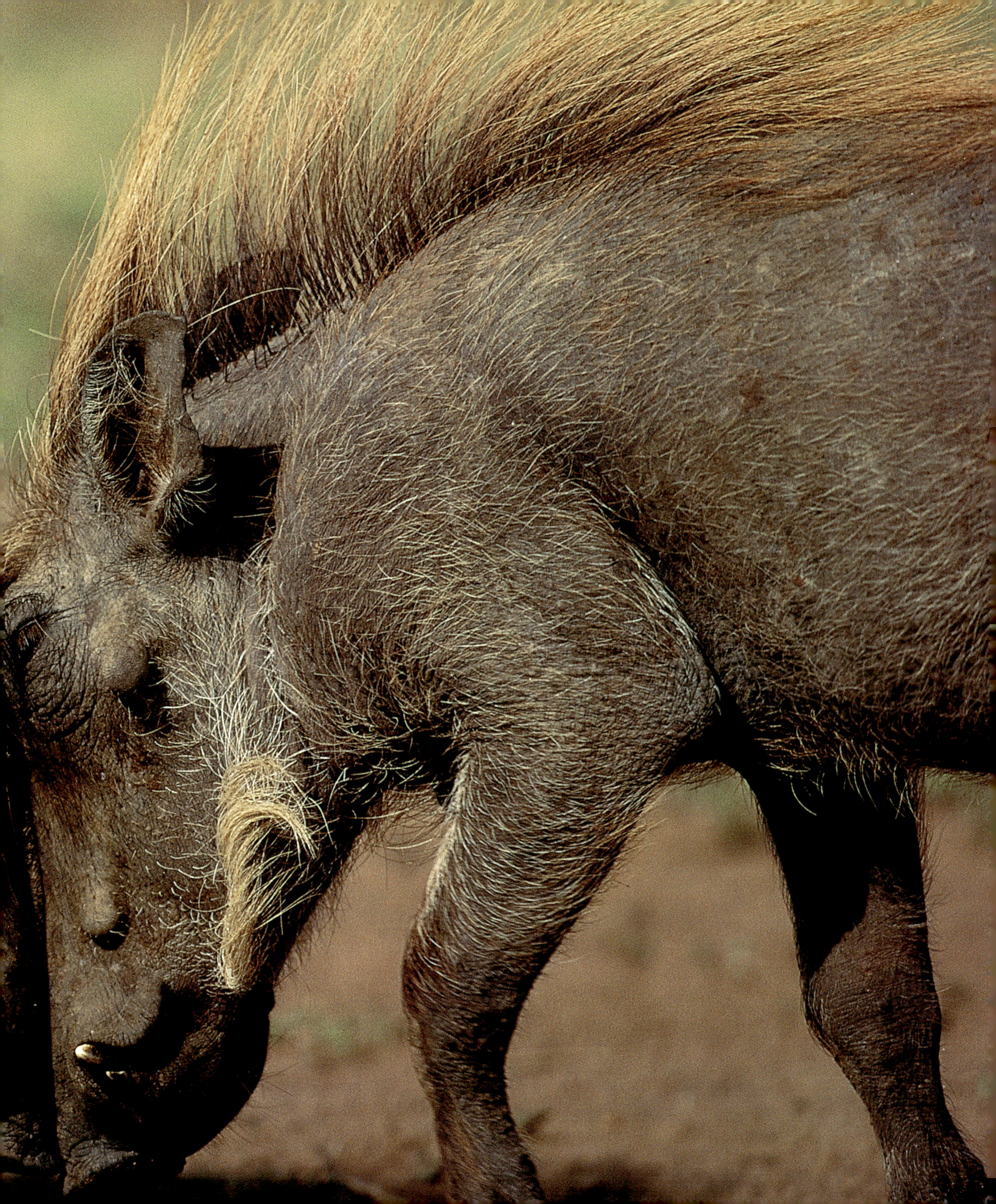

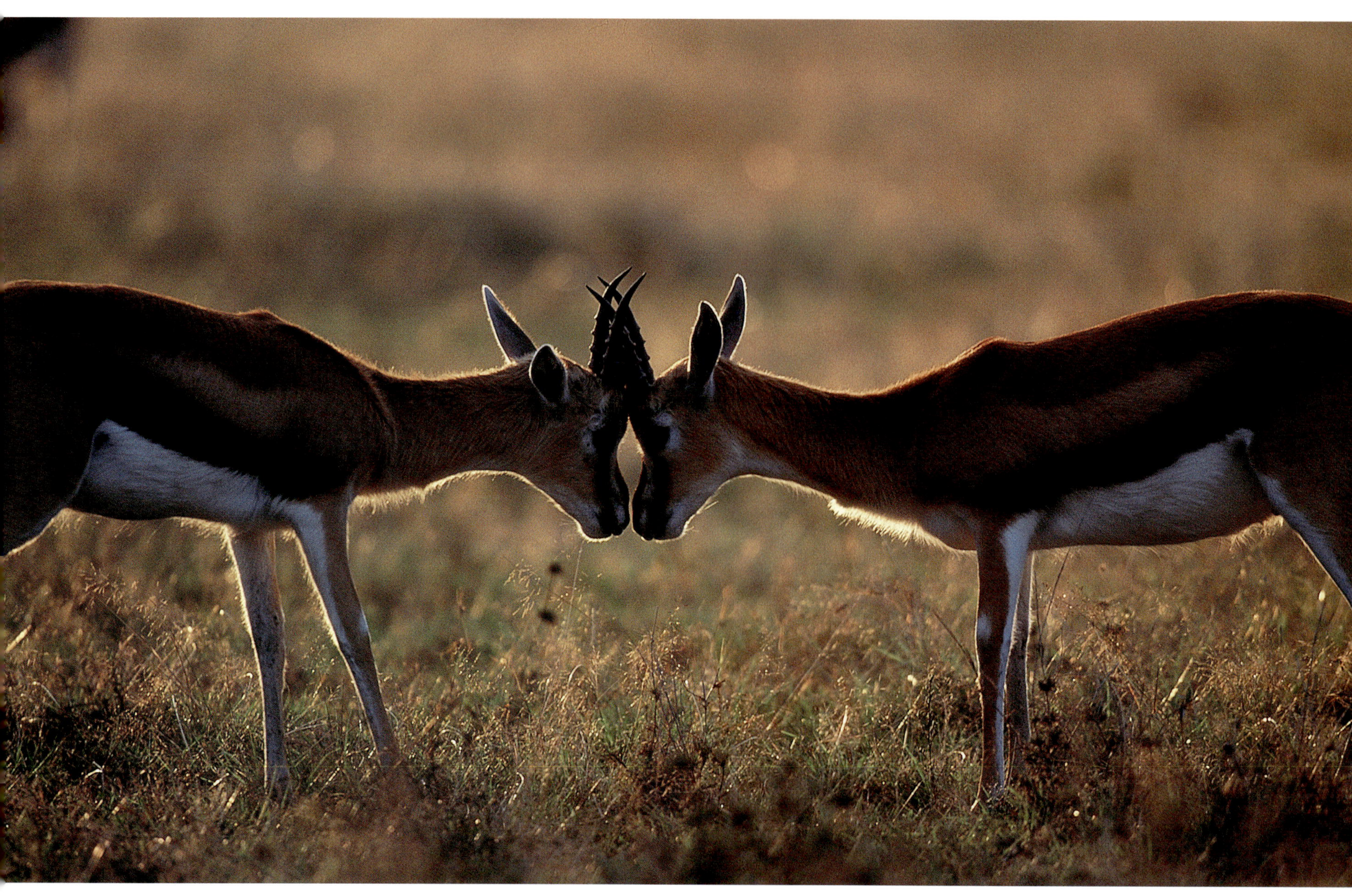

Out on the plains, a group of male Thomson's gazelles is actively competing for mates. The pair nearest to us first touches noses and foreheads, then springs back to commence a bout of head-butting. After only a few minutes, one gazelle runs off, but the victor doesn't bother to pursue him.

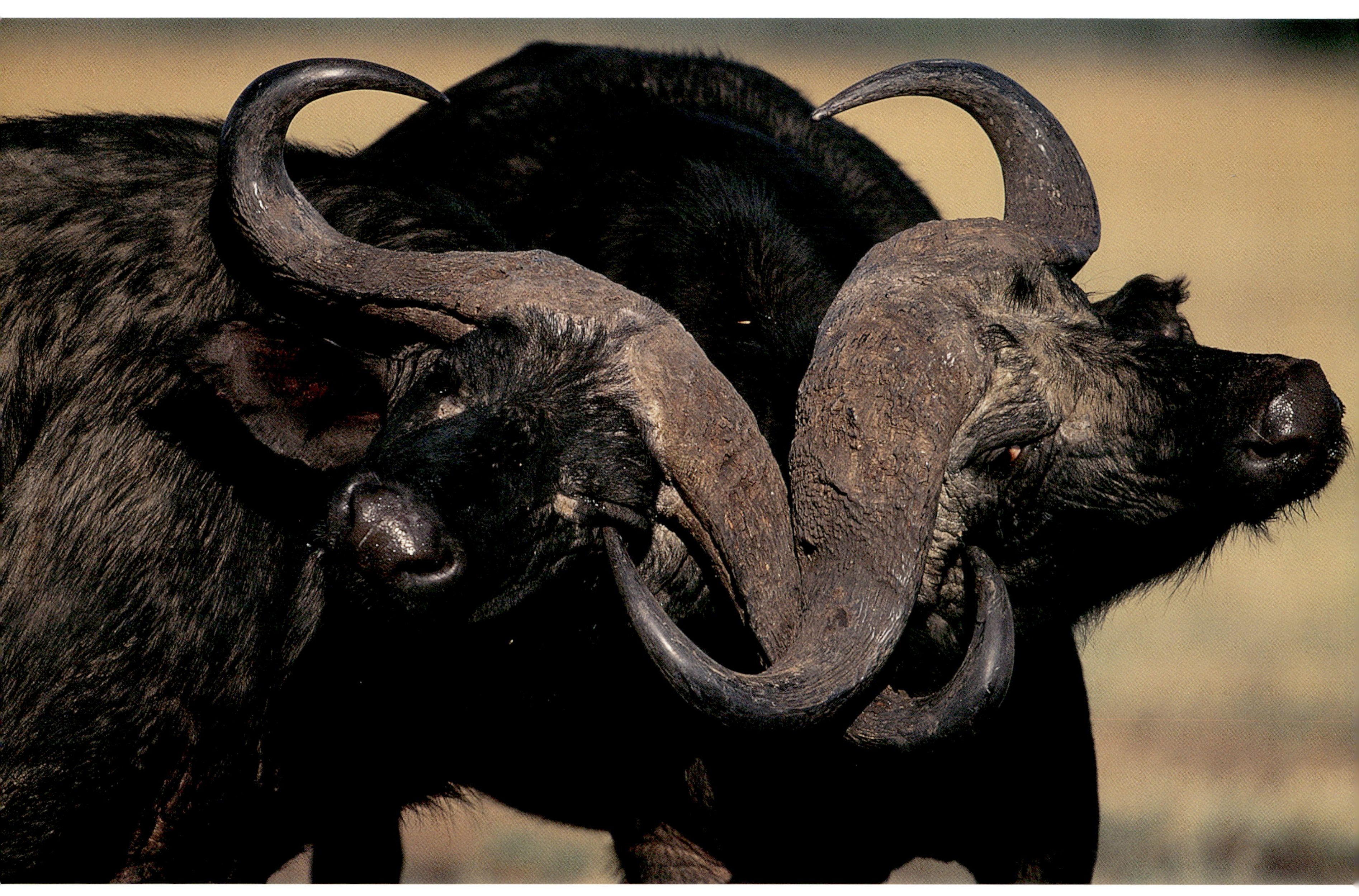

Two buffalo bulls lock horns in a ritualistic trial of strength. Their massive, heavily bossed horns have sharp ends and at times come perilously close to piercing an eye.

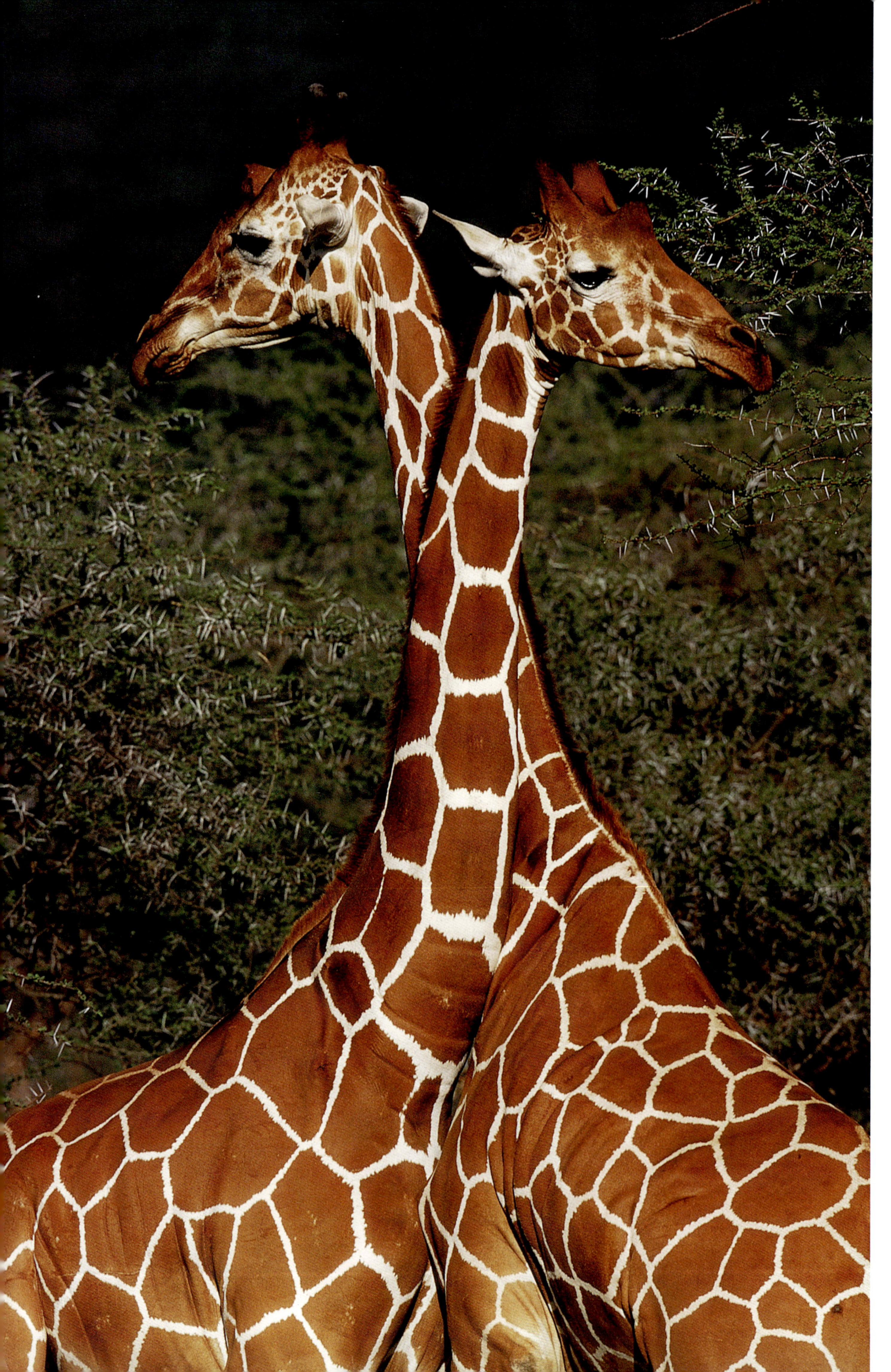

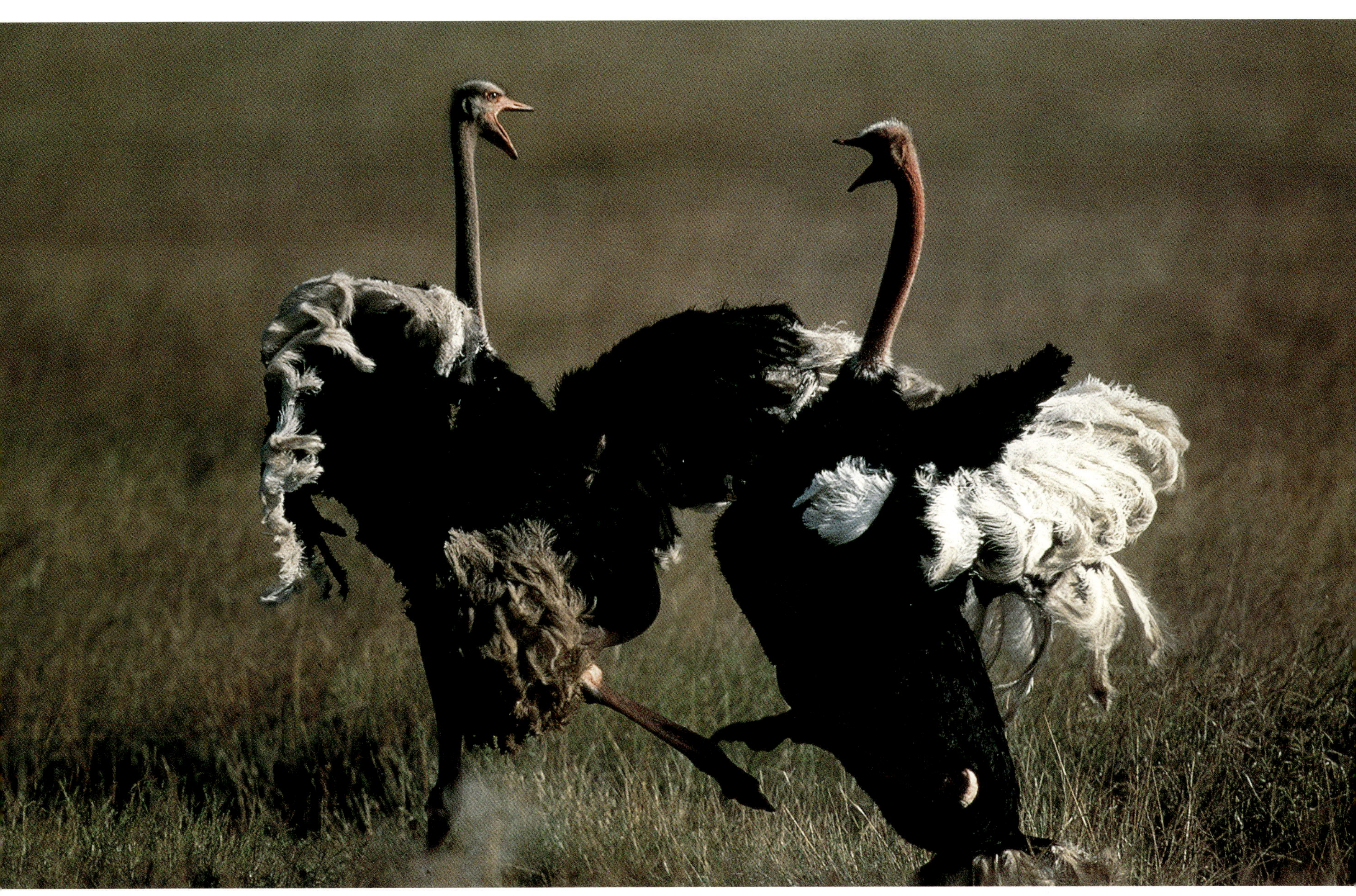

Opposite
Two reticulated giraffe bulls rub shoulders, entwine their necks, and bat each other on the flanks with the sides of their heads and padded horns. In this way they obtain information about each other's size and strength in a peaceful manner.

Love is in the air, but there is tension too. Two male and three female ostriches are picking their way across the plains. As the neck of one male changes color to red, the other moves in. They face each other, their feathers ruffled, wings waving. The fight is over in a twinkling of an eye, the victor having made his point. As the loser kneels, face buried in the grass, the triumphant one runs past, wings spread, mouth open to claim his hens.

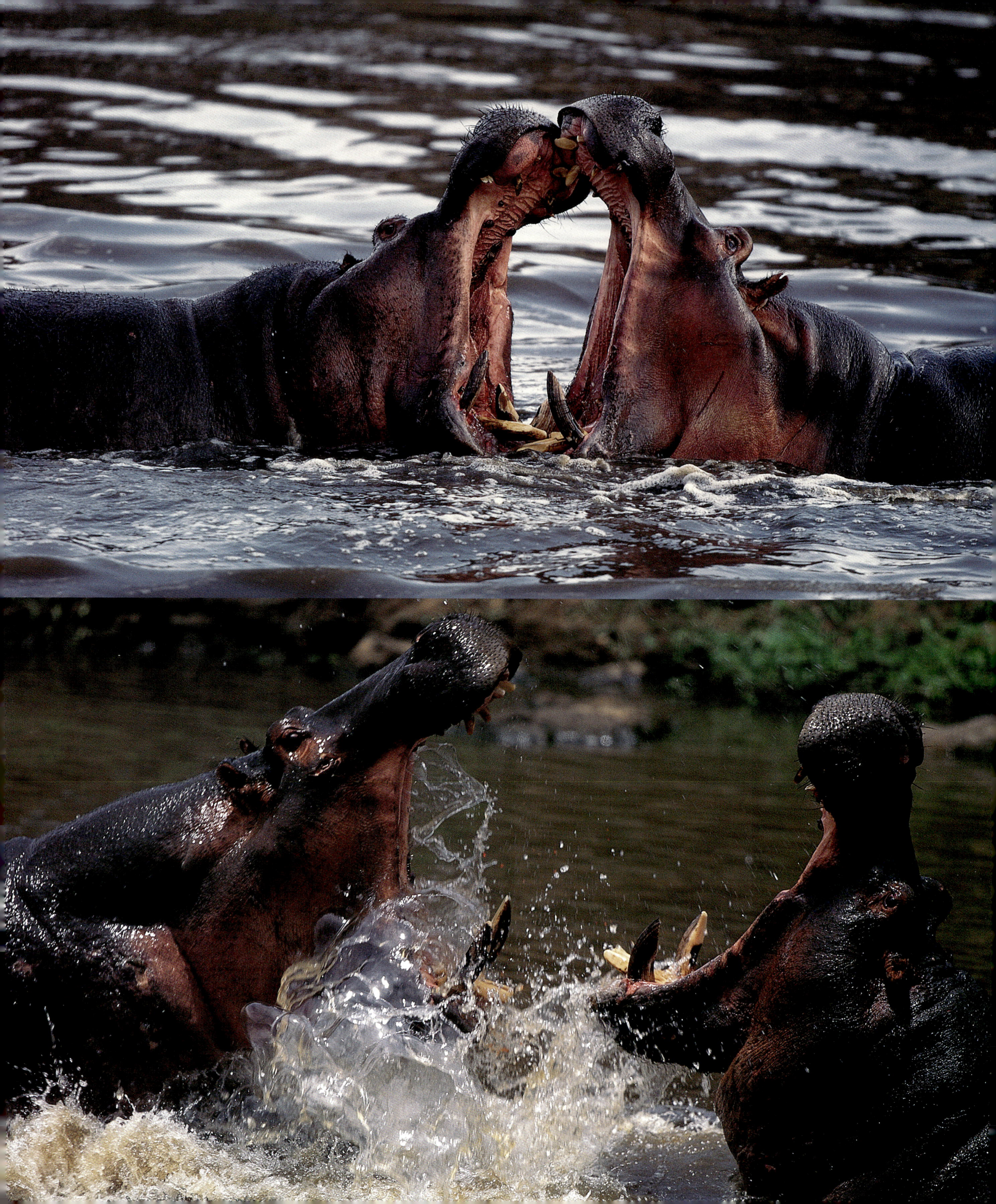

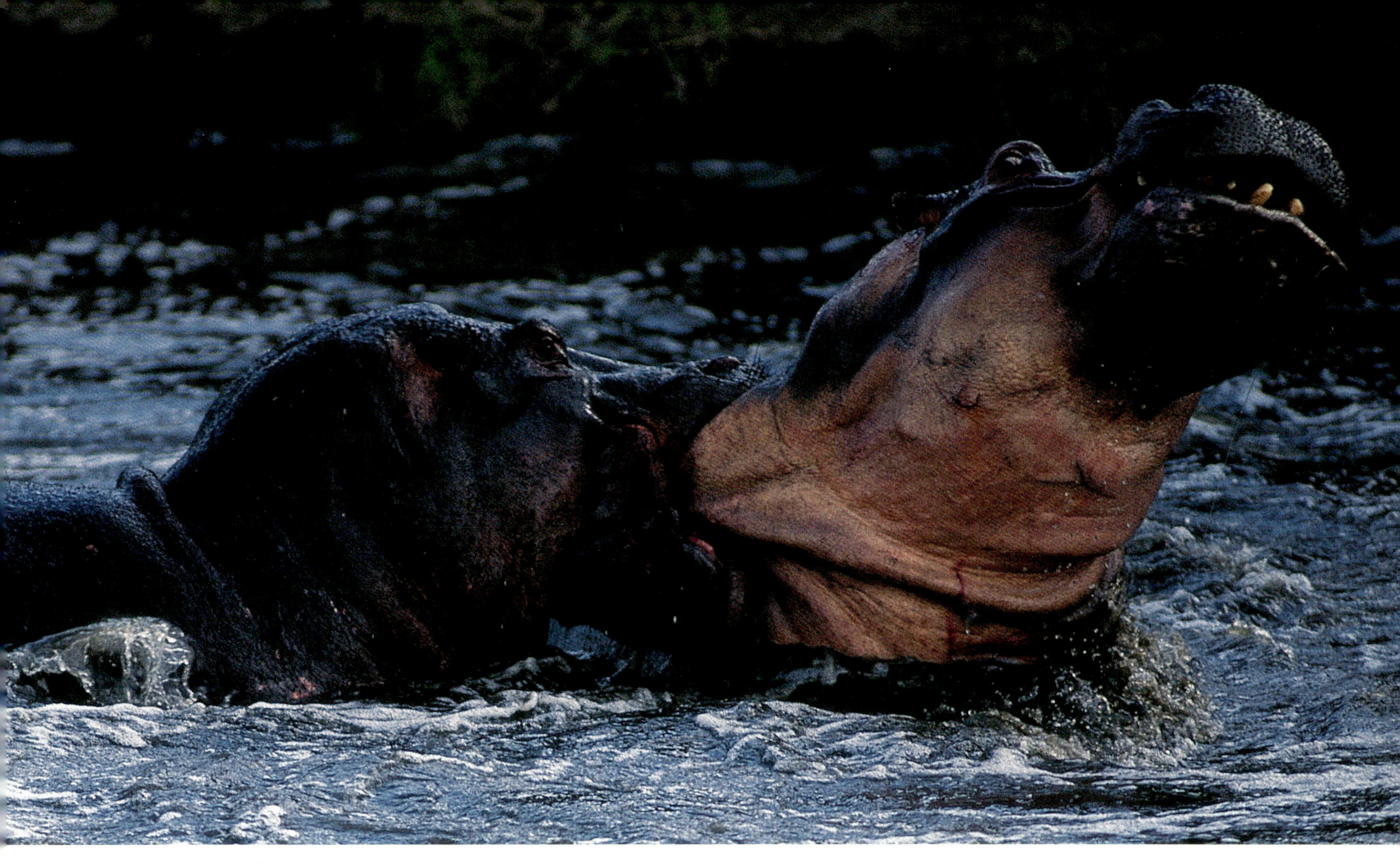

Hippos often posture, but rarely actually fight. This pair of bulls, however, is going at it with a vengeance, and judging from the look on the bull on the right, that bite on the neck is painful.

Opposite, above
These two hippo bulls are measuring each other's mouths. The one with the smaller span usually acknowledges the dominance of the other. At stake are territorial rights to an attractive stretch of the river.

Opposite, below
Two mature hippo bulls clash in a serious battle for supremacy. Hippo bulls will try to monopolize a stretch of water and mate with any cow that enters their territory. But territories are few and hippo bulls many, so competition is inevitable.

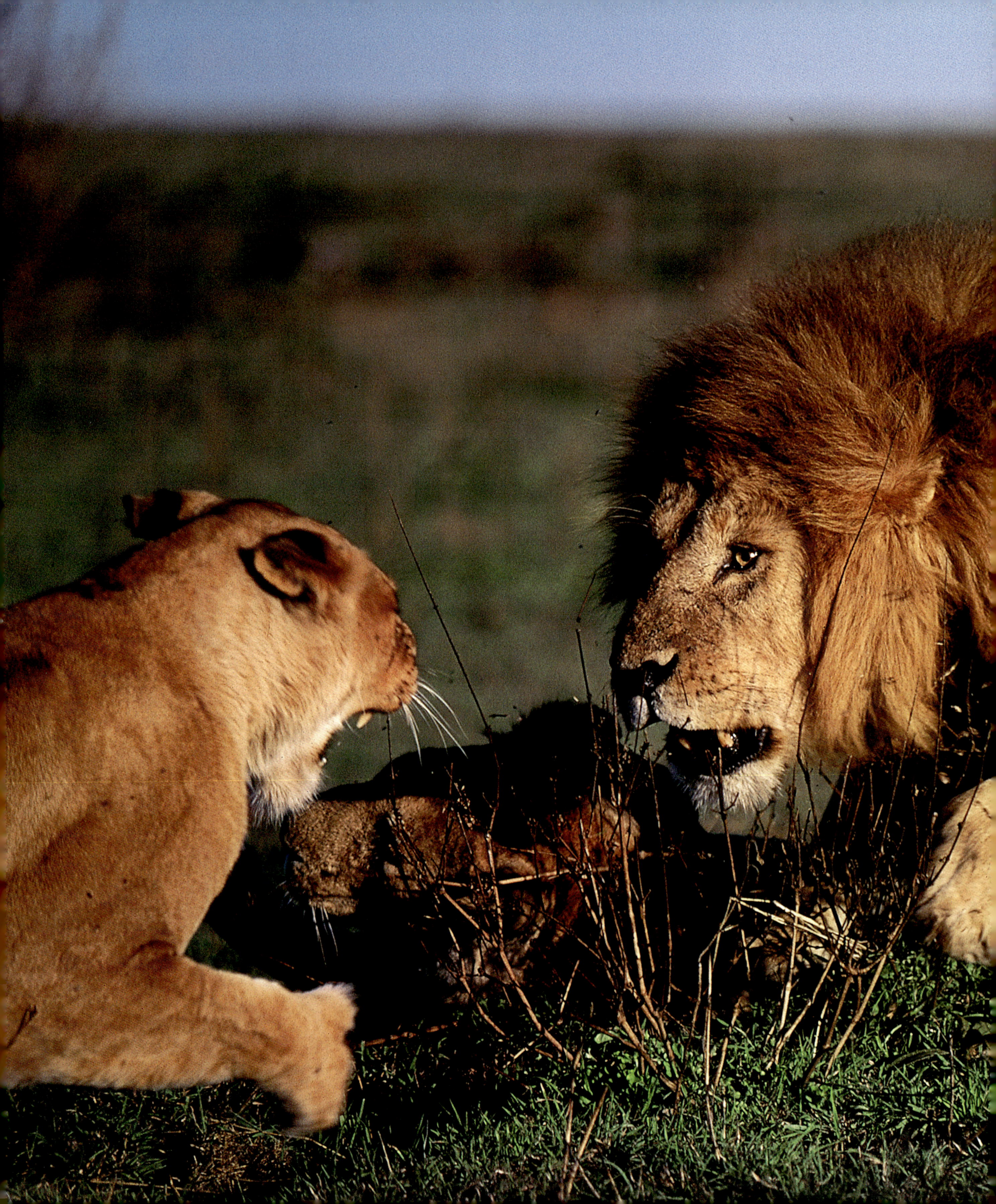

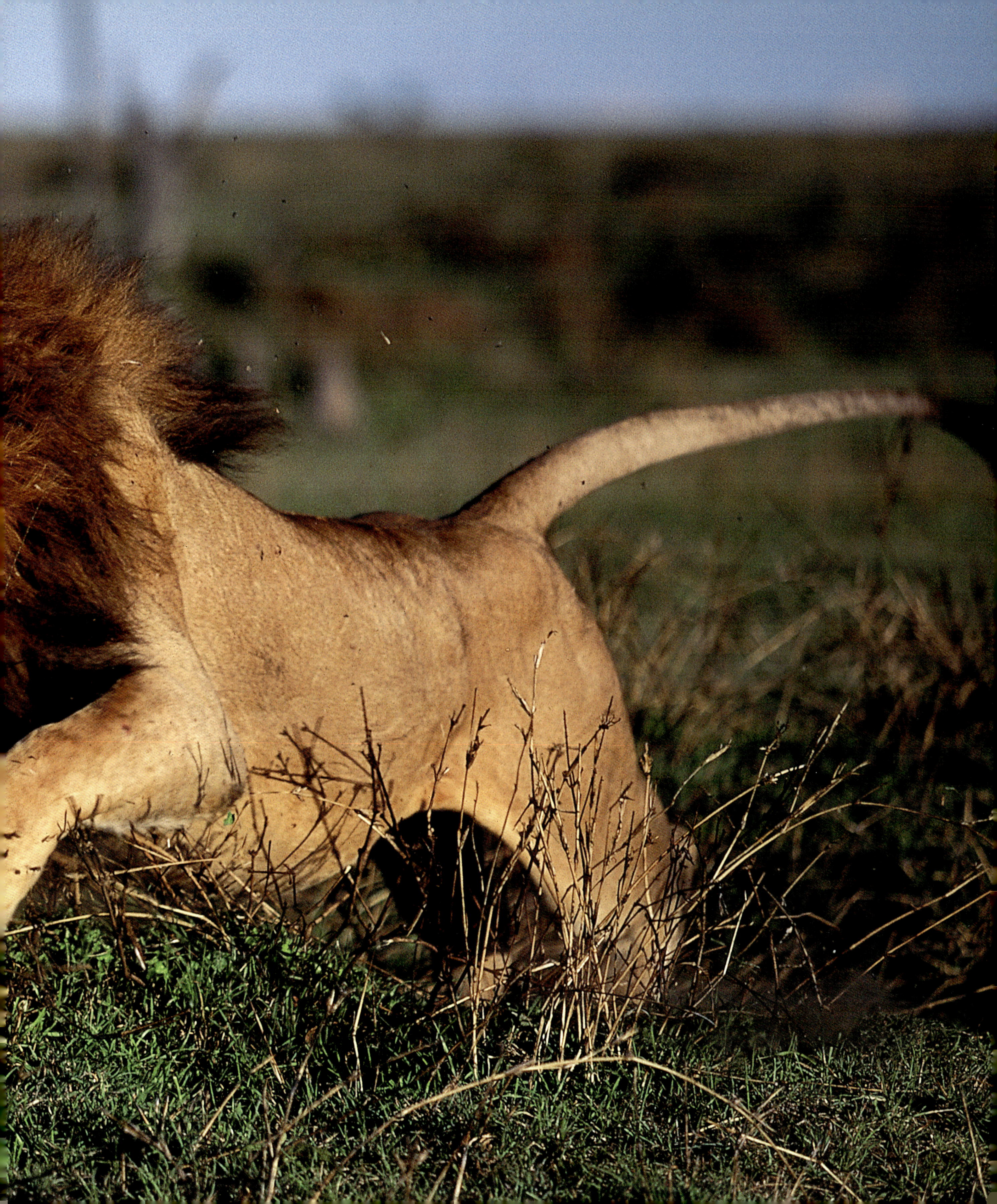

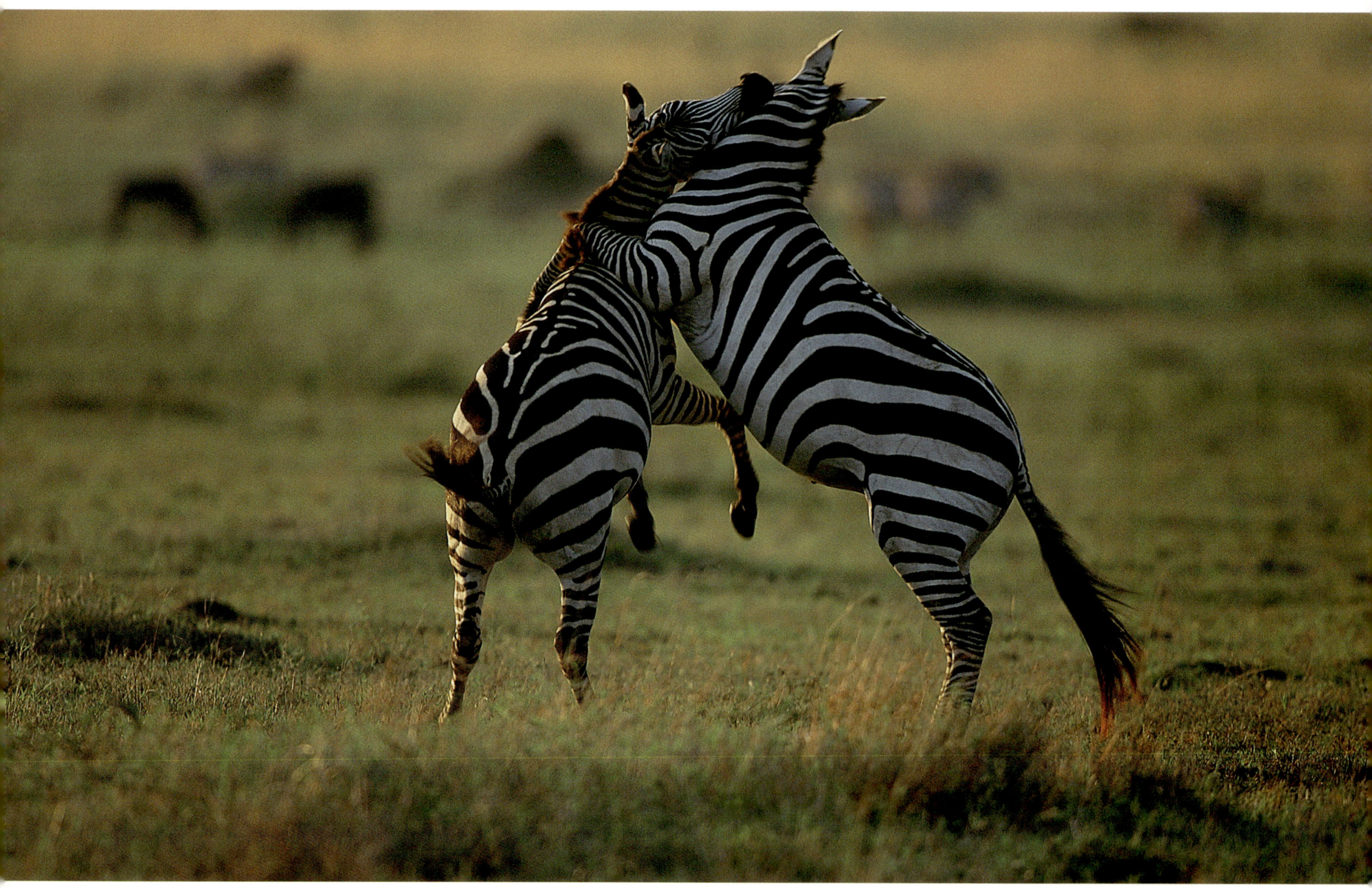

Early morning finds two plains zebra stallions engaged in "horse-play" fighting, which involves running, locking in combat, rearing up, and even biting. It is not a serious fight, however, merely a ritual to sort out who is stronger and more fit.

Pages 138–139
Frustrated in his courtship attempts with an unresponsive lioness, a male lion vents his anger by charging at her, stopping just short of bodily contact.

Opposite
Male weaver birds construct elaborate nests to impress and attract mates. This male is making some last-minute finishing touches to his nest. When he is ready to attract a female, he will hang upside down at the entrance of the nest and flutter his wings.

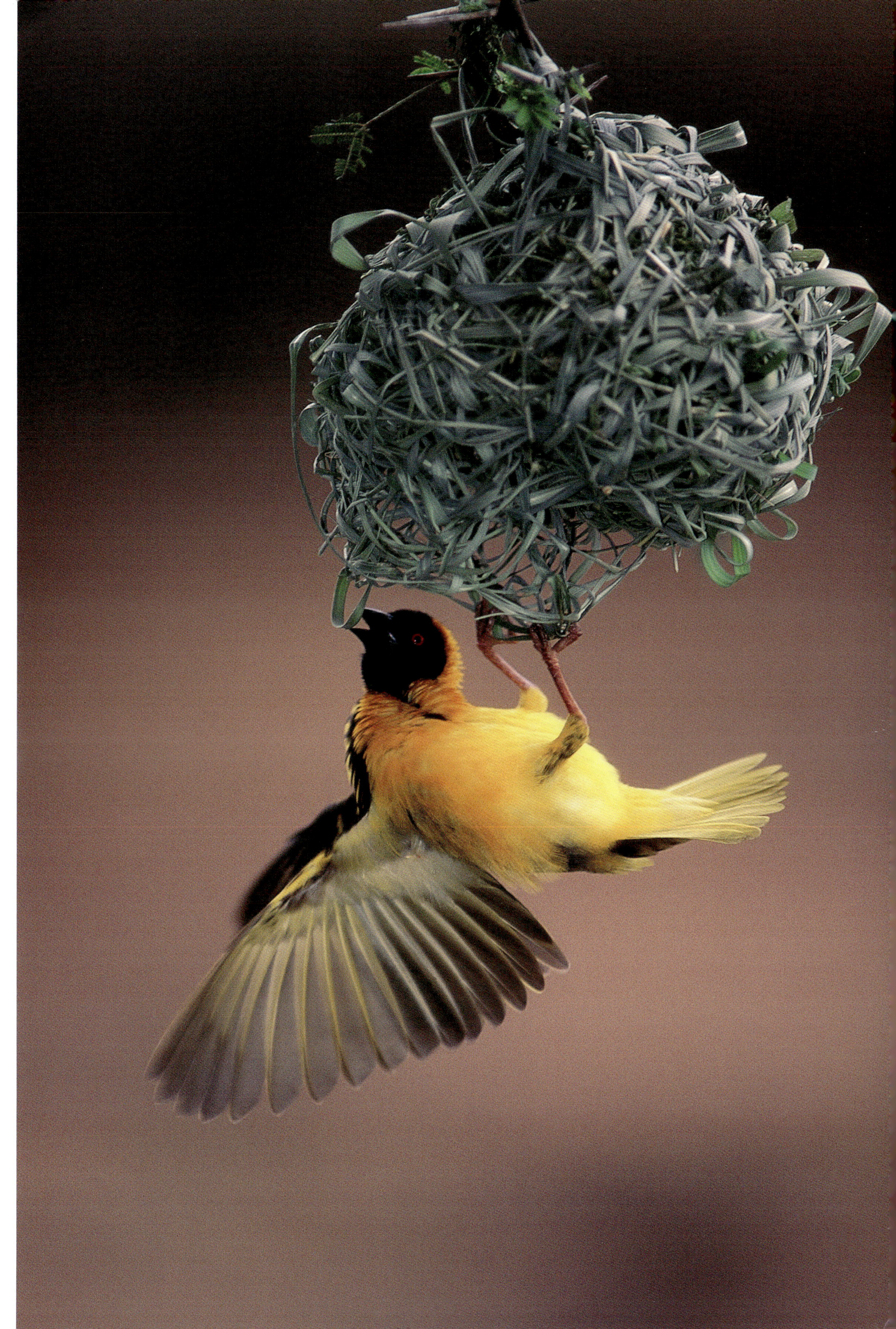

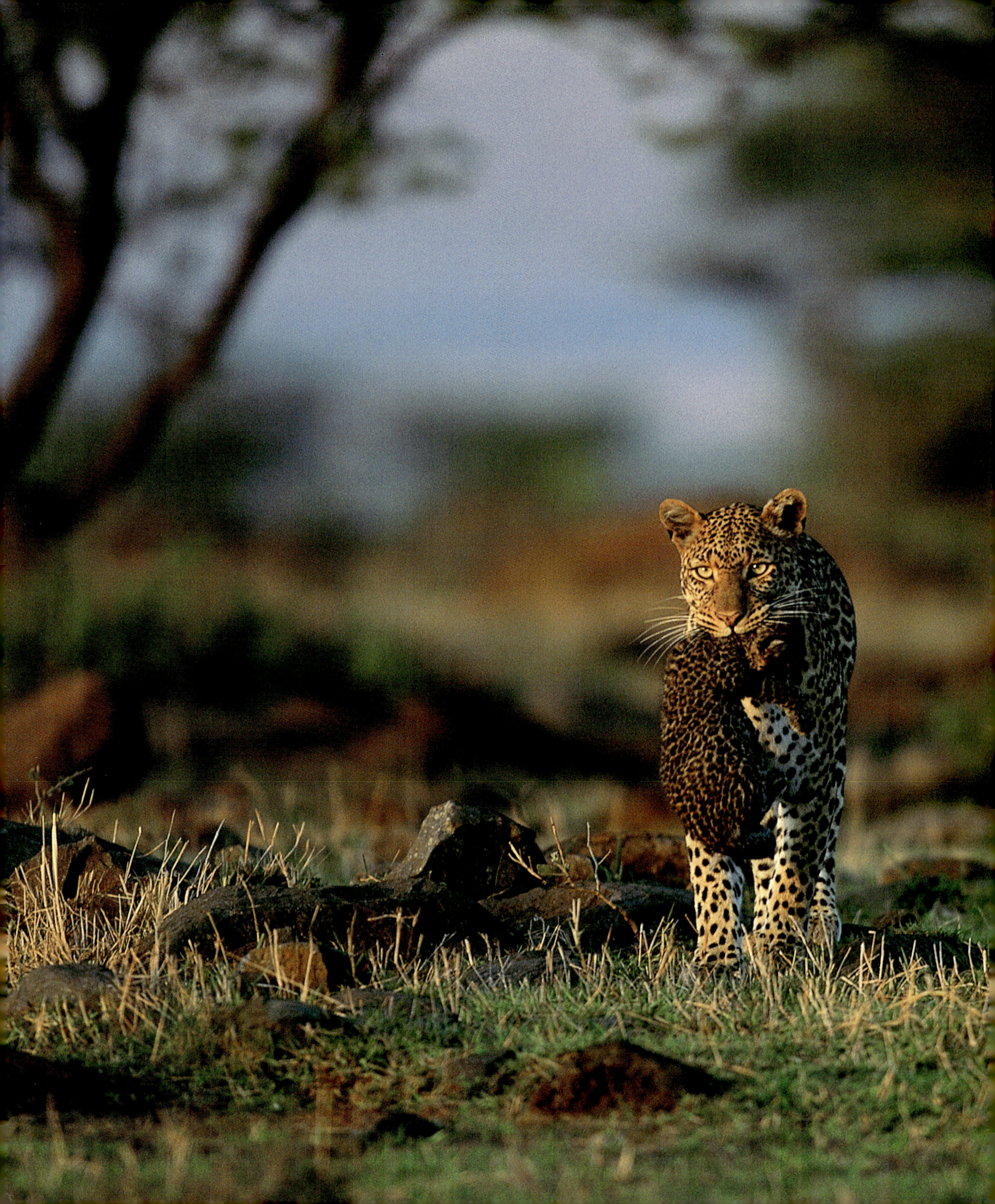

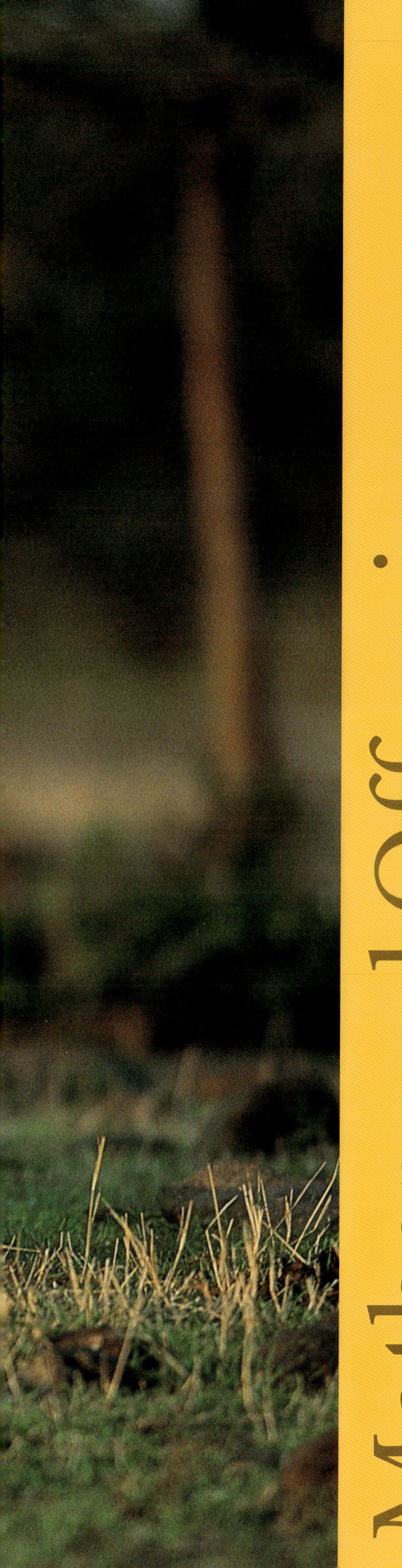

11

Mother and Offspring

In the Serengeti-Mara, some species give birth at certain times of the year. If you are there in August and September, you should see lots of gazelle newborn, and in October there are newly born topi; zebra foals are plentiful in January, and the young of wildebeests jostle for space in February. Other species give birth all year 'round, such as lions, cheetahs, and elephants. If you linger and watch closely, you may be rewarded with some unforgettable scenes: a cheetah mother pausing in her search for prey so that her tired cubs can rest; a giraffe keeping a lookout while her young one feeds; a gazelle turning to confront a jackal while shielding her fawn; a lioness visibly concerned when her cubs stray too far. I once saw a cheetah actually run toward a male lion, drawing his attention away from her cubs. Beside such images of devotion and duty, there are others of sheer tenacity: a wildebeest calf matching its running mother stride for stride; lion cubs too young to hunt following their mothers as they set out to find food; hyena pups pestering their mother for milk.

I read a long time ago that a lioness will defend her cubs with her life. It sparked my imagination and I wondered about wild mothers and altruism. What I saw out in the wild, however, put doubts in my mind about unbounded altruism. I watched a gazelle mother run away when a cheetah closed in on her fawn; she stood by bleating helplessly as the cheetah's cub toyed with it. I saw a cheetah abandon her four-week-old cubs when prey had become scarce and hunting and provisioning her cubs had become overwhelming. A lioness chooses to leave the scene come what may when a nomadic male lion attacks her cubs. A mother is considered the most altruistic entity in the wild, but there is a limit to how much she will give to her offspring – and for good reason.

A wild mother seeks to raise as many surviving offspring as possible, but she faces two trade-offs. First, she must strike a balance between being a well-endowed mother and reproduction. Hyena mothers could have strong bones that are massively reinforced, but there would be little calcium left over to make milk for the young. So, natural selection has limited the amount of calcium in her bones for the sake of her offspring. The health of the mother is not paramount.

Second, there is a trade-off between current and future litters as when a lioness breeds more than once. A lioness that devoted all her energy and resources to her first litter would in all probability have a first-class first litter, but her subsequent litters would suffer from a lack of resources. In order to maximize the number of surviving offspring, she will need to keep something in reserve when raising her initial litter.

A mother may not be all giving but, of course, her offspring want all of her resources. There is, then, a conflict between mother and child and, in fact, the conflict begins in the womb. In purely biological terms, the fetus must mine the mother's body for nutrients in order to survive, tapping into her bloodstream, forc-

Pages 142–143
A leopard mother is moving one of her two cubs to a new den. It's a tense situation for her since her cubs are vulnerable to a surprise attack from hyenas or lions.

ing nutrients its way at the expense of her health. The mother, weakened by pregnancy, struggles to keep her body in good shape for her own survival, which, of course, ensures future offspring.

The tug-of-war continues once the baby is born. The first decision of motherhood is whether to let the newborn live or die. Maternal investment is a precious resource, and if a newborn is likely to die, there is no point in committing resources to it. Better to keep the resources in reserve for the healthier, stronger littermates or future offspring. Thus mothers are prepared to neglect their runtish or sickly offspring. But the neglected baby was born with a survival instinct and does not give up easily. From my own observations, it seems to me that it is a struggle to decide when to give up, and it is with some anguish that a mother chooses to abandon her young.

Once an infant is allowed to live, the conflict between the generations continues. Since babies cannot suckle at will or win food from their mothers by force, they use psychological methods. I am positive lion and leopard cubs sometimes cry in order to manipulate their mother's genuine concern for their welfare, to induce her to give more than she would otherwise be willing to give. Most mothers are alert to cheating, however, and are not easily fooled.

At some point in every infant's life, there comes a time for weaning. The baby is reluctant – milk, after all, is a convenient and delicious food. But it's not a now or never situation – the offspring would eventually wean itself.

There is a reason why the conflict between mother and offspring is not a fierce one, as illustrated by a bleating wildebeest calf separated from its mother. The calf runs about in desperation searching for its mother – without her the frightened baby is utterly vulnerable. The mother can afford to bail out of the conflict, but the baby cannot.

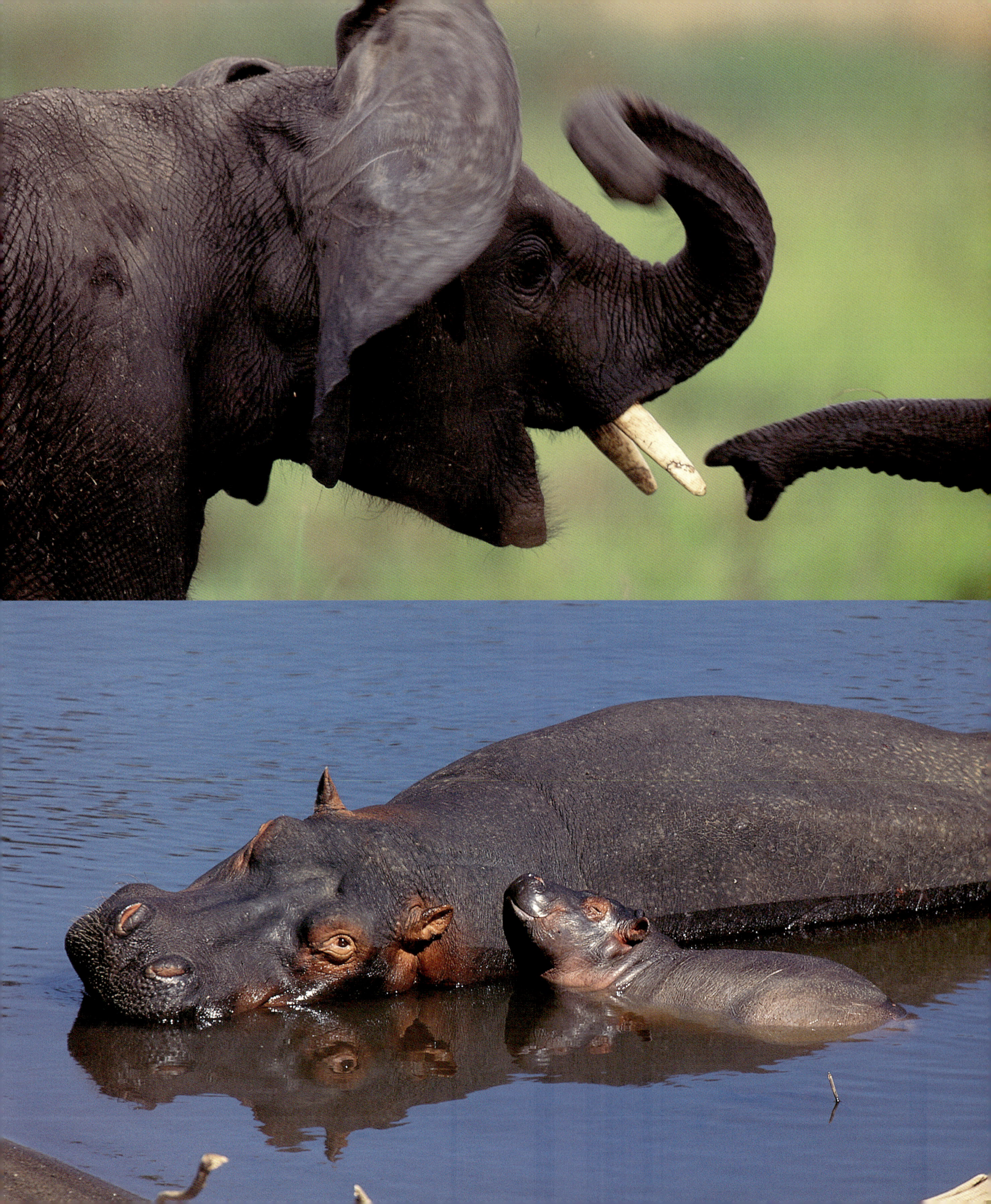

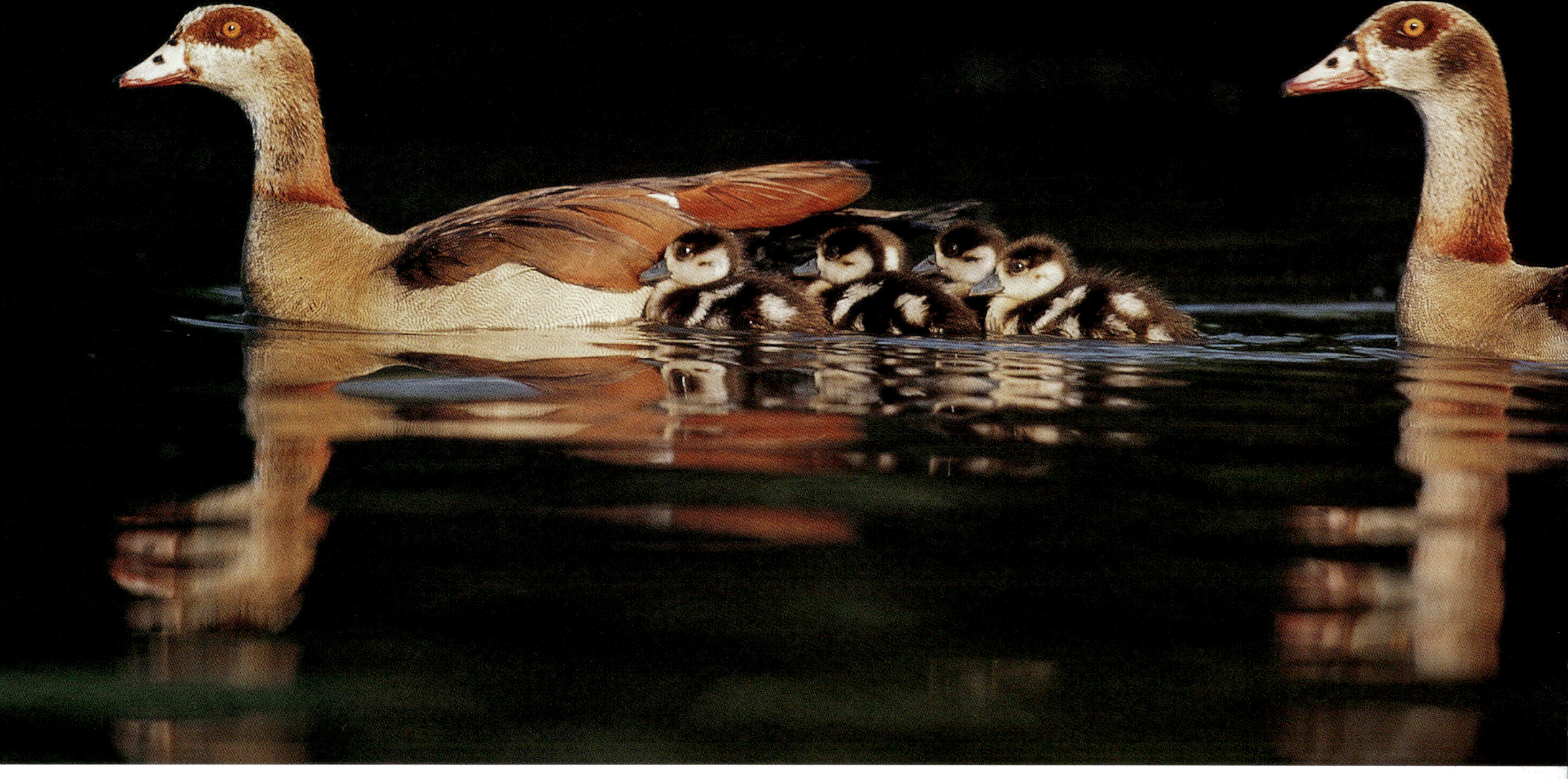

A family of Egyptian geese swimming on a river. Unlike in mammals, male birds tend to be more active in helping to raise a family.

Opposite, above
A playful elephant calf interacts with another while their mothers feed in the vicinity. Well-adjusted elephant babies of a family group are playful and inquisitive, characteristics that are conducive to learning.

Opposite, below
After nursing, mother and baby hippo rest in a shallow stretch of river. Hippos are social animals, and this pair is a part of a group of nearly 30 cows and their young, dominated by a large bull. With crocodiles on the prowl, the young stay close to their mothers.

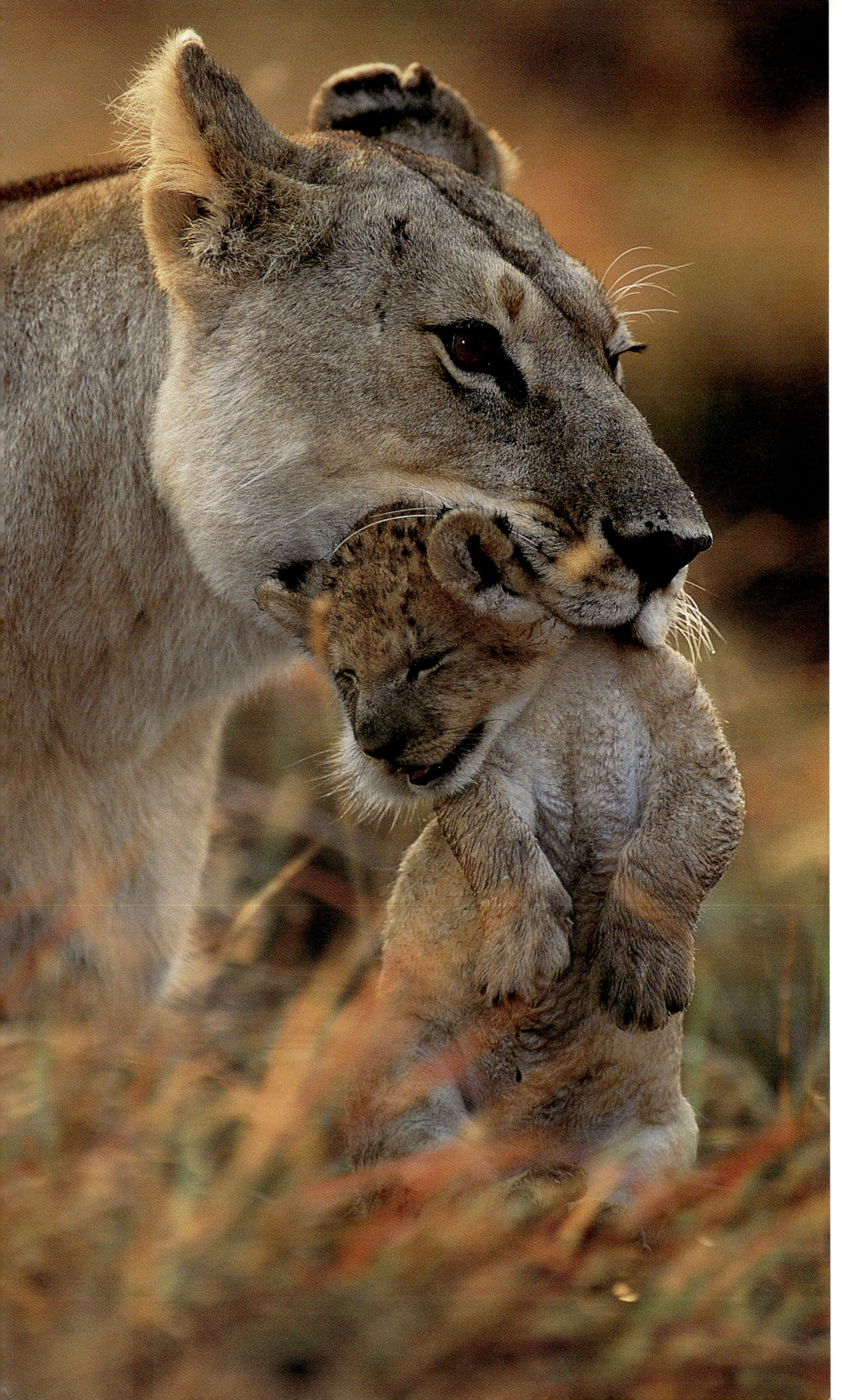

Though a lion's jaws are powerful enough to crush ribs and pierce elephant hide, a lioness carries her delicate cubs without a scratch.

Opposite, above
In search of a comfortable resting spot, one of the pride cubs finds the perfect place on its mother's broad rear. It is keenly watching the other cubs for an opportunity to play or some other entertaining activity.

Opposite, below
Lion cubs invariably find a way to get as close to mother as is physically possible.

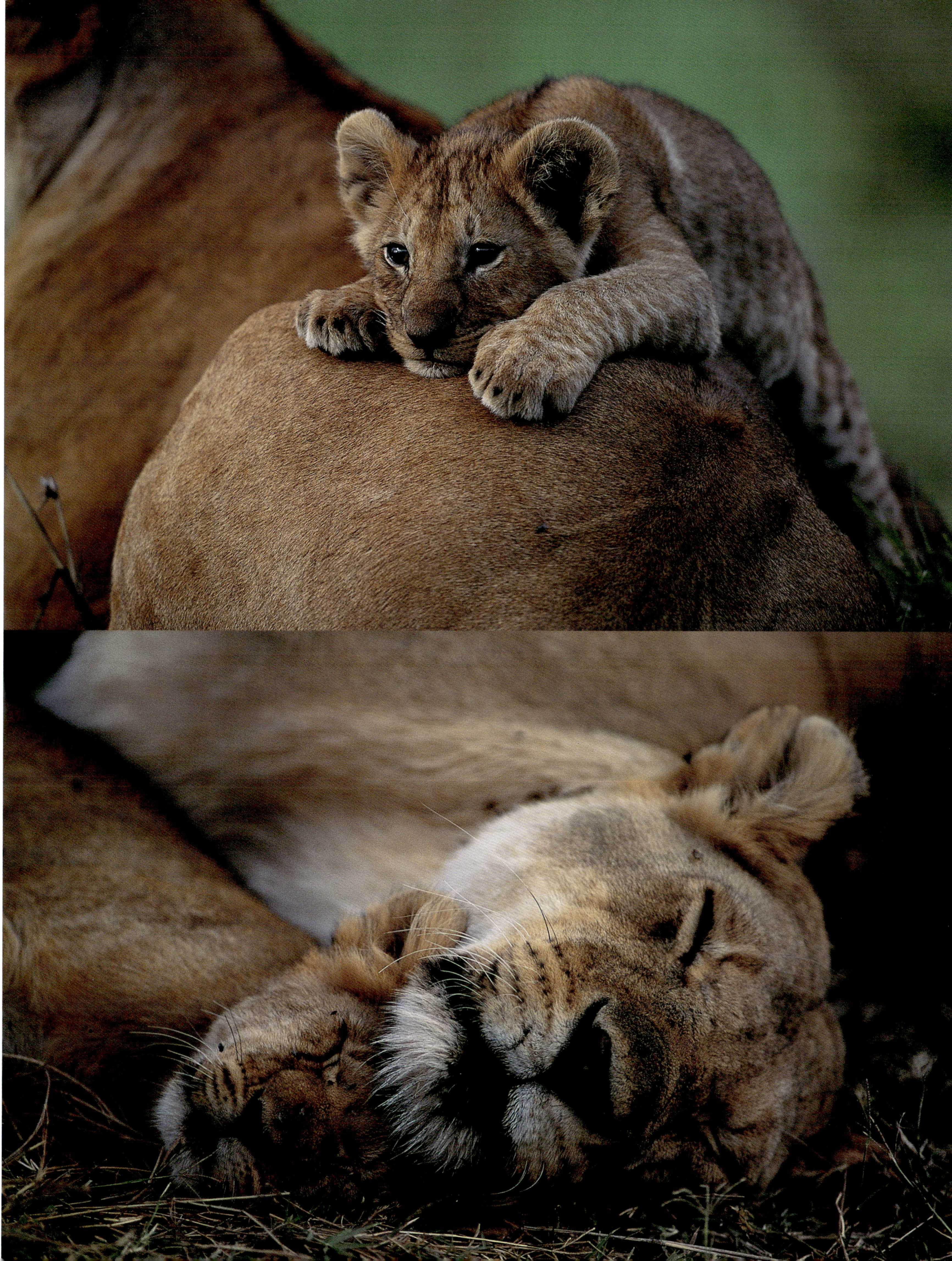

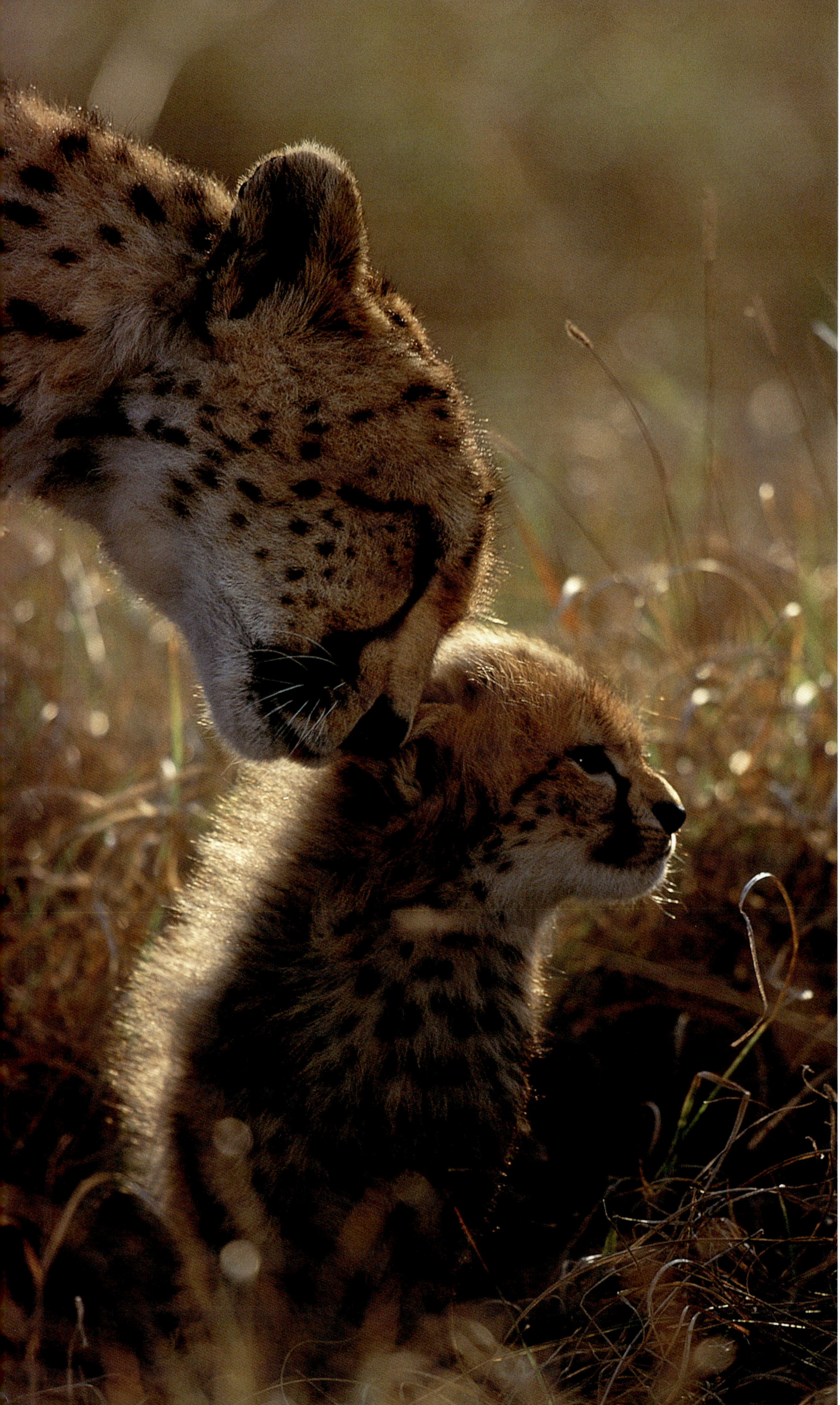

A cheetah mother reaches down to nuzzle and groom one of her two cubs, who is clearly relishing the attention. Cheetah mothers and cubs normally do not have as much physical contact as lions or leopards and their cubs.

Opposite, above
This cheetah cub, only a few months old, has awakened from a nap to greet its mother who is scanning the surrounding area.

Opposite, below
A leopard cub has finished suckling and is eager to join her brother in play, but mother is determined to finish grooming, despite the cub's protestations.

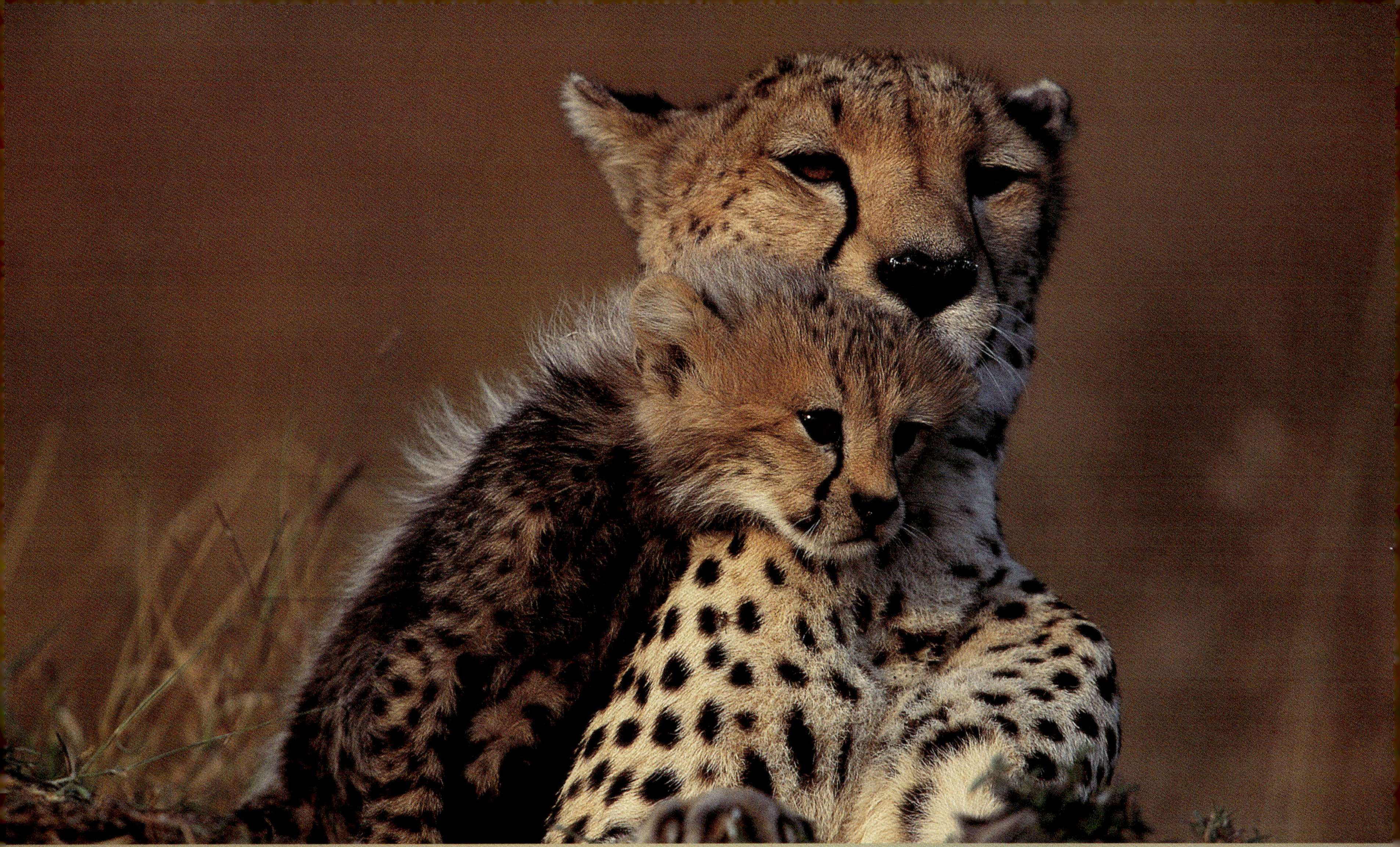

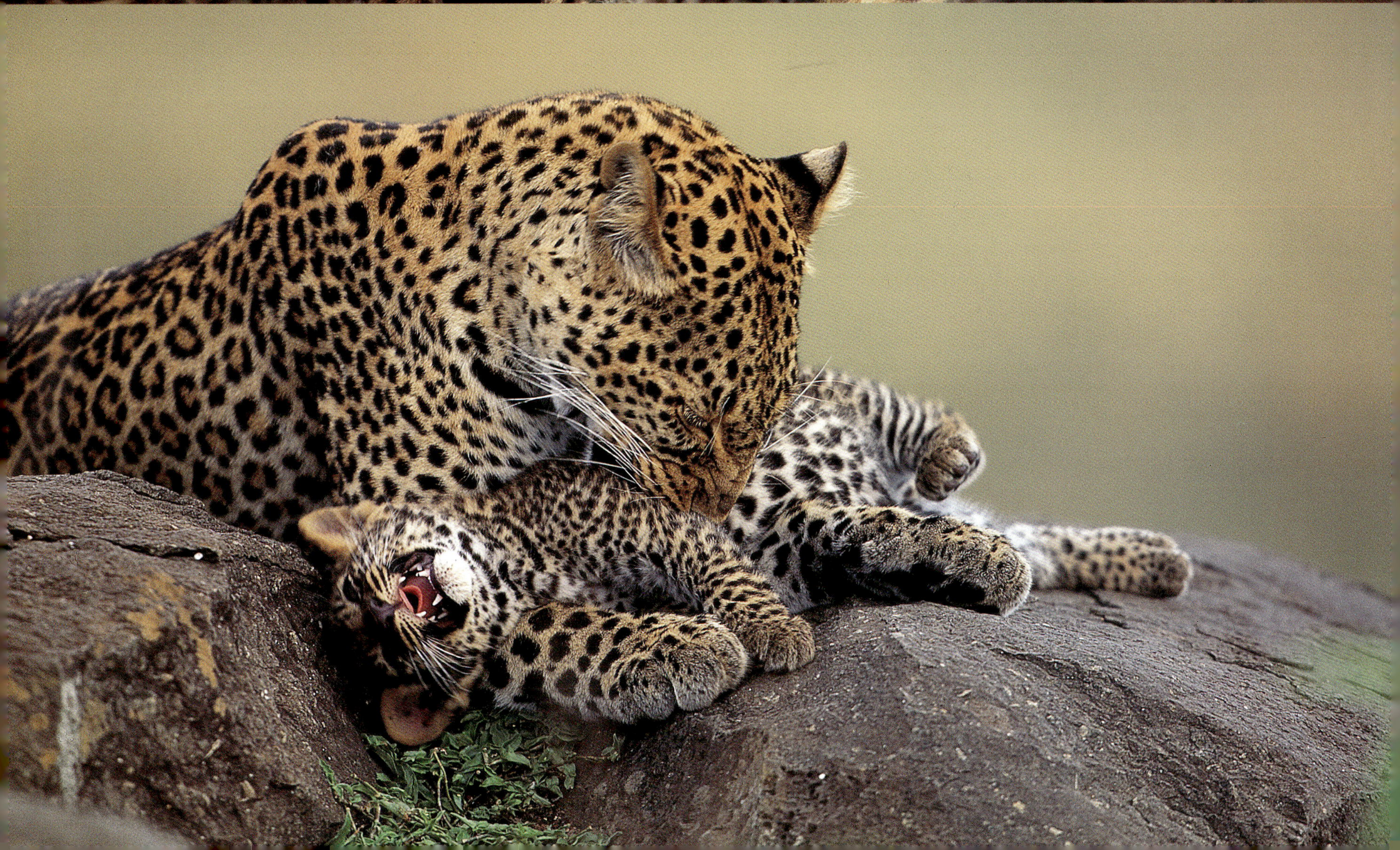

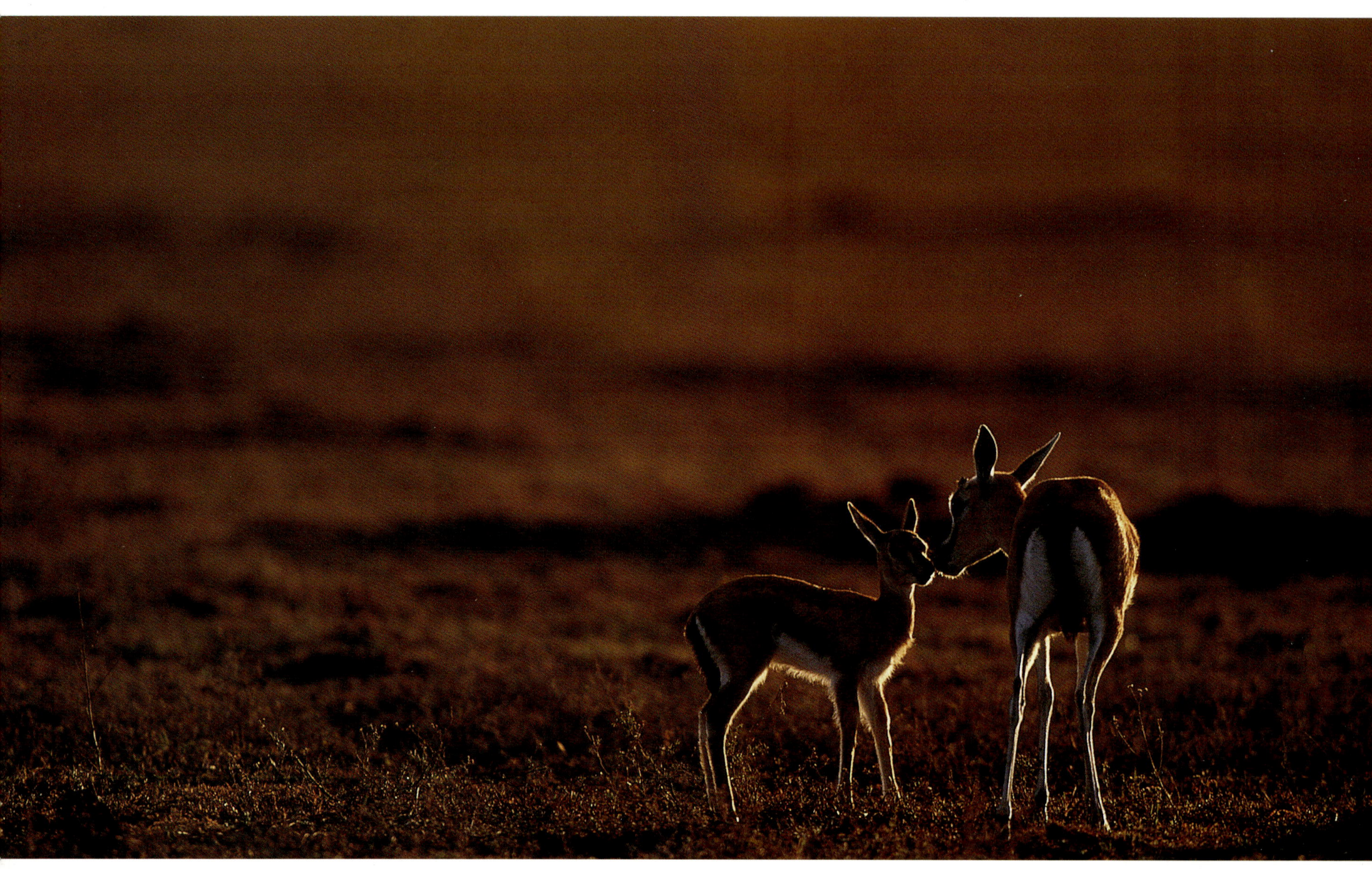

Having left her fawn hiding in the grass, a Thomson's gazelle mother, upon her return, first checks it over, using her sense of smell.

Opposite
While the mother sits resting after her meal of leaves, a young, utterly irrepressible Zanzibar red colobus monkey seeks an outlet for its boundless energy.

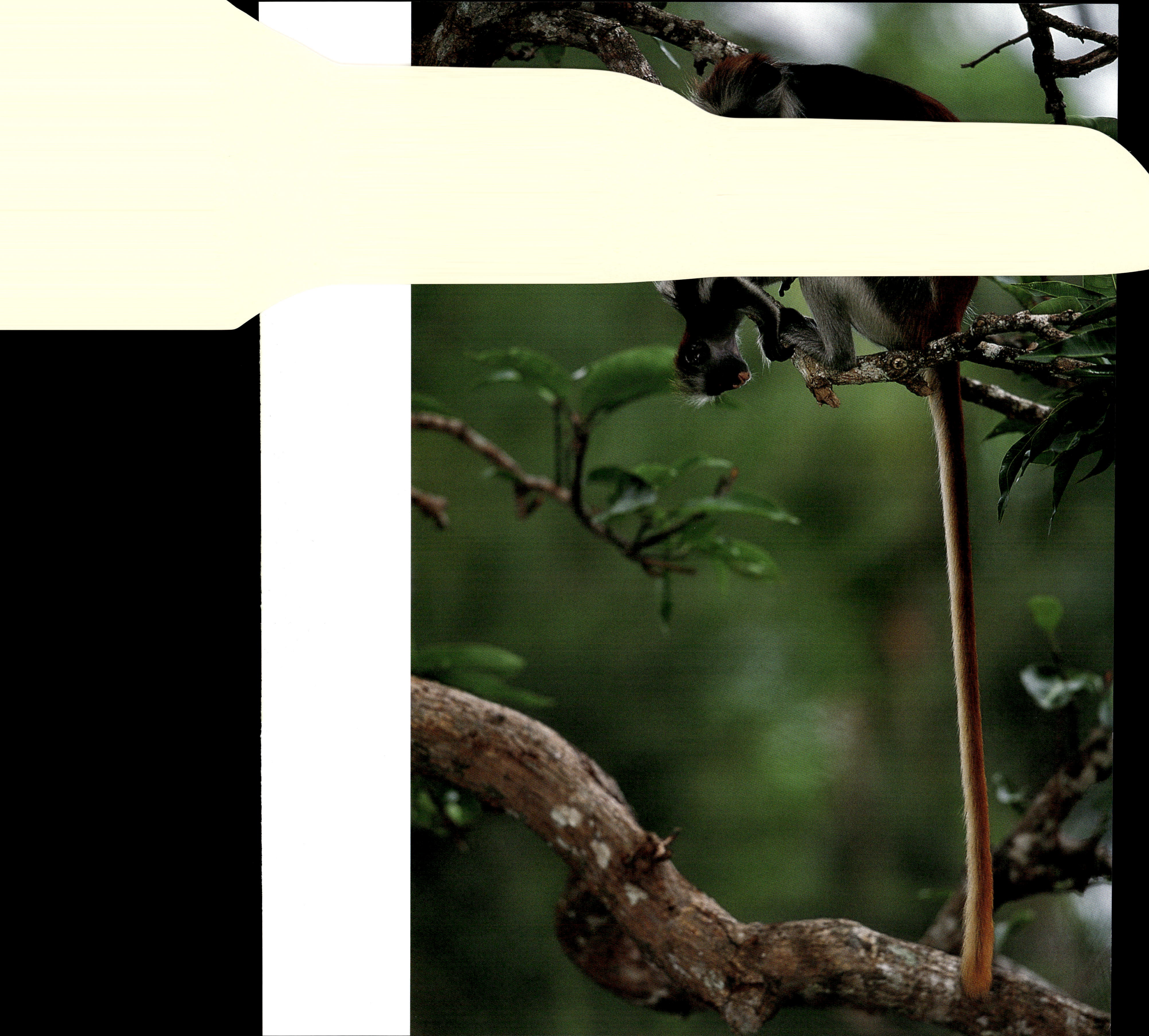

A rock hyrax youngster finds a comfortable perch on its mother's warm body. A rock hyrax litter may consist of as many as four young, but two or three is more common. The well-developed young are able to move around soon after birth.

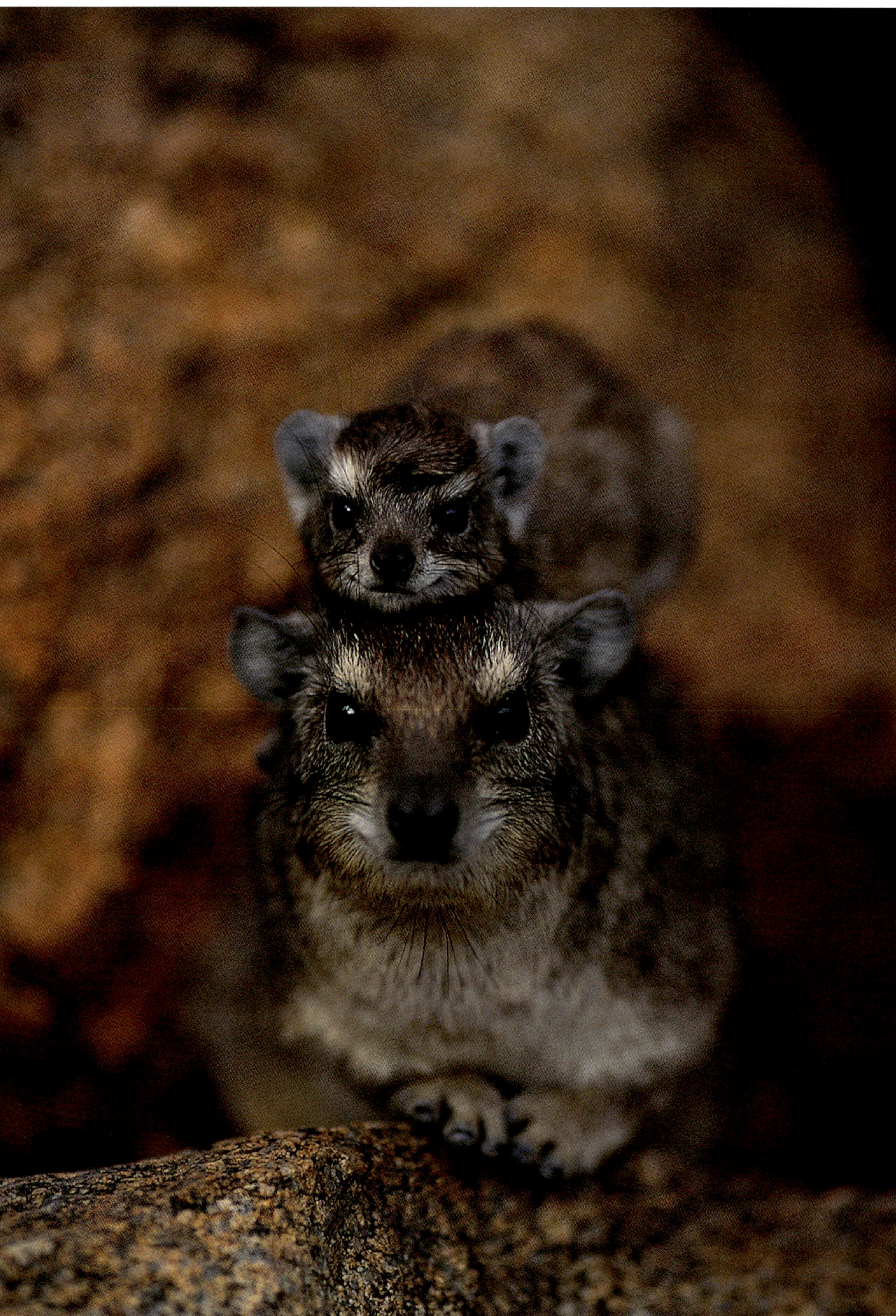

Opposite
A white rhino calf follows behind its mother. This is not a common sight: White rhino babies usually lead the way, while mother protects the rear and scans ahead, always on the lookout for danger.

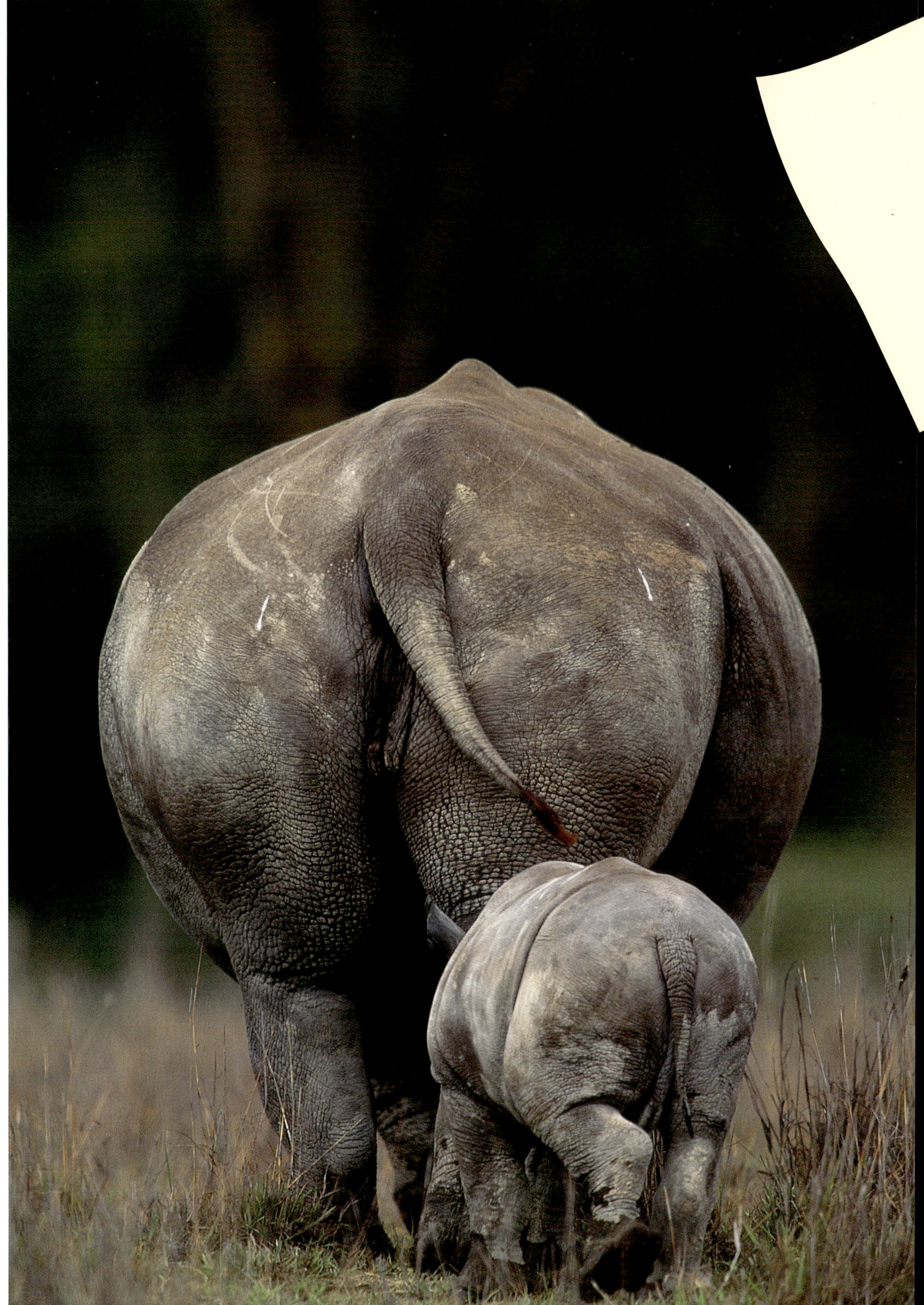

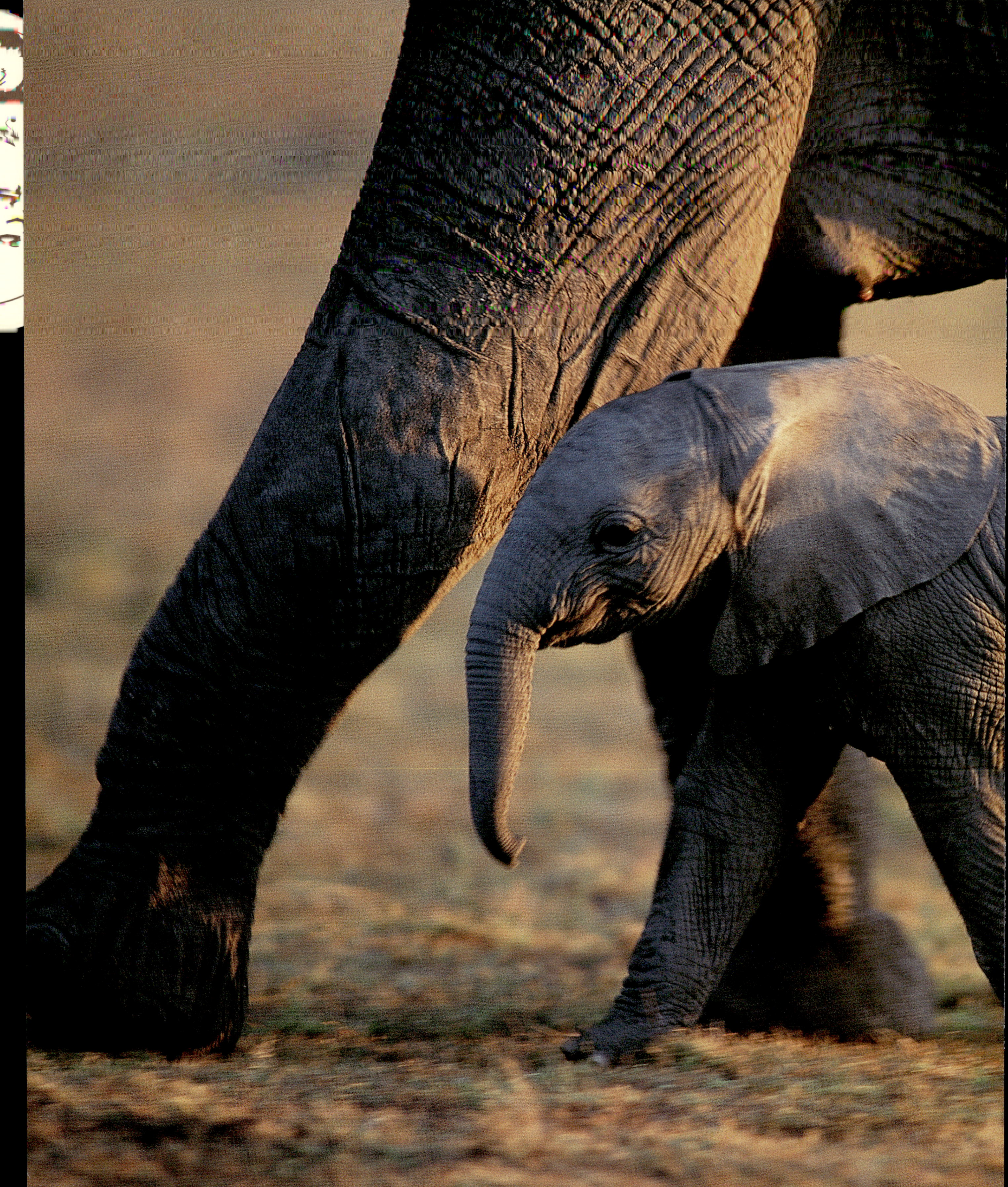

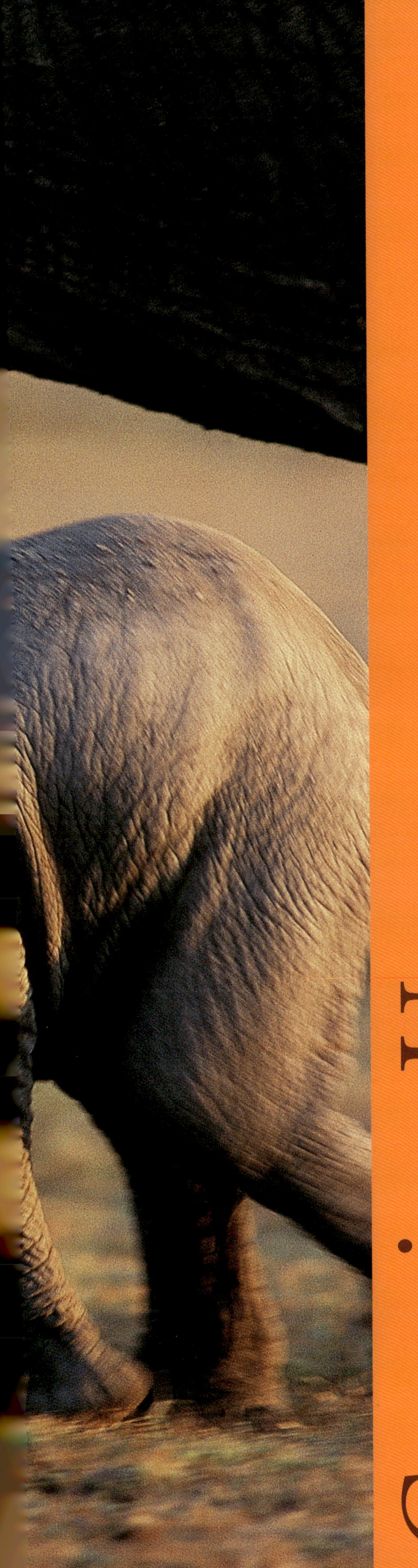

12

Growing Up

Infant mortality is very high on the savannah: In some areas, baboons lose half of their infants, and it's even worse for some grazers like the Thomson's gazelle. Twelve out of 20 lion cubs don't make it past the first few months, and 19 out of 20 cheetah cubs fail to survive to adulthood. Danger arises from a variety of sources: predation, accidents, flash floods, injury, disease, malnutrition, starvation, loss of mother, abandonment, infanticide. For the young who make it past the first critical period – two weeks for wildebeest calves, eight weeks for cheetah cubs – the tender scenes of nurturing and bonding are only the relative calm before the appearance of the many conflicts and hazards emanating from the harsh, dispassionate savannah.

Many animal species on the savannah have a home range or territory in which they carry out their daily lives sleeping, feeding, drinking, resting, wandering, raising their young, hiding. It is vital that the young learn the many useful features of their home in order to become efficient, functioning adults. We once observed a cheetah mother lead her eight-week-old cubs from the safety of their lair out into the big world. The vast plains must have seemed daunting to such tiny nomads, but the small cubs were too young to be fully aware of their utter vulnerability. Of course the mother was all too aware of the dangers and was intensely circumspect, staying with the cubs in whatever cover she could find. She seemed anxious as she cautiously traversed the plains, her irrepressible cubs running to keep up with her long, urgent strides. During the family's wanderings, the mother was often on the lookout for prey, but, in the process, she was also showing her cubs the details of her vast home range.

Can wild youngsters learn without a teacher? Although animals are born with appropriate instincts – giraffes have an inclination to eat leaves rather than grass – their natural tendencies still need to be refined and shaped by specific knowledge. It is not enough to like a certain type of food; it is also necessary to know where to find it and how to get it. If a young giraffe had to draw a map of where the choicest food is found by blundering about on its own, it would probably pay a high price for its youthful ignorance. But by following closely on its experienced mother's heels, the baby giraffe positions itself to feed on her knowledge, so to speak. The giraffe mother does not actively teach her young one; it learns through mother-infant togetherness. From the youngster's point of view, anything that interests its mother is worth checking out; anything that mother is wary of warrants a cautious observance from afar.

In order to learn how to survive, a wild young animal's impressionable brain simply needs to be receptive, attentive, and willing to experiment. The wonderful thing about learning in the wild is the ease of it – there is only occasional need for encouragement and discipline. It simply happens – young animals truly are little sponges, eager to absorb every piece of information they encounter. Cheetah cubs are highly inquisitive, adventurous, and playful. They'll examine anything that doesn't appear threatening with a great deal of enthusiasm – even lifeless objects are actively probed for life. To a varying degree, all

Pages 156–157
During the first year of life, a baby elephant rarely strays even a trunk's length away from its mother's side, seeking secure berth beneath her belly whenever it feels nervous.

the mammalian young of the savannah possess this potent mix of curiosity and energy: Zebra foals will not hesitate to take a detour to better examine bright stones; wildebeest calves will follow a small animal they have never seen before; elephant babies will chase birds; hyena pups will sniff at almost anything; and lion cubs will playfully attack leaves being blown about by the wind. In this way, the young get to know their home environment rather well.

Animals have also adapted to learn the essentials quickly. It doesn't take much time or experience for a newly born wildebeest to learn the route of the Great Migration. It appears that a young calf accompanying its mother once around the entire migratory trek can get all the navigational aids it needs to complete the route on its own the next time. Wildebeests and zebras in particular possess acute navigational instincts, and even seem to possess photographic memories.

Young animals of migratory species also learn survival language on the move by being attuned to the actions of the adults in their herd. When there is a sudden silence in the group, they absorb the message that a predator is suspected to be lurking close by. When the adults stop grazing, stand to attention, and become tense and ready for flight, the young can sense that some danger has been spotted. But when they see the grown-ups actually move closer en masse to a pride of lounging lions, the young understand that these particular lions, possibly full from a recent feeding, pose no threat.

Growing up involves a great deal of play. Mammalian play most often takes the form of play-fighting and exaggerated chasing and jumping. The cavorting of zebra foals and wildebeest calves is a familiar sight. The young of both herbivores and carnivores spar, joust, and contest. Carnivore young also play at stalking and prey capture, taking turns as hunter and hunted. Primates are particularly inventive at play, often devising new games on the spot.

However, play is a puzzle. While the costs of play – expenditure of energy, risk of injury, and risk of attracting dangerous predators – are easy to appreciate, the benefits are not immediately obvious. However, it seems that play develops and refines a wide variety of skills in relative safety before they are needed in critical situations. The head-butting of frisky male impala fawns and the trunk-wrestling of male elephant babies may be in preparation for the adult battles of the mating season; the playful ambushing of lion cubs and the delightful stalking of leopard cubs is perhaps schooling for real hunting and killing. It makes sense that the skills shaped by play would seep into adulthood, equipping the individual for survival and reproduction. We usually associate abundant and complex play with a highly developed nervous system. In other words, the species we tend to think of as "clever," are the most active players.

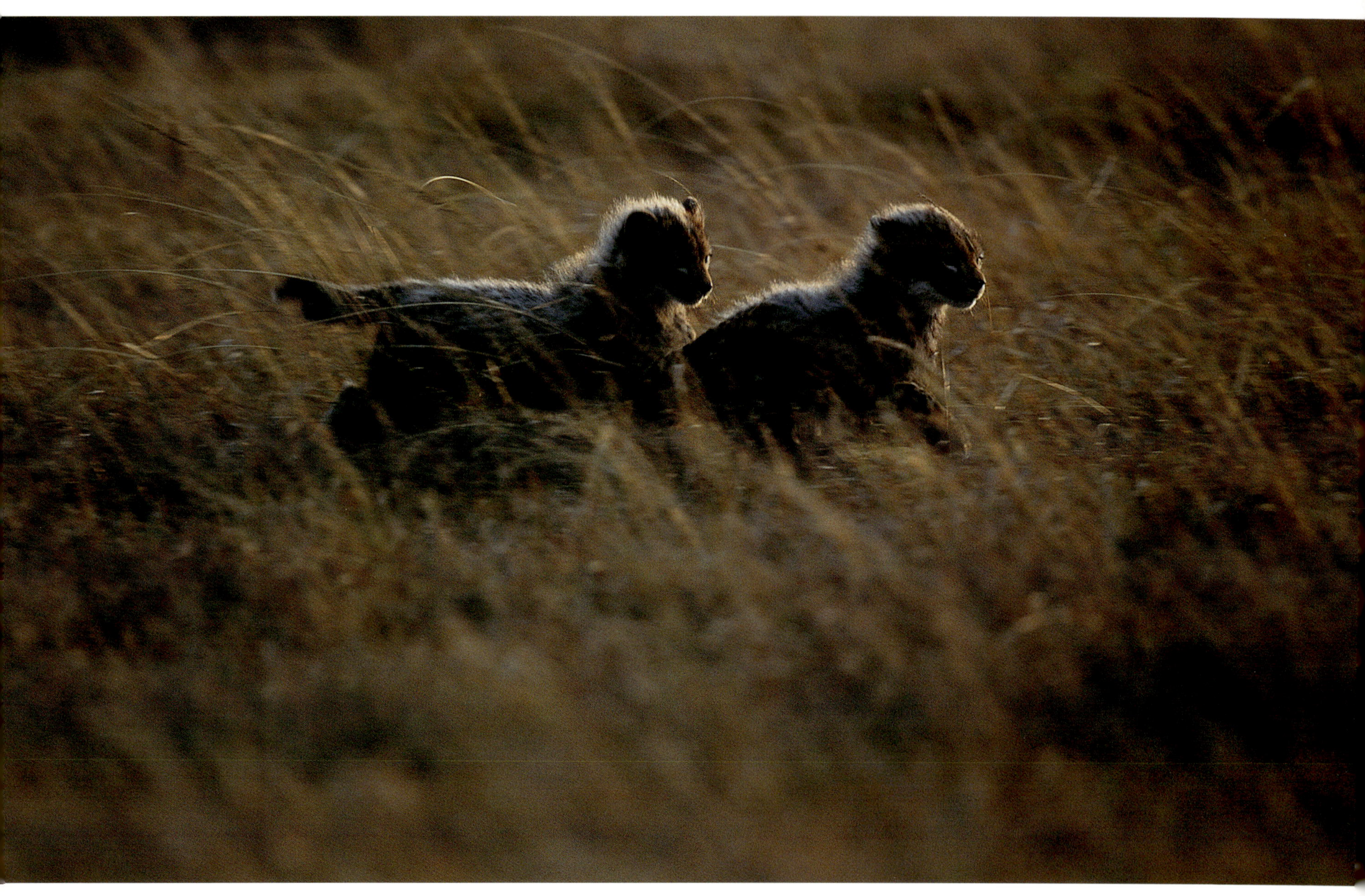

Brother and sister cheetah cubs play a game of chase. For this energetic pair, mother's rest time was their playtime.

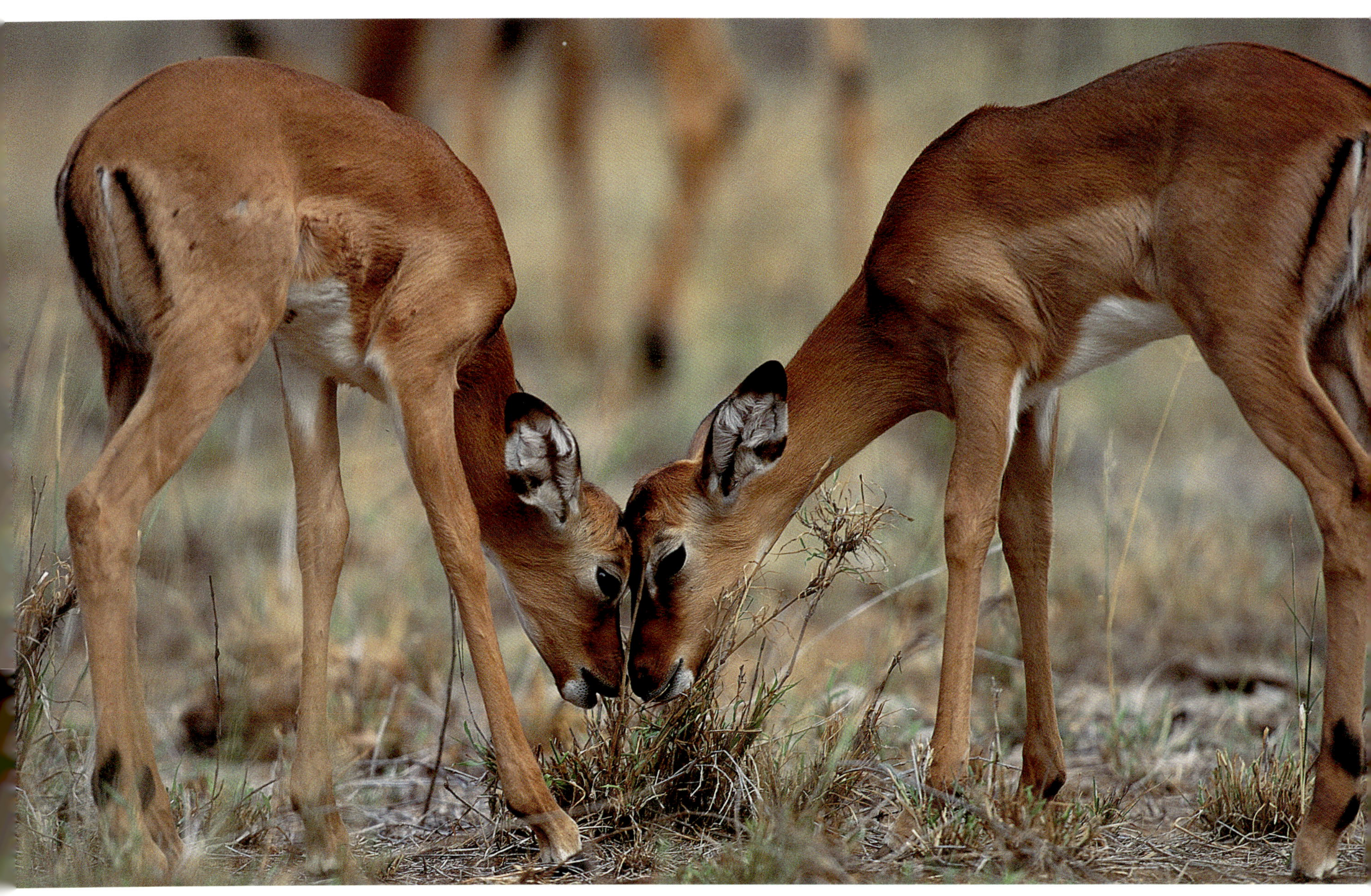

Two male impala fawns take time out to spar. Adult male impalas in bachelor groups do the same as they sort out positions in a fluid hierarchy. The prize is the right to challenge the male of an impala harem.

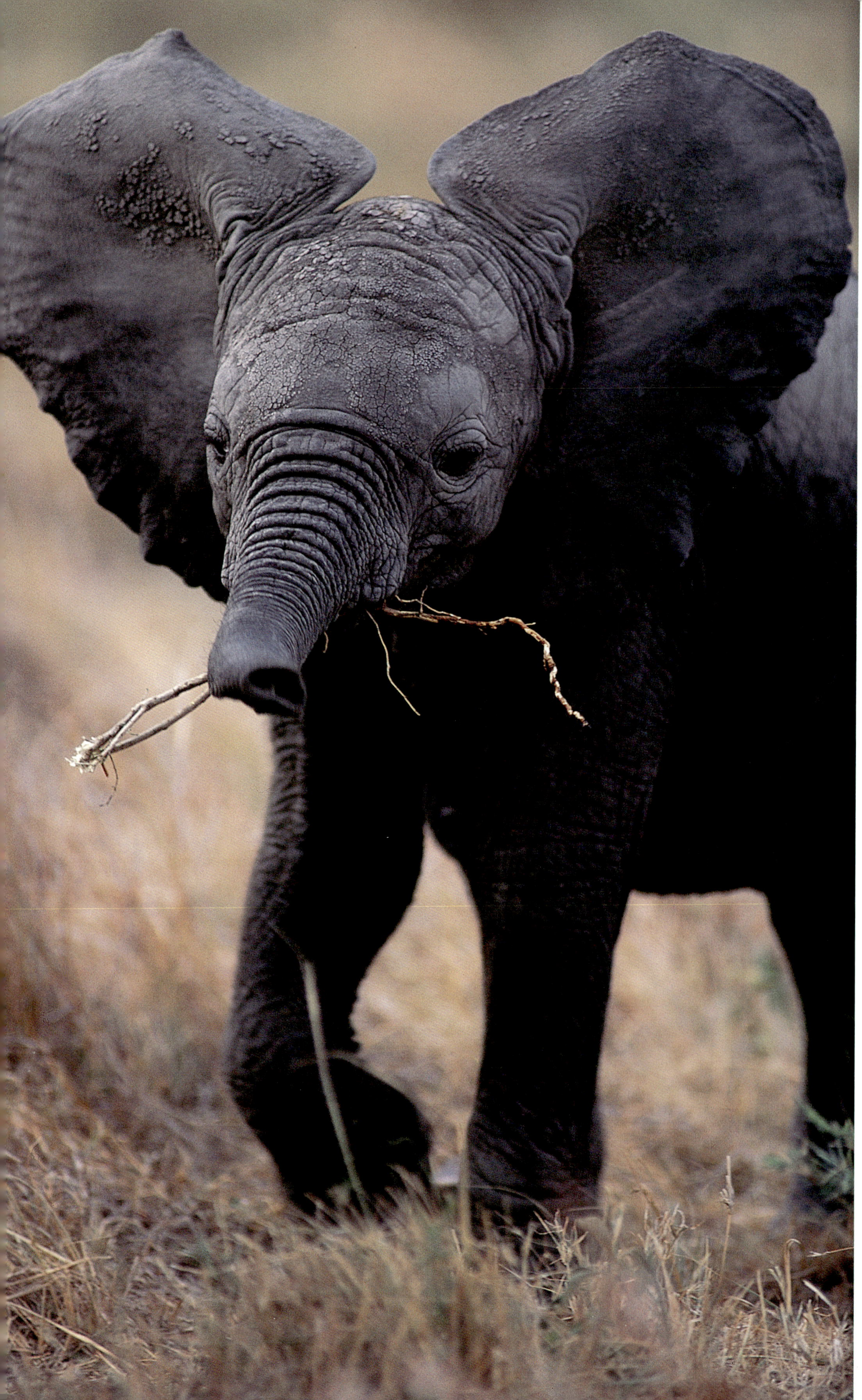

This young elephant wandered off to investigate something that caught its interest and became so engrossed that it was separated from its mother. Suddenly realizing that mother was nowhere near, it fanned out its ears in an act of self-protection and an attempt to bolster its own confidence, before running to catch up.

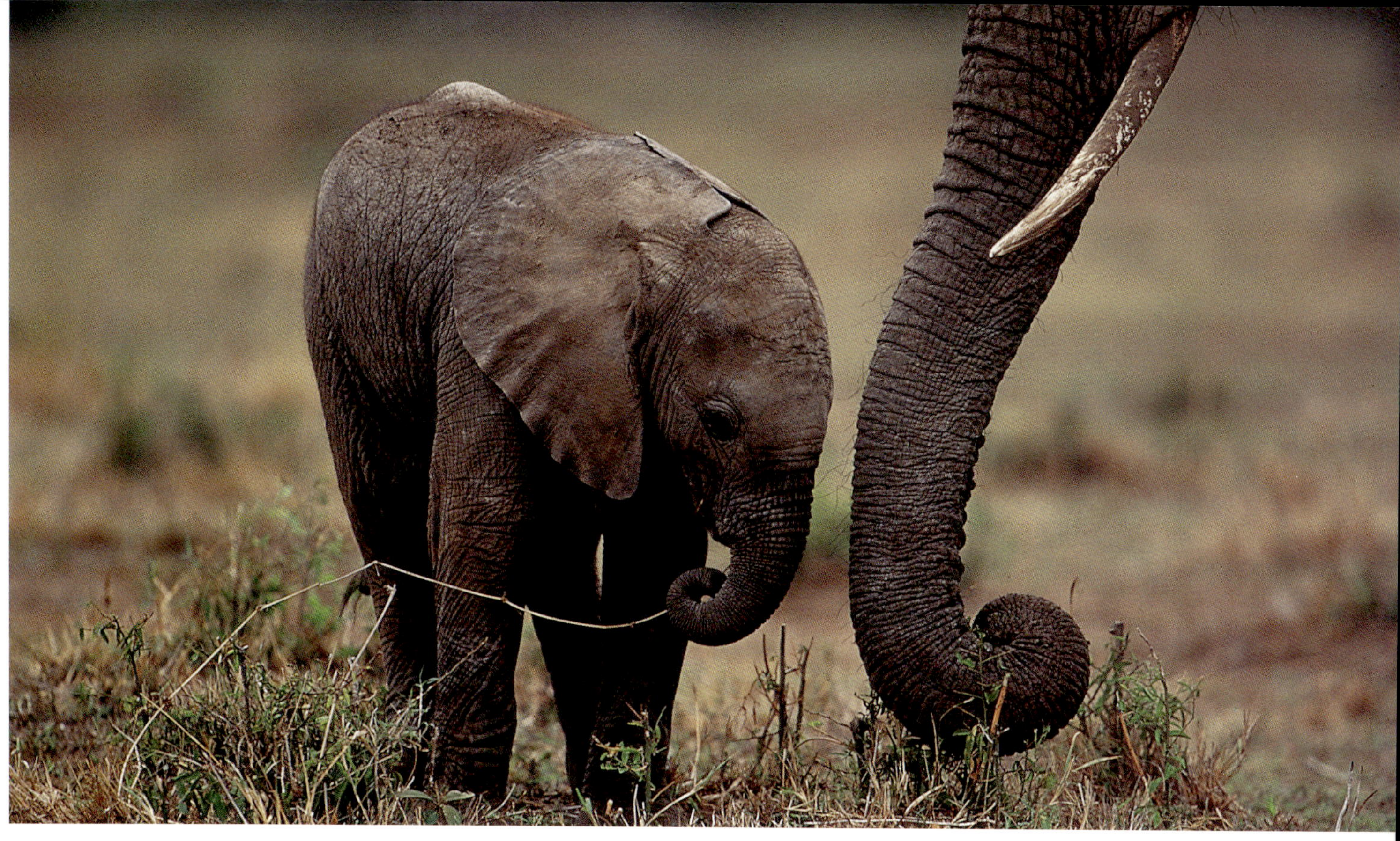

Feeling secure in the shadow of her mother, an elephant calf learns to use her trunk by experimentation and imitation.

This is the reaction of a young elephant when it feels threatened. It puffs itself up in a show of bravado, secure in the knowledge that its mother will come to the rescue should something go amiss.

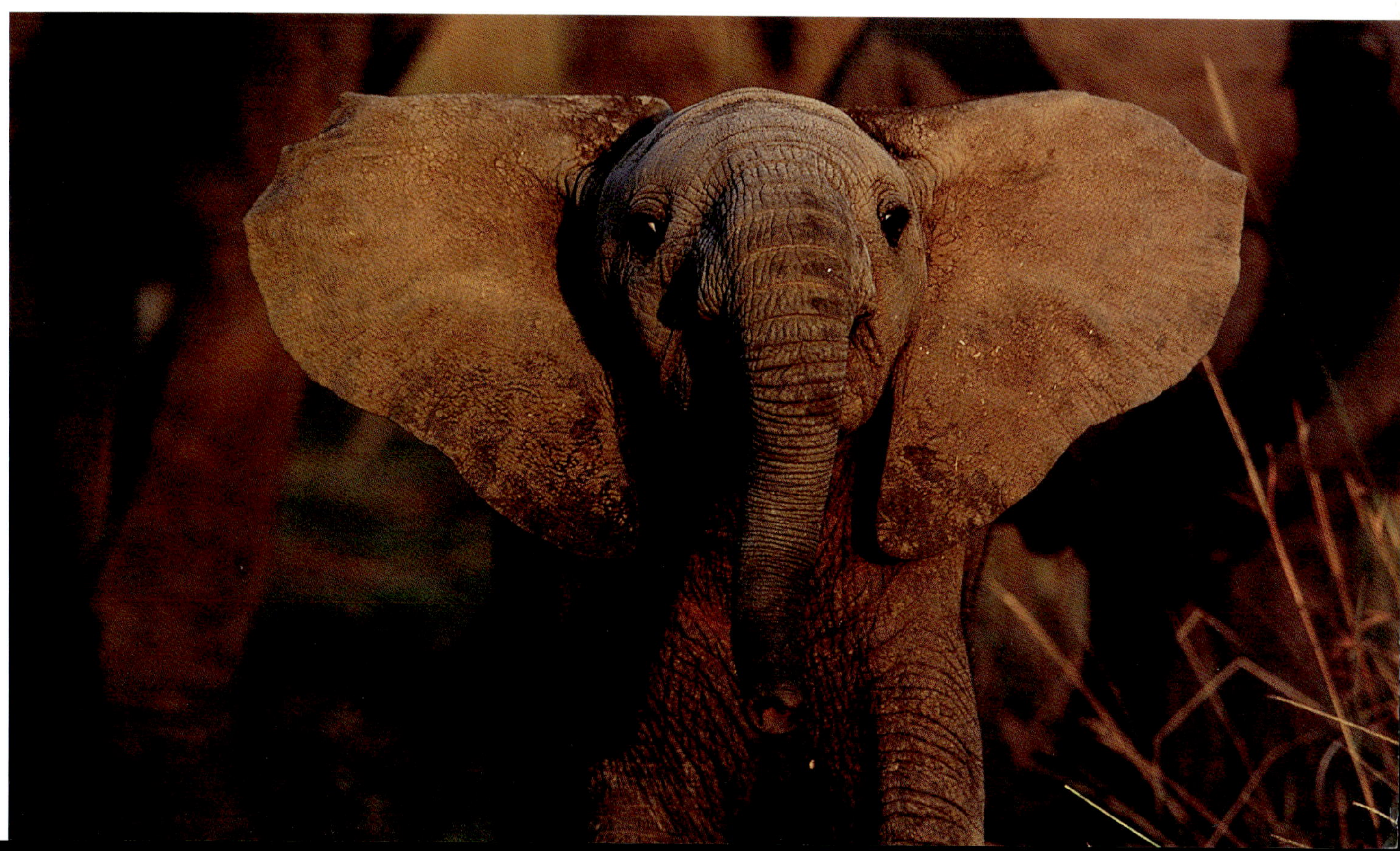

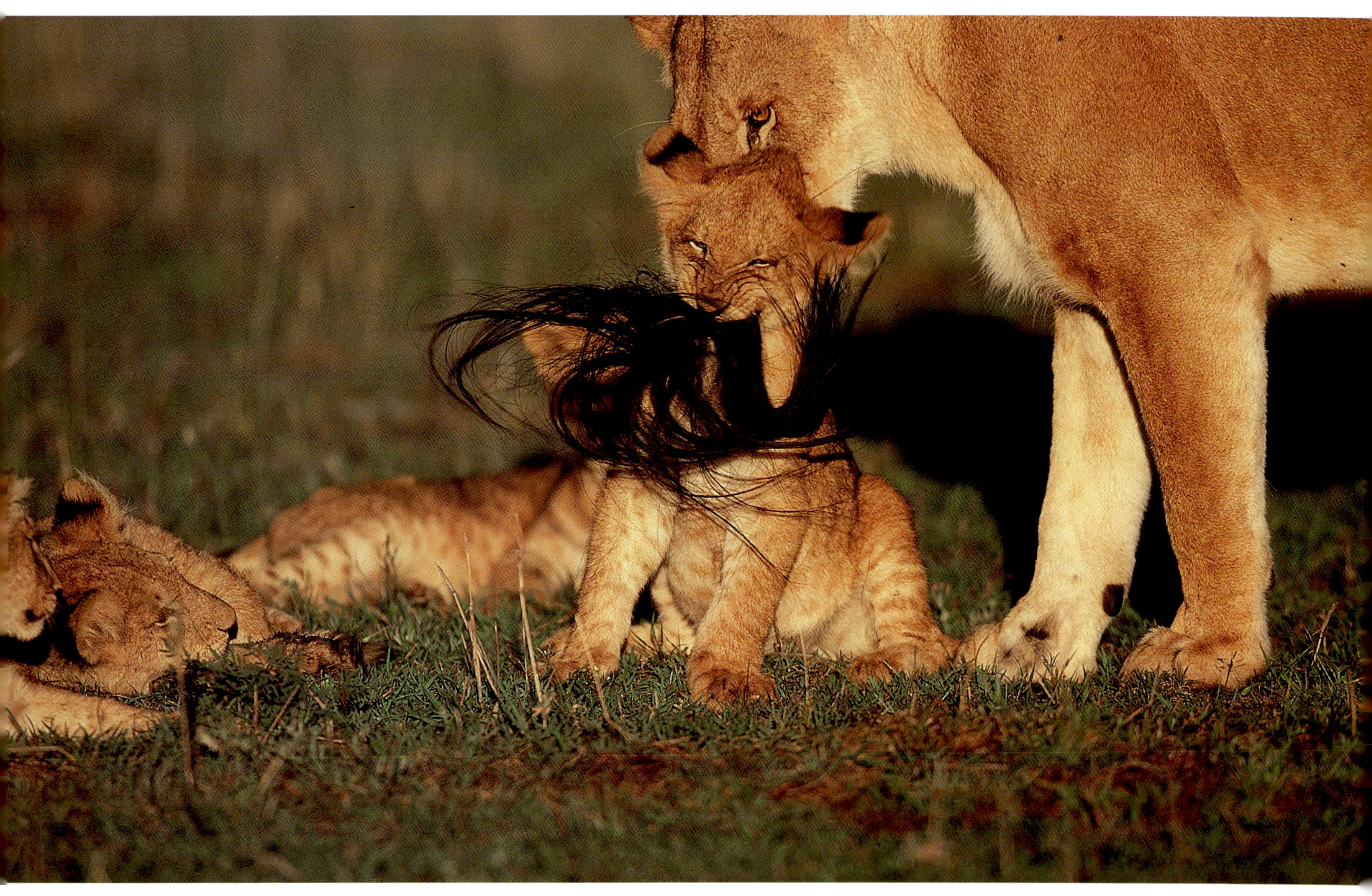

A lion cub has some fun with the hairy end of a wildebeest's tail. Lion cubs often engage in "predatory" play – stalking, chasing, and biting one another or playing with the remains of a kill.

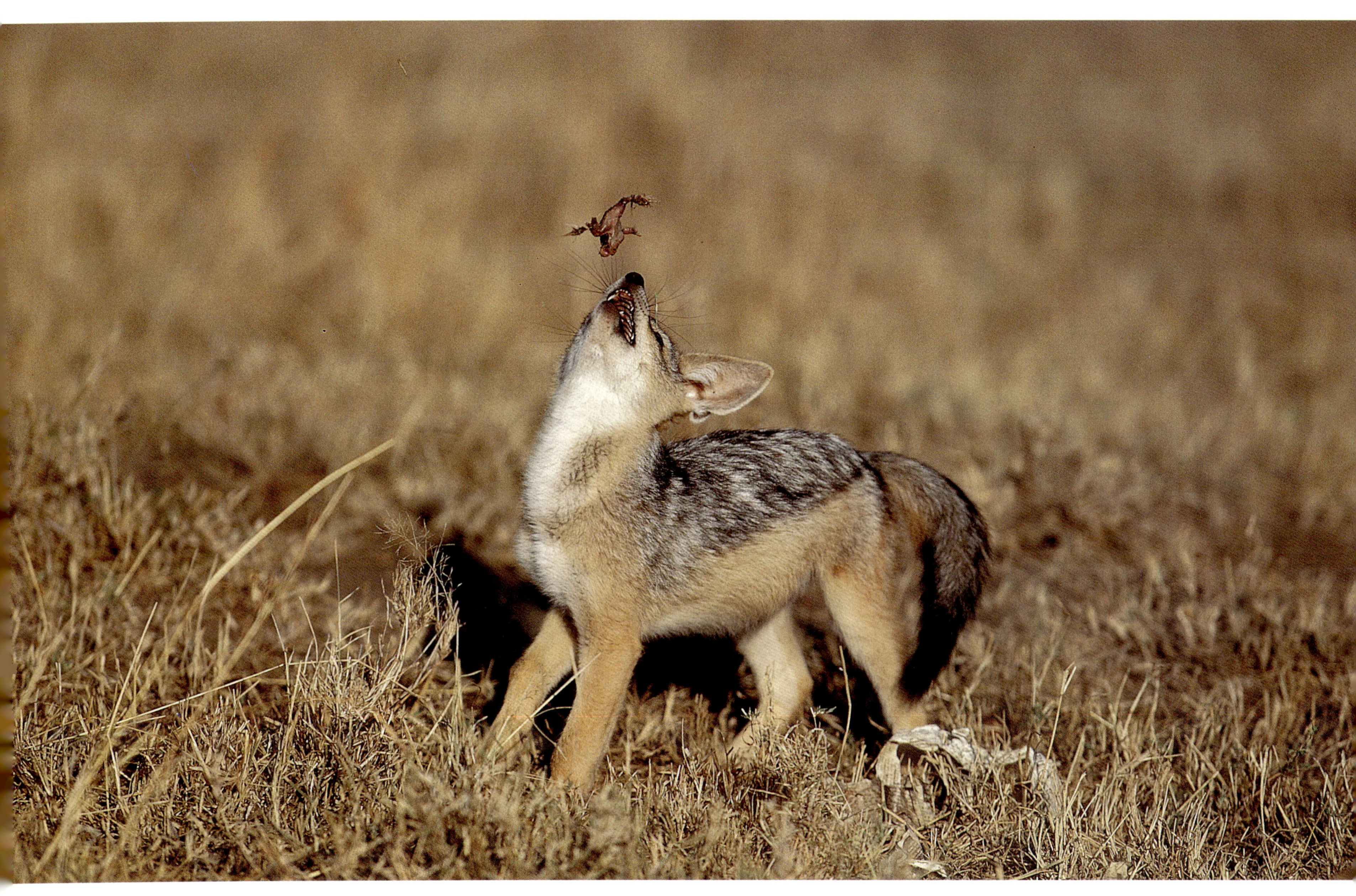

A black-backed jackal pup, exploring in the vicinity of its den, came across a piece of meat leftover from food brought to the den by its parents. It repeatedly tossed it into the air, attempting to catch it, but finally lost interest in the game and moved on.

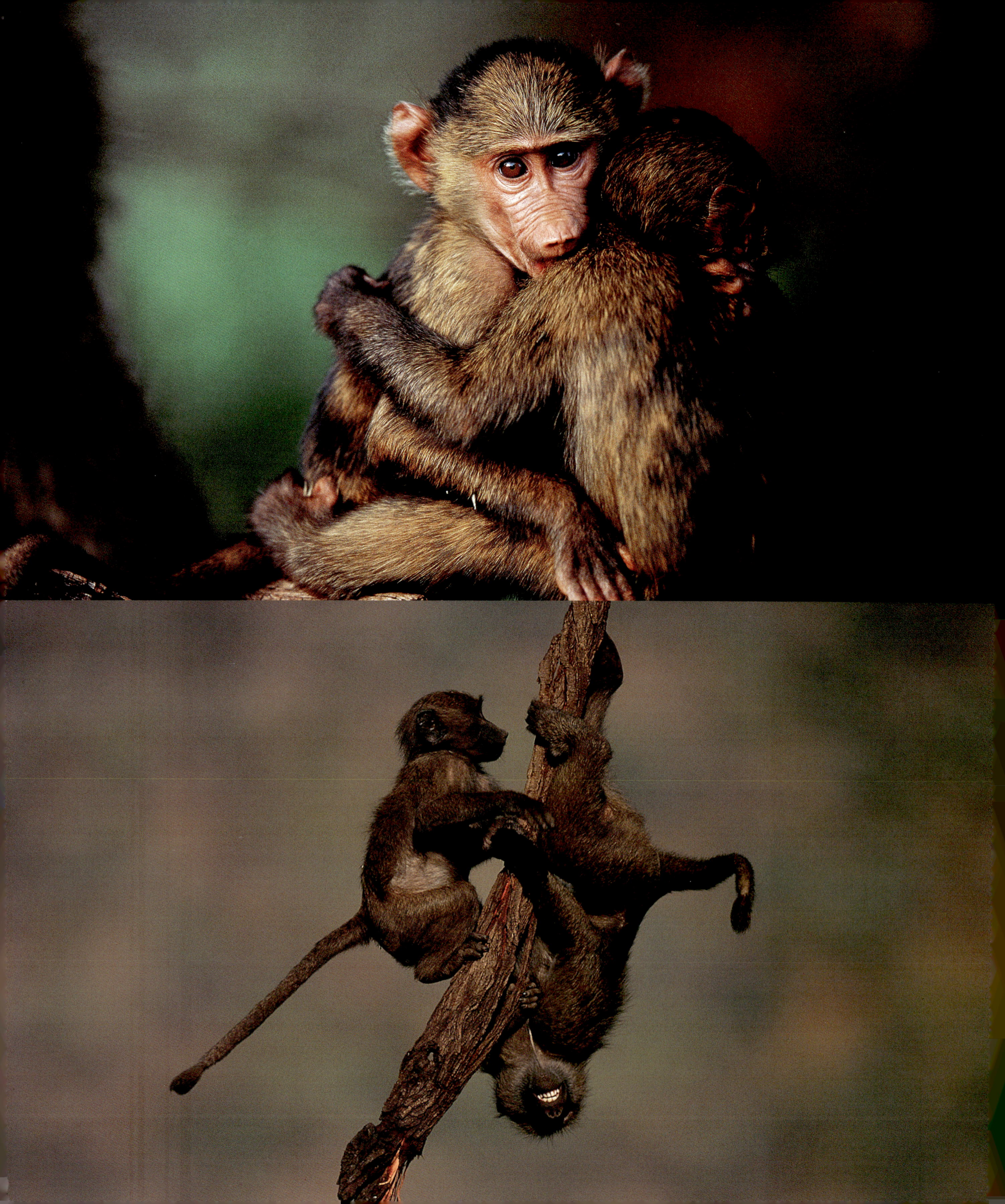

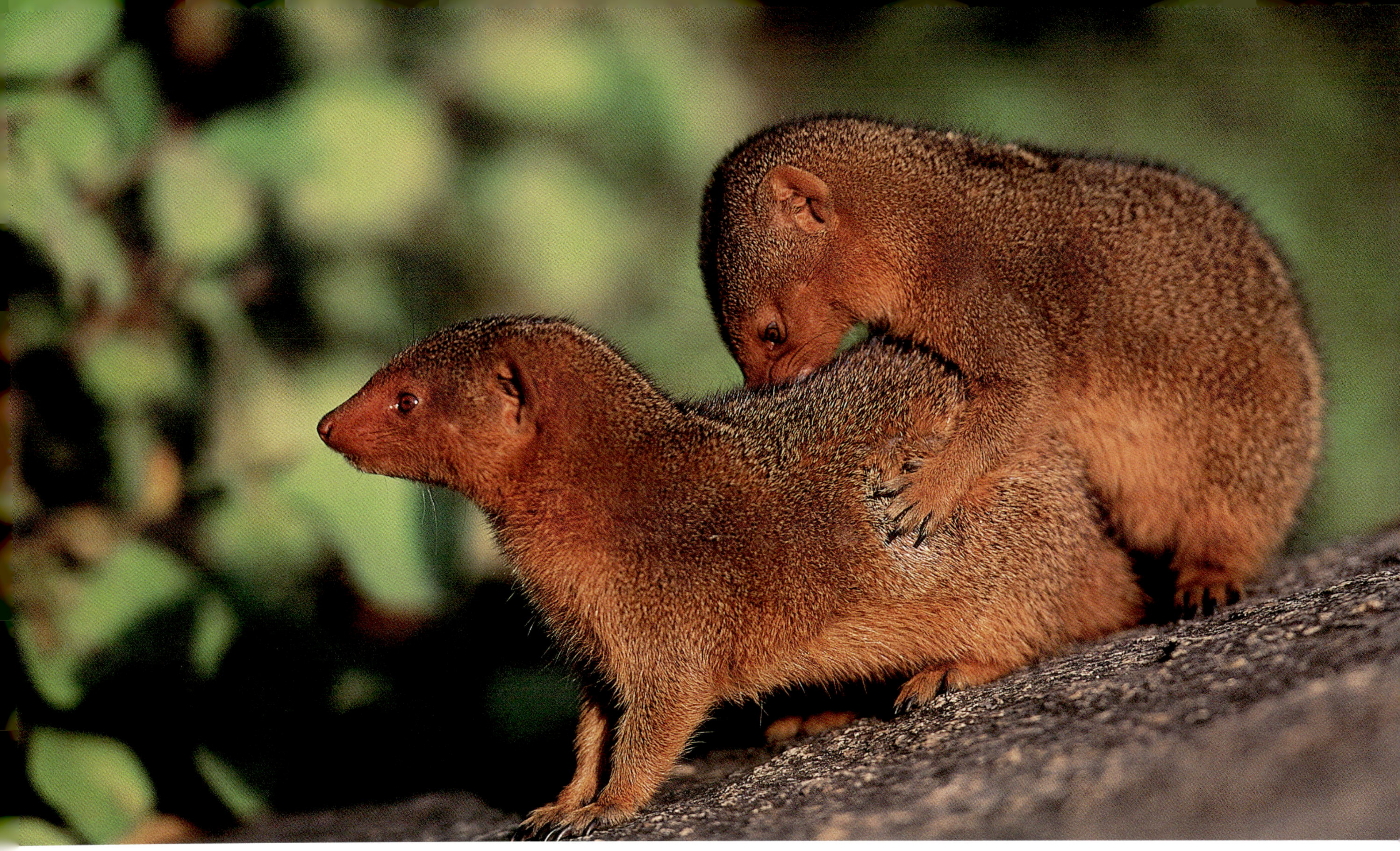

Two playful dwarf mongooses emerge from the bushes and their large social group onto the rock surface of a kopje. The young of different dwarf mongoose families within a social group will actively interact with one another.

Opposite, above
A few olive baboon mothers have gathered together to rest and groom, creating a secure environment in which youngsters can express themselves. Carried away in play, these two find themselves unexpectedly hugging each other.

Opposite, below
A hanging tree branch becomes a jungle gym for these mischievous olive baboon youngsters.

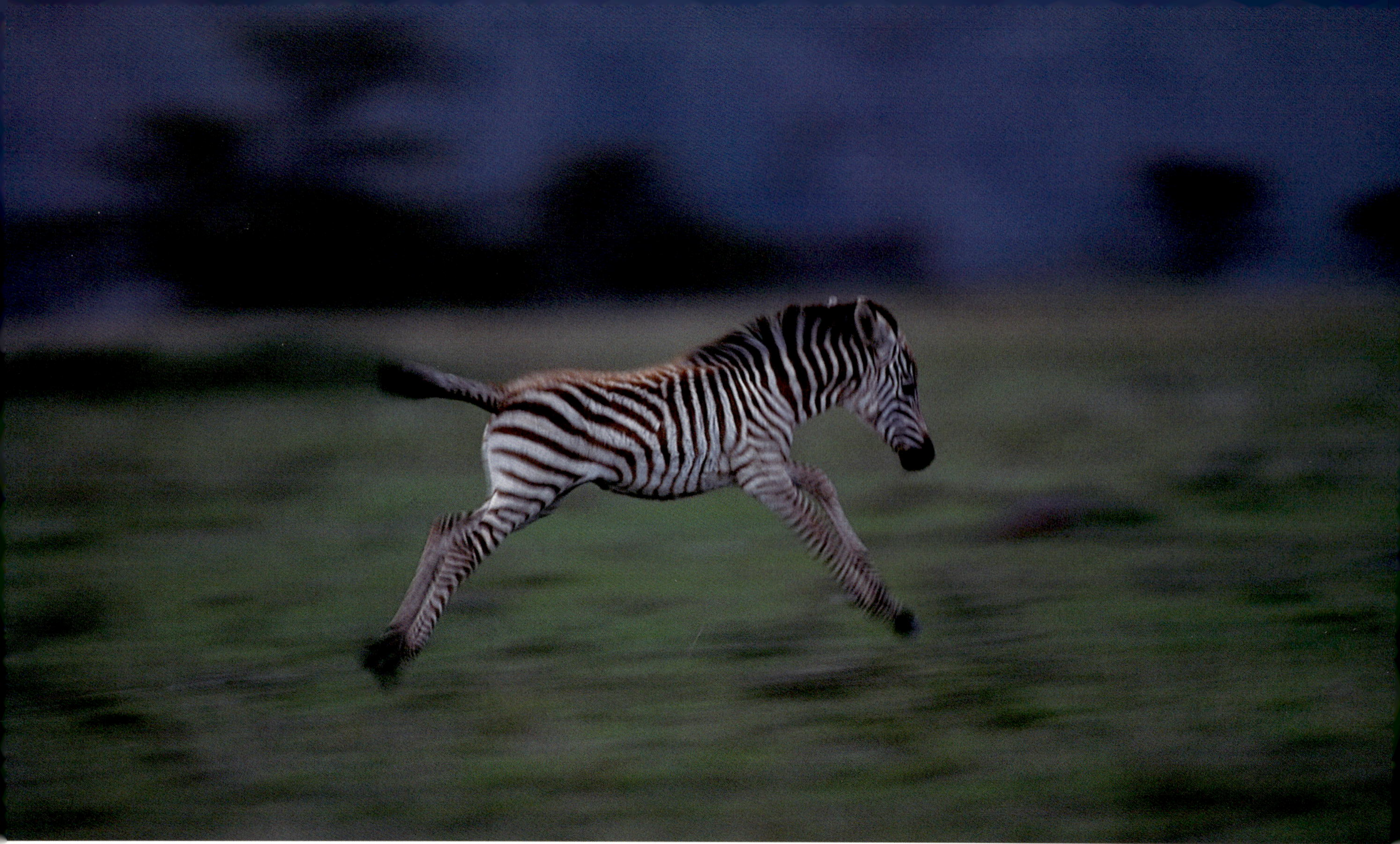

Zebra foals often perform "anti-predatory" behavior during solo play – leaping into the air, twisting their bodies, and fleeing as if trying to escape a predator. Could it be that the foal is reacting exuberantly to self-discovery as it explores a brand new world?

Opposite, above
There is frenzied activity outside a black-backed jackal den as the father plays with one of his offspring. In jackal society, the father is actively involved in raising pups.

Opposite, below
Pride lionesses often initiate play with pride cubs, such as mouthing and pulling a non-plussed cub's tail.

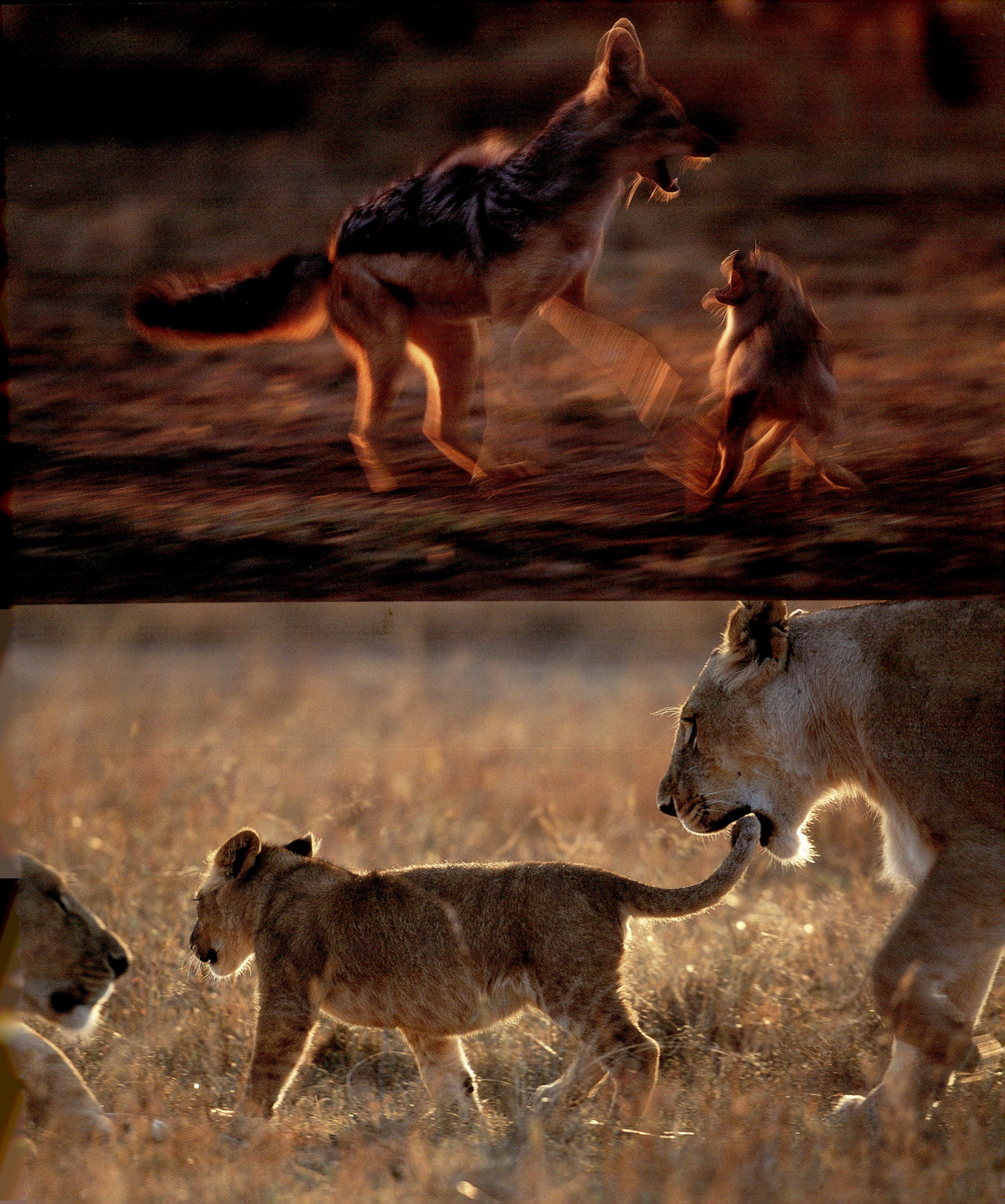

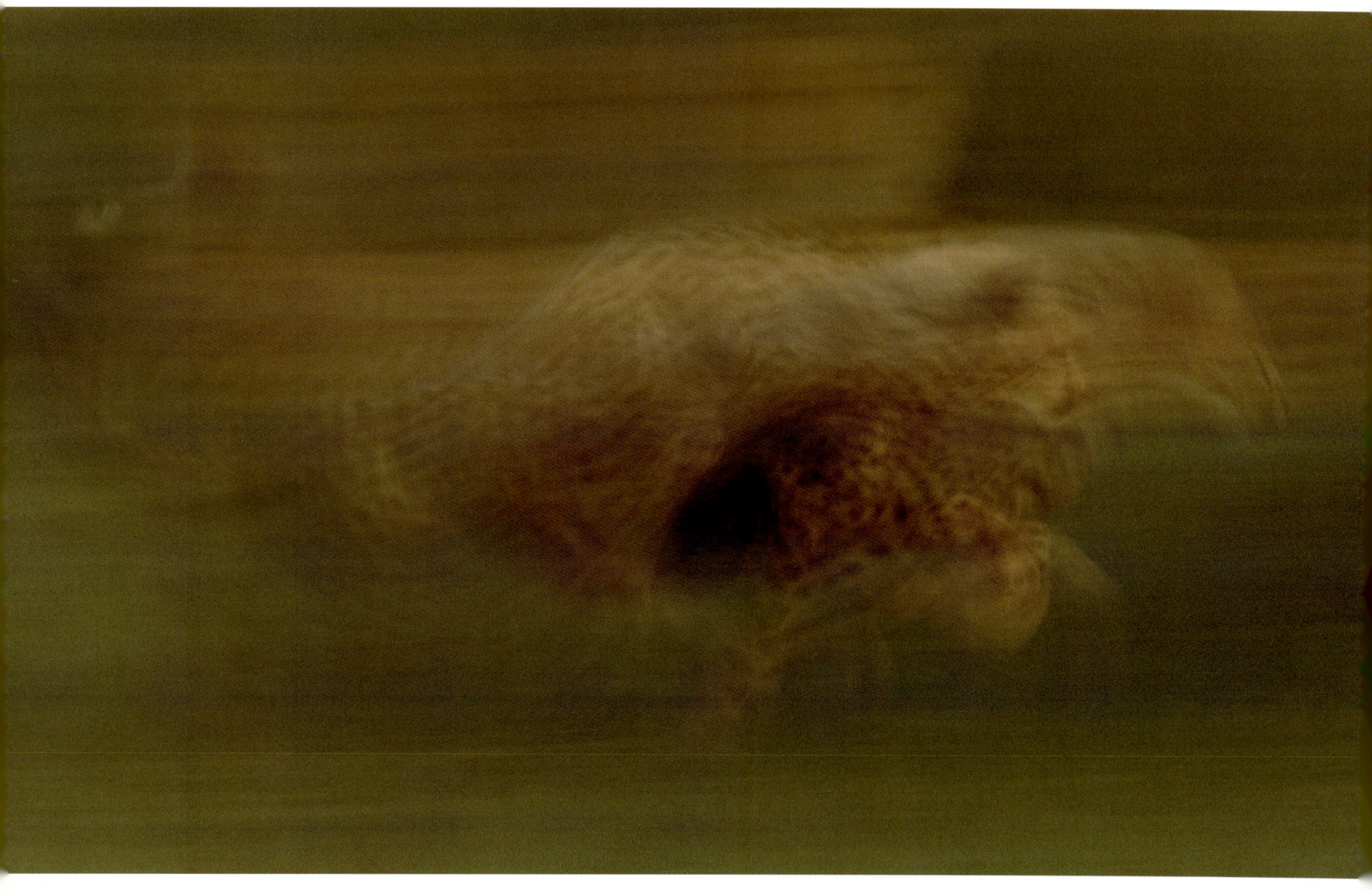

Running is extremely effective training for these budding champions of the high-speed sprint.

Opposite
After its mother stored the impala carcass up a tree, this highly charged leopard cub rehearsed the act of killing the animal.

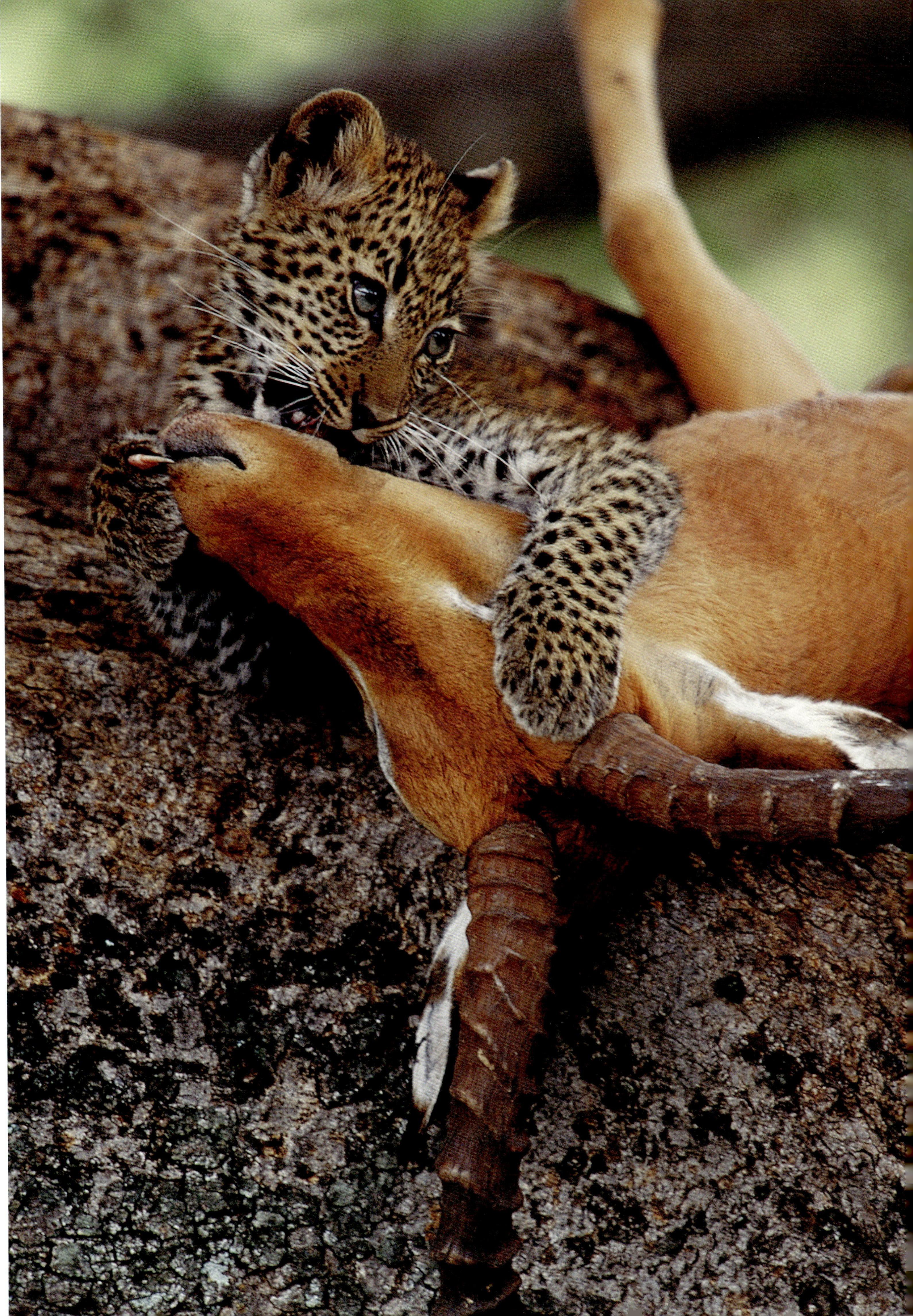

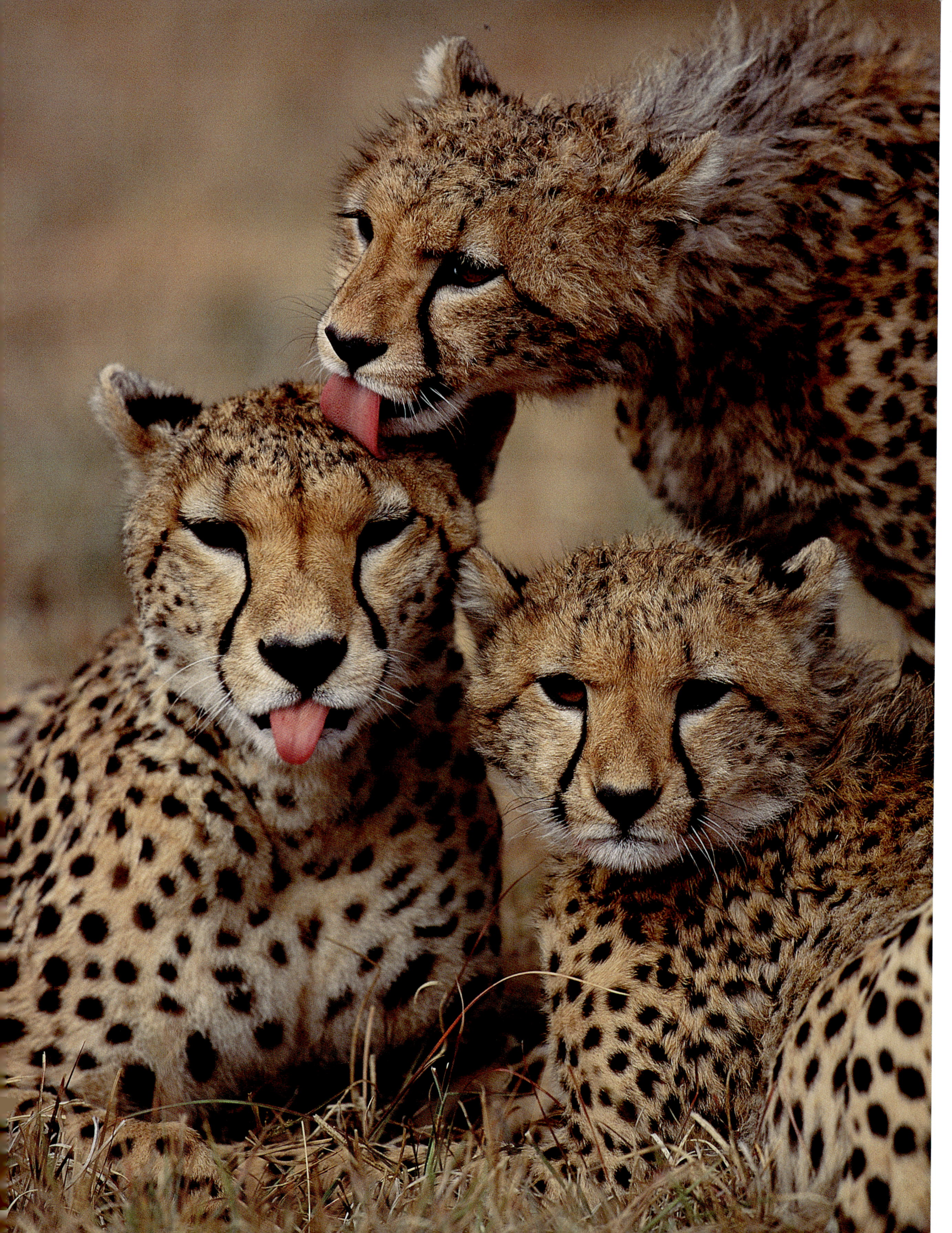

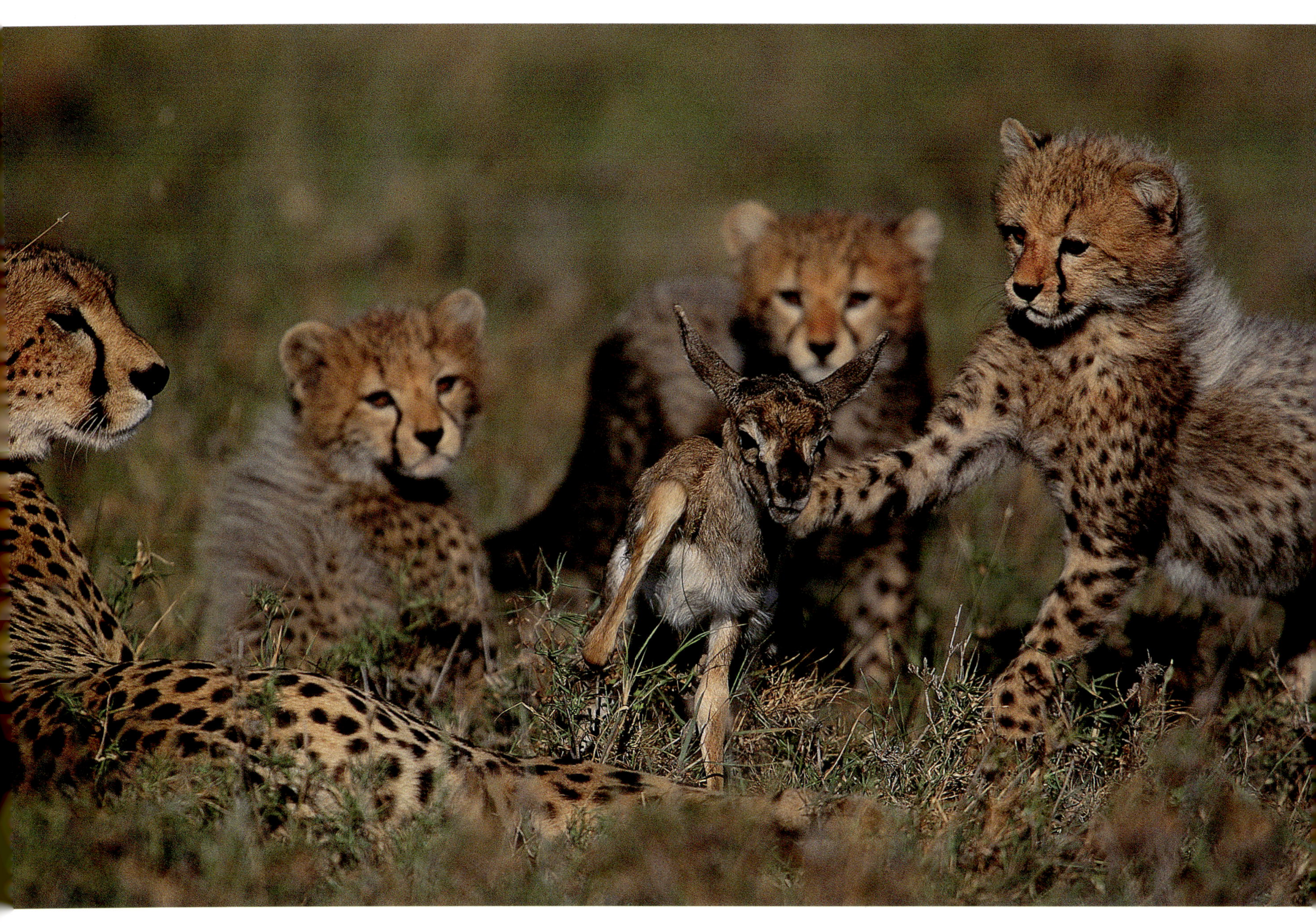

Seizing a learning opportunity for her cubs, a cheetah mother captured a gazelle fawn and released it, still alive, among her cubs. The fascinated cubs soon learned they could easily bring it down.

Opposite
Having fed on a Grant's gazelle during a passing thunderstorm, a cheetah mother and her eight-month-old cubs lick rainwater mixed with blood before the latter has had a chance to set and harden.

Pages 174–175
One evening, after having gorged themselves, a mother leopard and her adolescent cub emerged to rest, groom, and paw each other playfully in the soft evening light.

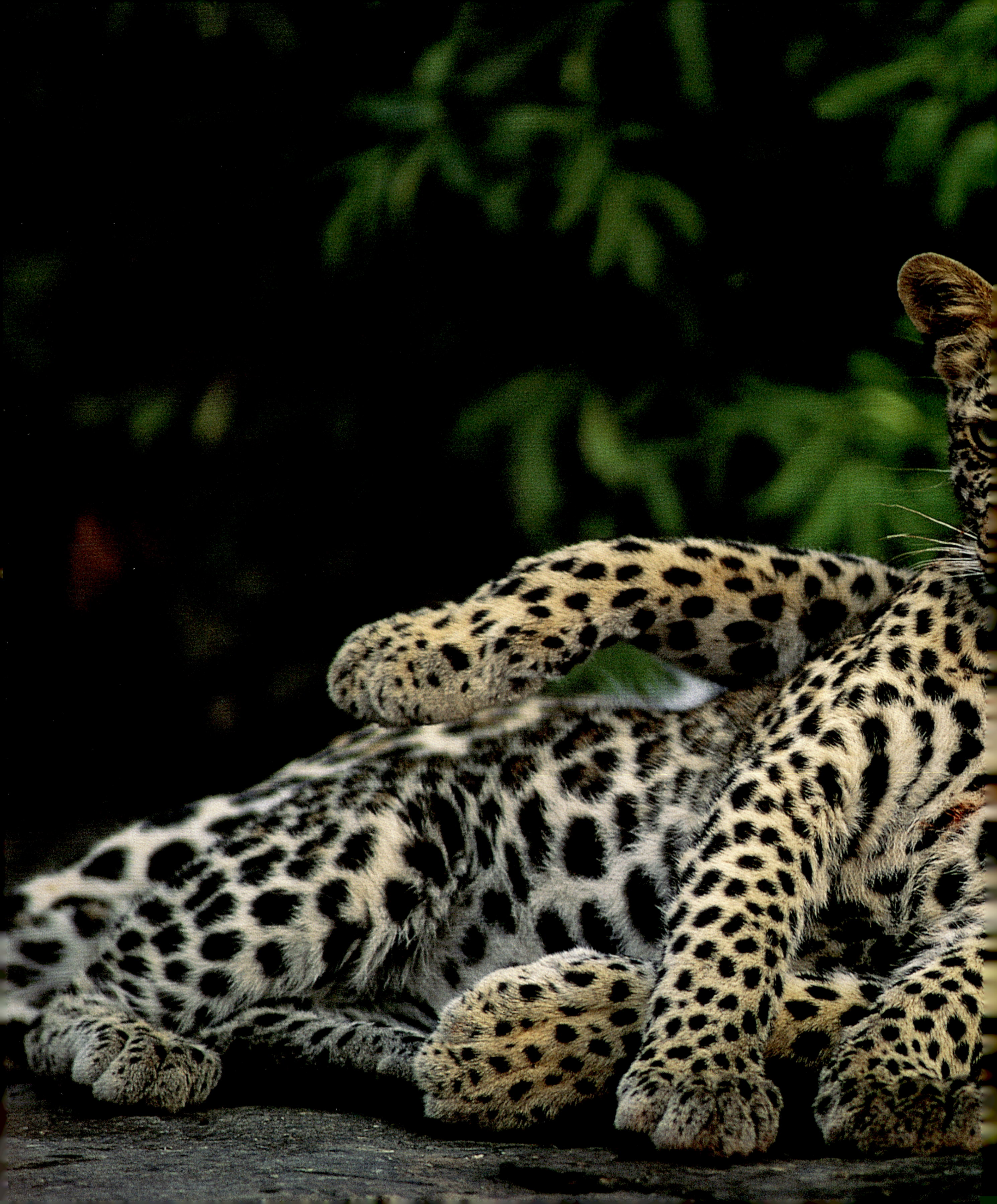

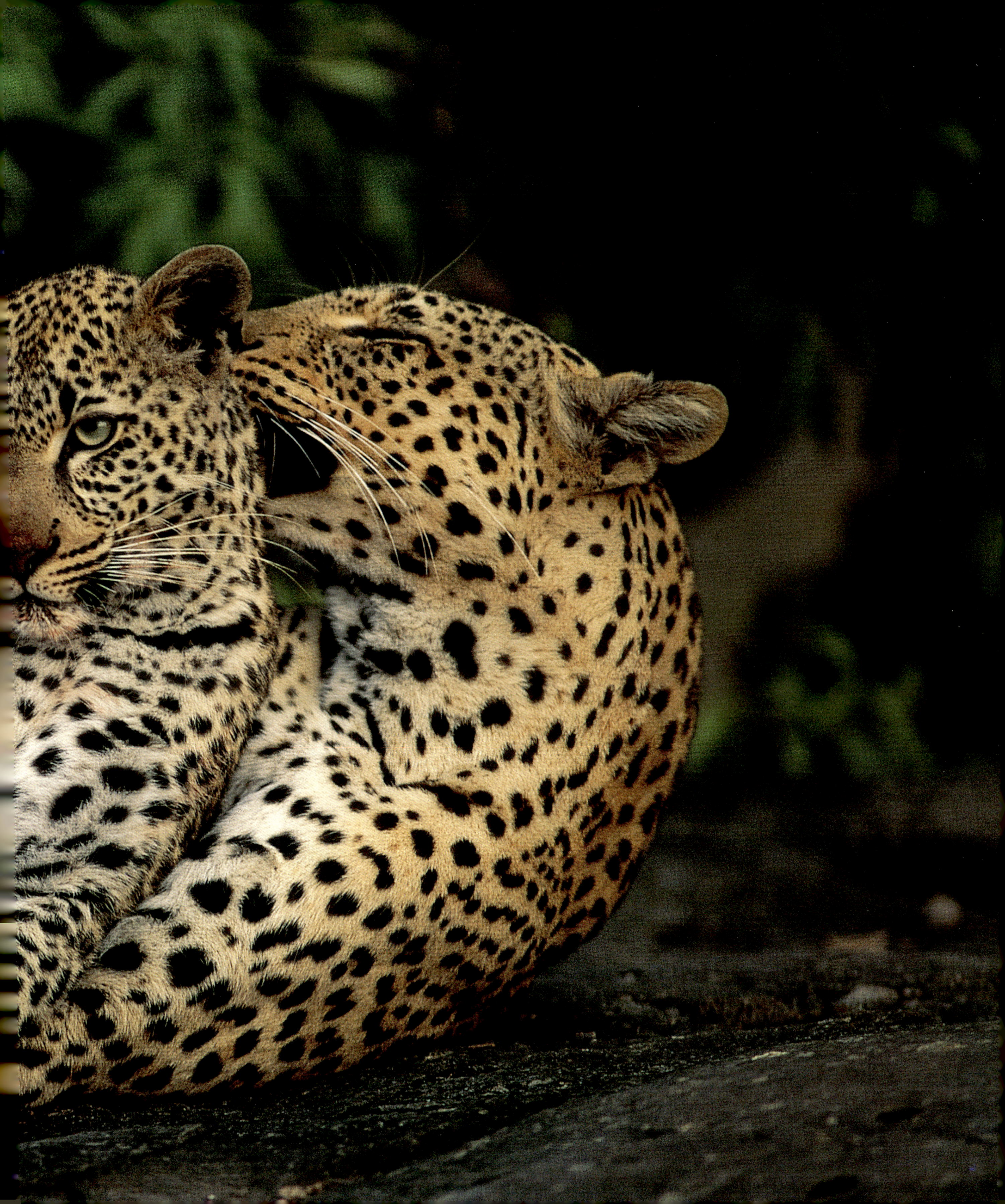

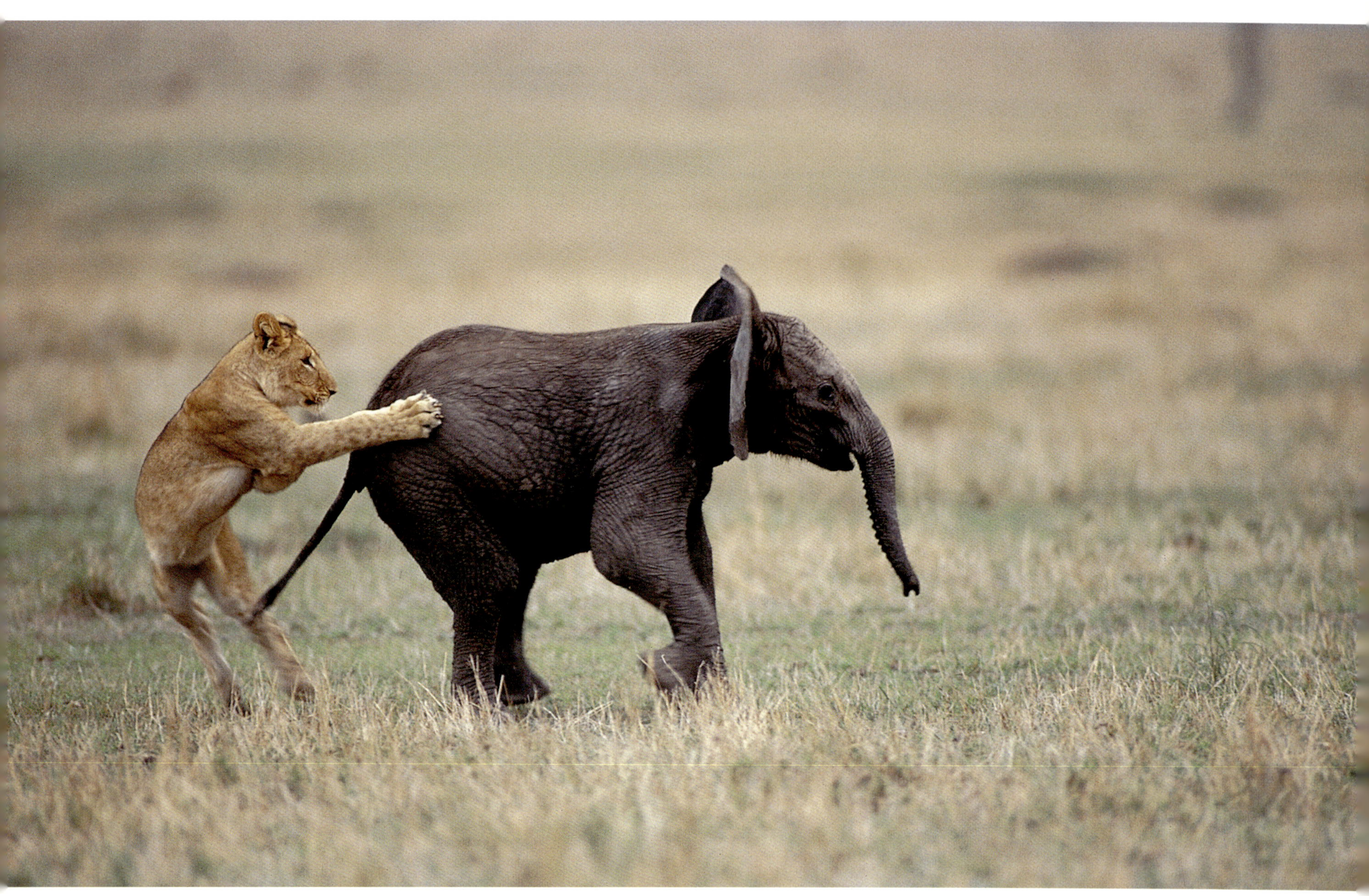

An adventurous lion cub tries to smack down a terror-stricken baby elephant. While the adults of the pride showed little interest in this vulnerable elephant wandering alone, the cubs became intrigued immediately, following it, play-stalking it. However, when the brave young elephant finally turned to face its antagonizers, flapped its ears, raised its trunk, and trumpeted, the cubs decided to leave it alone.

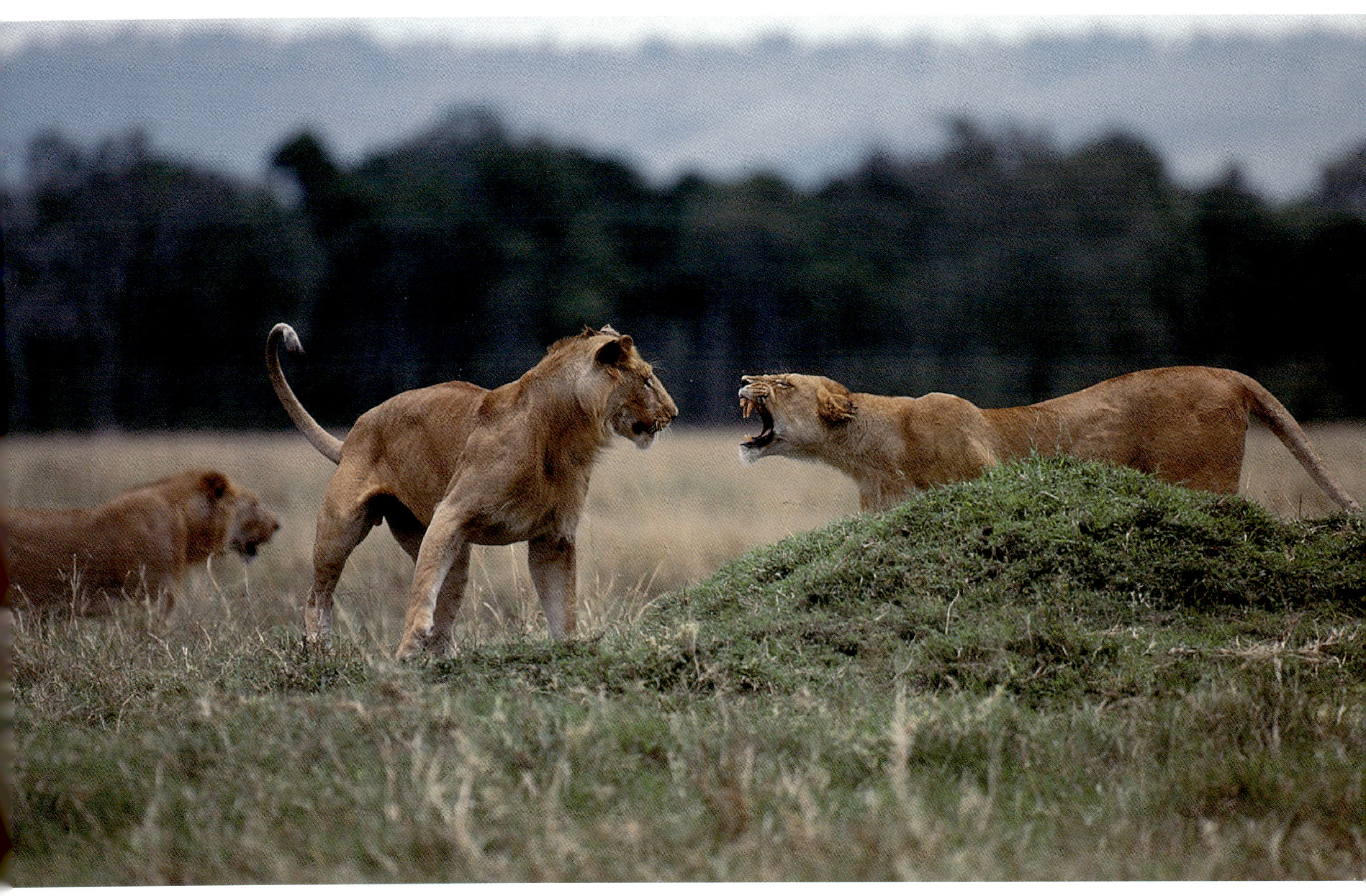

Too old to remain with their natal pride, these male lions have been ejected, but they are reluctant to leave. The maternal instinct of their mothers has been switched off, however, and this one is making it clear they are no longer welcome. The reality is that these young adults are now entirely on their own and will roam the plains as nomads until they find a pride that they can take over and which will accept them.

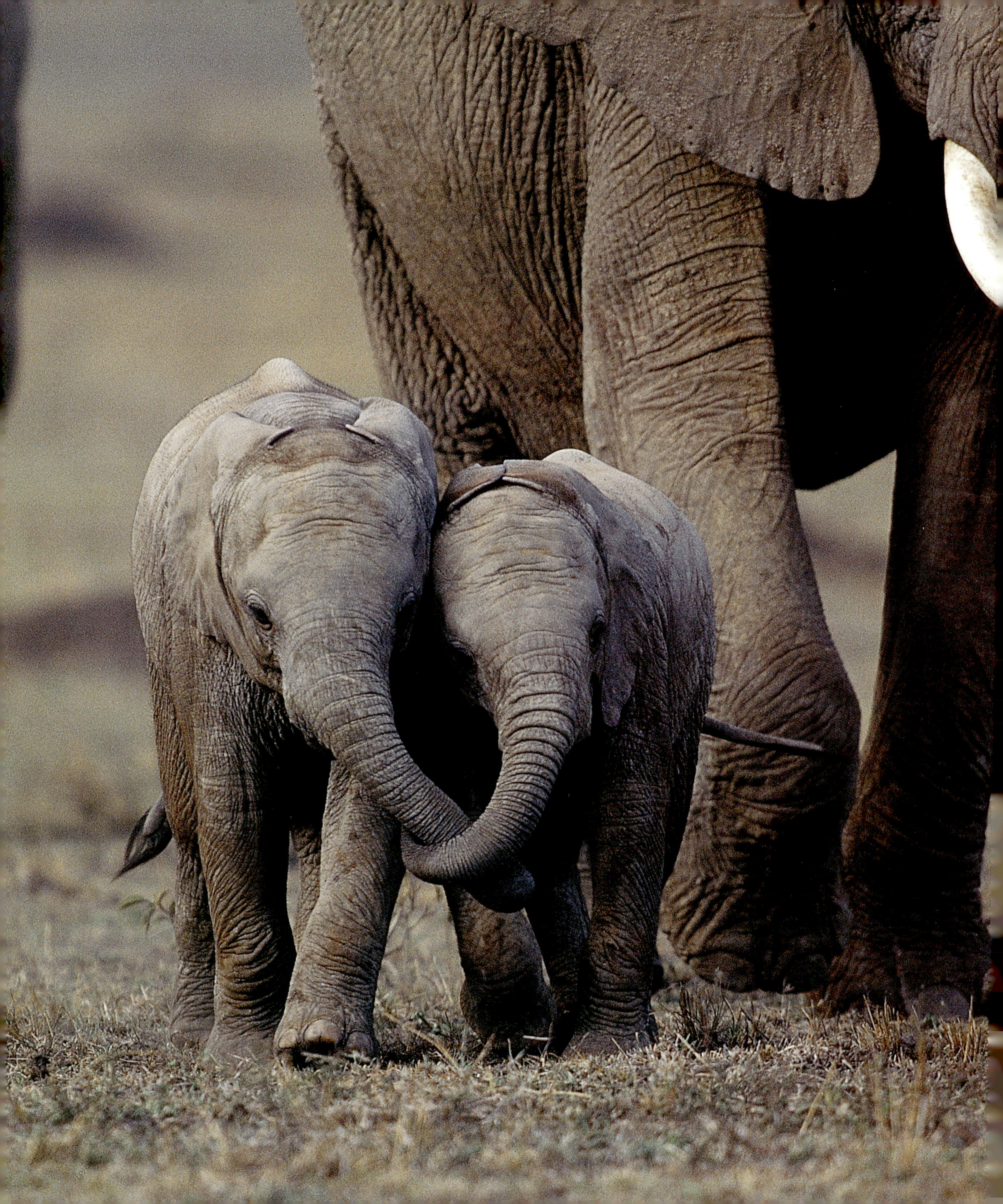

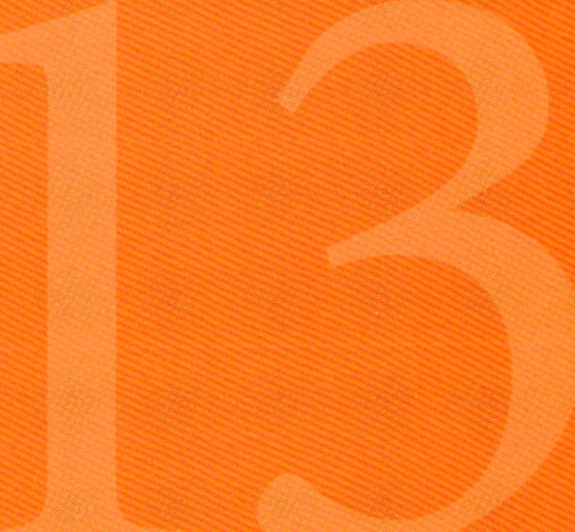

13

Getting Along

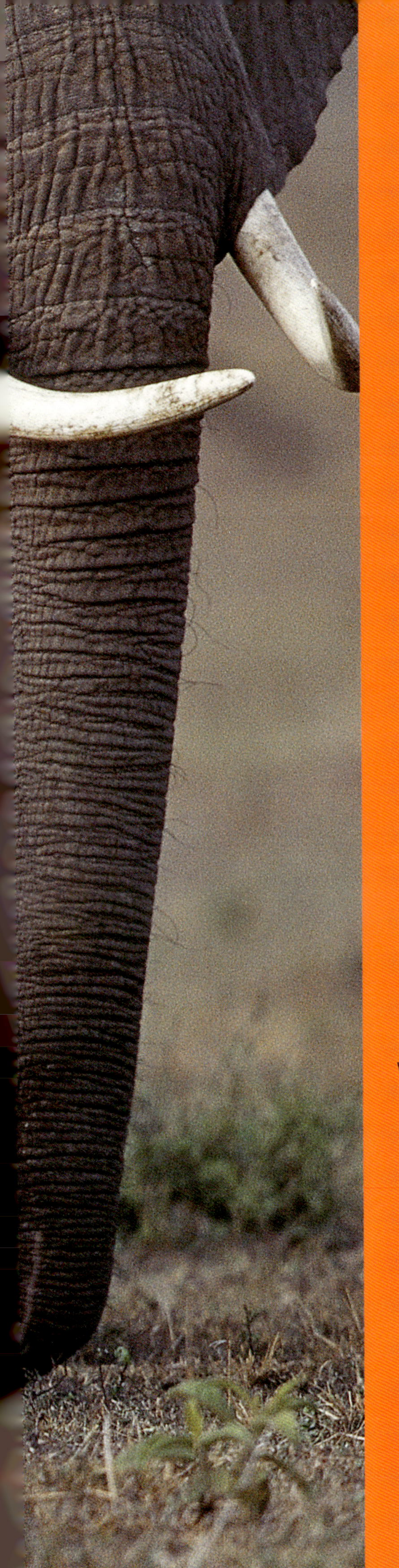

Newborn lion cubs are a rare sight on the savannah. Pregnant lionesses separate from the pride, find a secluded place, and give birth in private. For the next few weeks, the cubs are kept well hidden. This is a bonding period for mother and cubs, and while it is not too difficult for the cubs to learn to get along, each puts its own interests first. Thus you will find a male lion or leopard cub using its advantage in size and strength to hog most of the food, leaving a female cub crying in protest. A hyena pup will continually harass its weaker twin in order to corner all the mother's resources. In some instances, the weaker pup may even die of malnutrition or starvation.

It's a tricky balancing act: how to live in harmony with the others, and yet, how to promote one's own interests. It gets complicated for lion cubs that have recently been introduced into a pride already consisting of other youngsters – each has a short temper and is armed with claws and teeth. However, lion cubs have their own social instincts and are naturally drawn to one another, plus they learn more about sociality by watching how the mothers in a pride interact with the young. Lion cubs also watch mother when sizing up adults: A male lion of the pride may look forbidding, but he should not cause any harm if mother sits relaxed next to him, and there may even be a rare opportunity for play. There is actually an advantage for a brash young cub to liaison with one of the big guys in the pride: A male adult is likely to dominate at a kill and refuse to share with the lionesses, but he may allow cubs to feed alongside him.

In most social groups it is important for the young to learn the pecking order. Lion prides do not feature a hierarchy. A spotted hyena clan, on the other hand, is dominated by females, the most powerful being the alpha female. Next in rank are her pups, and below them are her sisters and their offspring. In this society, body language is used to convey submission, respect, aggression, and all the subtle messages in between. These social skills underpin this society in which the power structure depends on a network of complicated alliances. To recognize and reiterate each others' social status at an encounter, hyenas sniff each others' mouths, necks, and heads, then stand sideways-on and sniff the others' genitals. A subordinate hyena may feel compelled to make a submissive gesture by rolling on its back. Hyenas also signal their moods and intentions with body language: When undisturbed the tail is carried straight down; when aggressive it is vertically upright; and when frightened it is between the legs. When the ears are pointed forward, it is a sign of potential aggression; if backward then a retreat is intended.

One of the primary differences between humans and animals is that we humans make extensive use of verbal language, animals do not. Instead, they engage in the nonverbal language of rituals and body language. Rituals include males in combat such as giraffes necking; elephants trunk wrestling; warthogs head-butting; the greeting ceremonies of lions, elephants, and hyenas; or grooming in primates to signal friendship. Messages sent through body language include a gazelle stotting in full view of a cheetah; a

Pages 178–179
The youngsters in elephant groups form close relationships, spending hours together and displaying strong affections for one another.

wildebeest bull step dancing; a leopard walking along with tail raised after being spotted by prey animals; a subordinate baboon thrusting its rear in the face of a dominant baboon; a lion cub crawling on belly as it approaches a male lion; a lioness baring her teeth with ears flattened when in no mood to share food; an aggressive baboon flashing the white of its eyelids. The idea behind such nonverbal cues is to send clear, obvious signals of mood, intention, and fitness, which minimizes the expenditure of energy, reduces levels of aggression, and maintains a certain level of peace and harmony. For example, in ritualized combat in which a winner is established with no bloodshed, the message is "I am stronger, accept that, and this fight will not go beyond this rehearsal."

Nonverbal language comes into its own when the integrity of a social group is being maintained. The language is species-specific and the messages are unambiguous and involve using a set of visual, auditory, and olfactory signals. Physical contact and postures also play a role in social groups. Members of a lion pride often separate temporarily and then meet up again. When a lion encounters another, from a distance, each one watches the other attentively – friend or foe? Apparently lions consider body postures and mannerisms important in the confirmation of the identity of a friend. Even when a friend has been identified, lions will engage in a ritual of body brushing, nuzzling, licking, and sniffing to assure the other of friendly intentions.

Why do animals use nonverbal cues to communicate? Perhaps because the language of postures, gestures, touch, and rituals is simpler, more precise, and more reliable than verbal language. Without using an excessive amount of energy, wild animals are able to exchange information quickly and accurately and get along without acrimony, misunderstanding, or hassle.

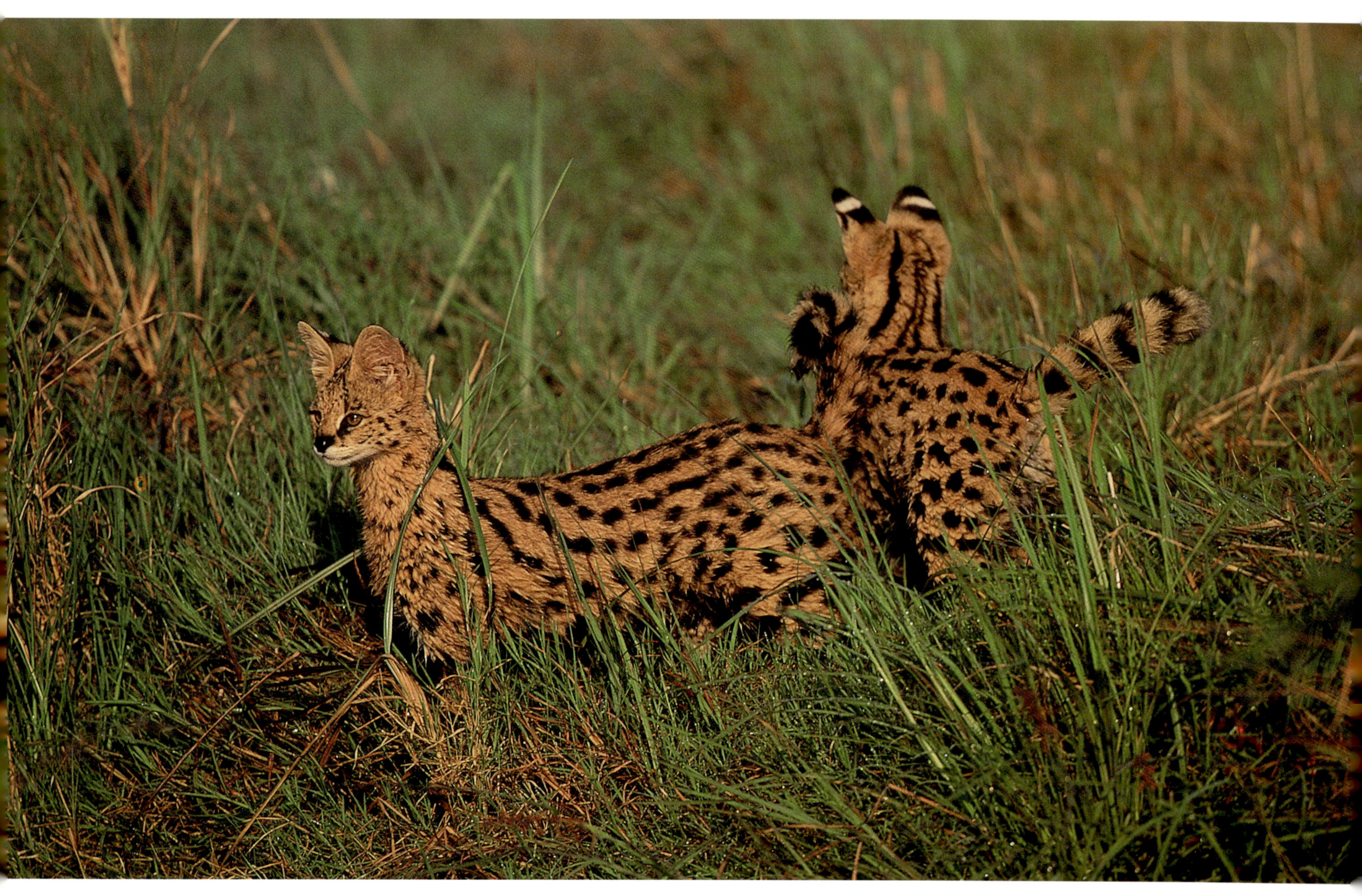

Two serval kittens left behind by their mother watch and wait for her return. To pass the time, they will play, sleep, and explore every nook and cranny of their immediate surroundings.

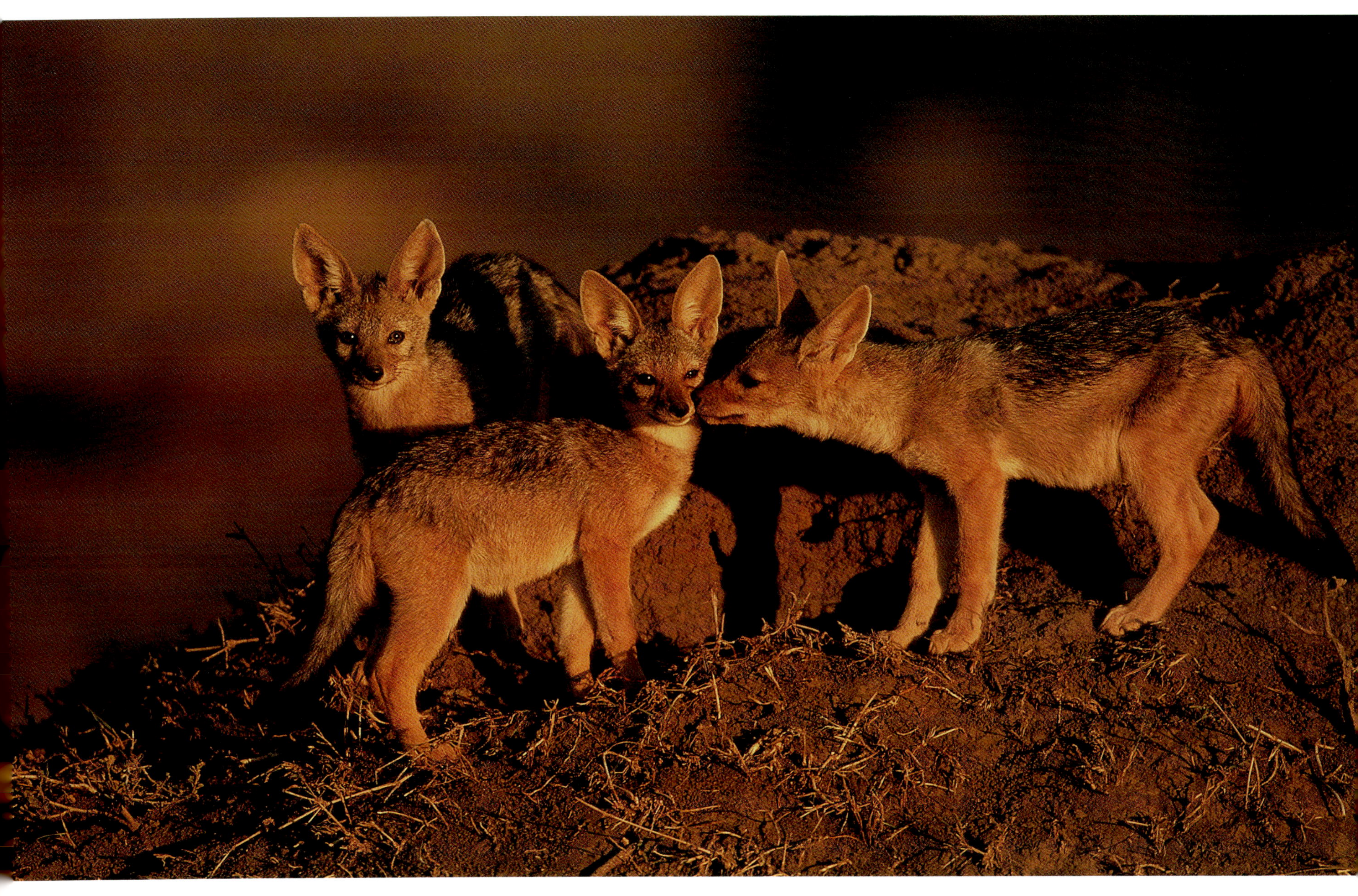

The early morning light reveals jackal pups playing outside their den.

Pages 184–185
As the cold dark gives way to the warmth of a new day on the savannah, three 10- to 12-week-old cheetah cubs snuggle up on their mother's belly, waiting for her to wake up.

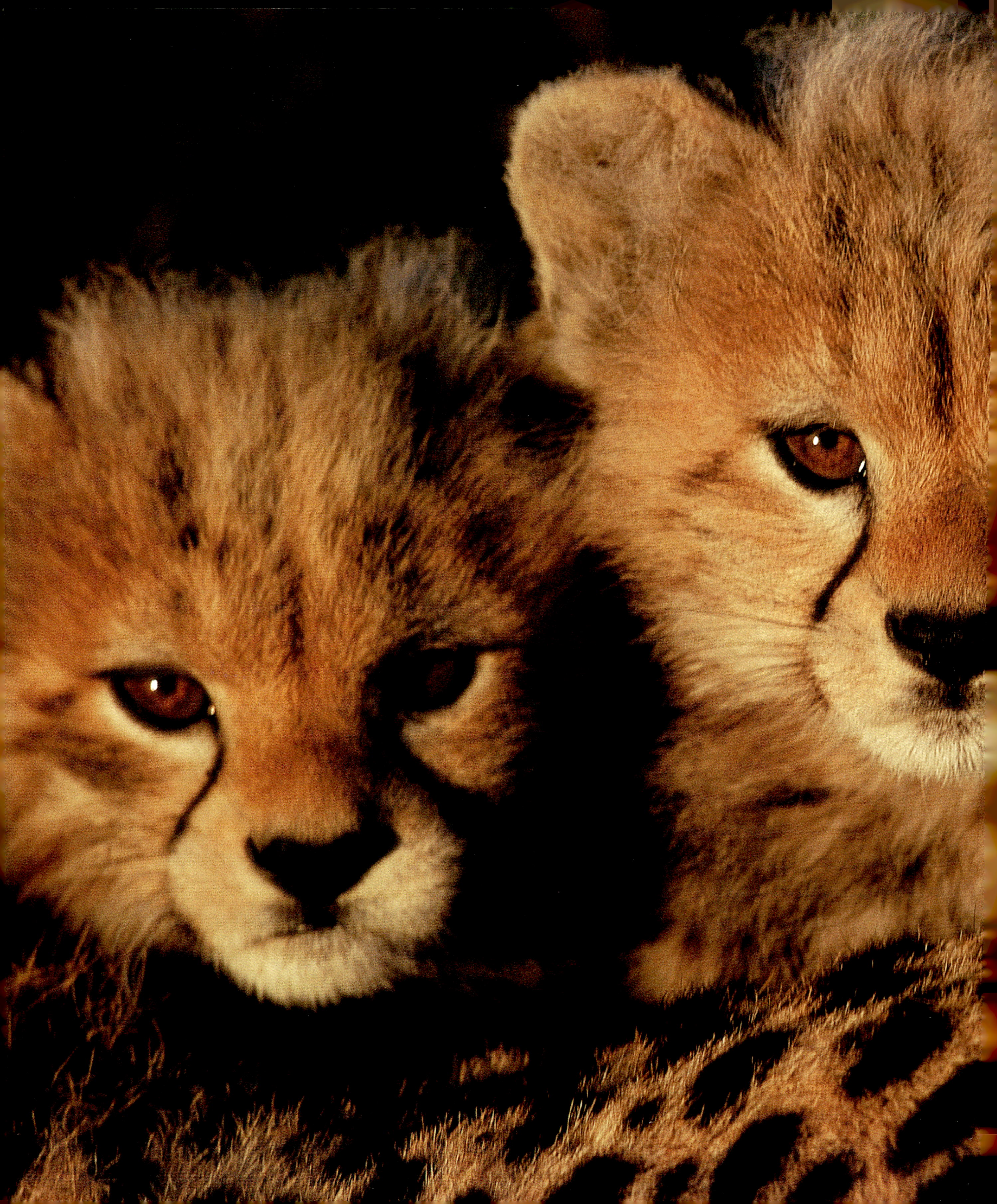

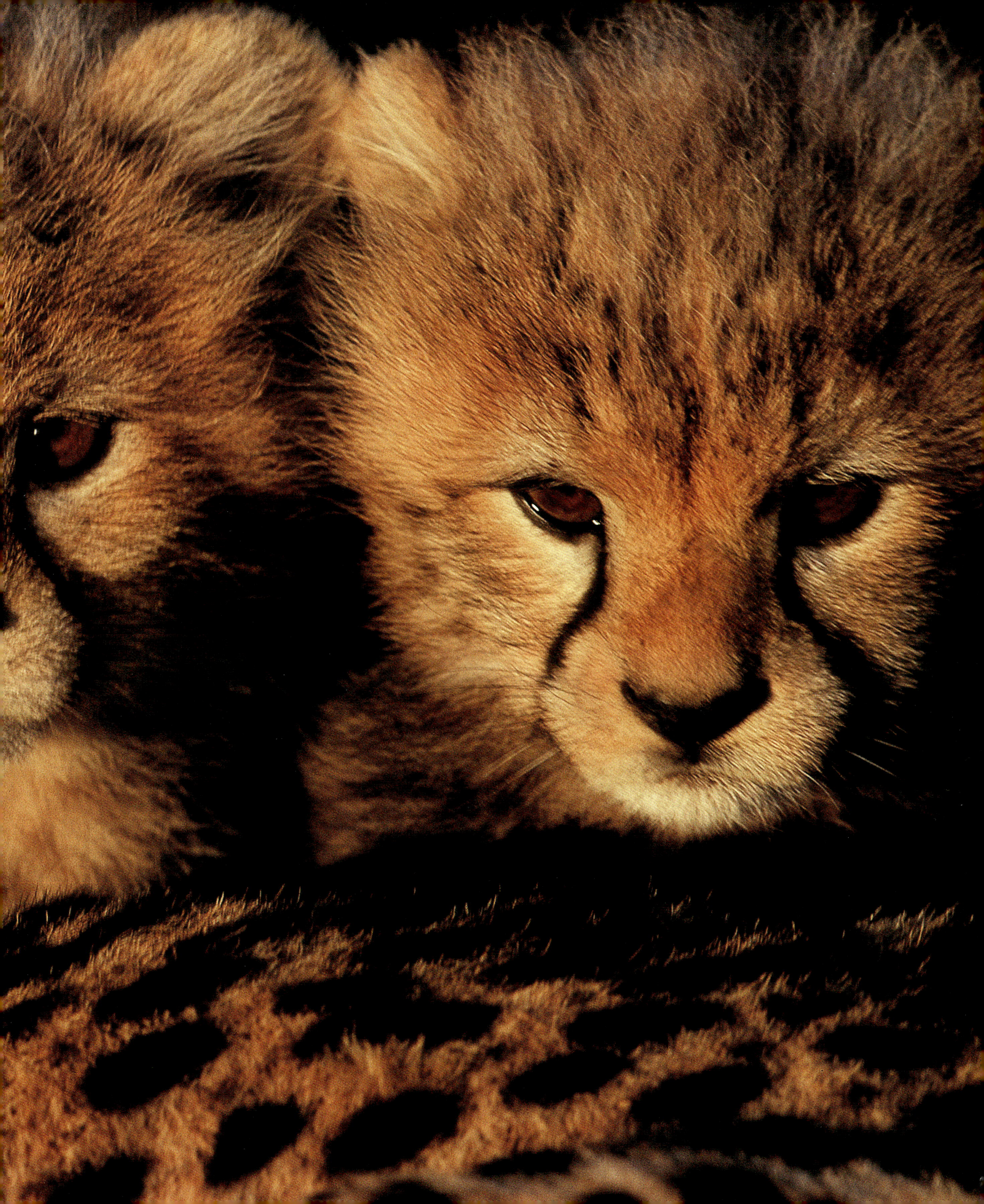

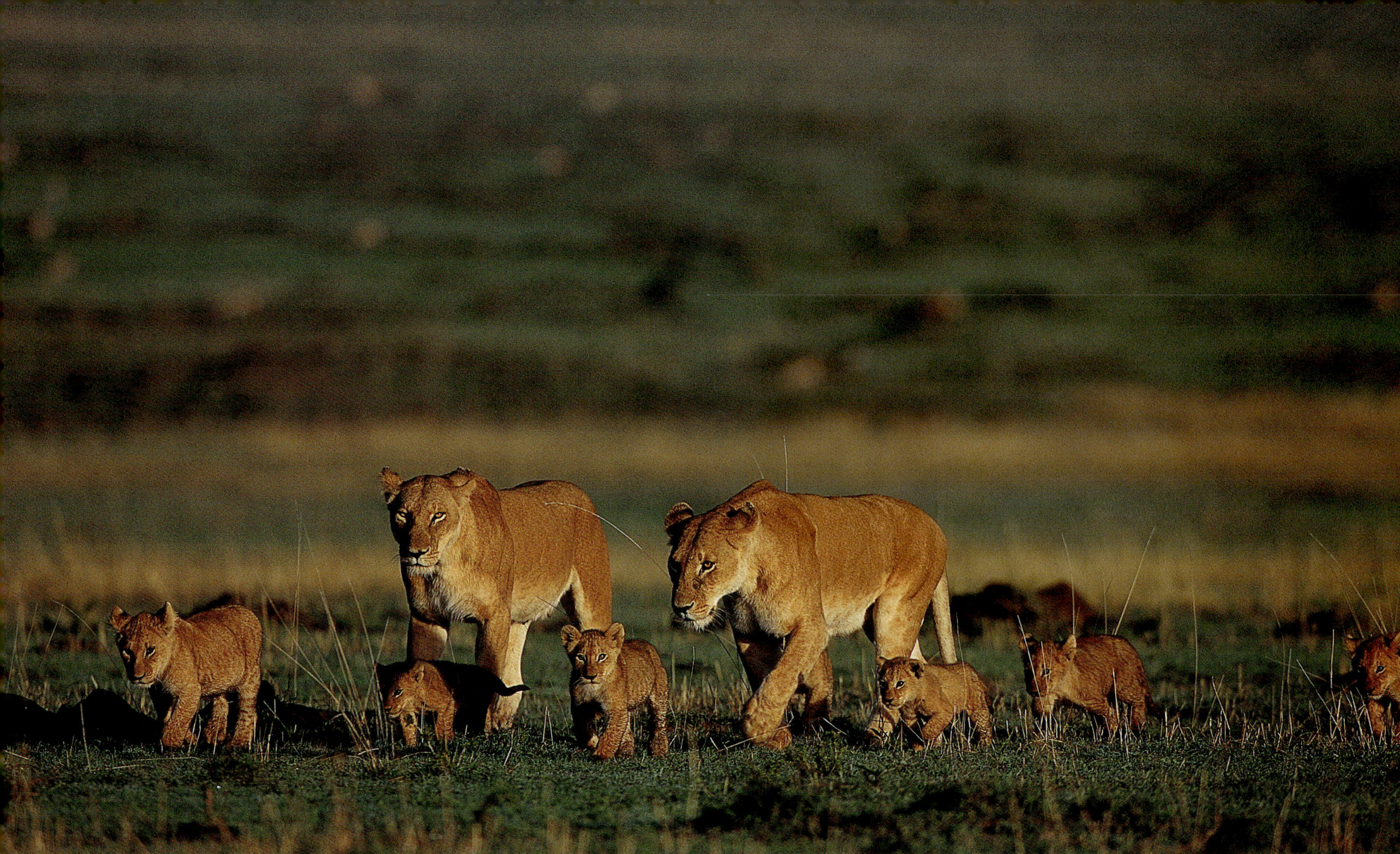

Pride lionesses escort their cubs to shelter as the morning temperature begins to rise. Lion cubs are often raised in crèches, which provide them with an opportunity to learn socialization.

Opposite, above
A pride male seems transfixed by a cub that a lioness presented to him during his siesta.

Opposite, below
Unsure of the mood of this resting male, the cub's body language is all submissive in a bid to ensure that the male will tolerate it and perhaps even reciprocate its overtures.

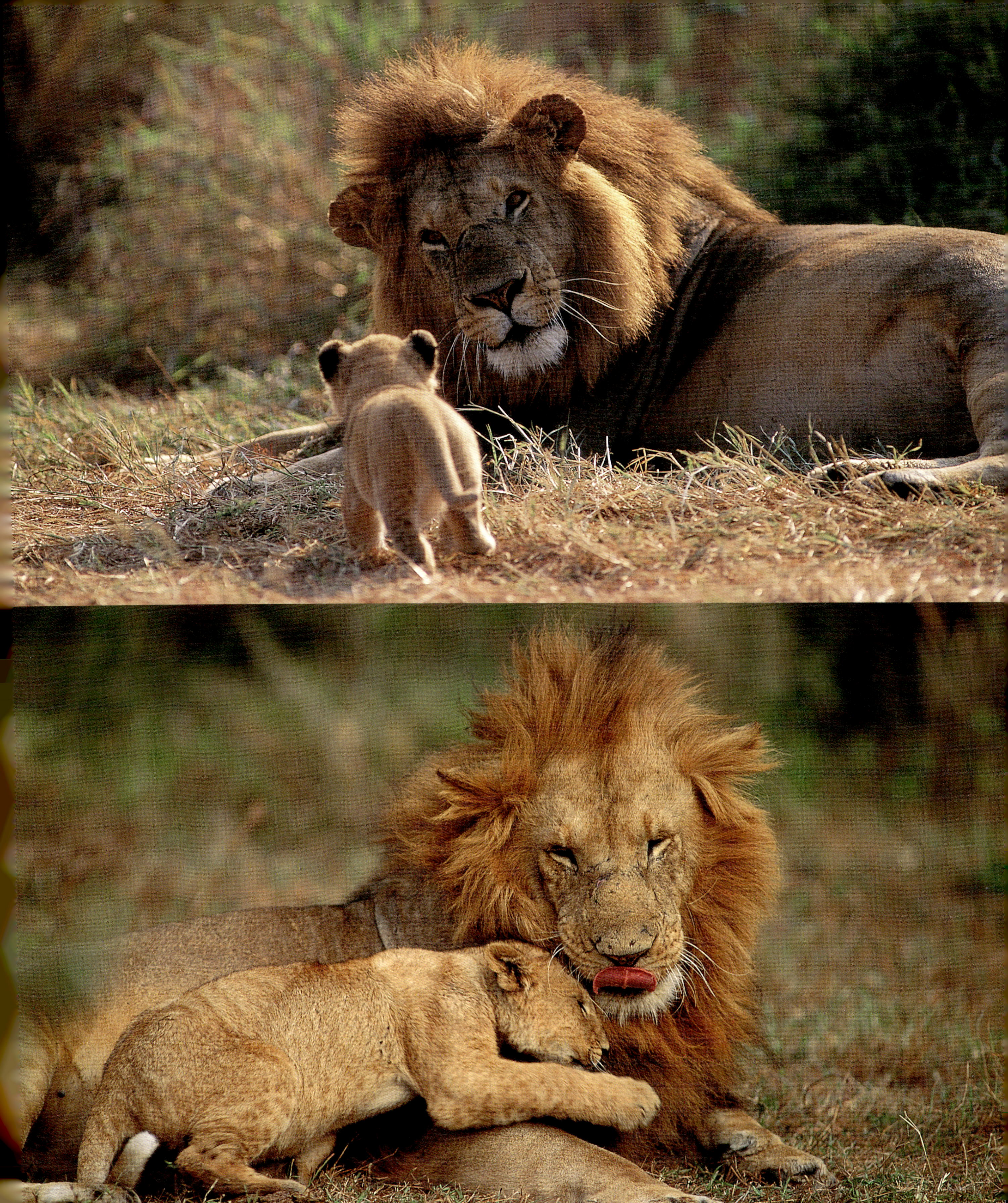

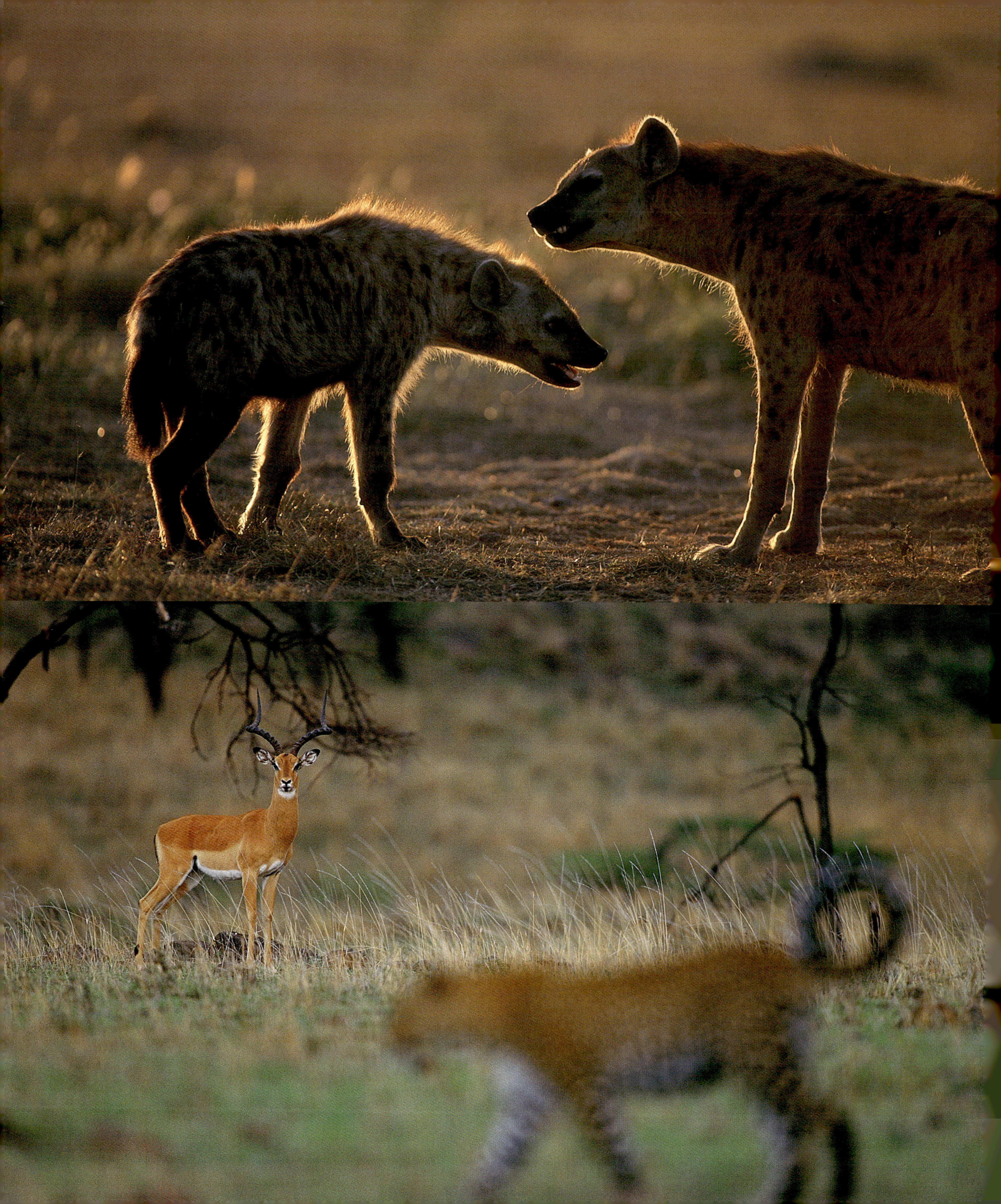

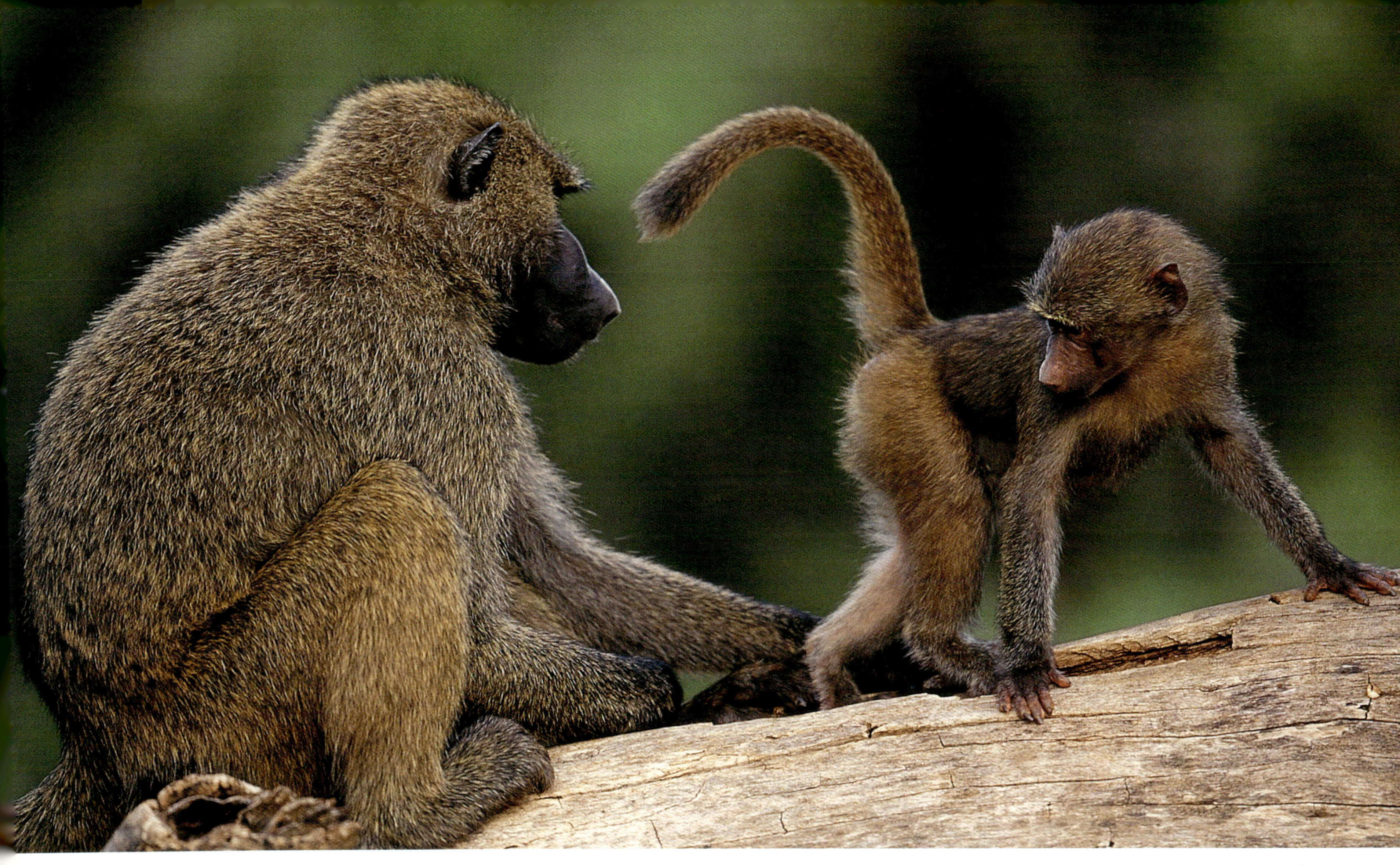

Although the adult olive baboon appears disinterested, the youngster is presenting its rear in a submissive gesture that is intended to preempt a reprimand.

Opposite, above
Two hyenas engage in an elaborate greeting ceremony. This ritual reconfirms their relative positions in the clan hierarchy, thus maintaining peace.

Opposite, below
A male impala has spotted a stalking leopard, at which point the leopard gives up the hunt and saunters away with her tail raised in the air, a signal to all that she has lost interest in this herd of watchful prey. The element of surprise is so vital to the success of a hunt that once they've been spotted, predators often abandon the attempt. Prey animals sometimes become enboldened and will even advance toward the predator and follow it to keep it in sight until satisfied that the danger has past.

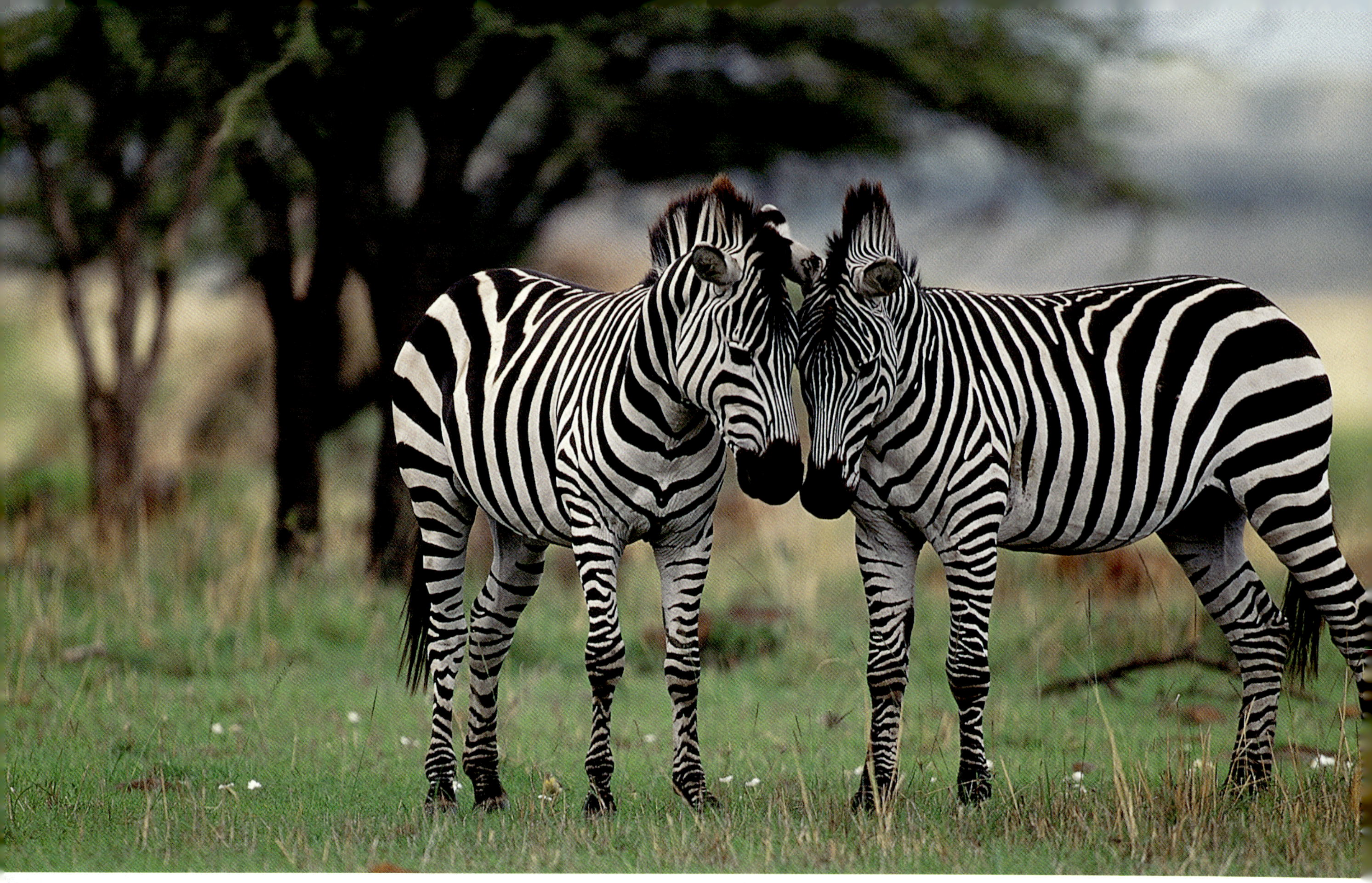

Two male zebras meet up and check each other out by nuzzling, smelling, and rubbing each other.

Opposite
A flamingo, its back feathers erect as porcupine quills, approaches a larger one to challenge its feeding spot. They go head-to-head, necks writhing in graceful arcs, but the larger bird claims victory by decisively elevating its head above the challenger. The smaller one concedes and returns to mining its own claim in the mud. Greater flamingoes feed on cyanobacteria, their primary source of food, by straining the silt through beaks held upside down in the water.

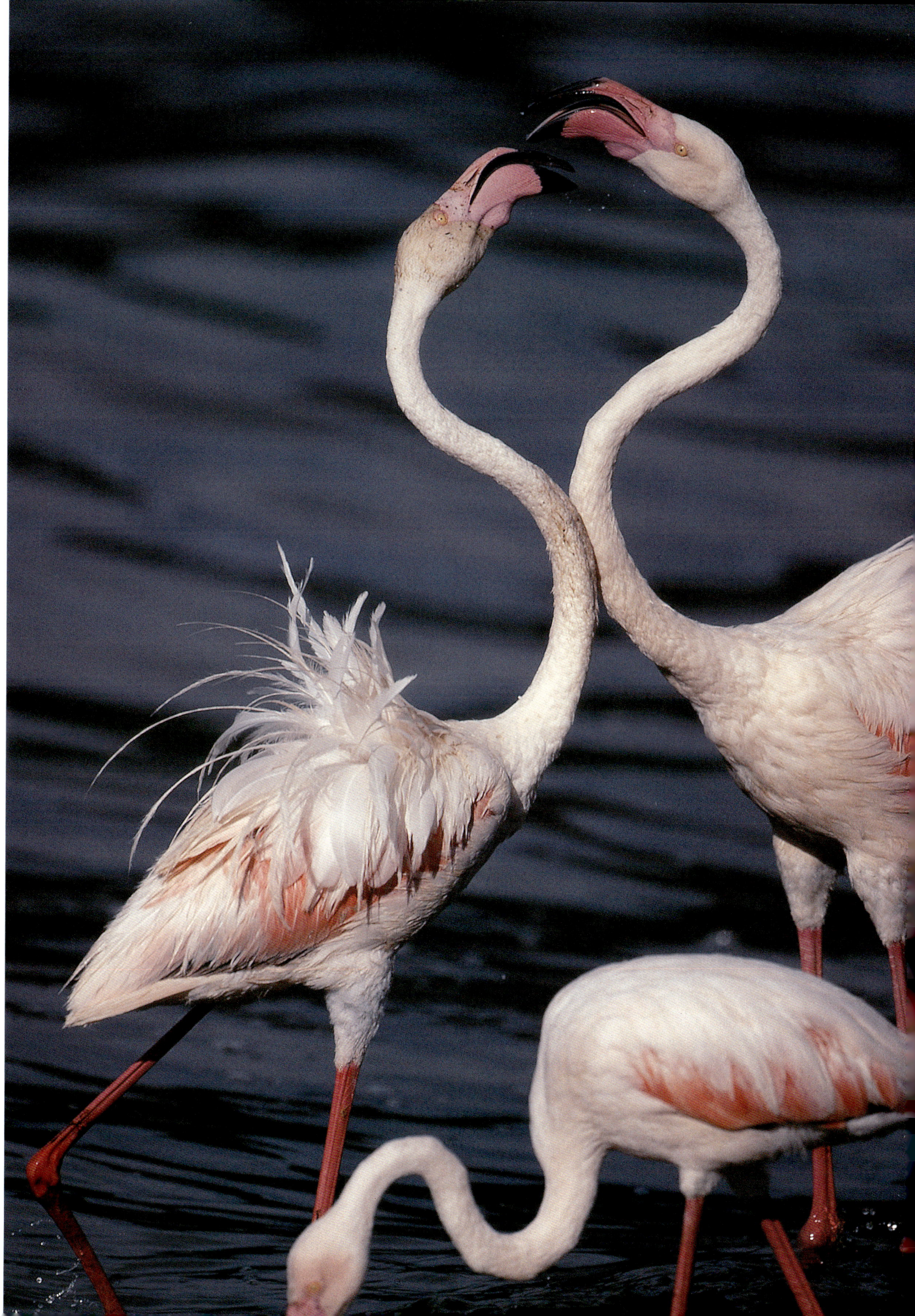

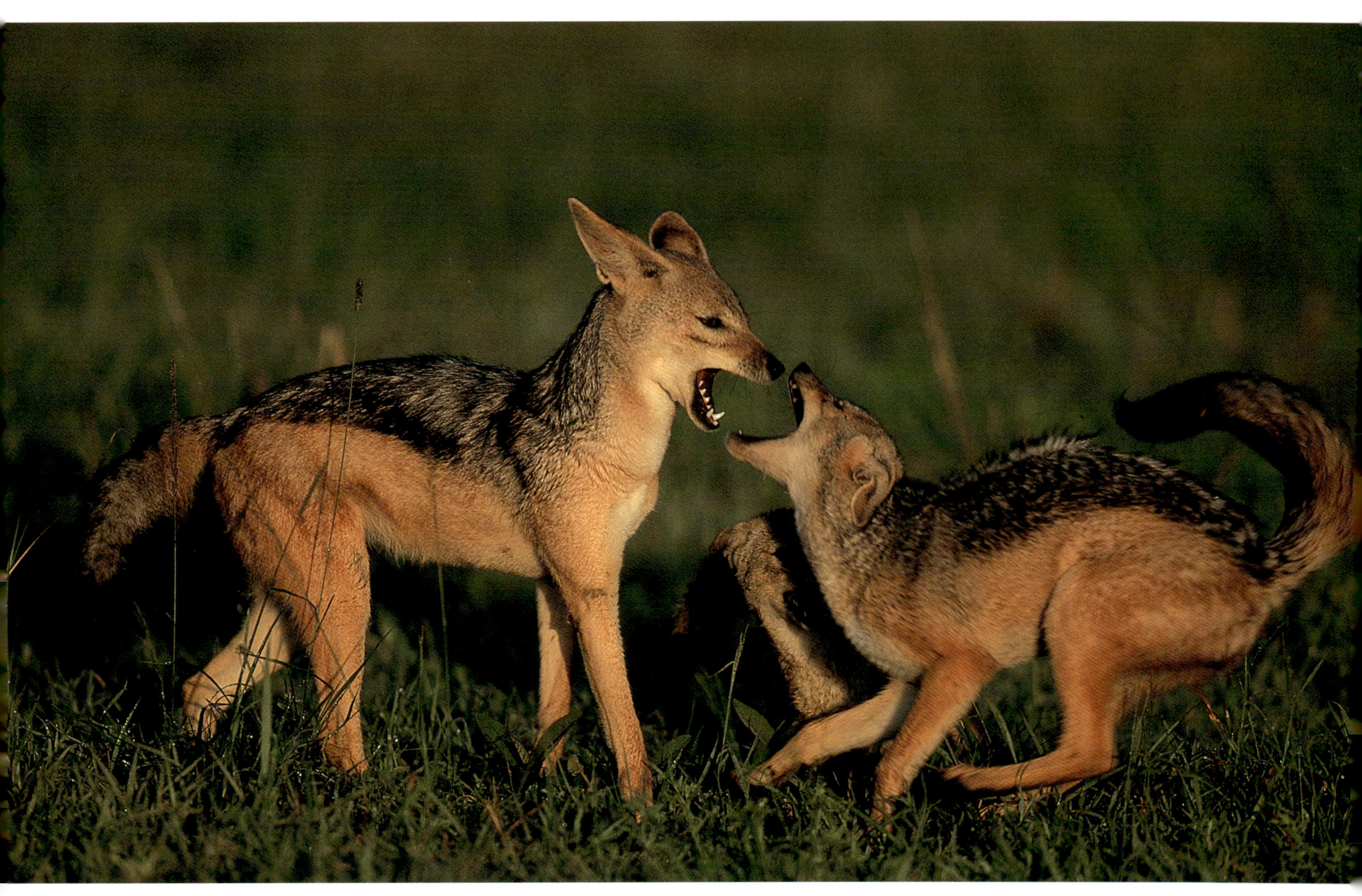

Adolescent black-backed jackals use body language to restore order after a particularly boisterous round of play gets out of hand.

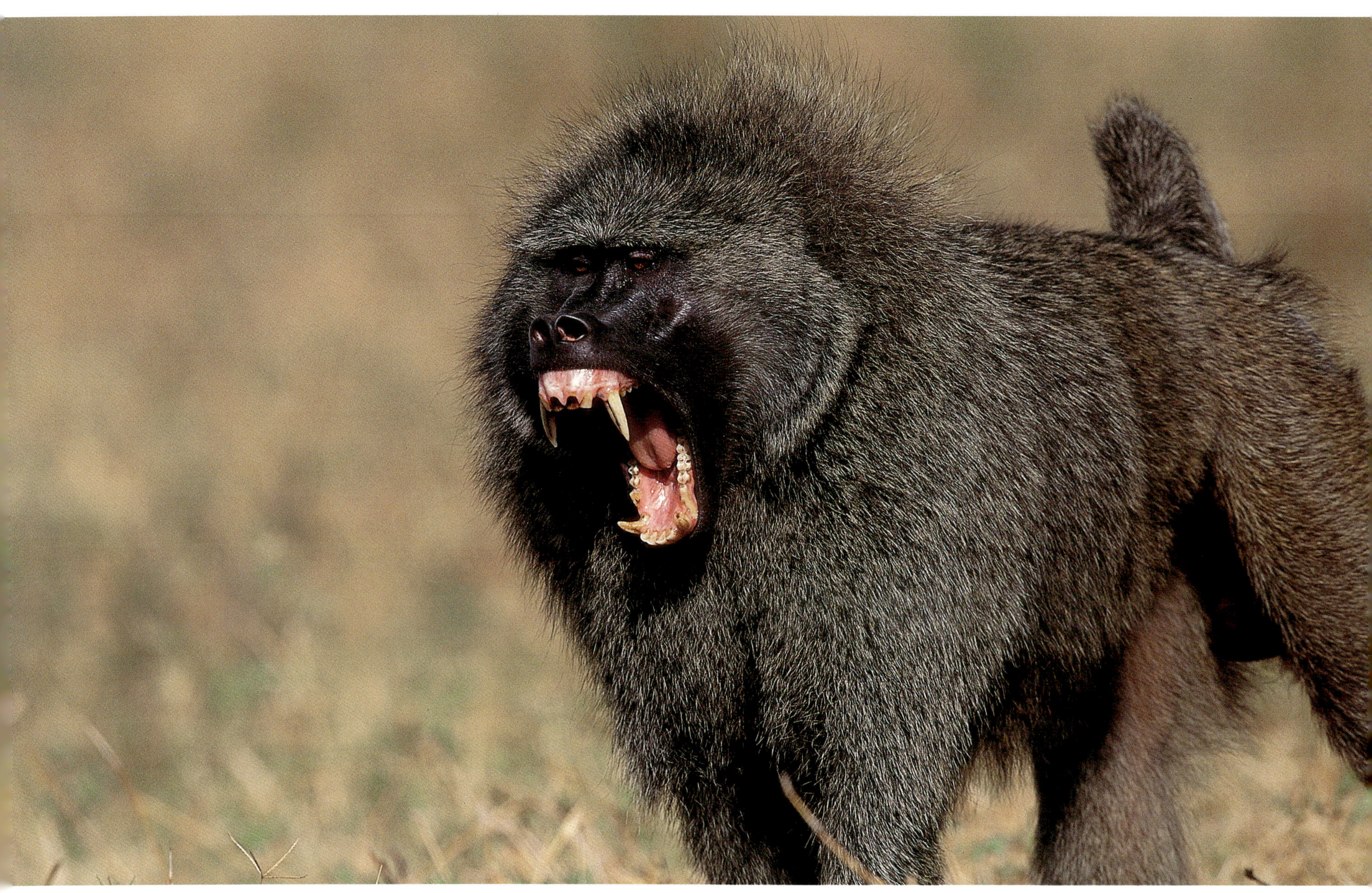

A strutting alpha male baboon shows his awesome canines. His aggressive gesture is meant for the other male baboons of his troop, for whom he must perform this ritual in order to affirm and retain his alpha-male status.

Pages 194–195
One late afternoon, a cheetah mother was leading her three adolescent cubs when they came across a patch of tall grass. Very often cheetahs won't walk through tall grass; they prefer to run through it, in case there is some hidden danger lurking there. The adolescents, true to their age, turned this into a game of chase.

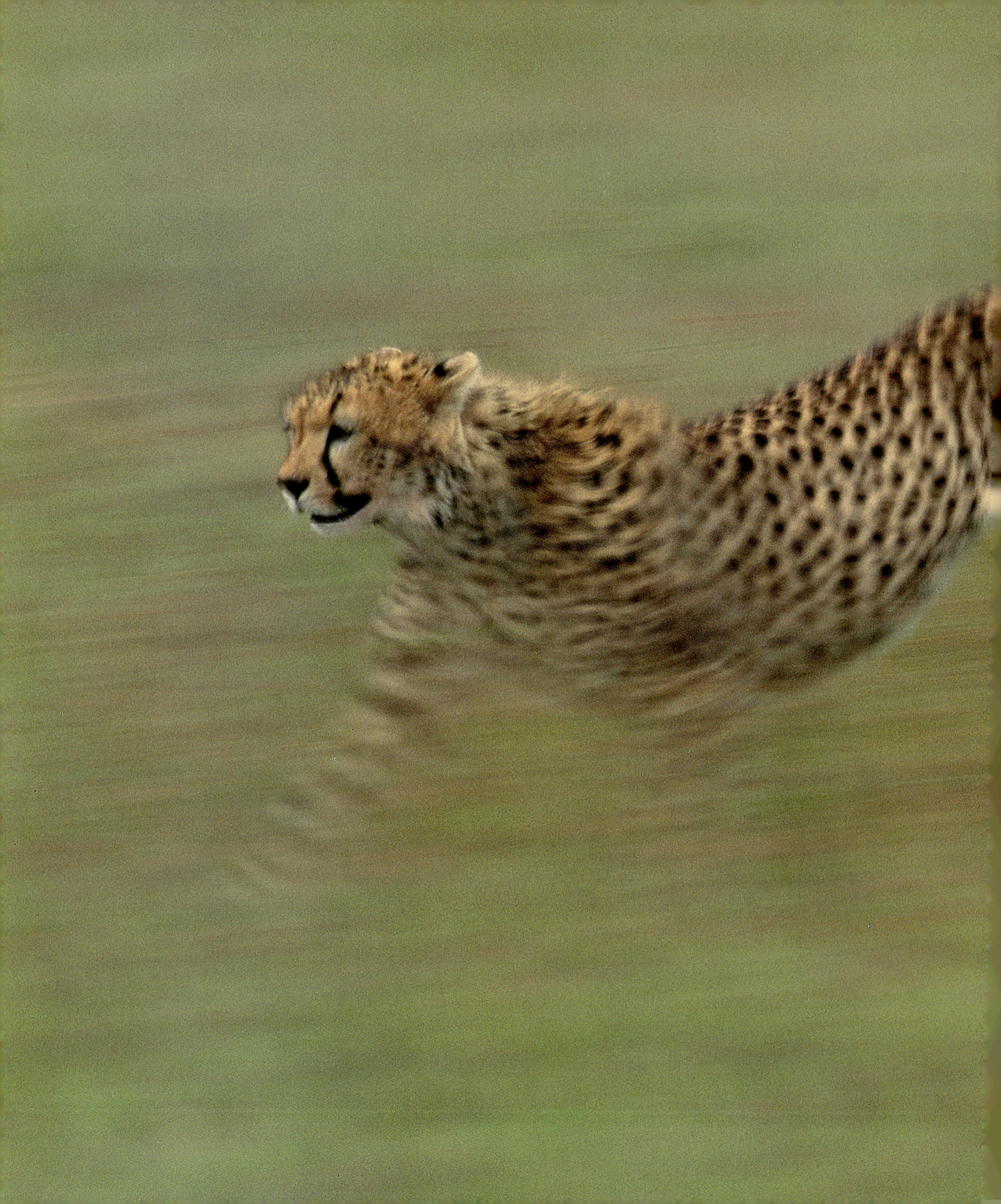

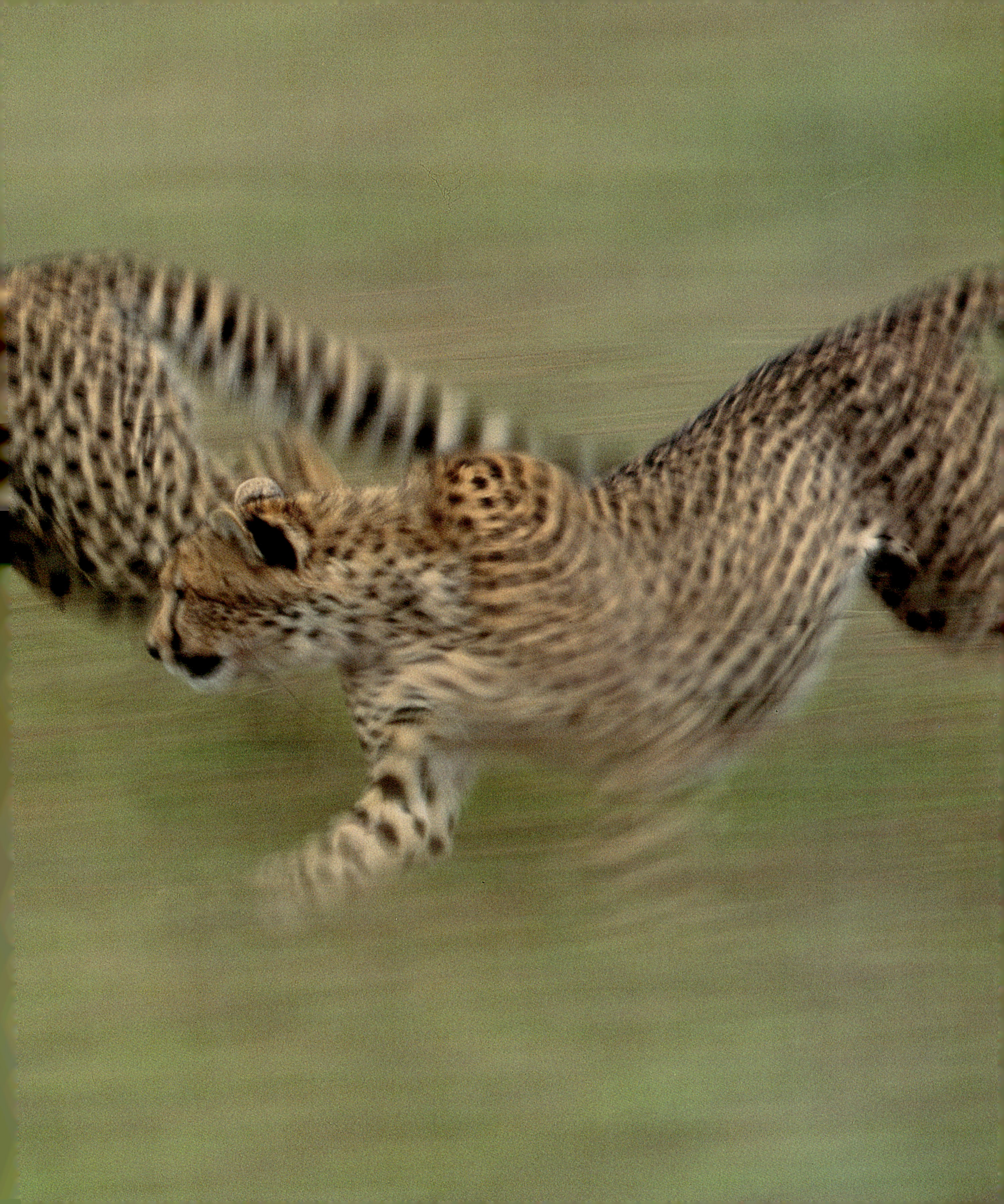

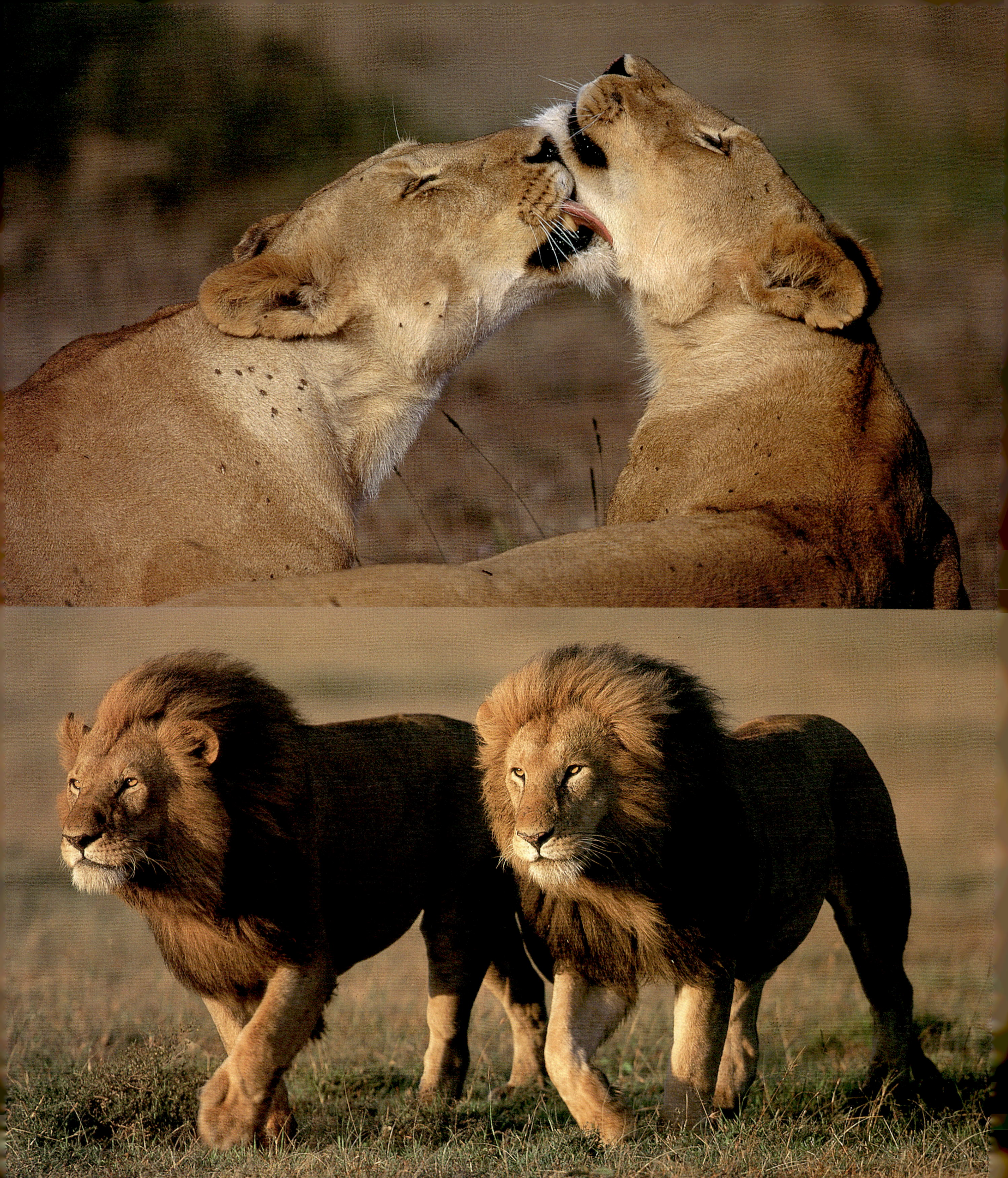

Two pride males reinforce friendship bonds by mock mating. It is thought that nomadic male lions who have met up in the bush and struck up a friendship are virtually inseparable. This deep bond continues even when they manage to take over a pride together.

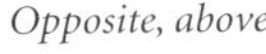

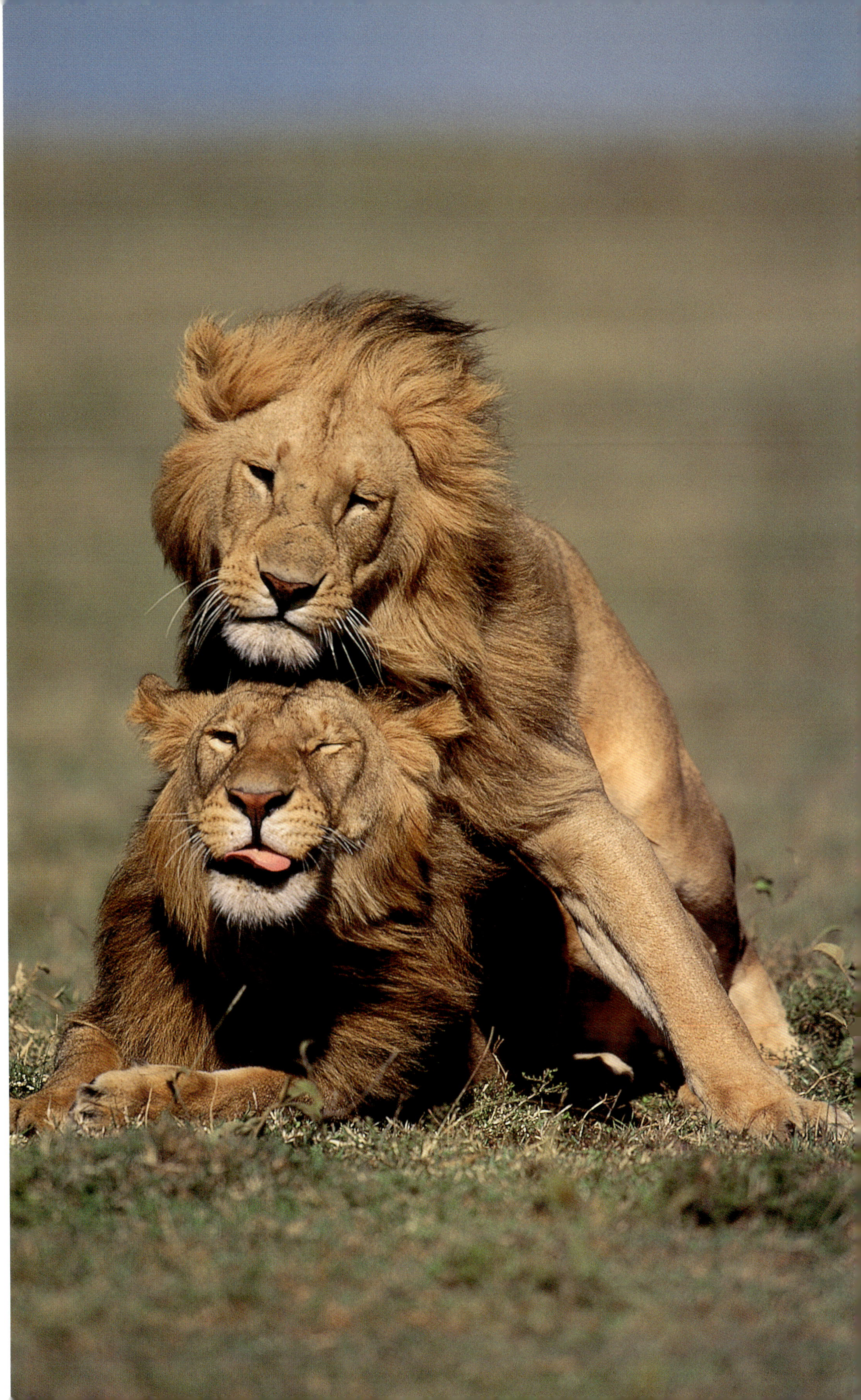

Opposite, above
In the morning hours, these two lionesses had acted aggressively toward one another while feeding on a wildebeest carcass. Now, in the evening, they appear to be making up. They took turns thoroughly licking each other's muzzles for close to ten minutes.

Opposite, below
Two handsome pride males, returning from a territorial patrol, have spotted an adolescent male consorting with one of his aunts. Since in-breeding is unacceptable behavior, these males are poised to race in and break things up – their whole bearing signals their intention to attack.

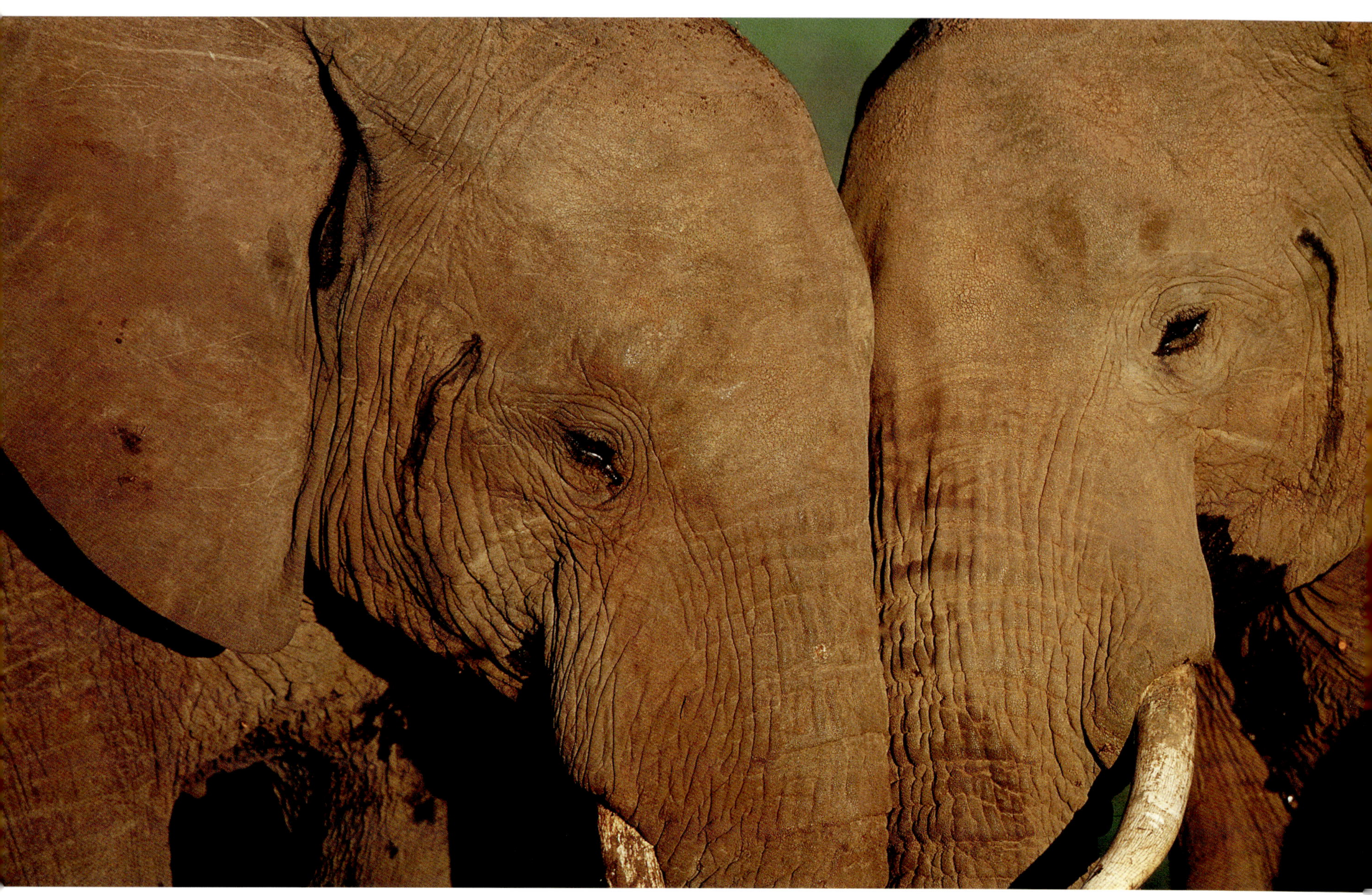

A family of elephants at a waterhole started socializing after they had drunk gallons and gallons of water. Elephants are most definitely contact animals. Family members often stand touching while resting or drinking, leaning and rubbing their bodies together or reaching out to caress one another with their trunks.

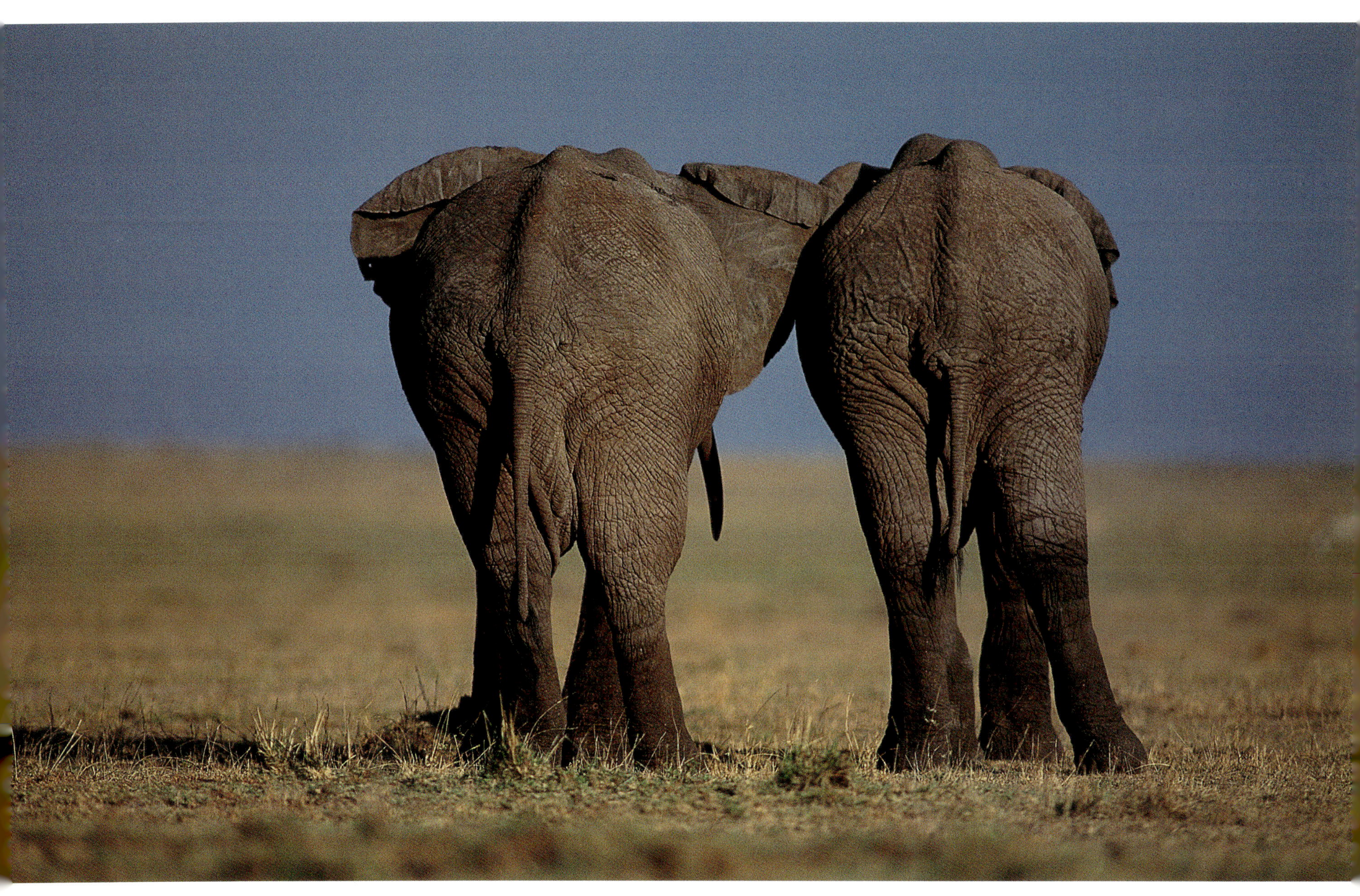

As a group of elephants made its way across the plains, these two adults detached themselves from the line and stood close together, feeling each other's foreheads with their trunks. Then, almost imperceptibly, one leaned its massive bulk toward its companion, who fanned its ears in response. After a minute or so, they moved on, side by side, perfectly in step.

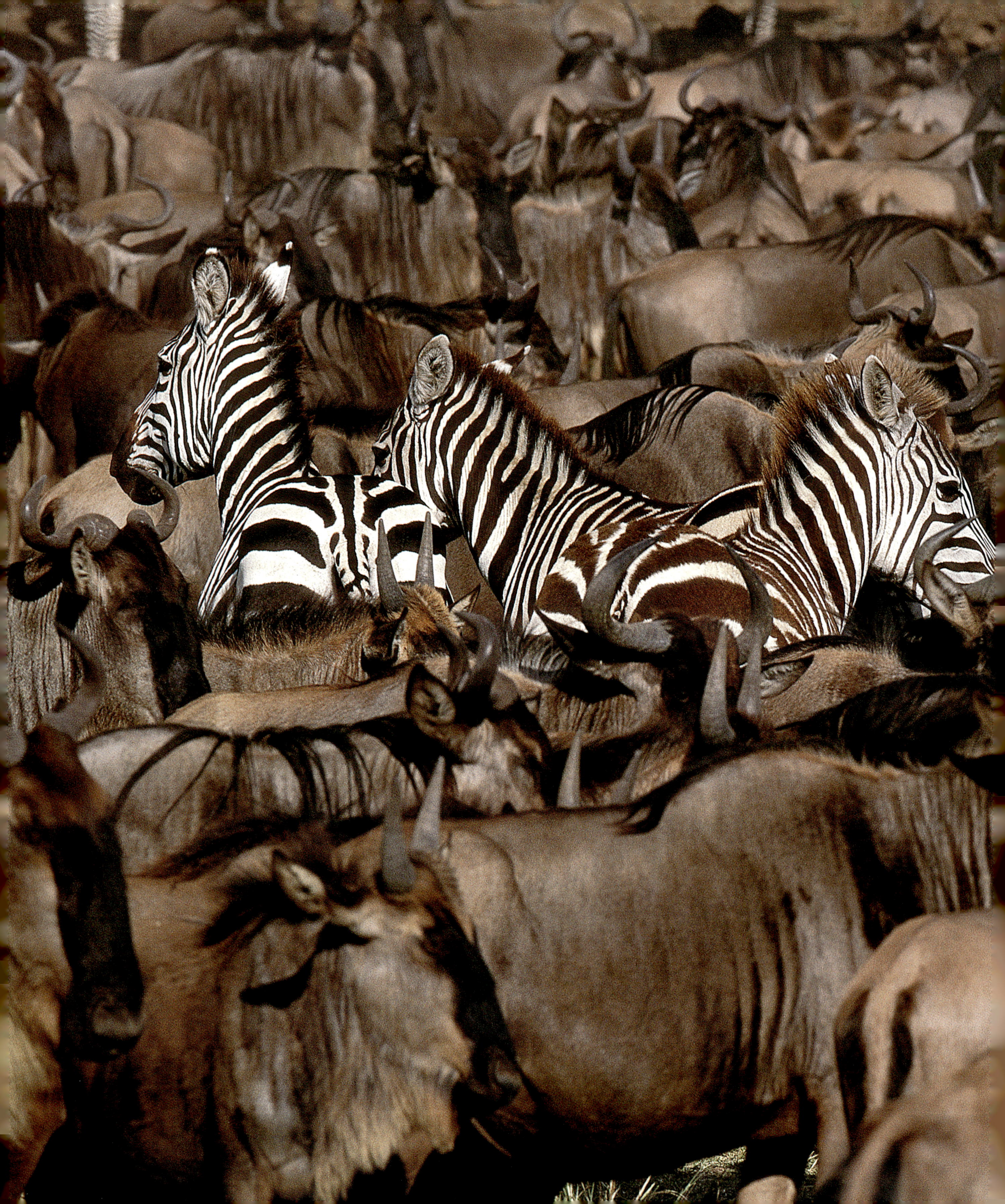

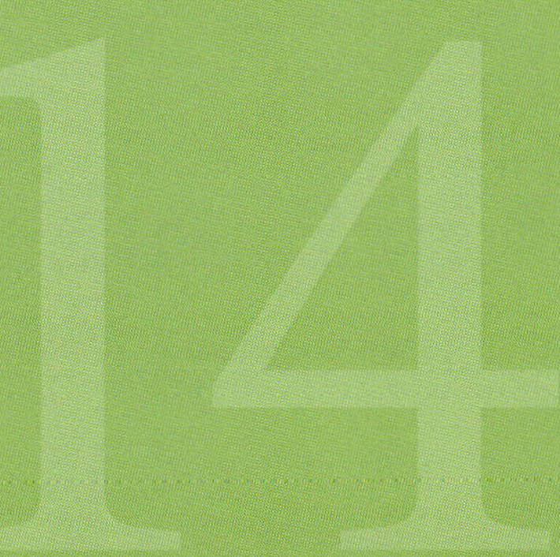

14

Herds and Social Groups

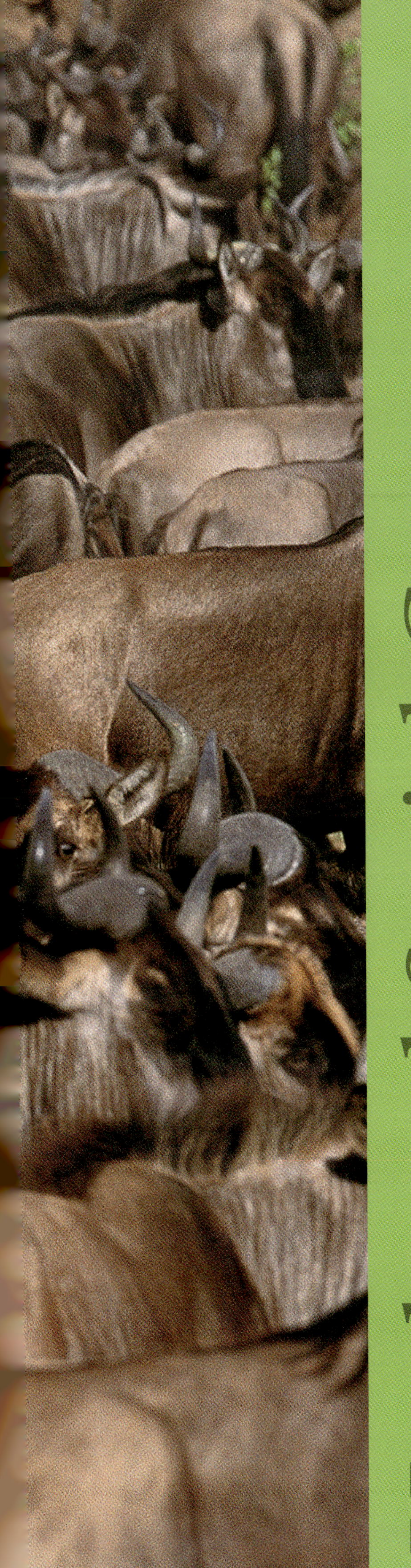

The wildebeest herd stood on the river bank, hesitating to cross. The possibility of lurking crocodiles was too great. If only one of them would wade in, the rest would know more about the crocodile danger, but none wanted to be the guinea pig, so they all waited, occasionally trying to nudge the ones on the water's edge into the river. Is this an example of selfish exploitation?

Wildebeests form huge, anonymous herds, especially when migrating. These herds are not social in the precise meaning of the word – the only enduring relationships within these milling masses are between mothers and their young ones, so exploitation is not an uncommon occurrence. Yet there are benefits to being part of a herd. There is safety in numbers: Not only are there many pairs of eyes to keep a lookout for danger, the sheer numbers of potential prey in a herd are so overwhelming to a predator that the odds of being selected as the victim are greatly reduced. In addition, living in large aggregations also means that the chances of both males and females finding a suitable mate are dramatically increased. Belonging to a herd allows a wildebeest to promote its own interests, so a wildebeest herd could be called a selfish herd.

Plains zebras are often seen in large herds on the open plains, but if you watch such a herd for a period of time or observe when lions threaten, you will see the herd break up into small mobile groups of up to a dozen, usually comprised of a stallion, his mares, and their young. It is these family groups that are truly social, not the large herds which disintegrate and re-form daily.

Herd membership in general is temporary, and herd members do not spend time getting to know each other. On the other hand, animals such as elephants and lions who live in family groups form far more permanent associations. A properly socialized animal living among relatives and companions is able to share in the great number of benefits made available through the social group's activities. A troop of olive baboons may be able to forage more efficiently in circumstances in which a loner would fail to survive. Among African wild dogs, cooperative hunting is a routine business. Fundamental to the success of the social group is that nearly all members of the group must cooperate in social activities, otherwise the advantages of gregariousness vanish.

To facilitate cooperation and harmonious living, relationships in social groups are usually governed by implicit conventions. In dwarf mongooses, one male has dominant status over other males regarding reproductive rights; in African wild dogs, there is one dominant female who is the main breeder. In many such groups, a complex hierarchy develops in which each member knows its place. Once established, this arrangement reduces aggression within the group. However, it has been found that those of high rank are more likely to survive life-threatening hardships than those at the bottom of the pile. When a high-

Pages 200–201
Biding their time, some zebras find themselves amid a sea of wildebeests gathered on a riverbank. When the animals finally pluck up the courage to wade in, zebras typically cross in orderly family groups, whereas wildebeests pour into the river in one huge disorganized wave.

ranking female baboon wants shade, the low-ranking baboon is conditioned to move out of the way; when she wants to eat where the pickings are best, the lowly baboon has to leave the dinner table.

There is one fundamental question that remains unanswered: Why do different species organize themselves in different ways? On the savannah, there is a wide variety of ways in which social groups organize themselves: a zebra family is a harem; a lion pride is a matriarchy; in baboon society it is the males that leave the natal group, whereas in chimpanzees it is the females that migrate; dikdiks and klipspringers pair for life. Another question is why are some species social and others not? For example, of all the big cats in the wild, lions are the only ones that live in social groups. It is thought that lions live in groups for a number of reasons: to be more competitive with hyenas whose niche environment overlaps with theirs, to defend their kills or steal kills from hyenas, cooperative hunting of big game in lean times, cooperative nursing of cubs, and possibly defense of territory from other lions. Yet the other big cats seem to survive quite well in the wild as loners. There are many speculations, but this remains a tough question for researchers to crack.

However, here's a thought: Lions are social, but leopards are solitary due to natural selection. Perhaps a chance mutation of genes occurred, introducing a gene for sociality into lions, which helped the animals adapt better to their environment. This selection of the mutation is then perhaps followed by more such mutations, and reinforced by more and more sociable lions surviving longer in groups than alone. Thus lions eventually specialize in sociality, while leopards do not because, for whatever reason, the same mutation did not occur in them. The same sort of reasoning may help to explain why the social structure of lions is a matriarchy as opposed to that of zebras, which is a harem. That's the way natural selection has worked – it's as simple as that.

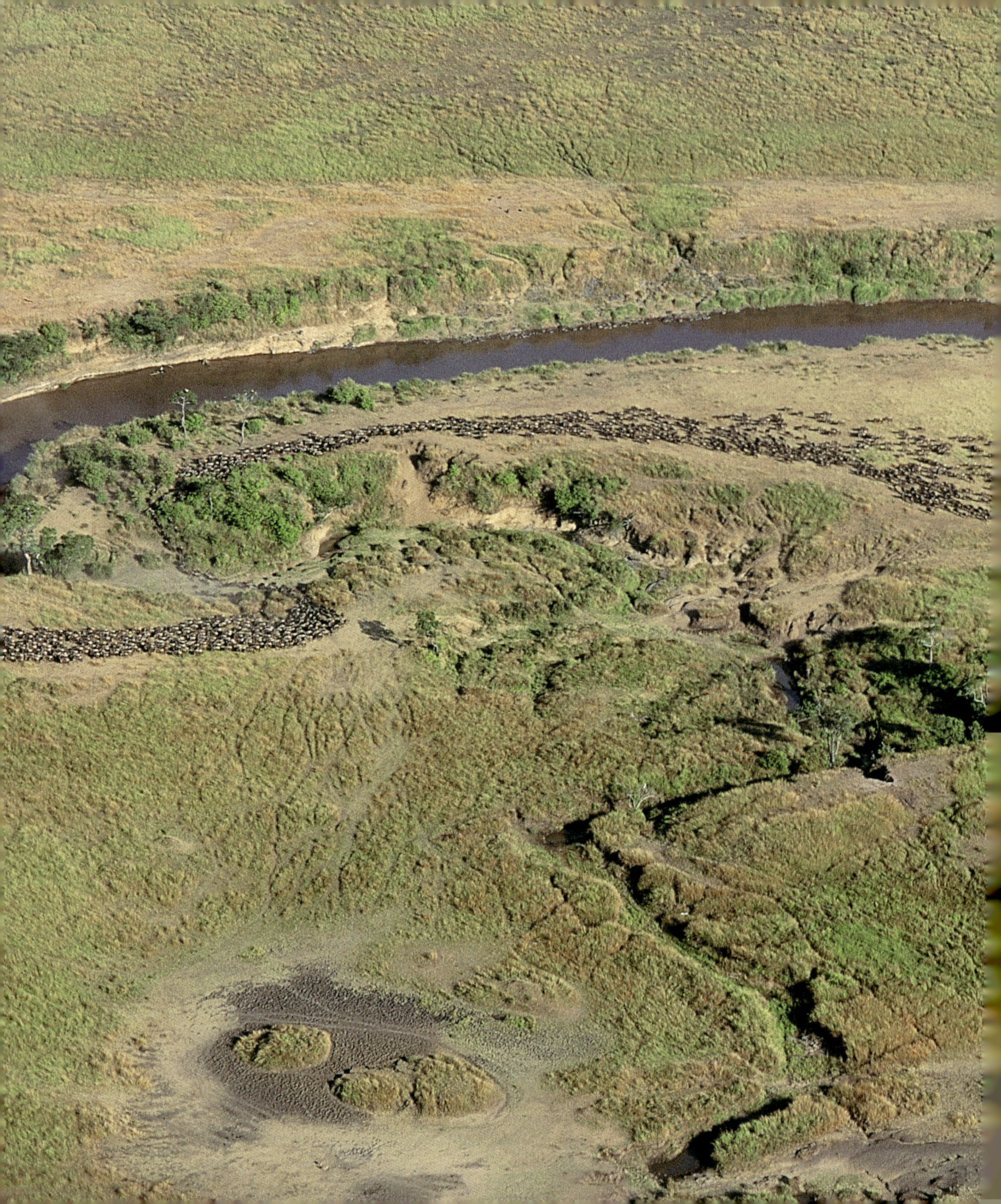

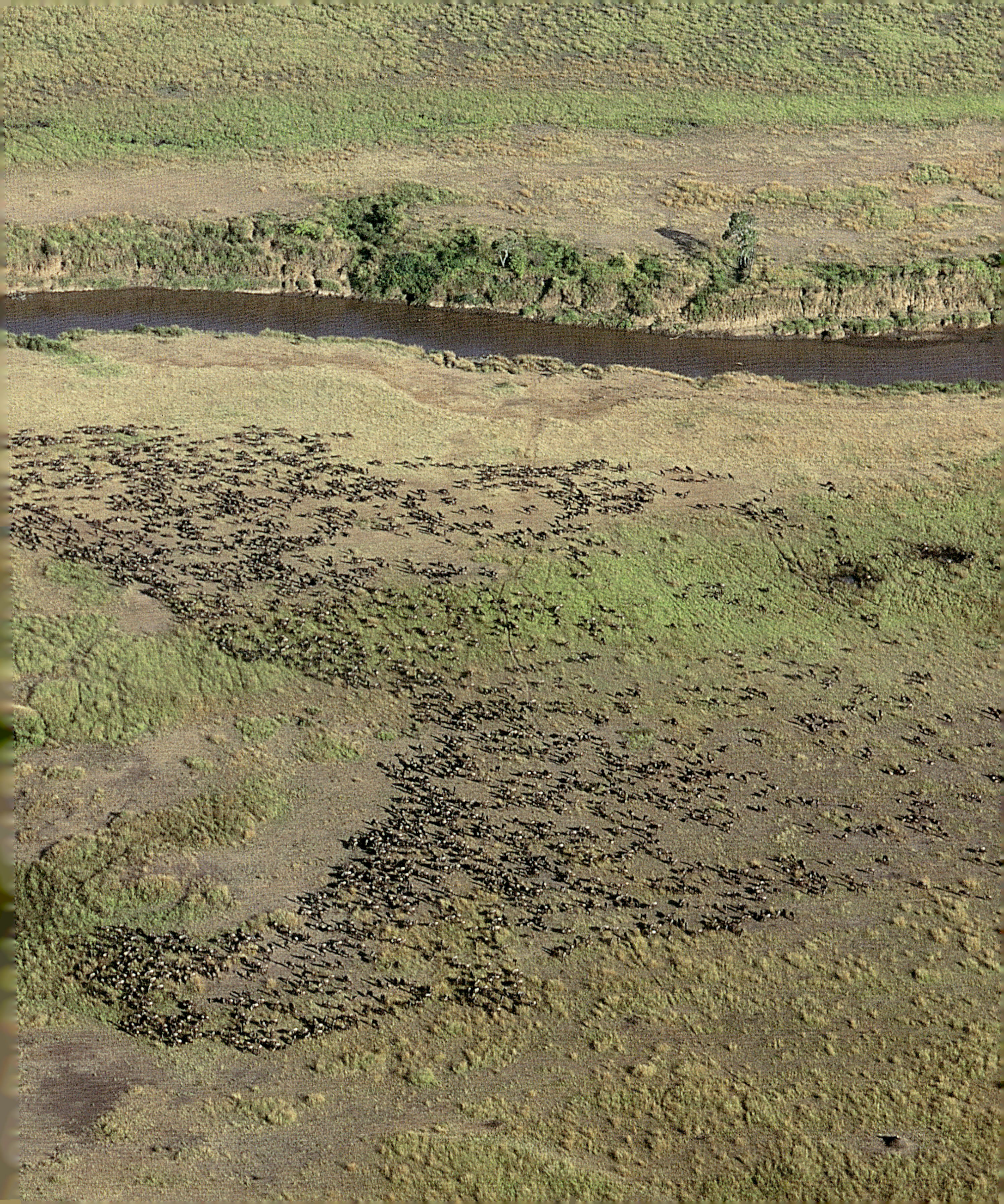

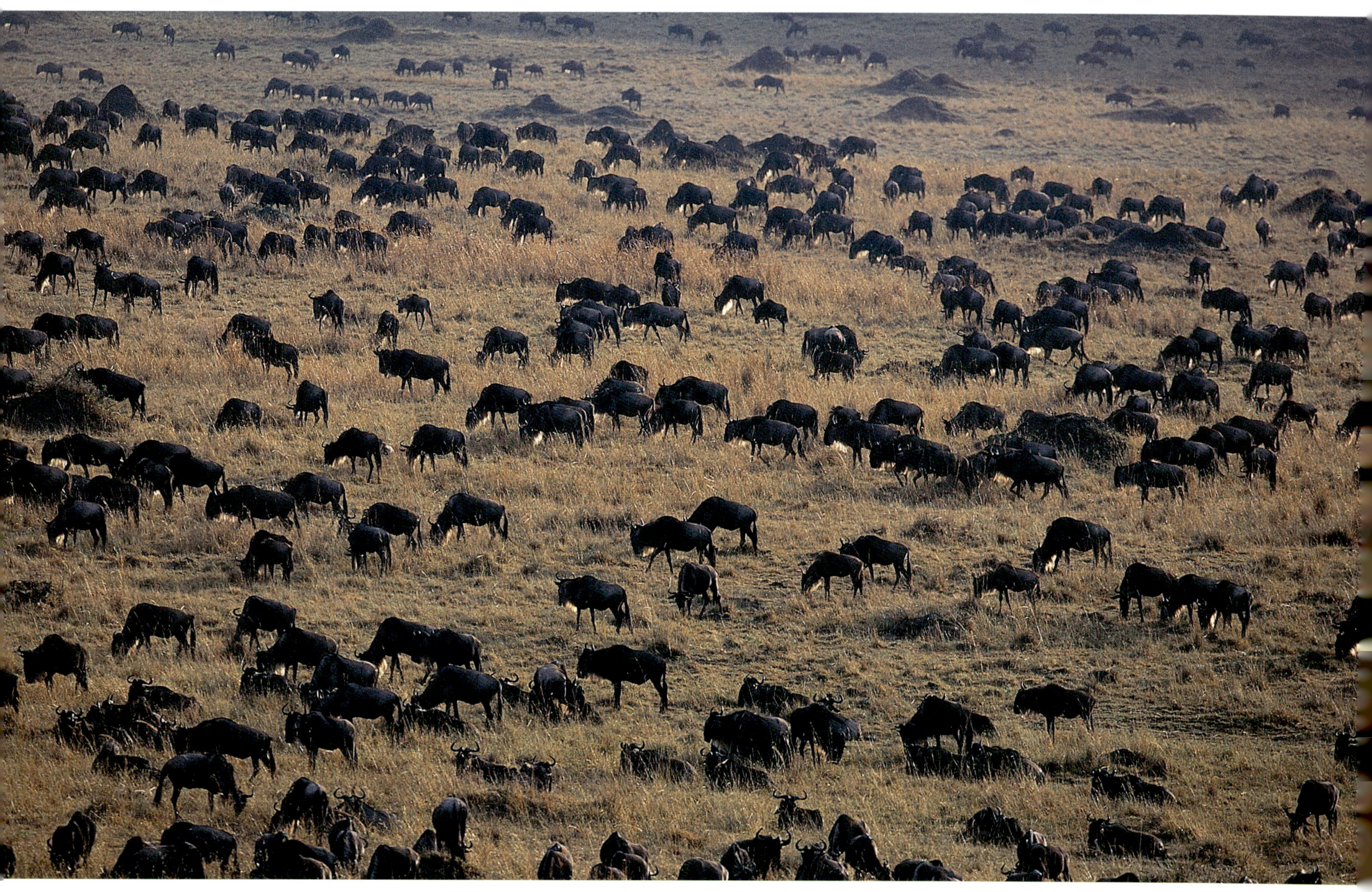

A grazing herd of wildebeests in the middle of the dry season.

Pages 204–205
A wildebeest herd heads for the river. Wildebeests coordinate their movements quite simply: Each keeps an eye on its neighbors and sticks close by them, quickly adjusting their own movements as necessary. In this way the herd moves as one.

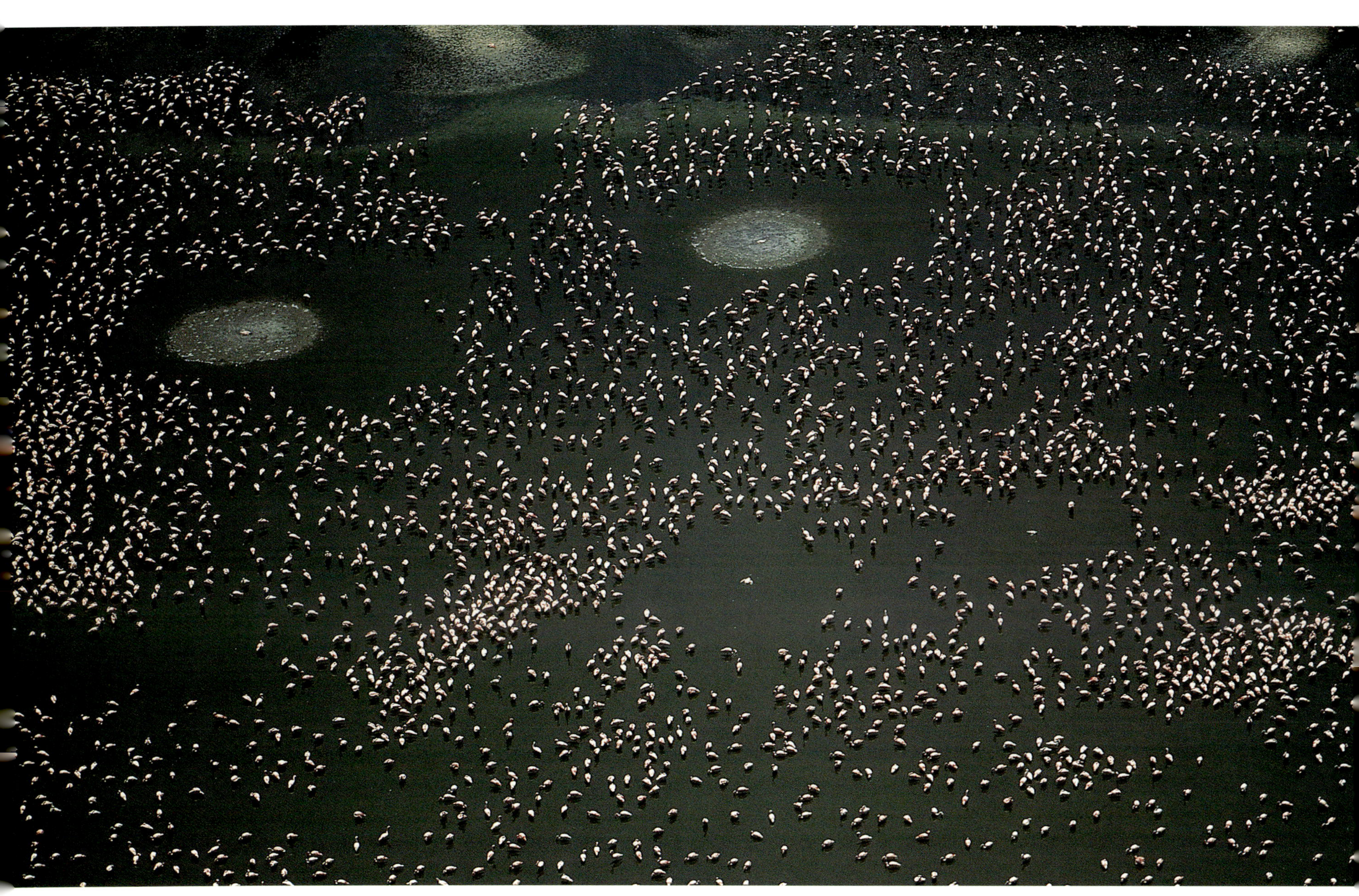

Lesser flamingoes in the highly alkaline waters of a Rift Valley lake.

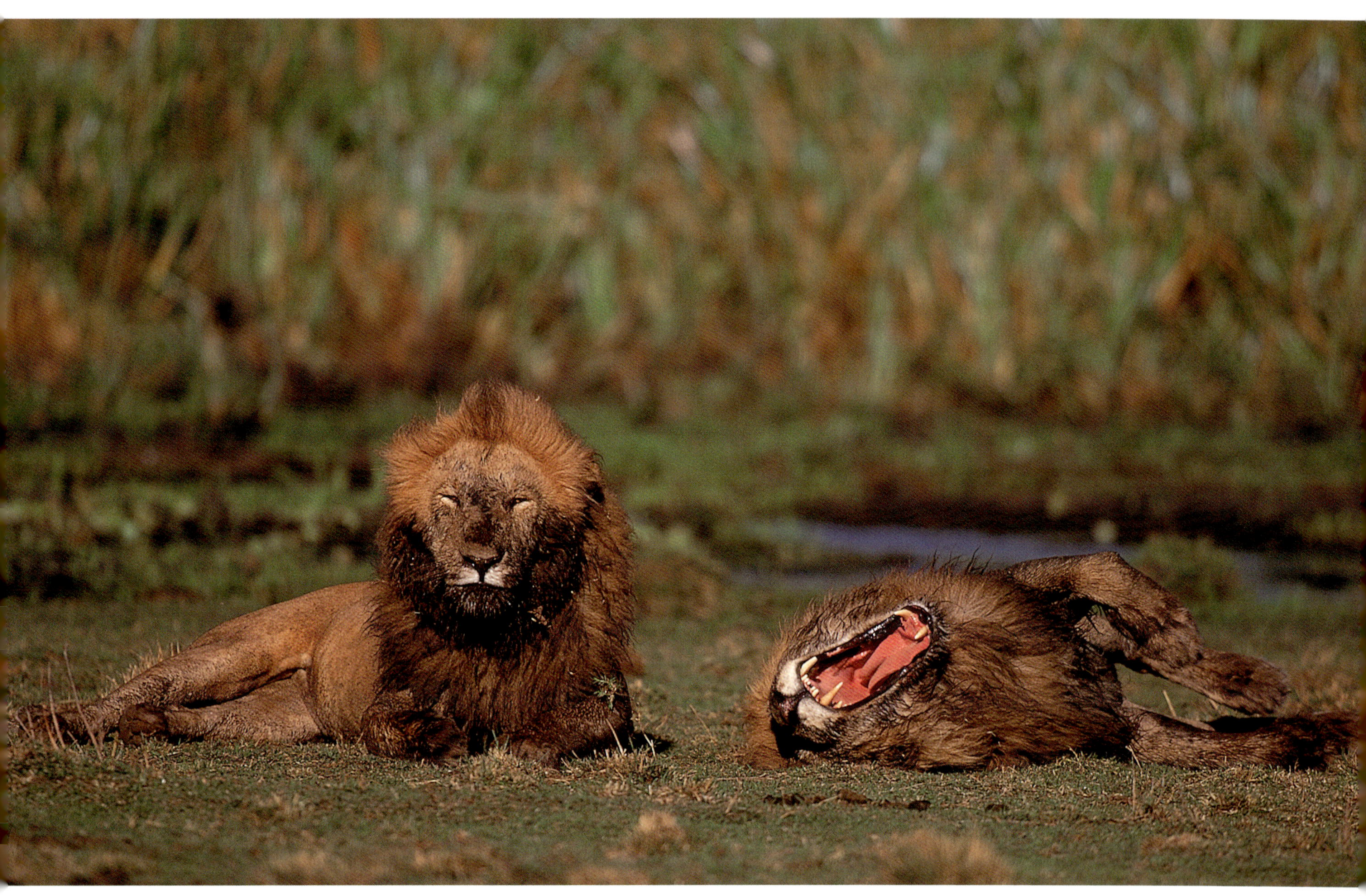

Having encroached on the territory of a neighboring pride and finding no evidence of the resident males, these lions have decided to settle in and stay for a while. This is risky behavior because the resident males could show up at any moment. During their stay, they nervously and continually reinforce their friendship bond to keep up their confidence level.

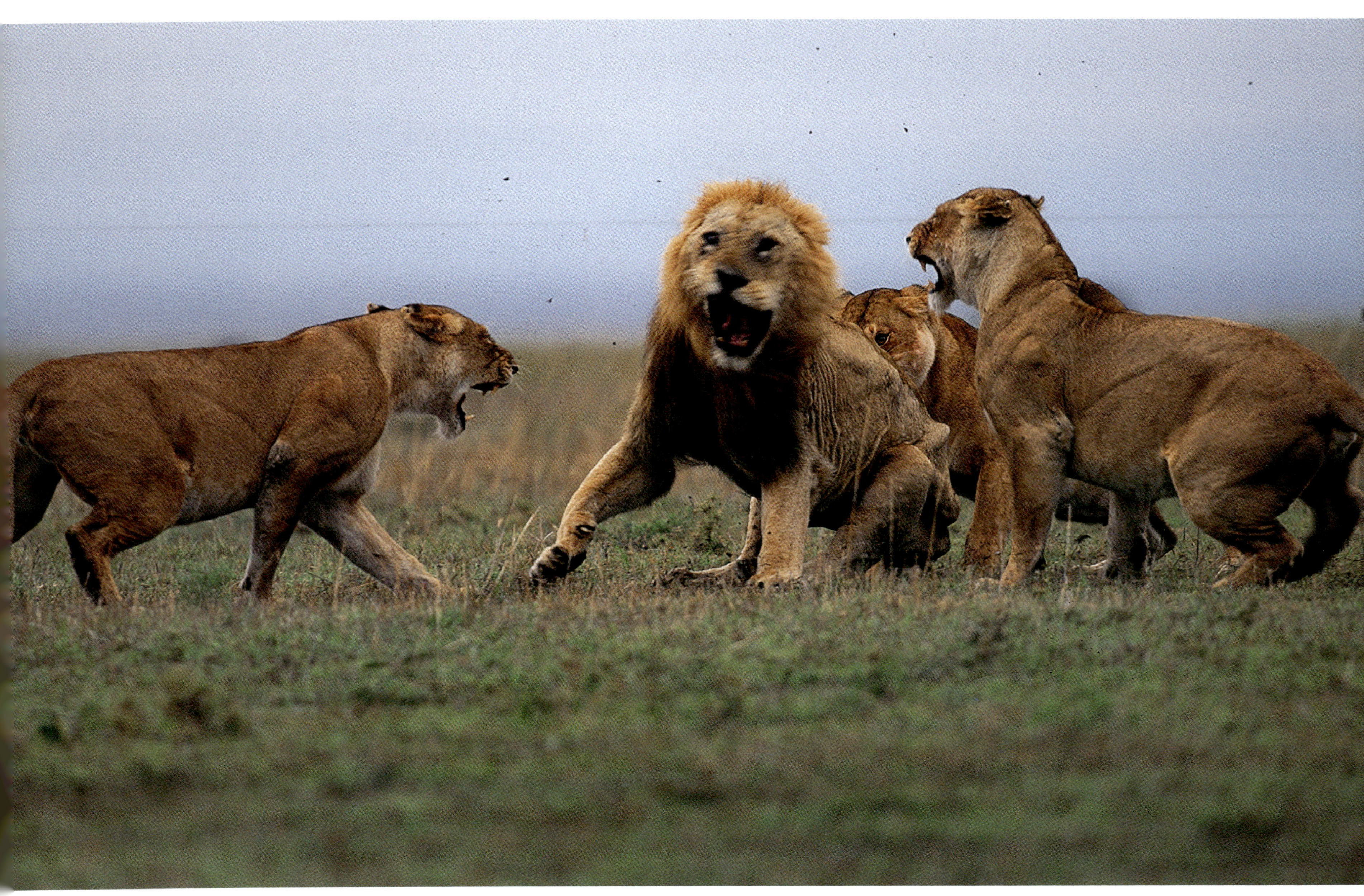

The mothers of a lion pride launch a preemptive attack on a male that could conceivably pose a threat to their cubs. While four of the lionesses went for the male, a fifth escorted the cubs away from the scene to safety. They were successful in their bid to scare him away.

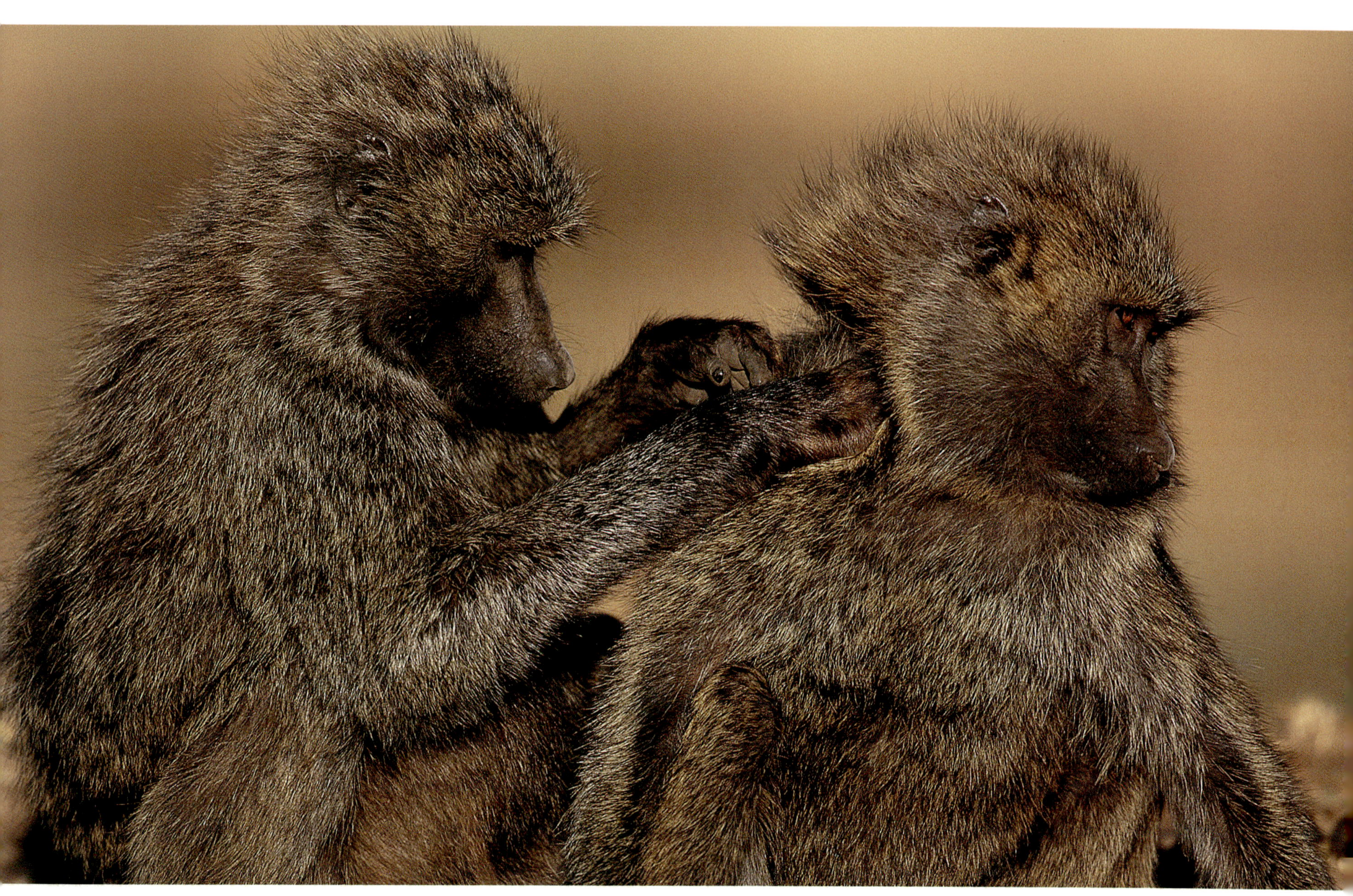

Grooming is so pleasurable and relaxing to monkeys like these olive baboons that they'll often nod off during a lengthy session. Grooming is also a means of promoting social cohesion within the group, and it is thought to sometimes limit the size of a troop, as it becomes more difficult in terms of time to ensure that everyone in a large group is well groomed. Friendships can become strained and groups break apart when some are not giving or receiving their fair share of the grooming.

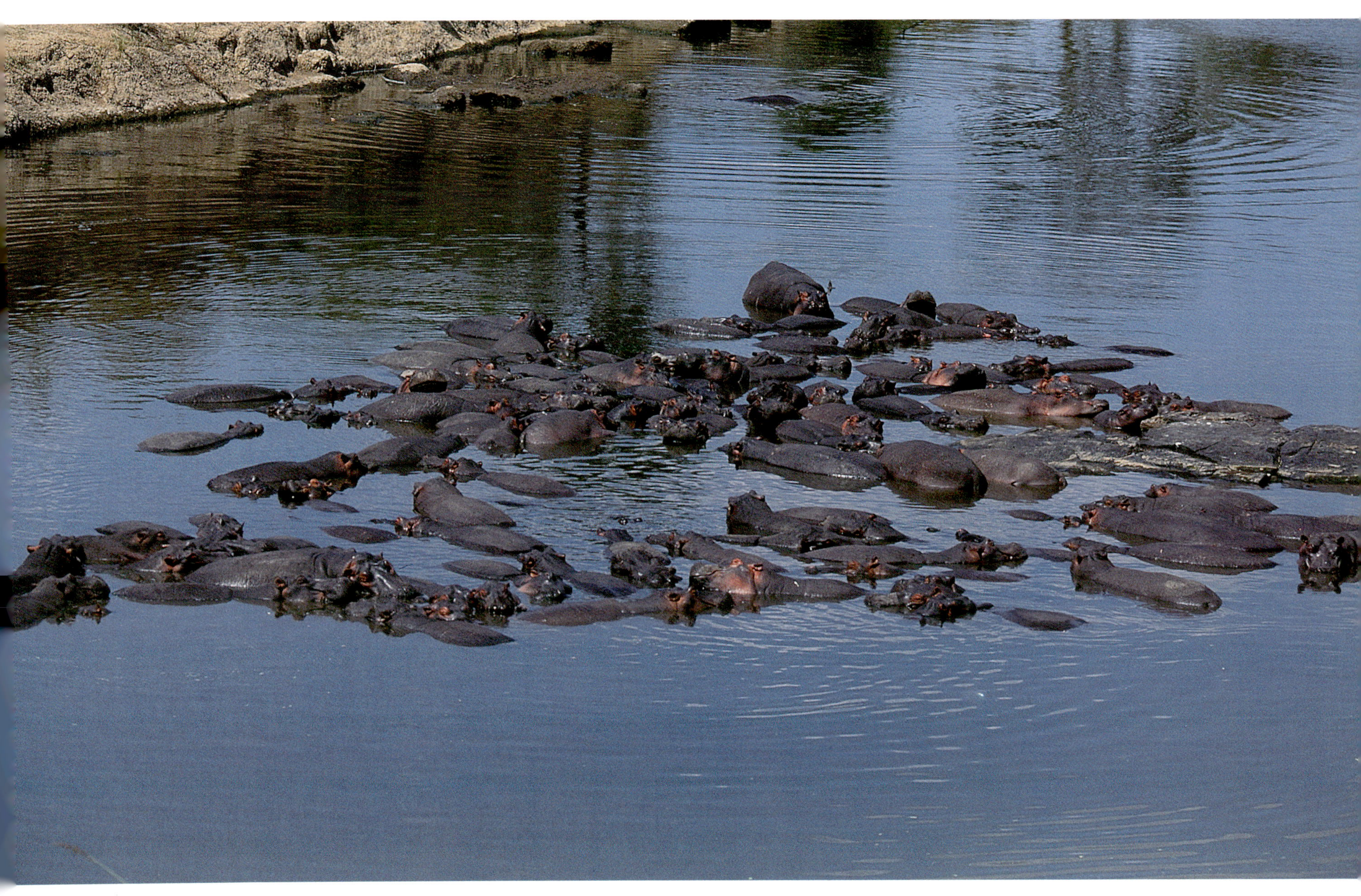

A group of hippos, called a pod, sleeping in the river. Pods of 10 to 15 hippos, including a dominant bull and cows with their calves, are typical. However, when the river starts drying up and resting spots diminish, larger groups will form.

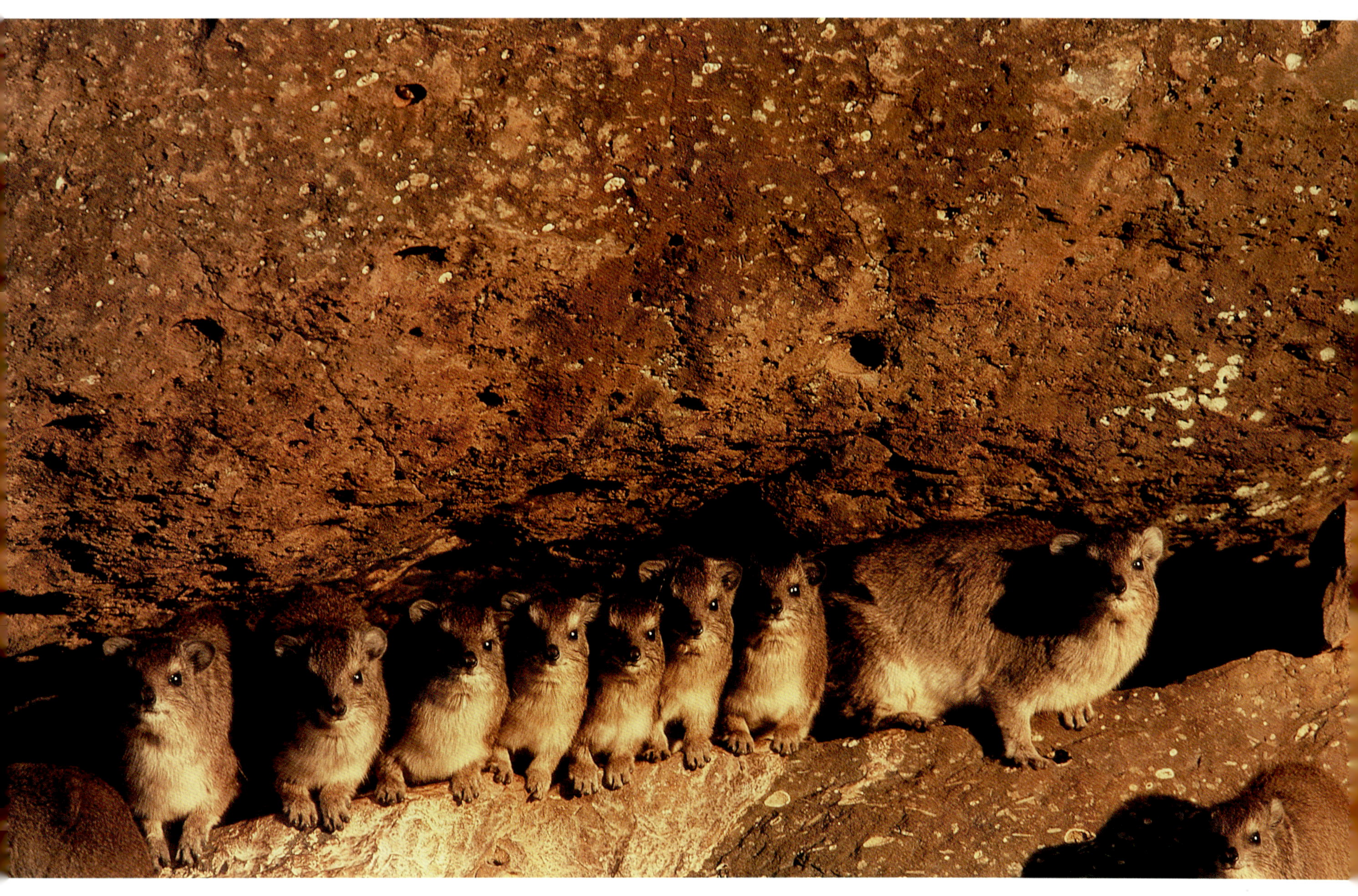

A row of hyraxes are catching the first rays of the sun. These highly social mammals are similar in appearance to the American woodchuck, or marmot.

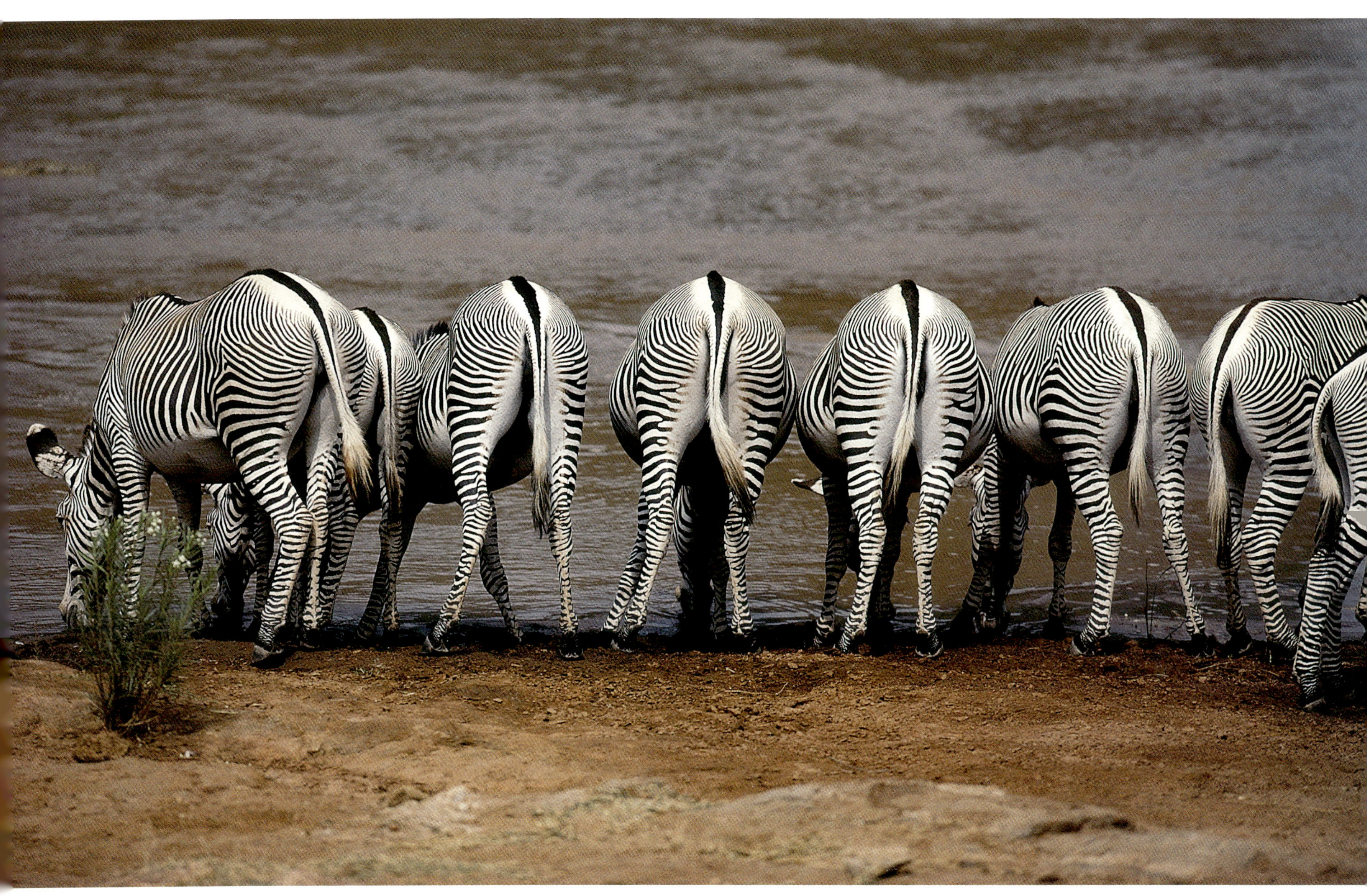

A slow-flowing river cutting through the savannah draws a wide spectrum of animals such as these Gevy's zebras, which can be distinguished from other zebra species by their extremely thin black stripes. While the group is drinking, one zebra usually acts as a lookout for trouble, holding its head high, while the others drink. The zebras will not linger since water sources attract predators.

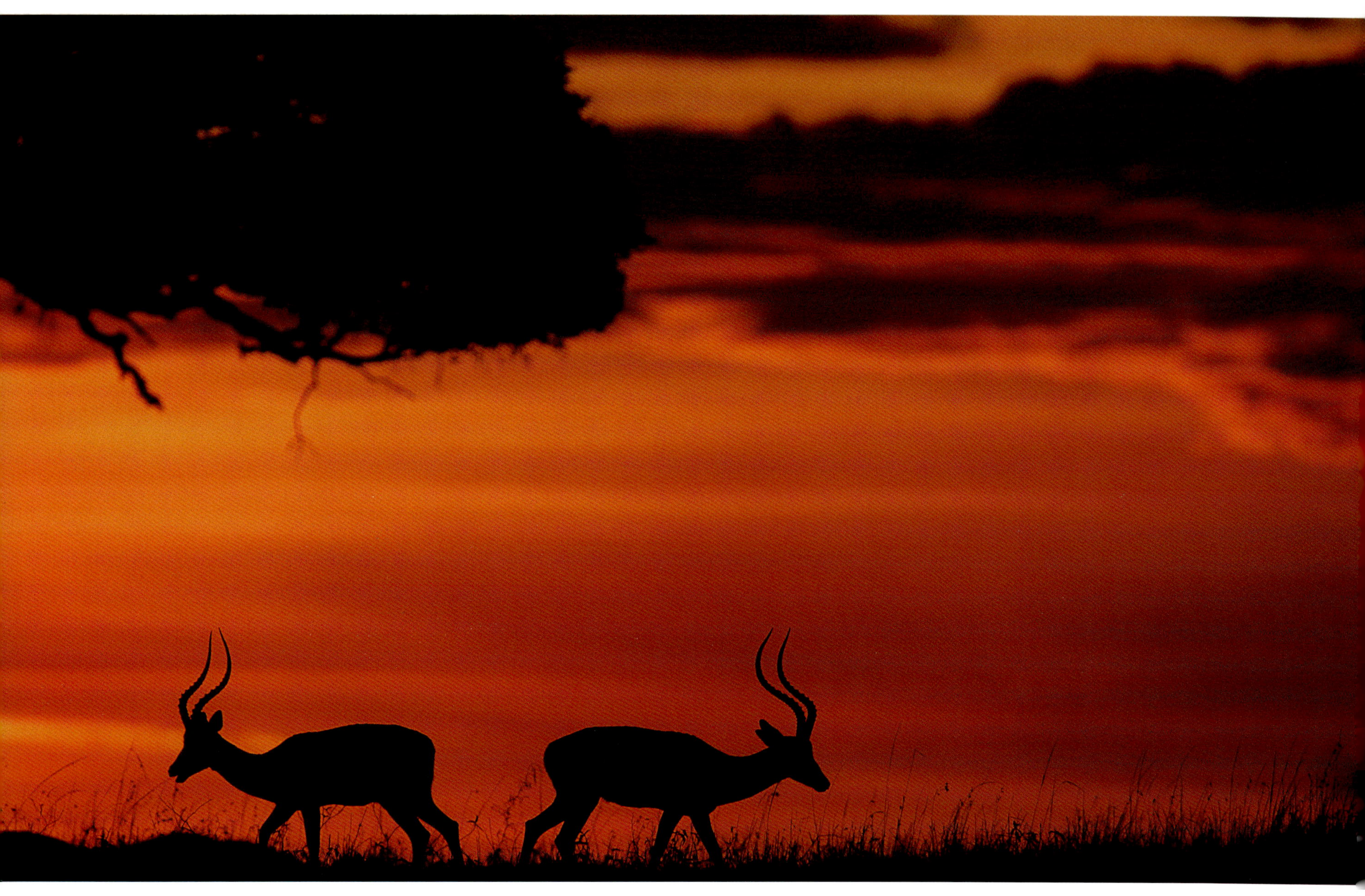

Two impala males pause during a friendly duel. Impala bachelors have a fluid hierarchy within their bachelor groups. Their position in the hierarchy is either reaffirmed or adjusted through these sparring matches.

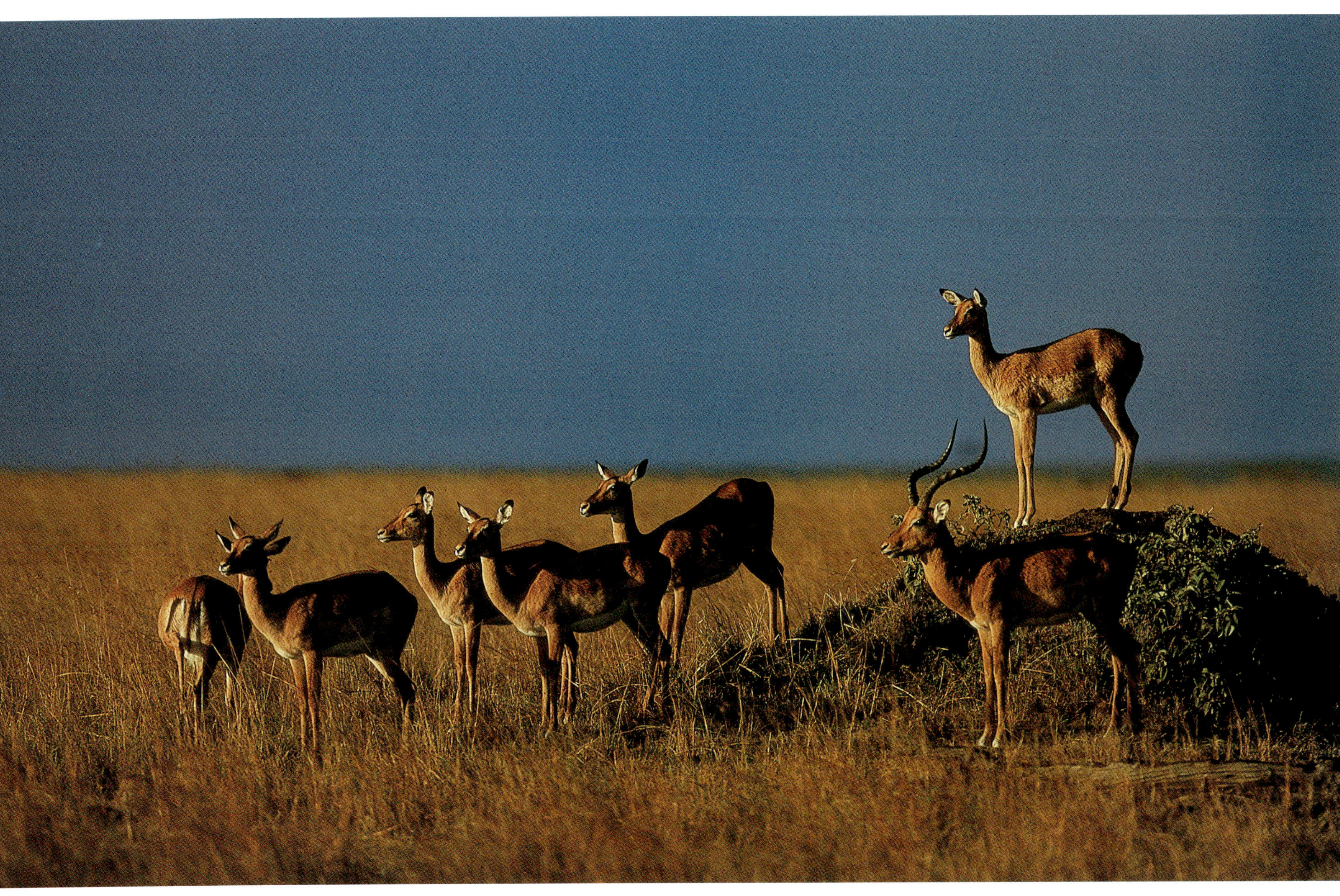

A male impala with his small harem, waits in anticipation of rain. There is no permanent bond between a male and the females of his harem. If the male is ousted by a rival, the females will accept the victor.

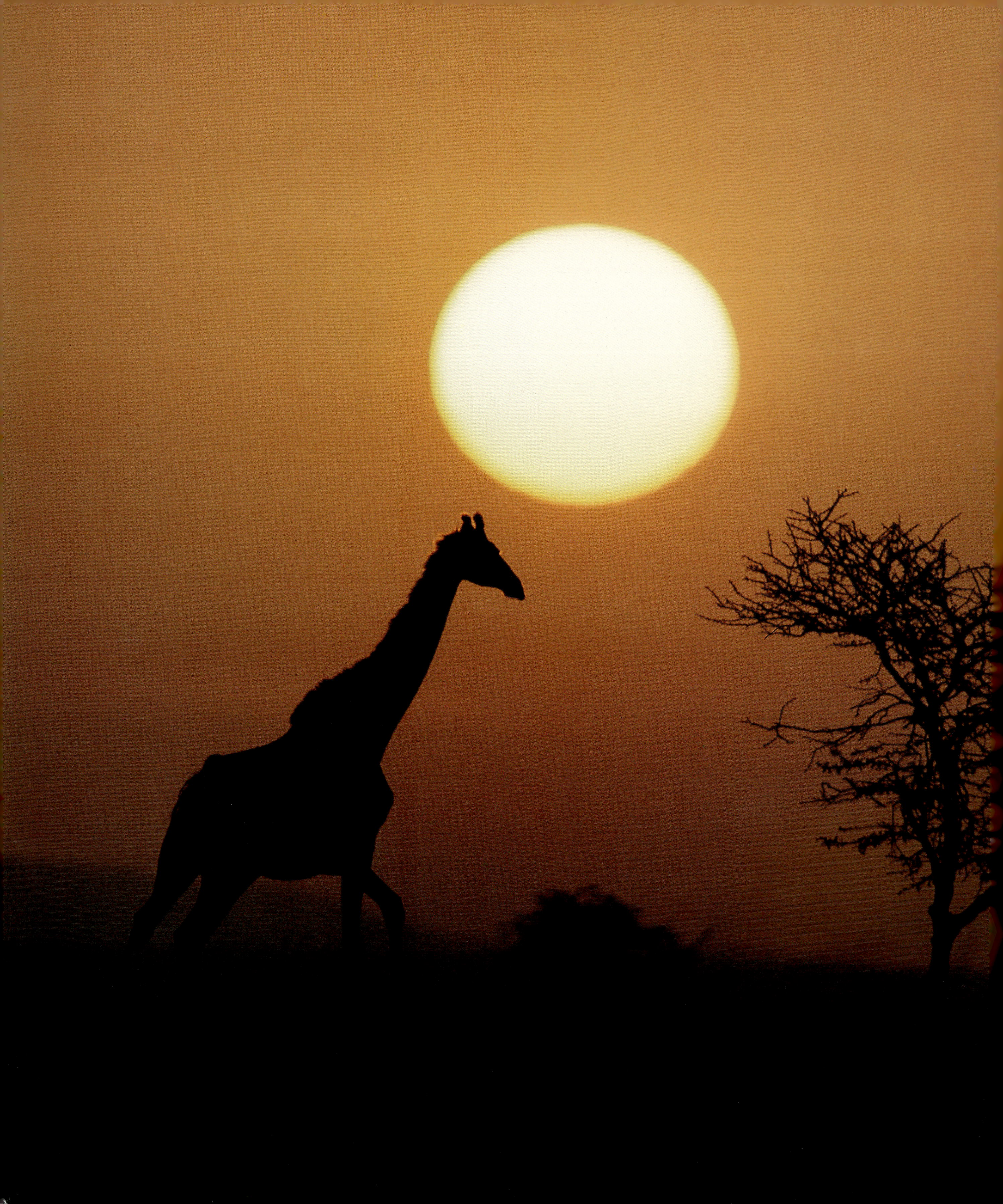

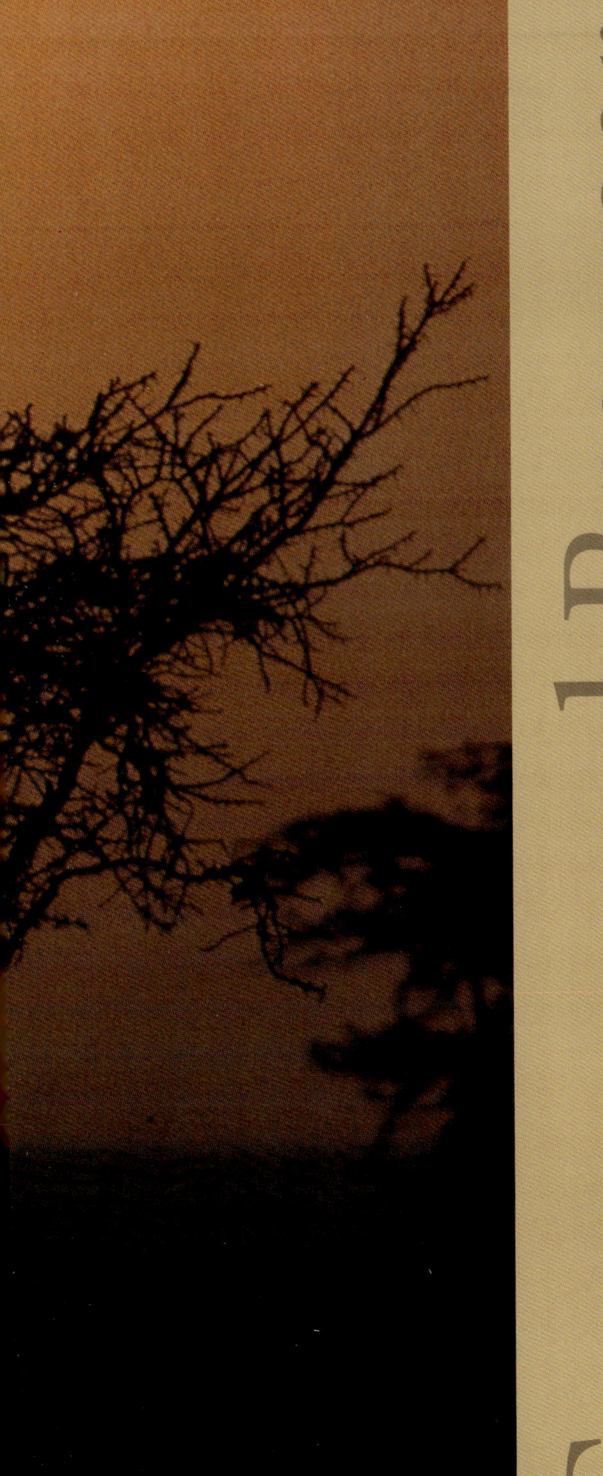

15

Grazers and Browsers

There's a lot of grass in the savannah. For every 100 gazelles, there is one square mile of grassland. Why so much more grass than gazelles?

The ultimate source of energy for life is the sun. Plants synthesize solar energy to build their bodies and to do the work of living. Grazers feed only on grass, but they do not get at all the grass tissue. Nor can grazers get at the fuel the grasses have already burned. Furthermore, much of the grass eaten remains undigested and passes out as waste, and some grass is broken down in respiration to supply energy for the animal's own use. All in all, less than ten percent of plant food is converted into body tissue. So there is much more of grass than there is of grazers in the grasslands.

But of course grass is not the only vegetation. Trees and bushes and other types of vegetation are distributed over the savannah as well, and these are eaten by the browsers such as giraffes and dikdiks. Throughout the mosaic of savannah habitats, there are fewer browsers than grazers, fewer giraffes than gazelles. This is simply because there are fewer leaves than grass.

The bodies of grazers and browsers have adapted to their respective tasks of feeding. Unlike grazers, who have wide muzzles to gather grass – a hippo's mouth, for example – browsers such as the giraffe have long, narrow mouths to select single leaves. The black rhino with its pointed upper lip is a browser and is most commonly found in bushy savannah, whereas the white rhino, as its broad lips indicate, is a grazer and lives in predominantly open grasslands.

Within the browser group there is specialization, thereby reducing competition for the available food. A giraffe's remarkably long neck enables it to feed on the nutritious tufts of acacia leaves up to 20 feet high, well out of reach of other browsers. Gerenuks are long-necked antelopes that browse at a level below that of giraffes. In addition to using their long necks, they regularly rise on their hind legs, using their front legs to manipulate the branches to within easier reach. Bushbuck browse at a lower level, black rhinos still lower, and the tiny dikdik feeds on the leaves at the lowest levels.

The bushes and trees that comprise the habitat of browsers provide many areas where both browsers and their predators can easily conceal themselves. This is perhaps why you don't find browsers in large aggregations. But on the open plains, where cover is practically nonexistent, grazers gather in groups of ten, twenty, and sometimes well over a thousand for greater protection.

Pages 216–217
A giraffe ambles across the Maasai Mara plain. Giraffes are exclusively browsers so they inhabit those areas of the savannah that have a liberal supply of bushes and trees.

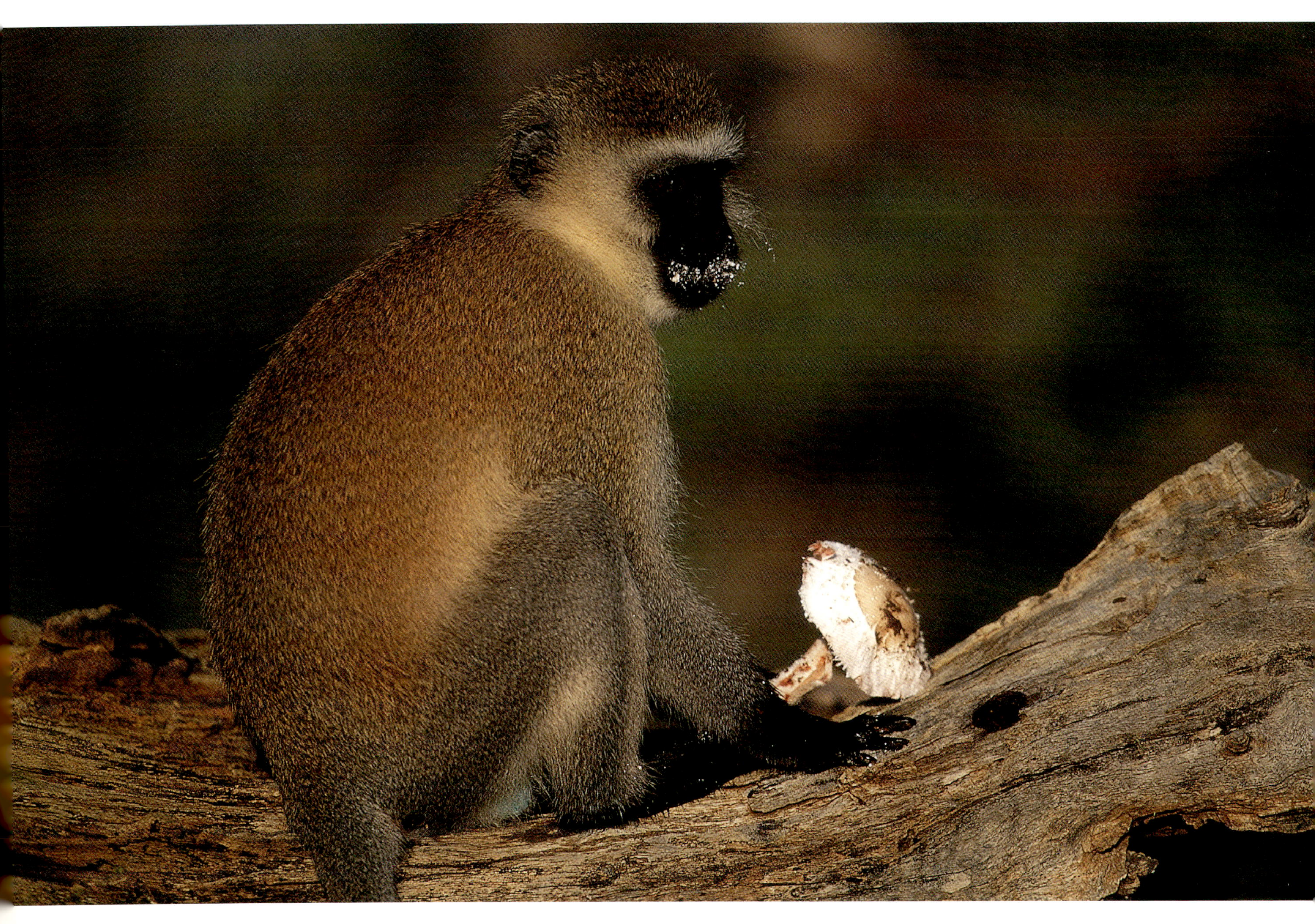

This vervet monkey found a local delicacy – wild mushrooms – soon after descending from its roosting tree. A dusting of mushroom bits surrounds its mouth. Vervets are equally at home foraging on the ground or in trees. When they feed on the ground they never stray far from trees so they can make a quick escape if danger arises.

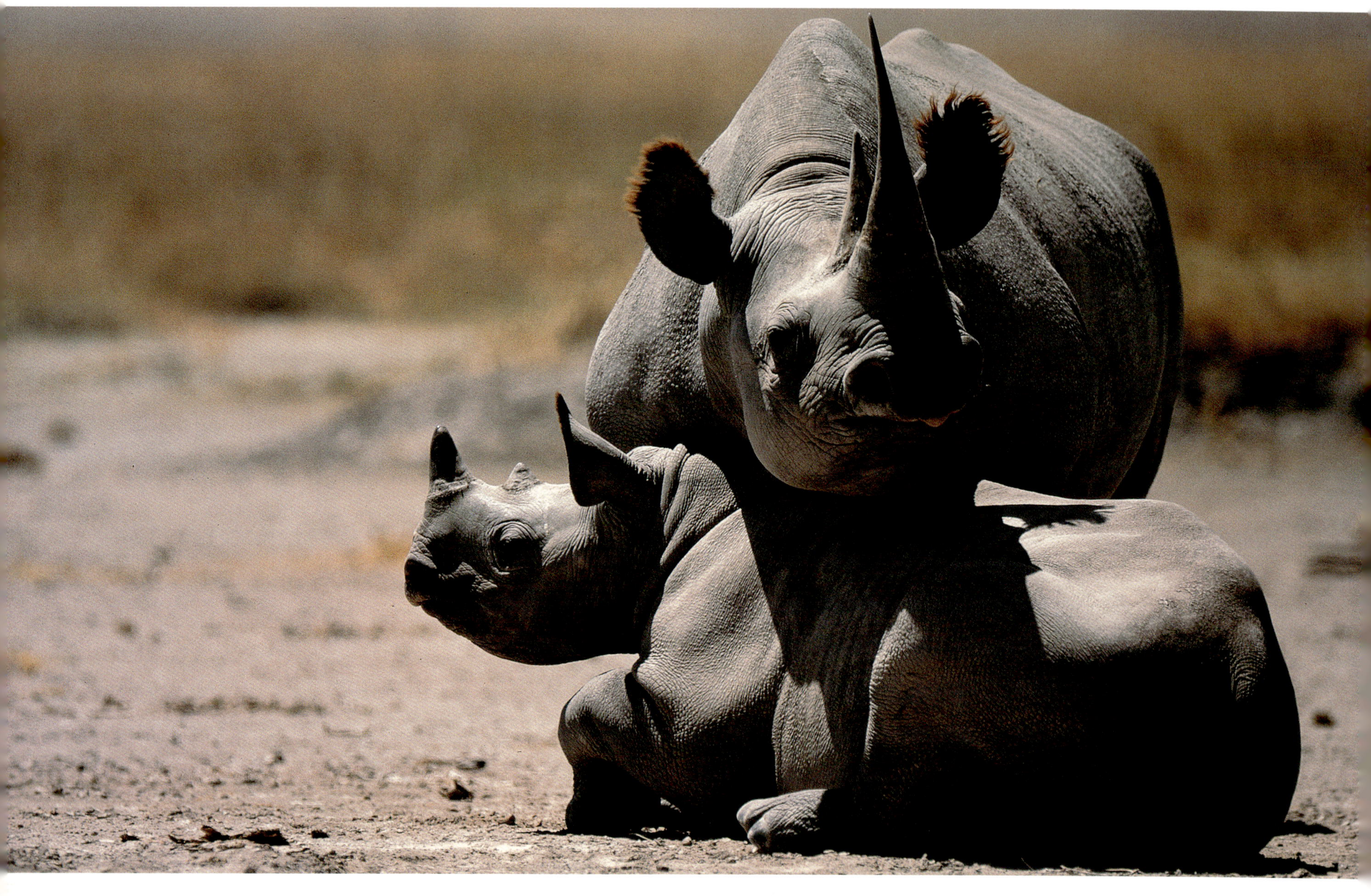

A black rhino mother rests her head on the back of her baby. The pointed mouth of this rhino species is adapted for browsing on the leaves of shrubs and bushes.

Opposite
The mouth of this white rhino is squarish, which is an adaptation for grazing on grass.

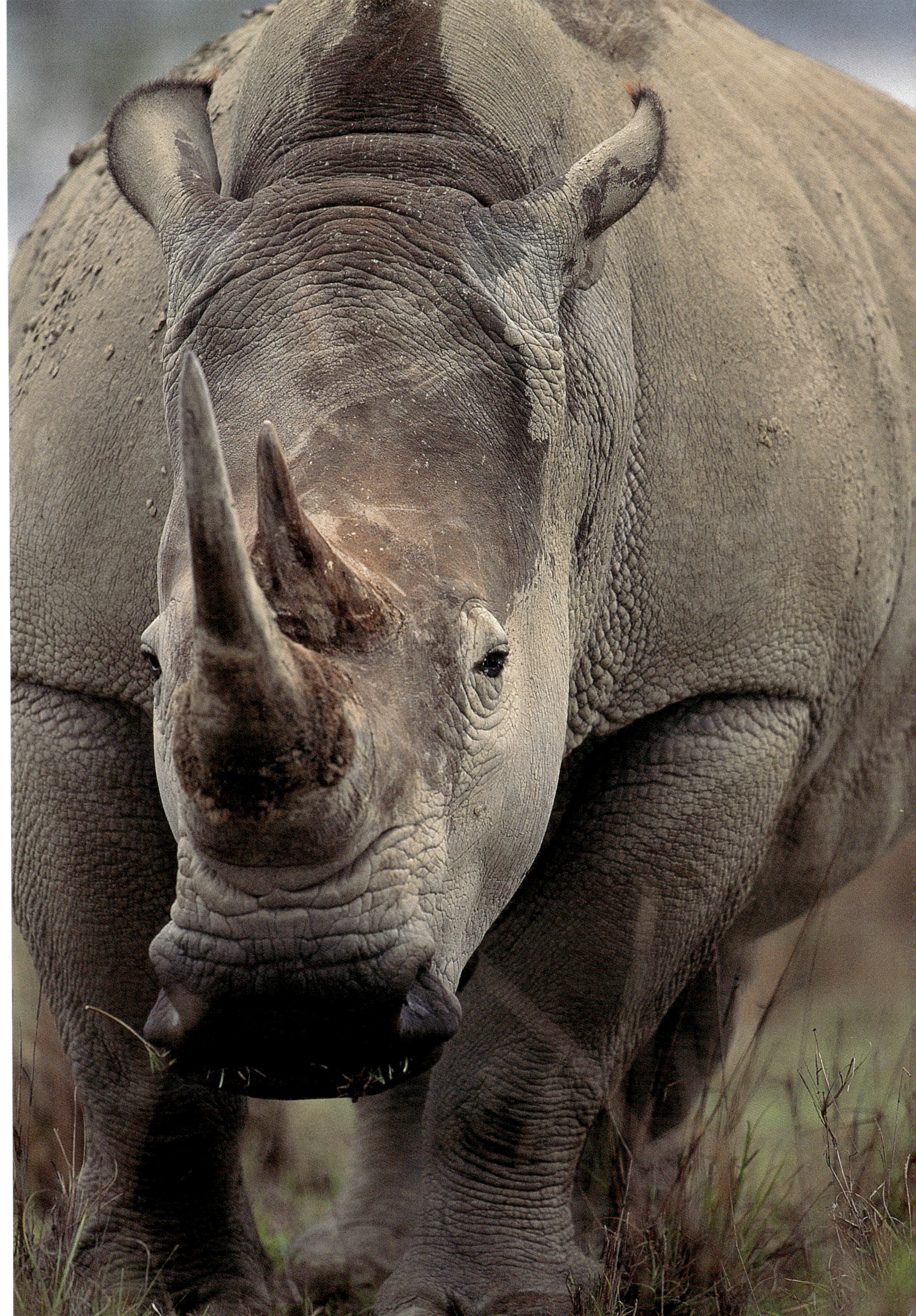

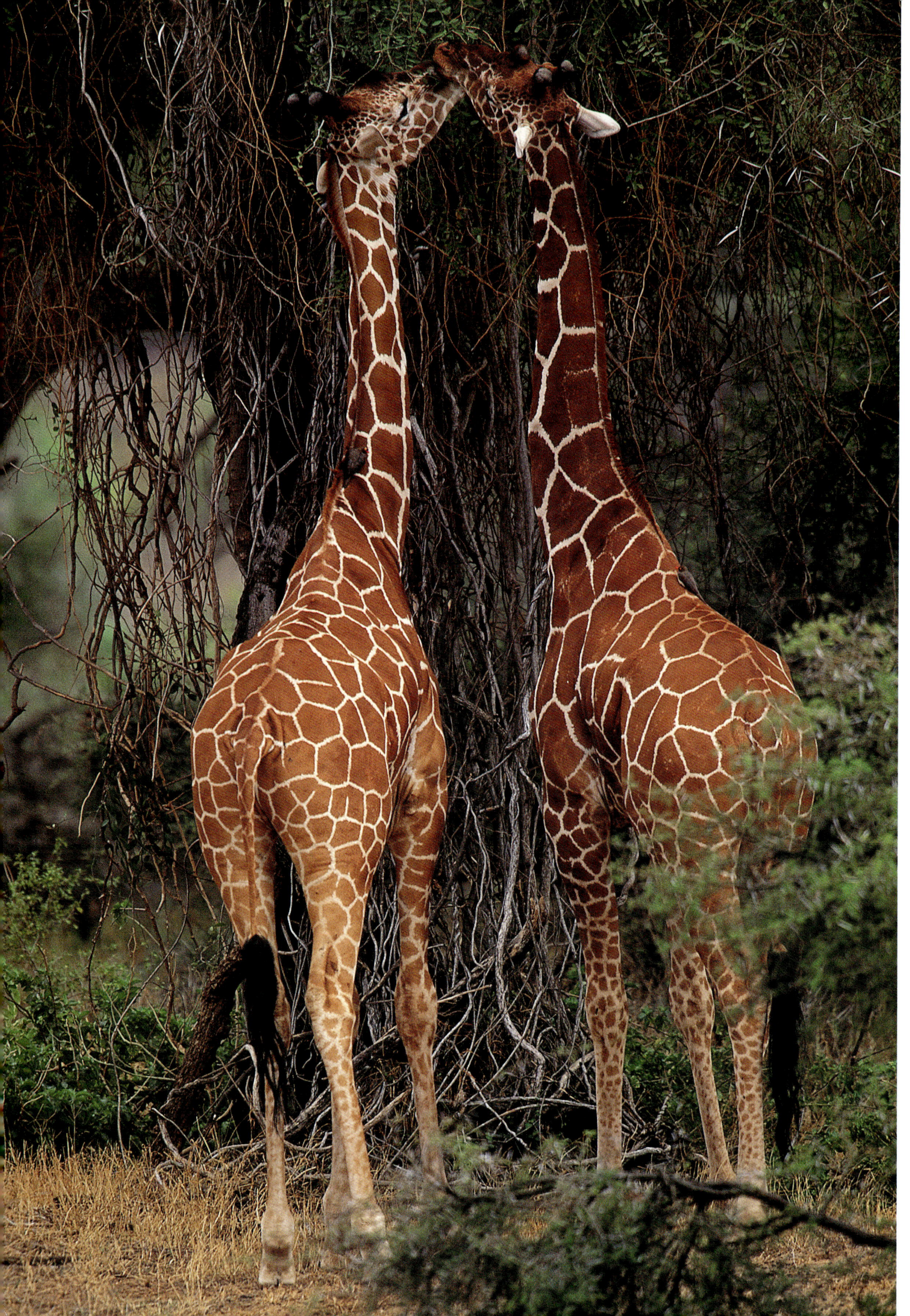

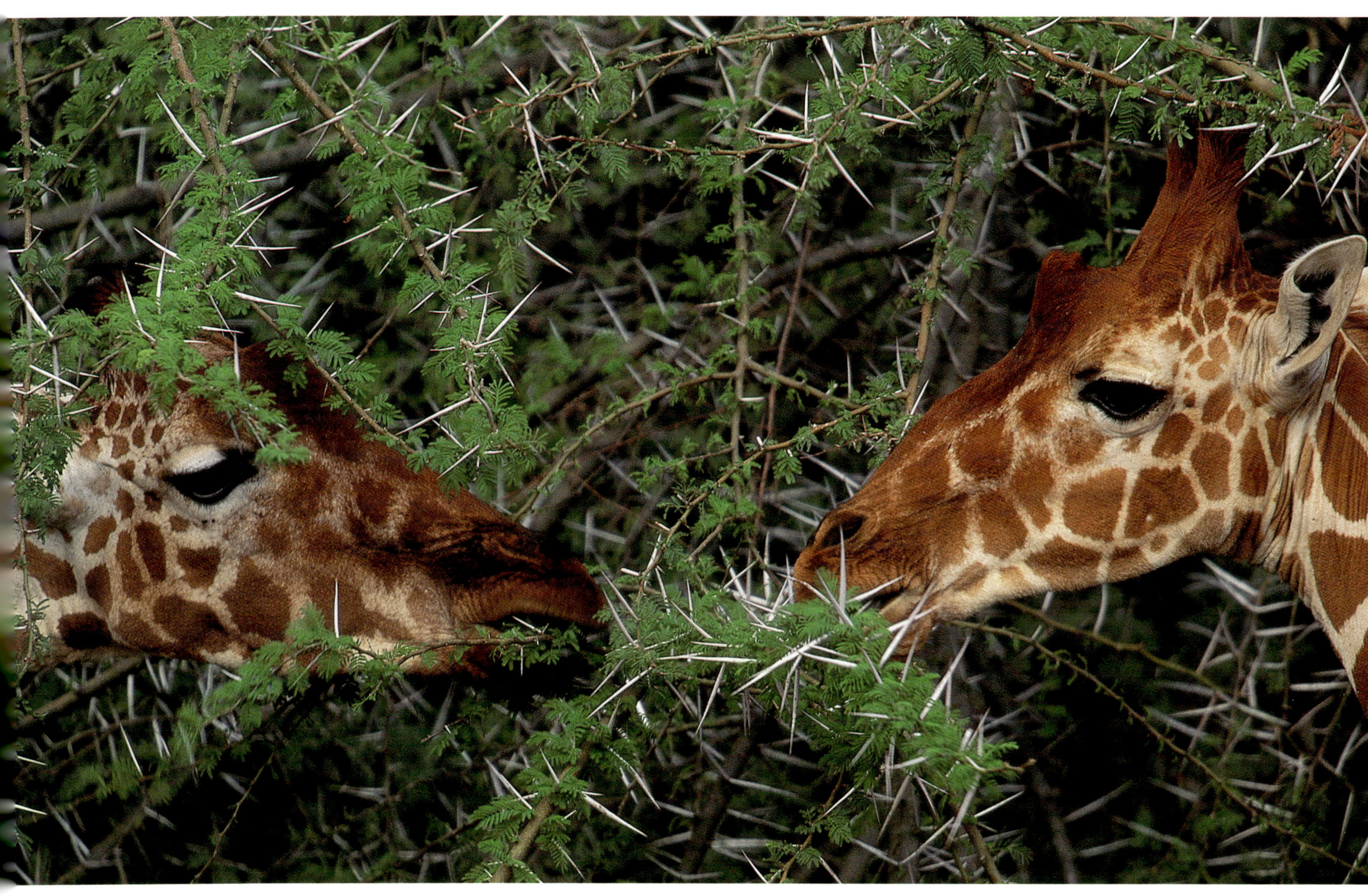

Undeterred by the thorns of an acacia tree, reticulated giraffes, with their narrow muzzles and long flicking tongues, can easily get at the lush, hard-to-reach leaves.

Opposite
Evolution has solved a number of problems for the giraffe through elongation. One of those problems is competition for food – its long neck and legs lift it into a food niche that no other species can reach.

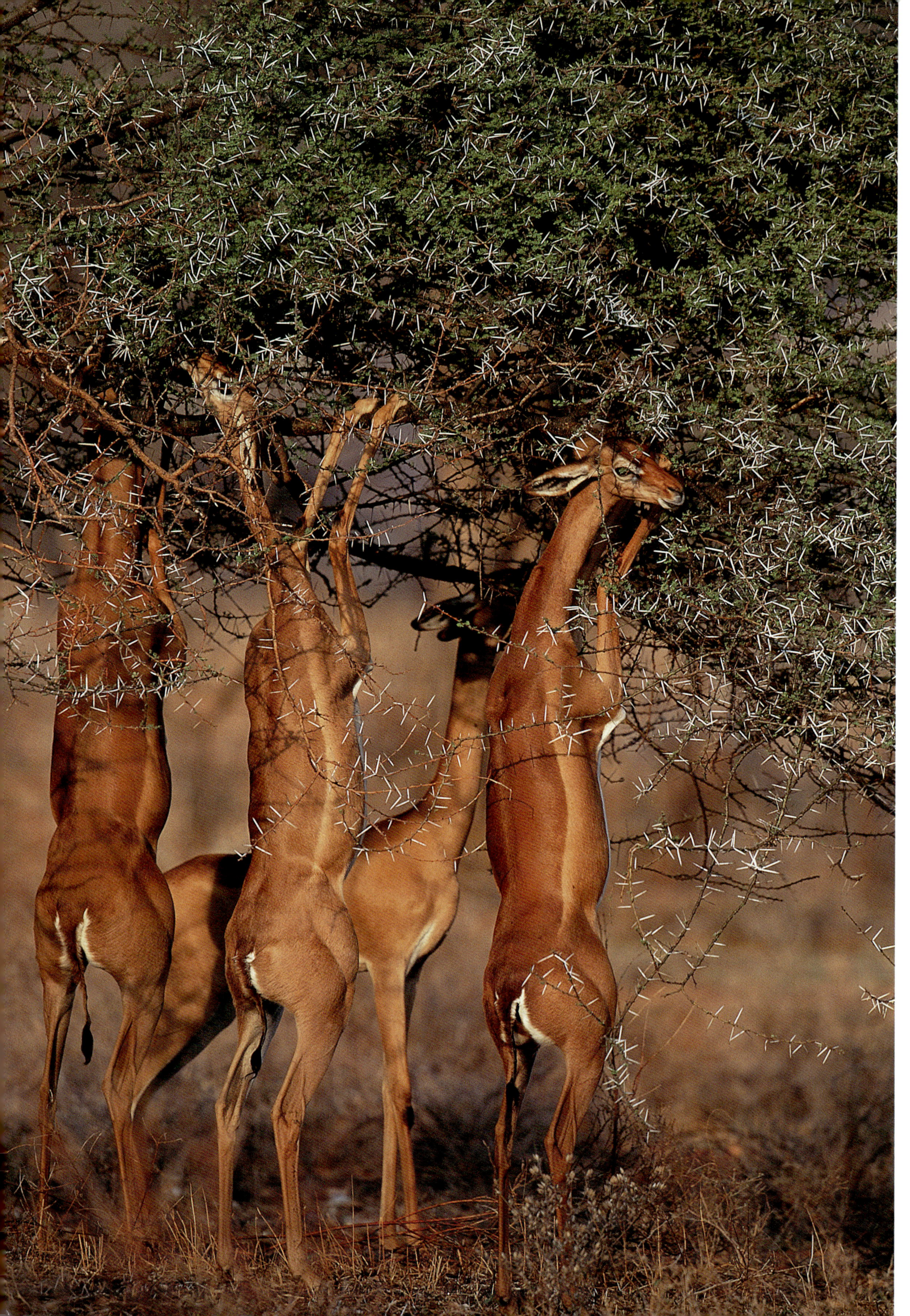

Opposite
Gerenuks feed on leaves high up on thorn trees by balancing on their hind legs. The gerenuk inhabits arid savannah where it gets all the water it needs by feeding on the juiciest leaves of a wide range of plants.

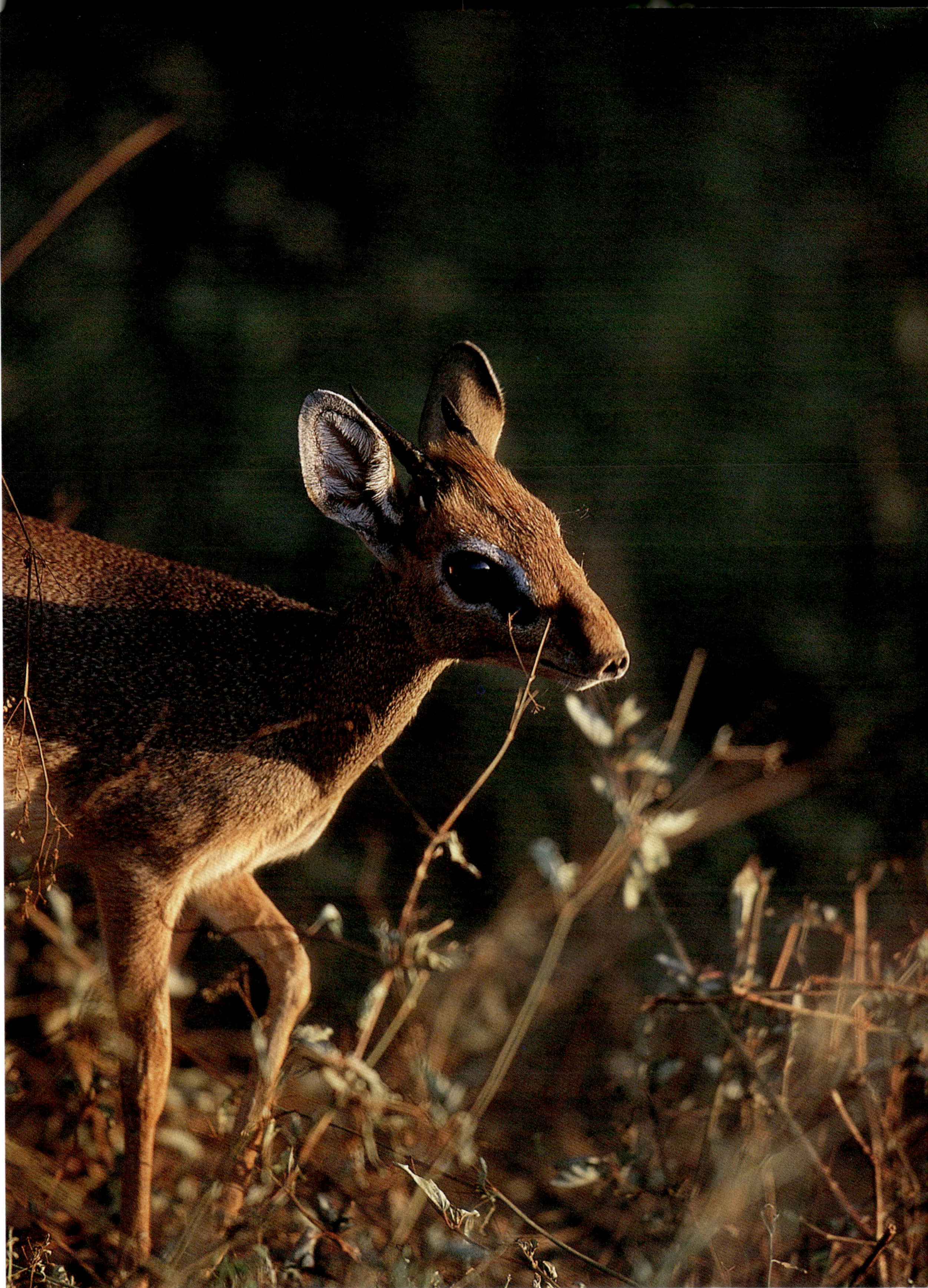

Smaller in size than gerenuks but sharing the same habitat, dikdiks in the scrubland savannah browse on vegetation that grows closer to the ground and beneath the favorite leaves of the gerenuks.

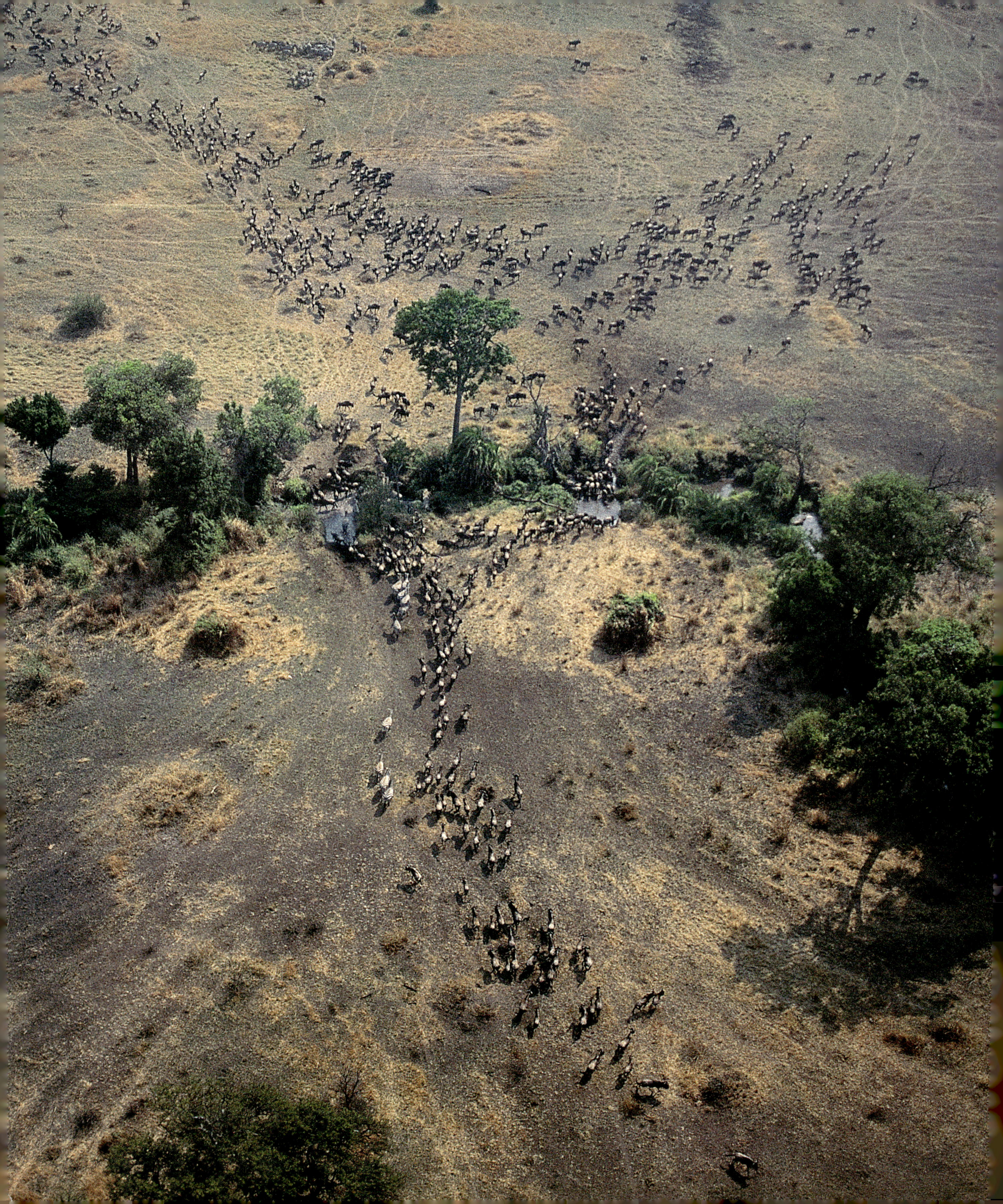

16

The Great Migration

Most grazers migrate. Although grass does not move, its availability changes over time and space. Grazers seek quality grass and migrate in the expectation of finding it elsewhere after the local supply is exhausted. So, migration is a feeding adaptation that allows grazers to exploit a habitat according to the season. Some migrate short distances, others engage in migration on a massive scale.

During the Great Migration, a million or so wildebeest cover approximately 9,600 square miles in their 300- to 500-mile round trip of the Serengeti-Mara conservation area in East Africa. Toward the end of the calendar year, in the last few weeks of the long dry season, the herds are in the northwestern woodland area of the savannah of the Serengeti. When the rains start around November-December, the herds start moving to the short-grass plains in the southeast. The grass there is rich in minerals, just right for grazing during the breeding season. Calving also takes place here in February-March, and with thousands upon thousands of newborn, the plains that once gave the illusion of vast open space into infinity, now look busy and crowded. The herds hang around until the end of May, the end of the wet season. For months the wildebeests have stayed put, but now that the grass is drying up and water is getting scarce – there is no permanent water on the short-grass plains – the herds start getting itchy feet and the migration begins. By June this area is brown and dusty, and the herds have already left for the dry season refuges. Over the long dry season, the herds are continually seeking out new pastures, moving west and north. In late June and early July, they are in wooded savannah, where there is permanent water. During this phase, rutting takes place with males competing for mating rights over groups of females. Then the herds move north to the greener Maasai Mara where permanent water is also found. The herds linger on in Maasai Mara, but by September, the journey south is well under way.

About 250,000 zebras also migrate, usually preceding the wildebeests. The zebras eat the coarser tops of the grass, exposing the juicier lower portions preferred by the wildebeest. About 400,000 Thomson's gazelles also migrate along the same route, but they do not travel the full course.

Why must the wildebeests expend such an enormous amount of energy and risk their lives on such an arduous journey? Why not some other antelope species? A short answer is that typically two species cannot occupy a single niche, and the wildebeest was the first to adapt to the migratory niche. This niche requires constant movement in the long dry season, and the body of the wildebeest is such that it can run for great lengths without using up any more energy than if it were walking. Its behavior is also adapted to save time: A calf is up and running within minutes of birth, able to keep up with its mother in a moving herd. Wildebeests even rut on the move. These and other adaptations enable them to have access to huge resources of food – no wonder there are a million of them!

Pages 226–227
This river winding through the bushland savannah of northern Serengeti is a typical obstacle to migrating wildebeests.

It is difficult to imagine the life of a wildebeest on the move, but chances are the journey is difficult and hazardous, especially in a very dry year when the progress of the herds is relentless in its search for food and water among the diminishing pastures and shrinking water supplies. There is the stinging dry wind and the chilling rain, the unbearable midday heat and cold nights, the inhospitable thorn trees, and the ever-present flies. The desperate desire to slake their thirst in the river must be tempered by the knowledge that the river may be infested with crocodiles. The grass near the bushes is inviting, but lions may be lurking behind them. And wildebeest mothers must care for and protect their highly dependent babies. Separation can occur when the herd stampedes or crosses a river in a frenzy – it is a poignant sight to see a cow and her calf galloping to and fro, grunting and bleating, trying to locate one another. In the frenetic, hectic pace of the migrating herd, however, the chances of being reunited are slim. Then there is the long trek itself in which there are rivers to ford, hills to scale, plains with waist-high grass to traverse. The amazing thing in all this is that nothing stops the wildebeests in their powerful urge to migrate. No river is too wide or deep, no plain too broad – they do what's got to be done to survive and reproduce.

When thousands of wildebeests gather in a herd, there is great potential for confusion. Yet the herd appears to move in effortless synchrony. To achieve this, each individual in the herd pays attention to local information, such as the action of its immediate neighbors, and follows simple rules. Thus, when moving from one place to another the rule is "follow your neighbor," and a long line of wildebeests results. When the herd is running away from suspected danger the rules are "don't bump into your neighbor, match your neighbor's speed, and keep close together." The result is a herd, twisting and turning, in unison. Thus, the outcome is global behavior that is neither random nor chaotic. On the contrary, it is intelligent, well-suited to the environment, and even poetic.

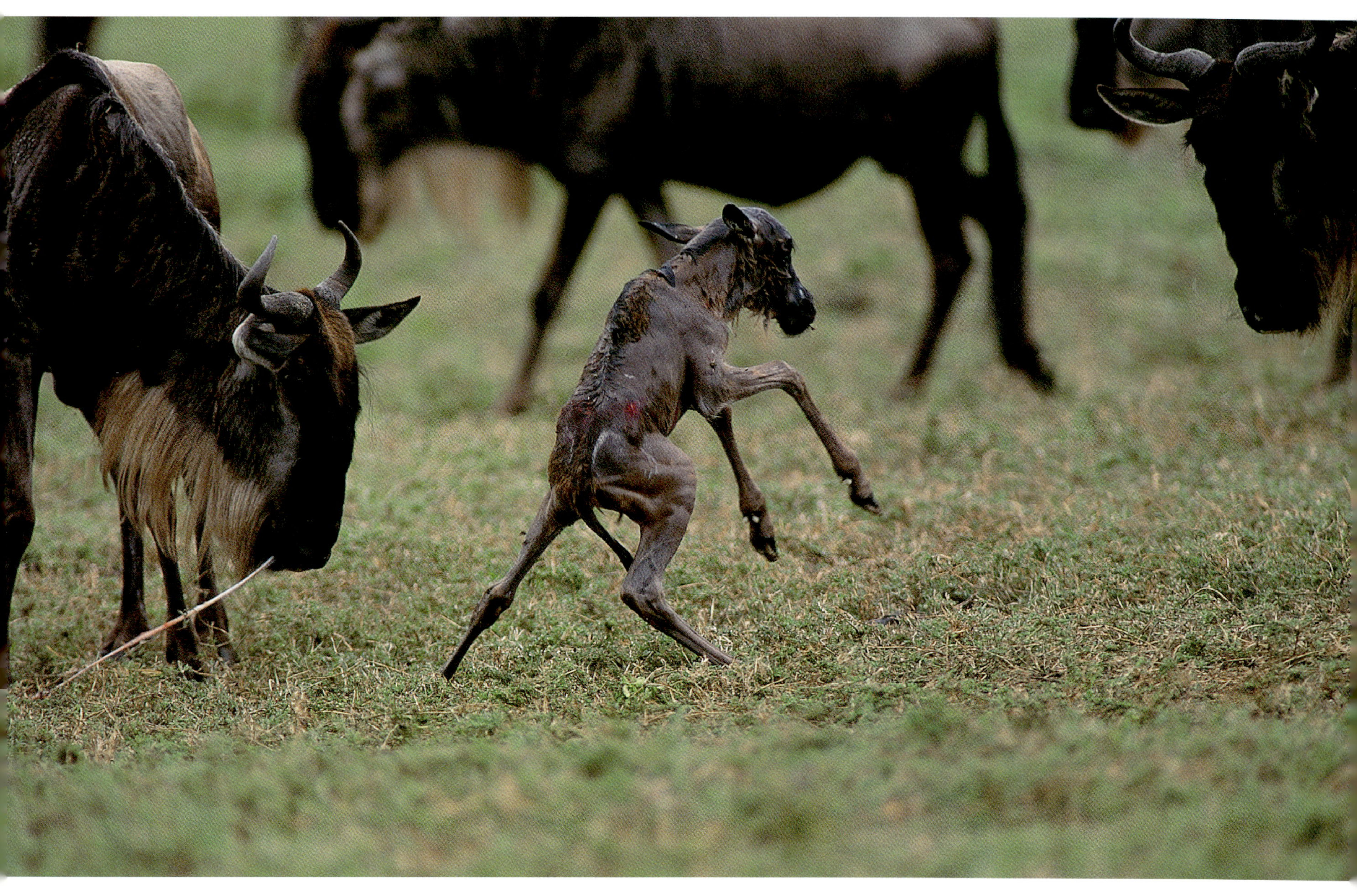

A wildebeest calf, only a few minutes after birth, takes its first steps in life. The calf managed to walk on its third attempt, then staggered over to mother, at left, to suckle.

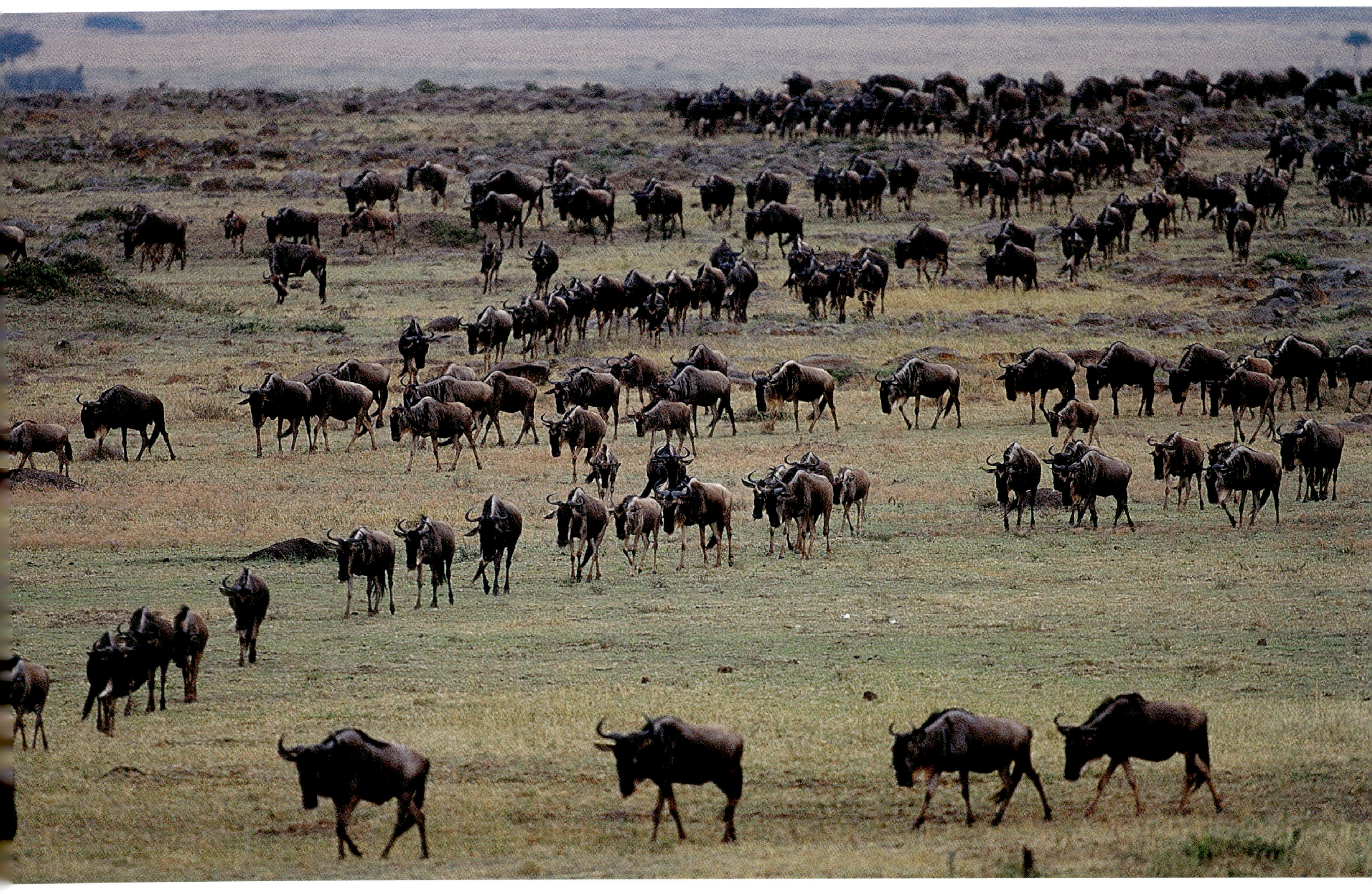

From beyond the horizon, thousands of wildebeests approach in long lines, beating paths to greener pastures.

Pages 232–233
Male wildebeests invest a good deal of energy into ritual fighting to establish a hierarchy for mating access, to maintain a territory, and to corner females in heat.

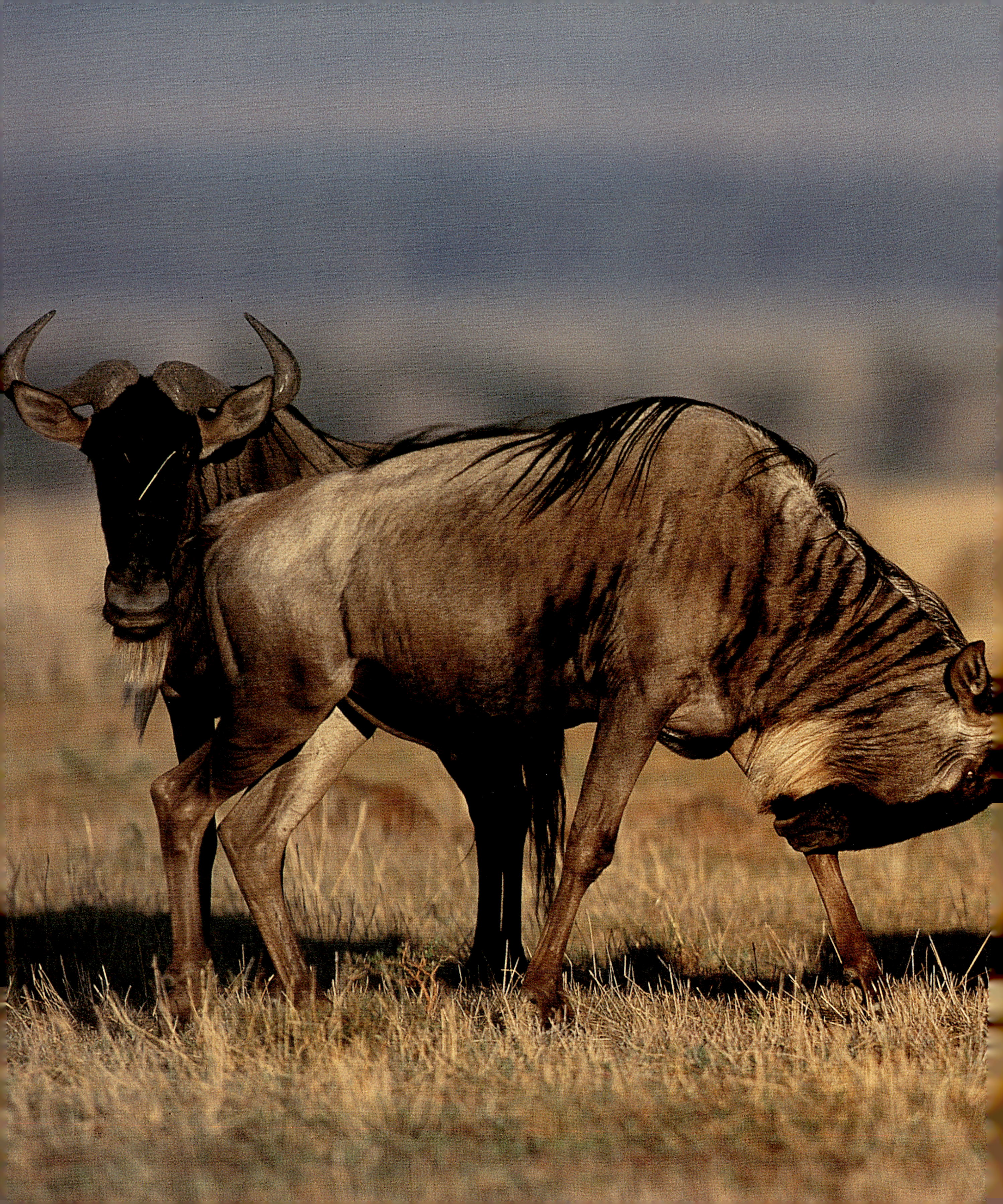

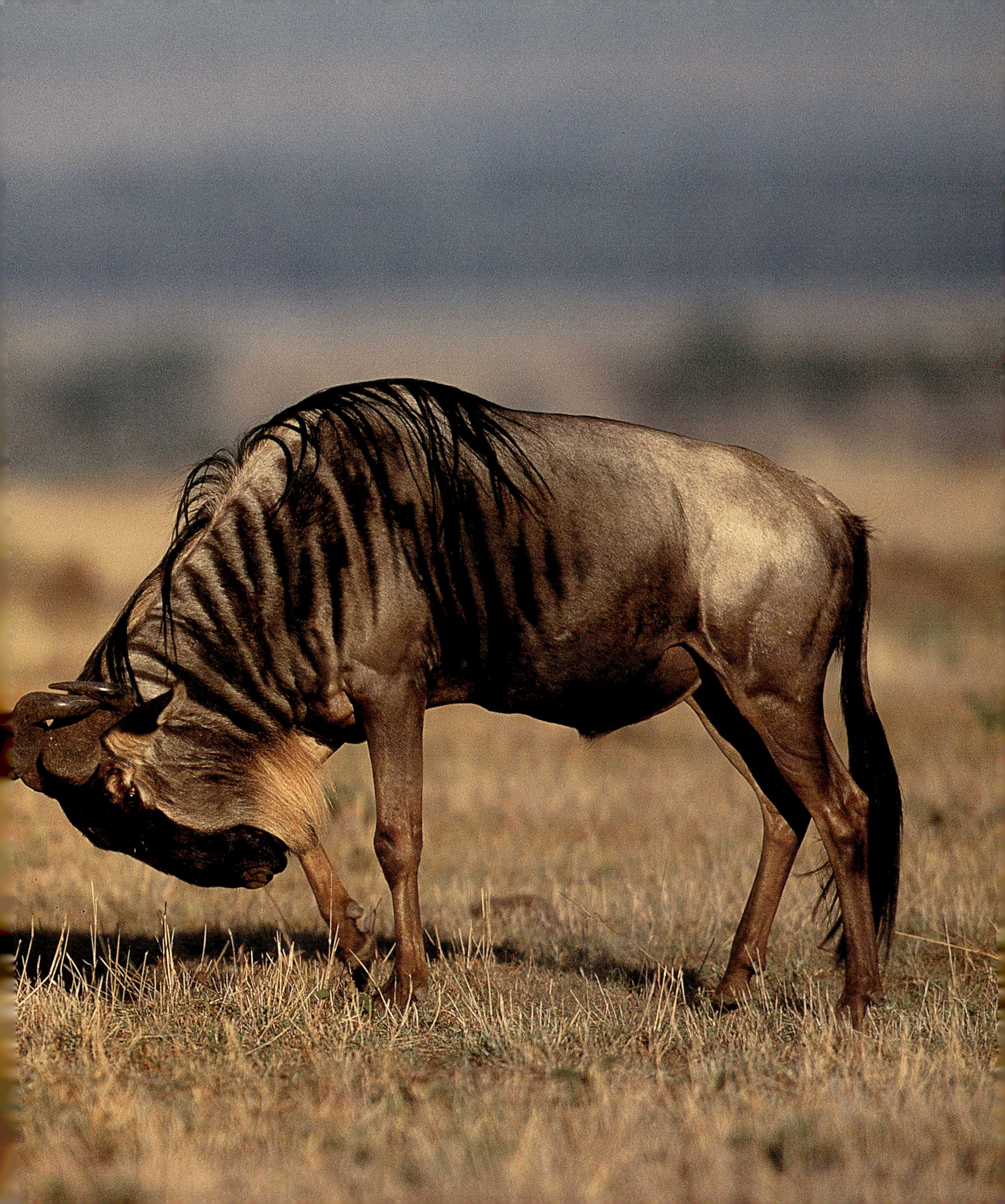

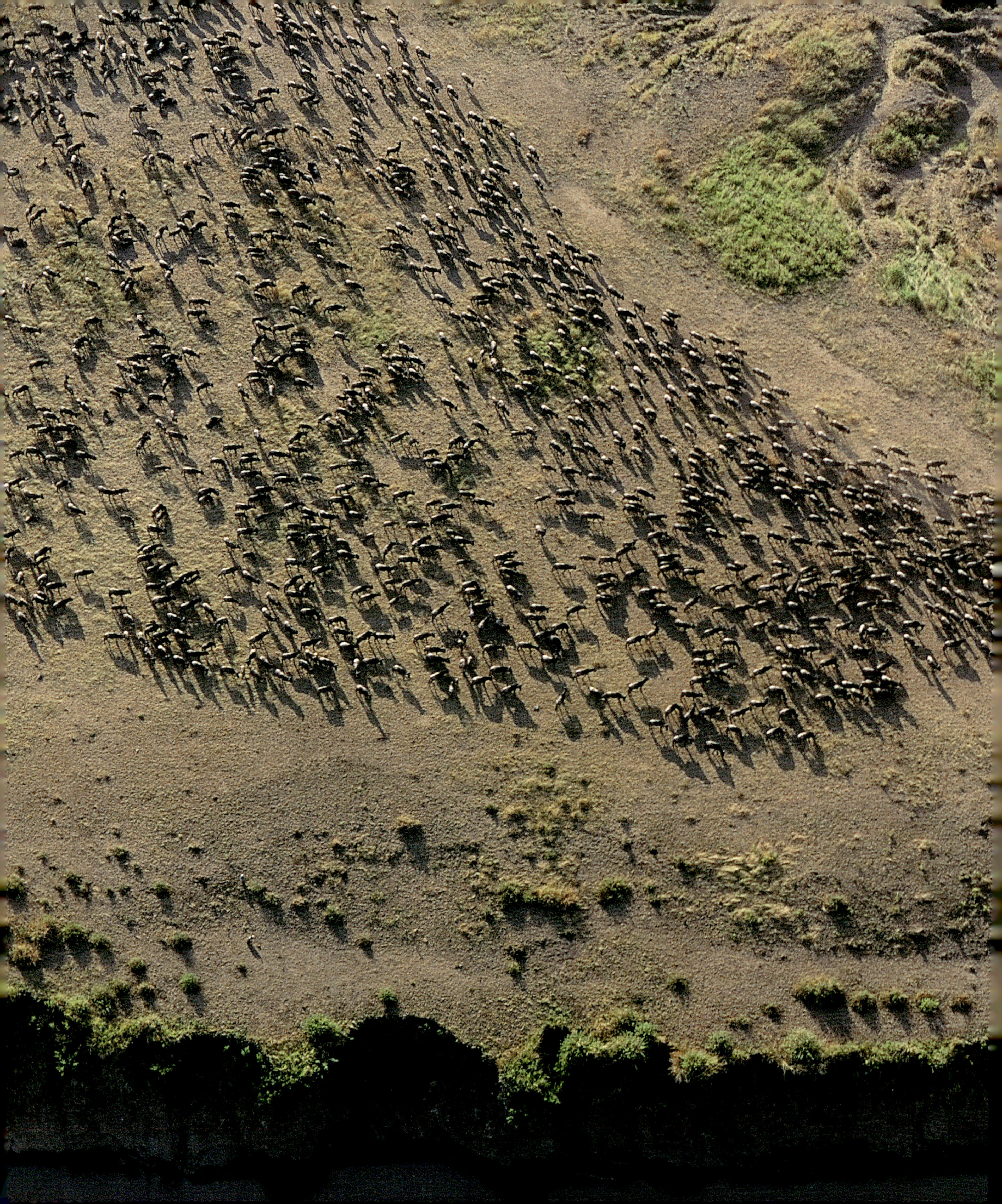

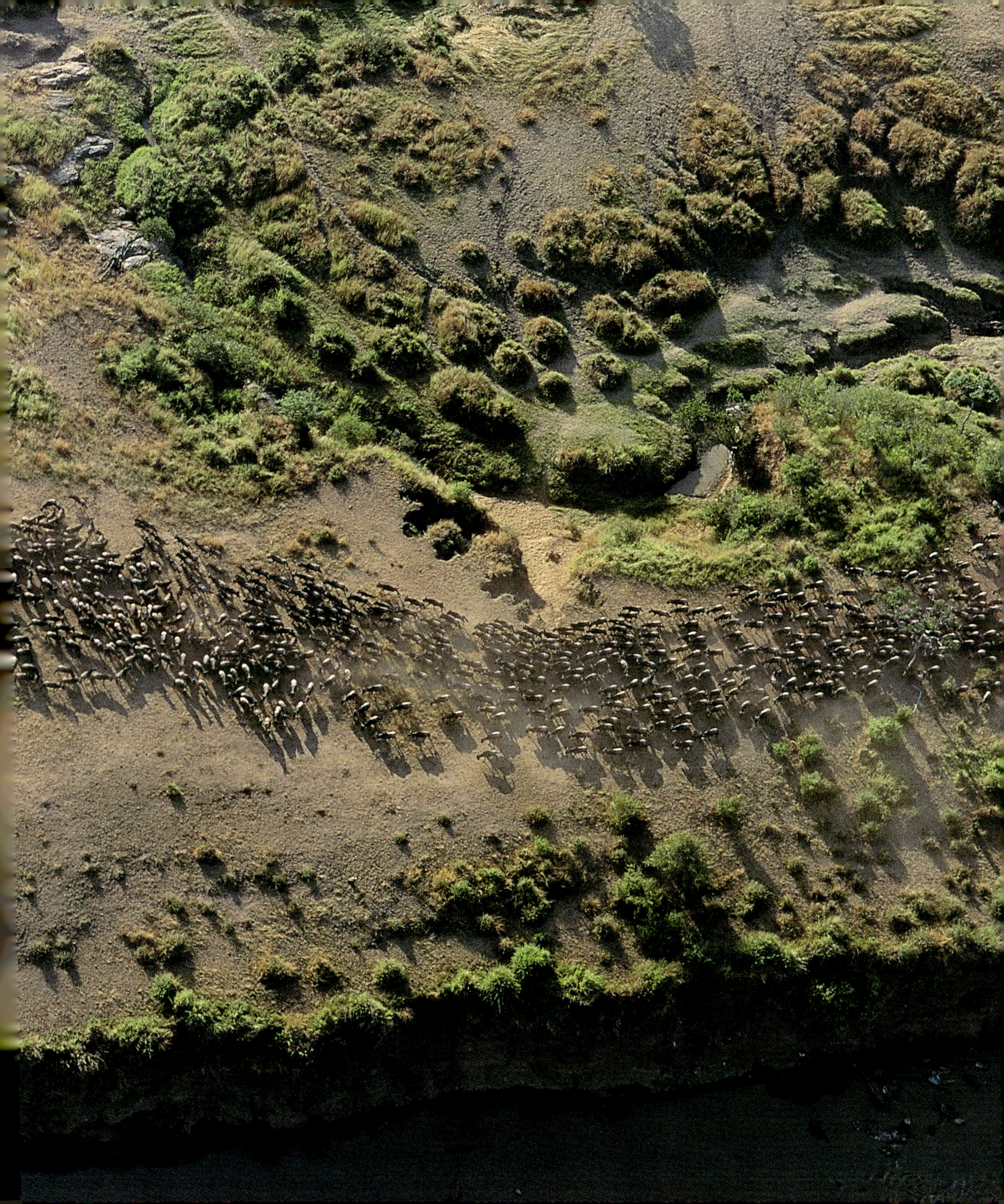

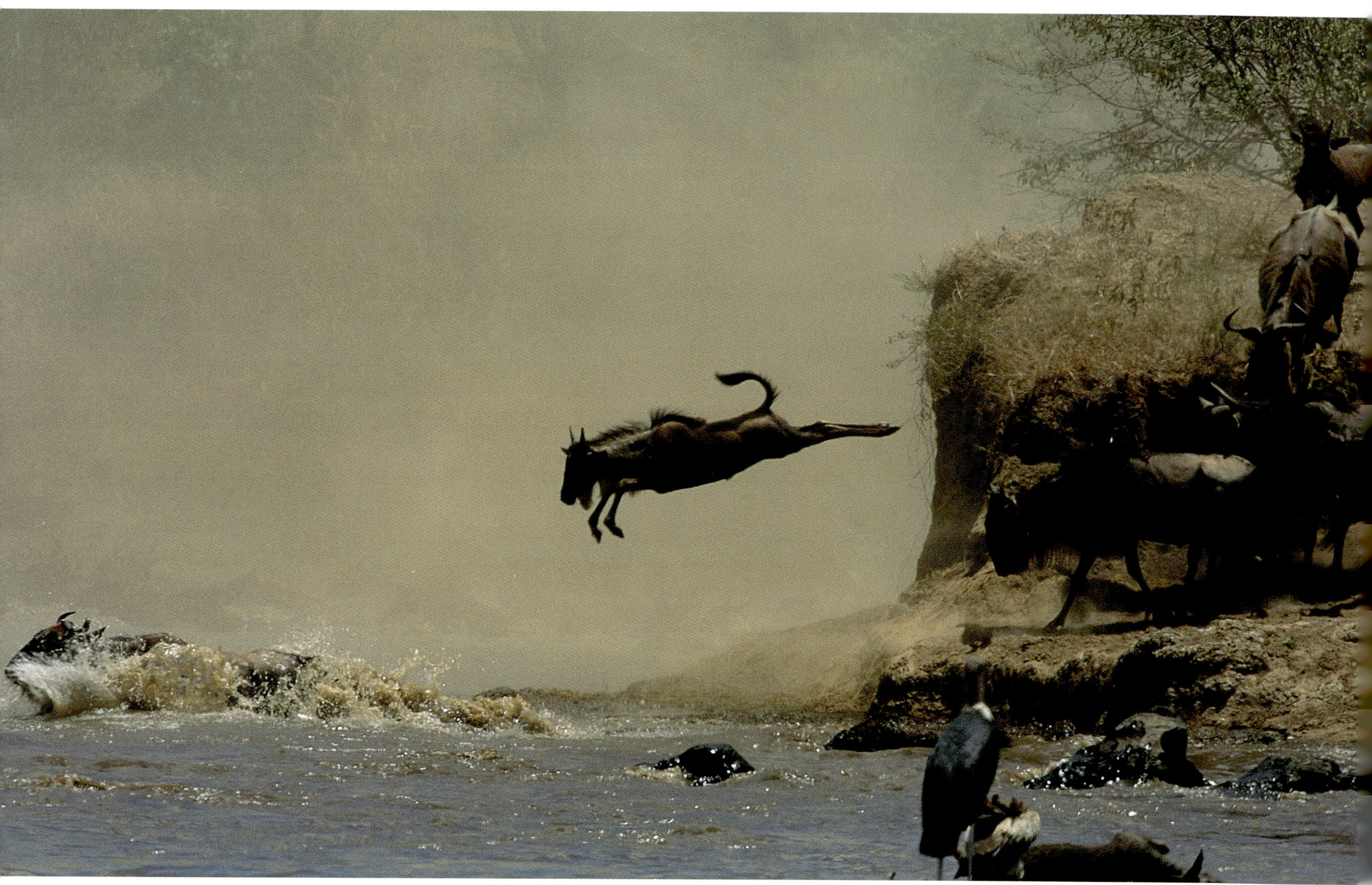

Sometimes, as the wildebeests cross the Mara River, they leap into the river one after the other, and desperately struggle through the fast-flowing waters as if terrified of some lurking danger. The instinct is right, for, in fact, there are dangers beneath the water's surface. Notice here how, despite its haste, the calf's hind legs are stretched and the fore legs folded – here is a born athlete.

Pages 234–235
A herd of wildebeests makes a run for the mighty Mara River. Seen from the air, the migrating beasts resemble the marching safari ants that emerge in their millions during the rainy season.

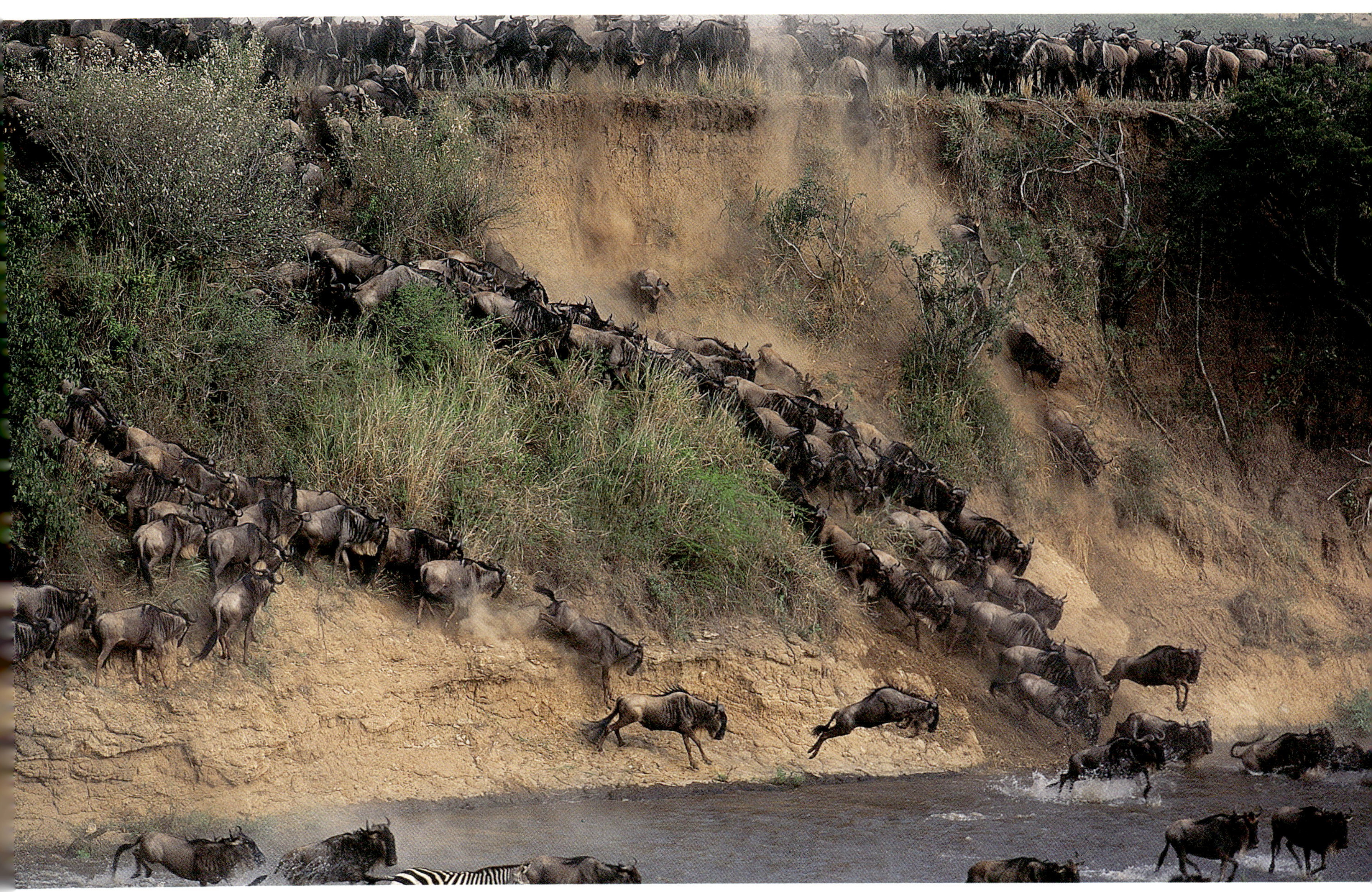

Once the crossing has begun, it quickly gains momentum. Wildebeest after wildebeest pours down the steep bank and into the river.

Pages 238–239
It's almost impossible to stop the tidal wave of wildebeests once it's begun. When those in the front along the water's edge are unwilling to enter, and the jostling from behind becomes too intense, a few are bound to get shoved in before they're ready. But the animals will often spread out along the bank and cross the river as a broad front.

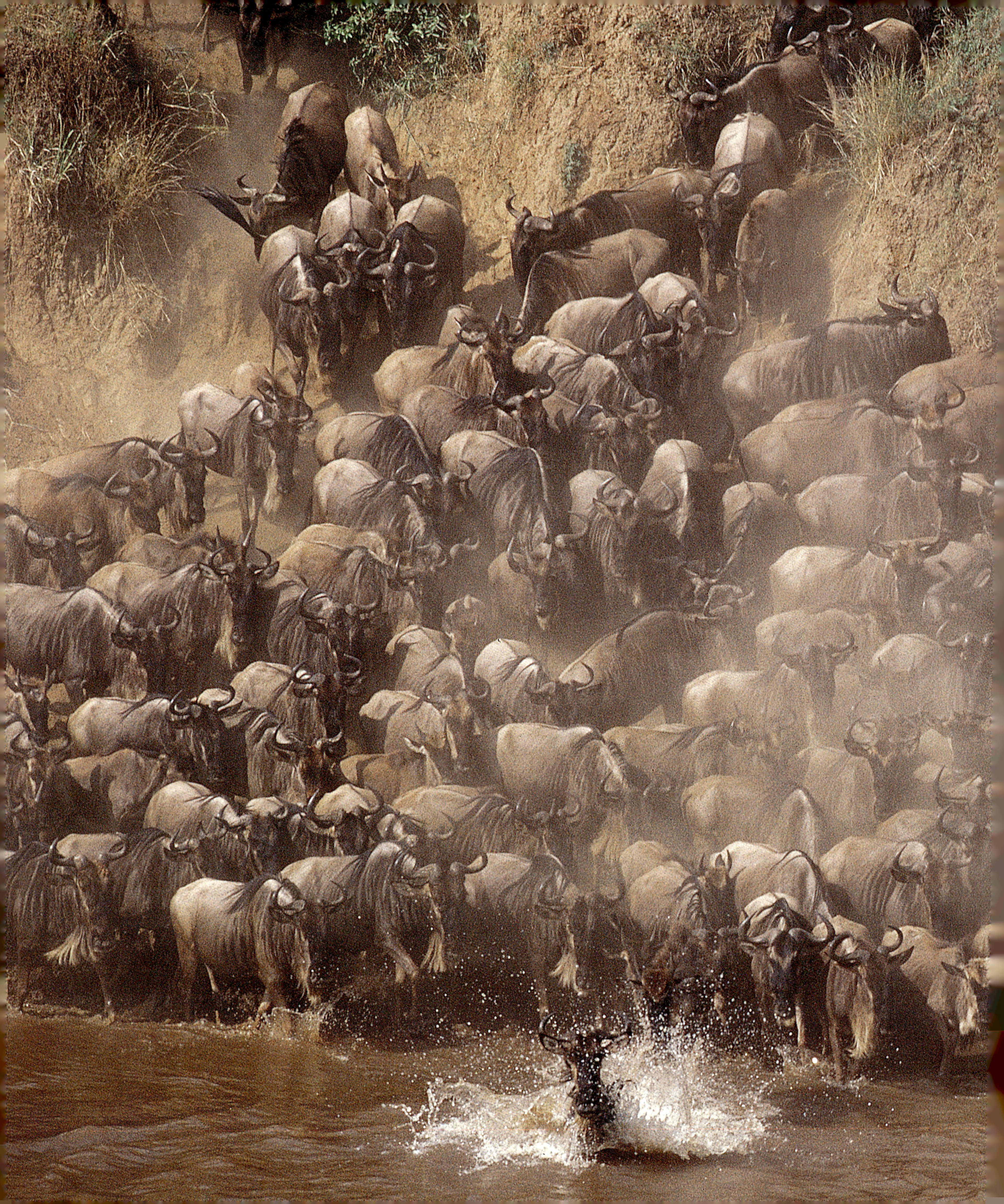

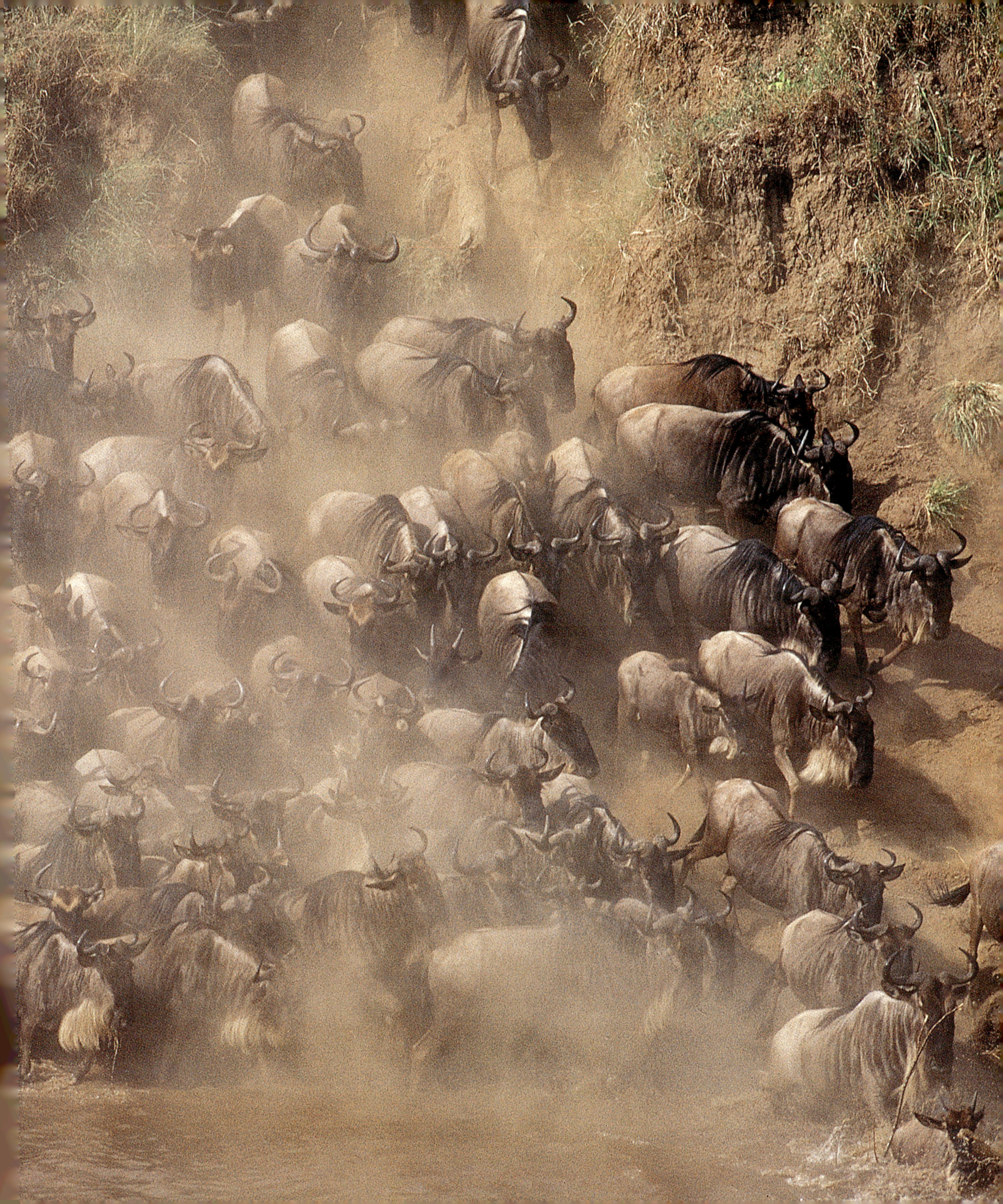

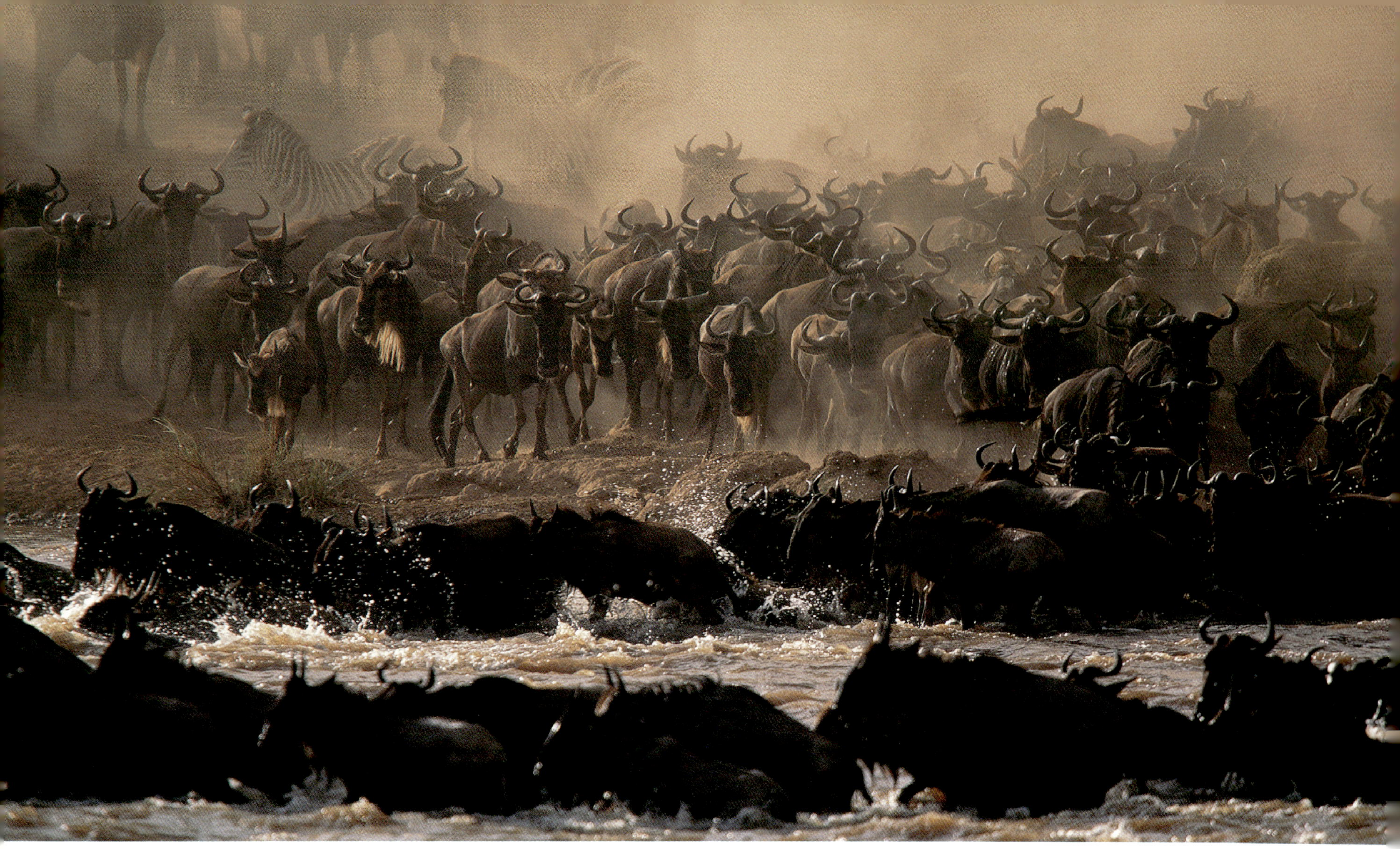

The sheer numbers of animals, both zebras and wildebeests, had built up throughout the day, and by evening the pressure of the bottleneck at the river's edge had become too much. But there is safety in numbers: crocodiles shy away from confusion caused by a large number of crossing animals.

Opposite
Wildebeests have found a hippo trail and try to climb up the steep embankment. Such trails are established by hippos who leave the rivers under the cover and safety of night to graze.

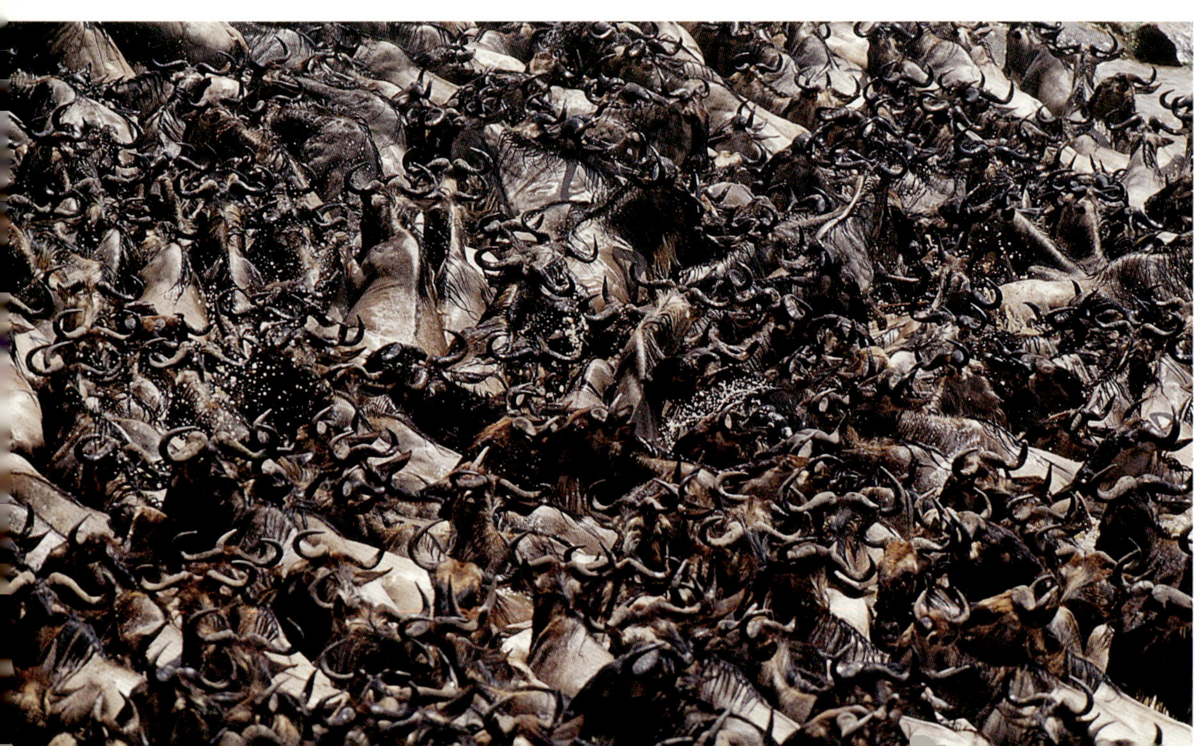

Left
These crossing wildebeests have chosen a narrow exit point so a bottleneck has formed. In a state of panic, they try to climb over each other to get out of the river. To compound their difficulties, the leading wildebeests' hooves have turned the bank into a slippery paste, with no firm hold.

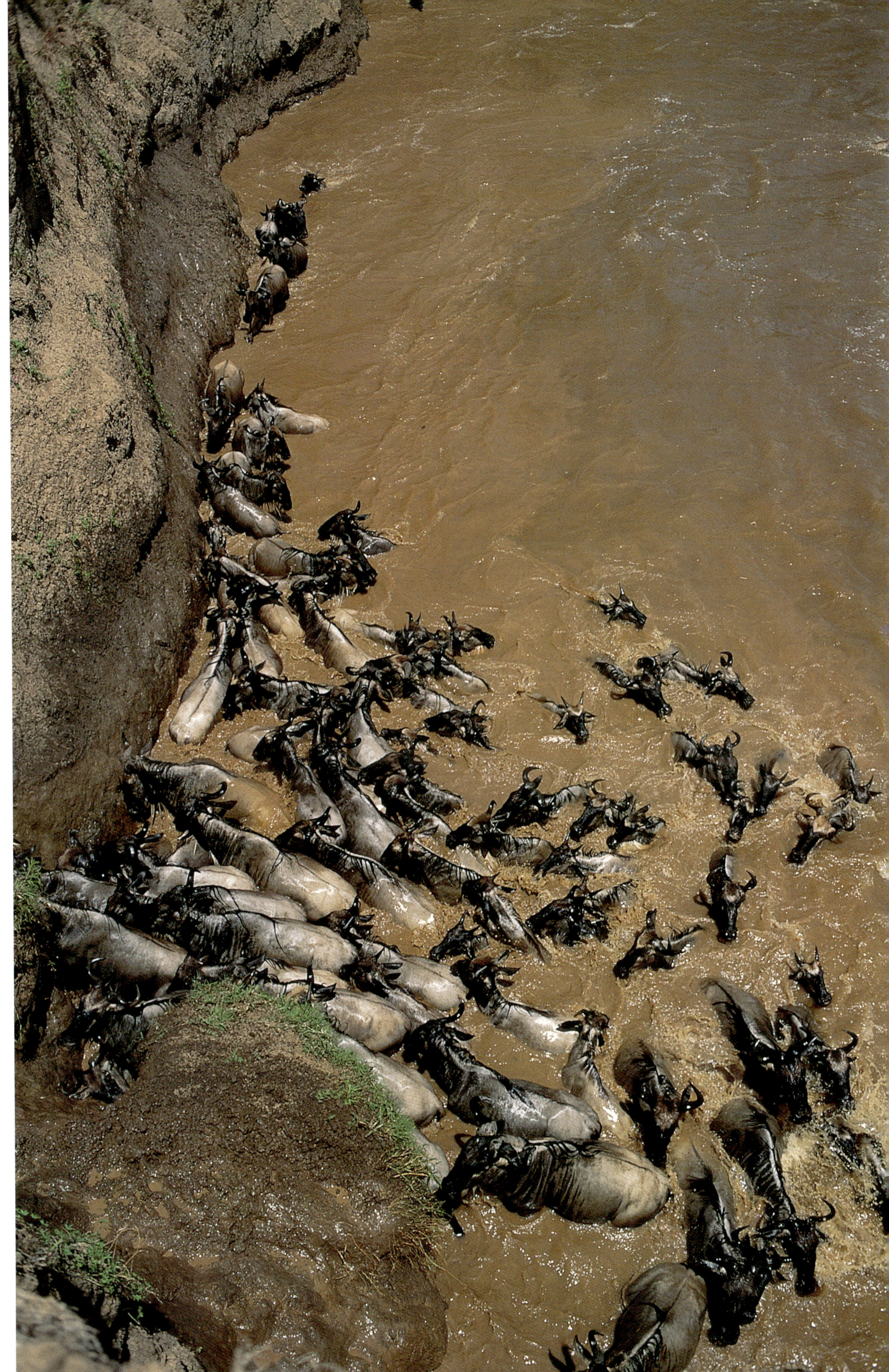

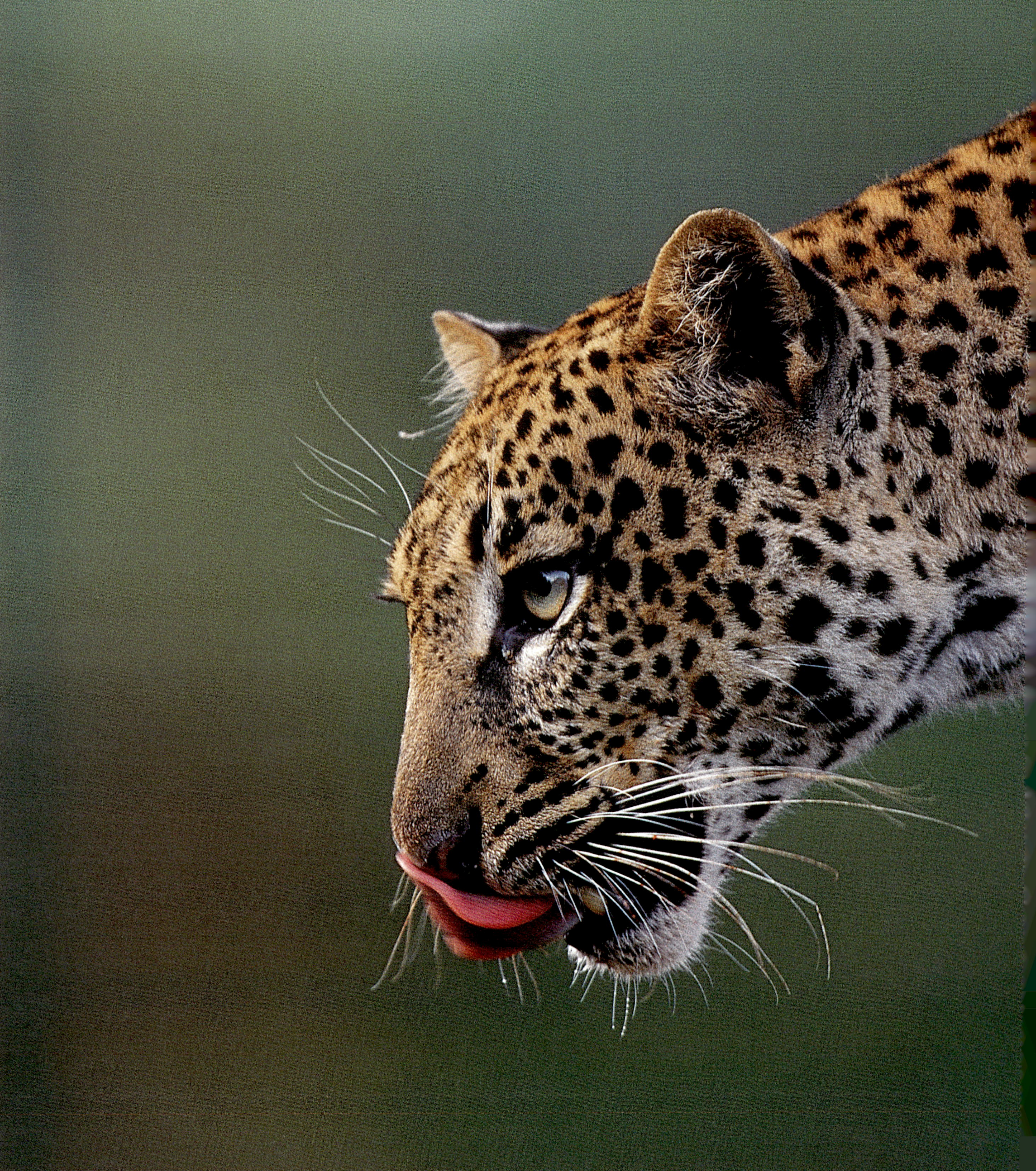

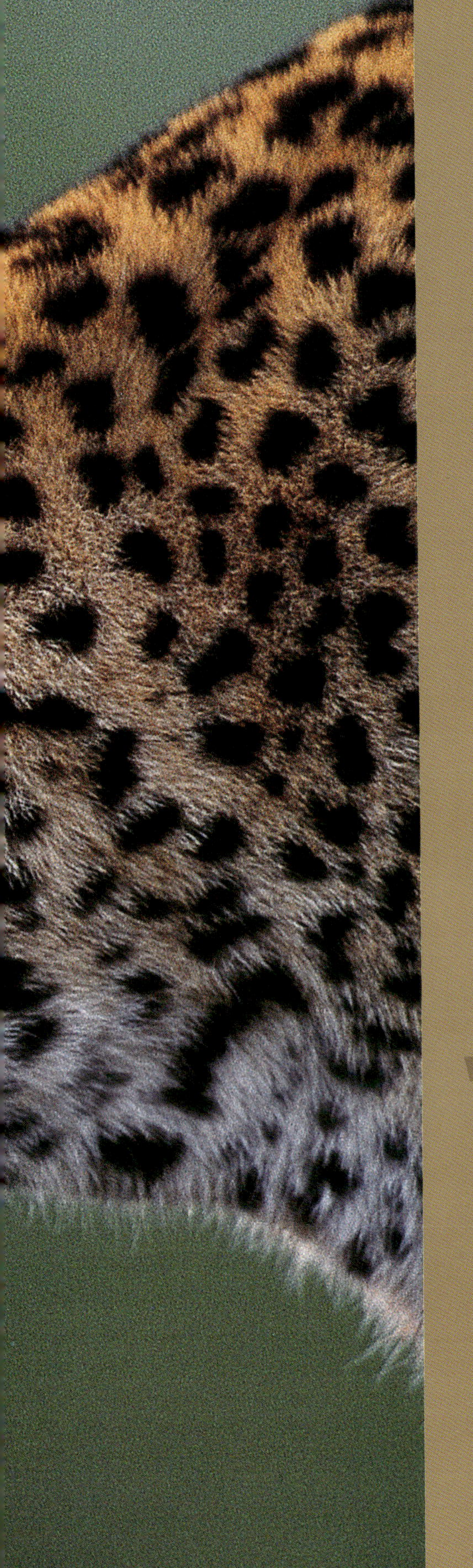

17 Escaping Predators

Herbivores face the difficult problem of survival in the unpredictable savannah. The food supply can be unreliable in availability and variable in quality. Diseases can break out. Predators can strike at any moment. Fortunately, herbivores have instincts finely tuned to their uncertain environment, serving as the first screen of all the information their acute senses absorb. Those that possess keener instincts escape the predators and are more successful at survival.

The more successful herbivores tend not to be big risk-takers. They are cautious and their descendants are likely to inherit genes that encourage caution. However, when circumstances force risk-taking, especially when they are protecting their young, herbivores will fight furiously. Zebras have been known to injure lions that are moments away from pouncing on them, and wildebeest bulls have been observed turning to face lions head on, trying to butt them with their horns in a desperate attempt at self-defense. Enraged warthogs have even been seen chasing cheetahs. The fearless warthog, if it survives, is more likely to pass on the genes that encode such determination than more passive animals.

The open plains present very few hiding places, so when taken by surprise, running is the usual method of escape for most herbivores. This method is made more effective by certain unique adaptations. For example, a Thomson's gazelle, when chased by a cheetah, will run in a zigzag pattern. This not only throws the less agile cheetah off balance, but also enables the gazelle to increase its peripheral vision so that it can see directly behind itself. Another technique is used by zebras when attacked by a lion: The zebras sometimes will take off in all directions. It is likely their stripe patterns add to the confused picture, making it difficult for the lion to focus on a single individual. Impalas carry out a similar maneuver, making prodigious leaps into the air to escape from an attacking leopard.

One of the major hazards faced by a herbivore is its need for water. In the rivers there are crocodiles, and predators often lie in wait near sources of water. No wonder herbivores, except for elephants, approach water with such caution and trepidation. As a few of the braver animals venture nearer the water's edge, the rest will stand and watch, ready to bound away at the slightest sign of danger, real or imagined. With eyes, ears, and nostrils all on red alert, others will approach when sufficiently assured that it is safe, and still others will anxiously keep watch as they wait their turn.

Animals are also alert when feeding: Not all the gazelles in a grazing group have their heads down at the same time, and when zebras take time to rest out on the plains, one zebra may lean its neck on another so that the combined field of view covers 360 degrees. Giraffes and ostriches have an advantage in spotting danger because of their height: When they interrupt their feeding to stare at something, the rest of the herbivore community pays attention.

Pages 242–243
From the vantage point of a tall tree, a leopard watches a browsing herd of impala. As long as the leopard remains in the tree, it has the advantage of surprise.

With all these watchful herbivores primed to leap out of harm's way at a moment's notice, the element of surprise is critical for a successful catch. Once, out in the savannah, when my car refused to move, I had to walk for help. I wasn't trying to hide, so all the grazing animals saw me and kept moving away as I approached. I realized that a predator hunting singly would be hard-pressed to catch an alert adult animal. There are rare exceptions, as when African hunting dogs hunt in packs using a relay technique in which one rested dog picks up where another tired one leaves off as they wear the targeted animal down to exhaustion.

Once a predator has been sighted, it is often "escorted out." When Thomson's gazelles spot a cheetah on the prowl, they will snort with alarm, hold their heads stiffly up, and twitch their striped flanks. Then they will move en masse closer to the cheetah, gradually attracting more and more gazelles from the neighborhood. The staring, twitching mob might move quite close to the cat, but it will always maintain the crucial flight distance. In this manner, they will escort the danger out of the neighborhood, having spoilt any chance it might have had of catching an unwary gazelle. It is not uncommon to see a pride of lions resting with herds of game wandering close by; lions have learnt not to waste precious calories in the hopeless pursuit of game that is aware of their presence.

However, herbivores are vulnerable during the reproductive season. Mothers in late pregnancy are less speedy, and the newborns are easy prey. Yet there are examples of reproductive strategies to counteract these predator pressures. The best-known instance is the short duration of the calving season of wildebeests as well as the speed with which their calves become mobile after birth. Wildebeest calves can walk within seven minutes of birth, and many other newborn antelopes, including the eland, which is the largest antelope, can do so within an hour.

Since wildebeest calves can follow and keep up with their mothers within minutes of birth, they are known as followers. Many antelope species, such as waterbucks, are called hiders, because soon after birth the mother leaves the newborn hidden and lying motionless in the vegetation. She will feed some distance away from where the baby lies and will visit it periodically to suckle, but she is careful not to suckle the baby when predators are near, for that would reveal its location. Predators, of course, look for signs of hidden babies. Cheetahs will studiously scrutinize a gazelle group from a distance, looking for clues to hidden fawns, and will often crisscross an area looking for fawns in the brush.

The healthy adult savannah herbivore probably lives with less fear of being killed than we suppose because it is surprisingly well-equipped with the tools it needs to protect itself. It is the very young, the very old, and the disabled that are usually targeted by the big predators.

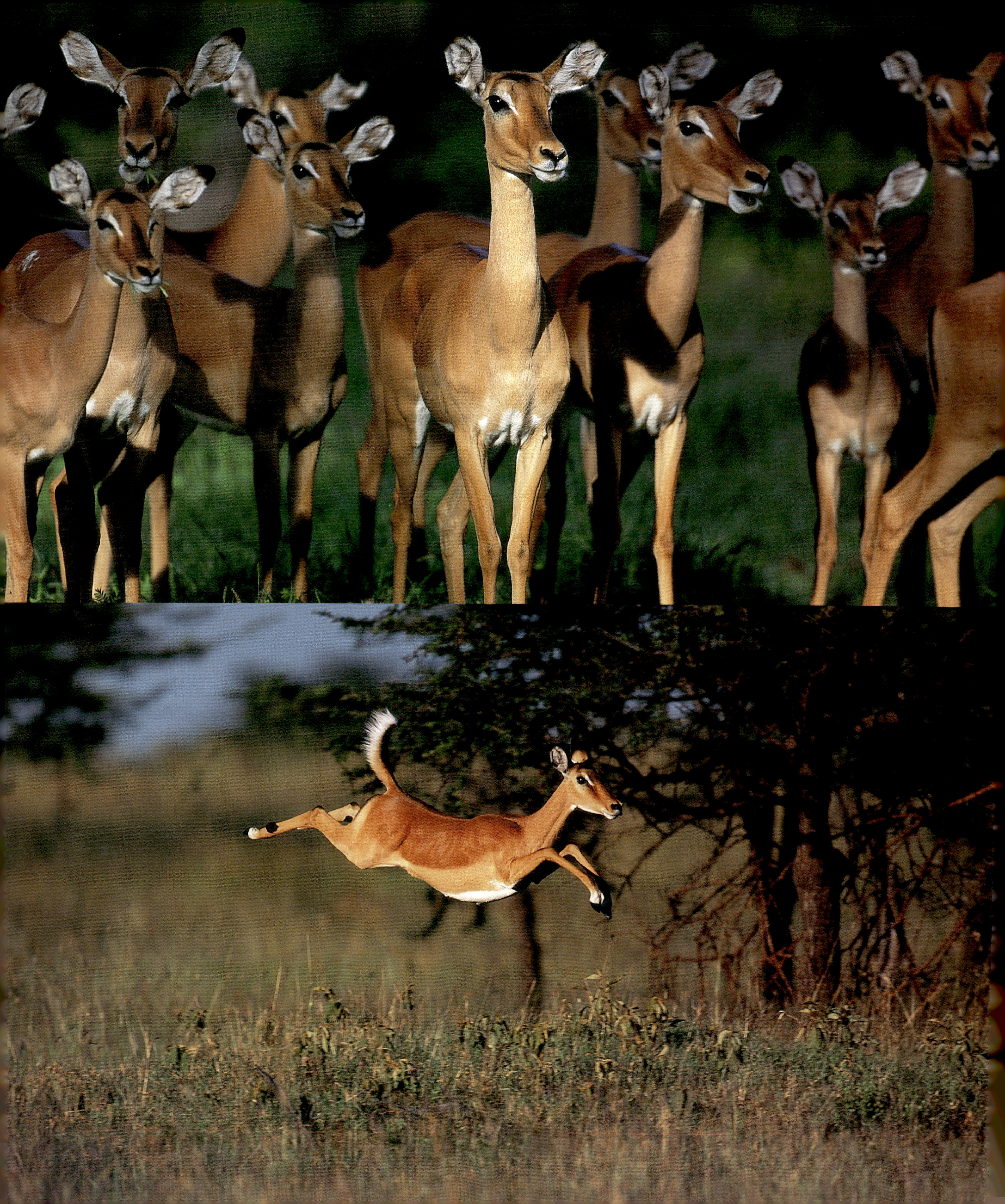

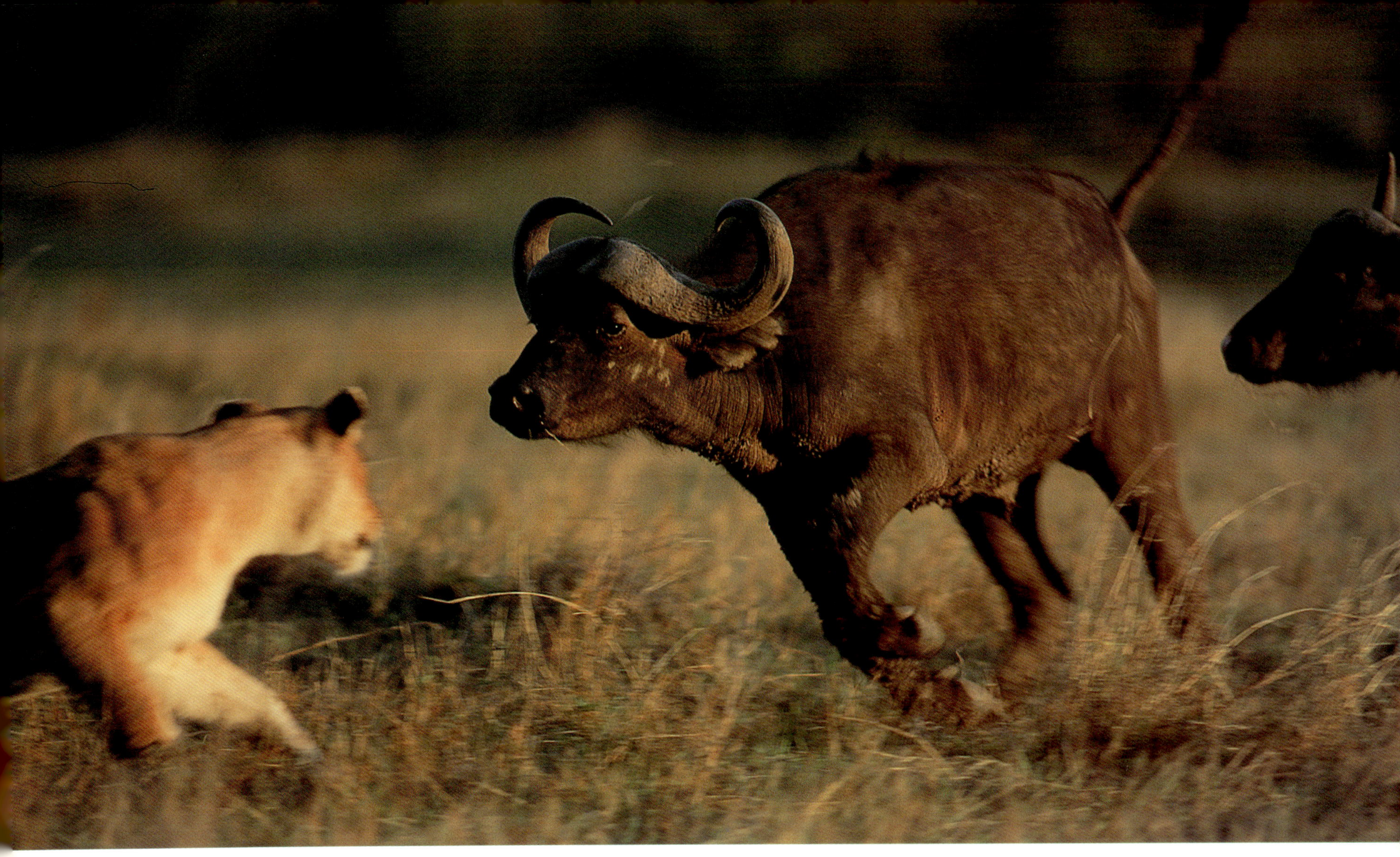

When this spirited buffalo turned and charged head on at the lioness, who had failed to catch it from the rear, the lioness was forced to give way. On impact, a charging buffalo can hit with the force of a car traveling faster than 35 mph.

Opposite, above
An alert harem of impala making use of their collective ears, noses, and eyes to detect possible danger. When they have pinpointed what they consider a safety threat, impala herds will adopt tense postures and all will turn to face toward the potential danger.

Opposite, below
The gravity-defying leaps of adult impalas can reach as high as ten feet over a span of some 32 feet. Such spectacular leaps carry the animal over rough terrain, such as bushes and rocks, with relative ease.

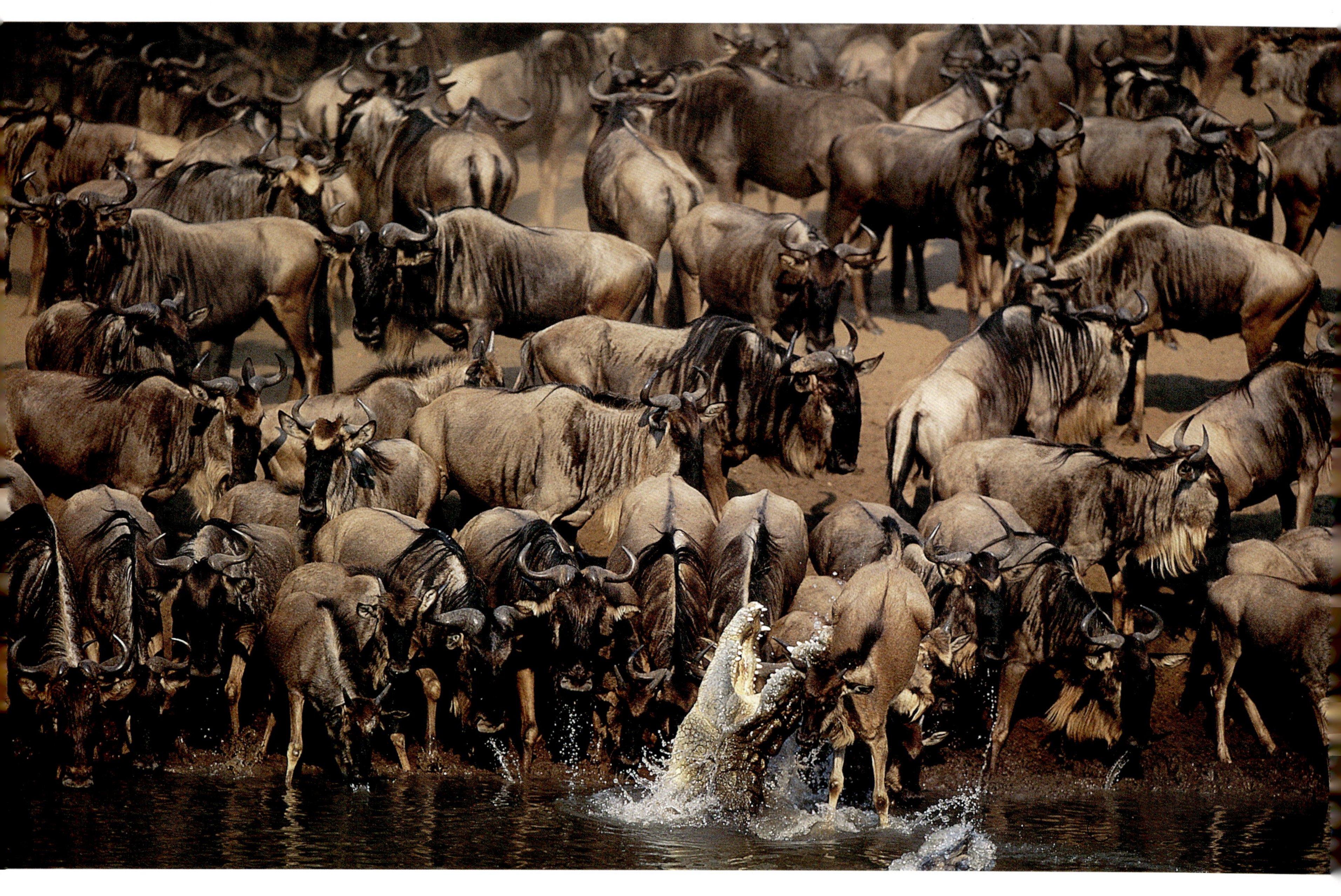

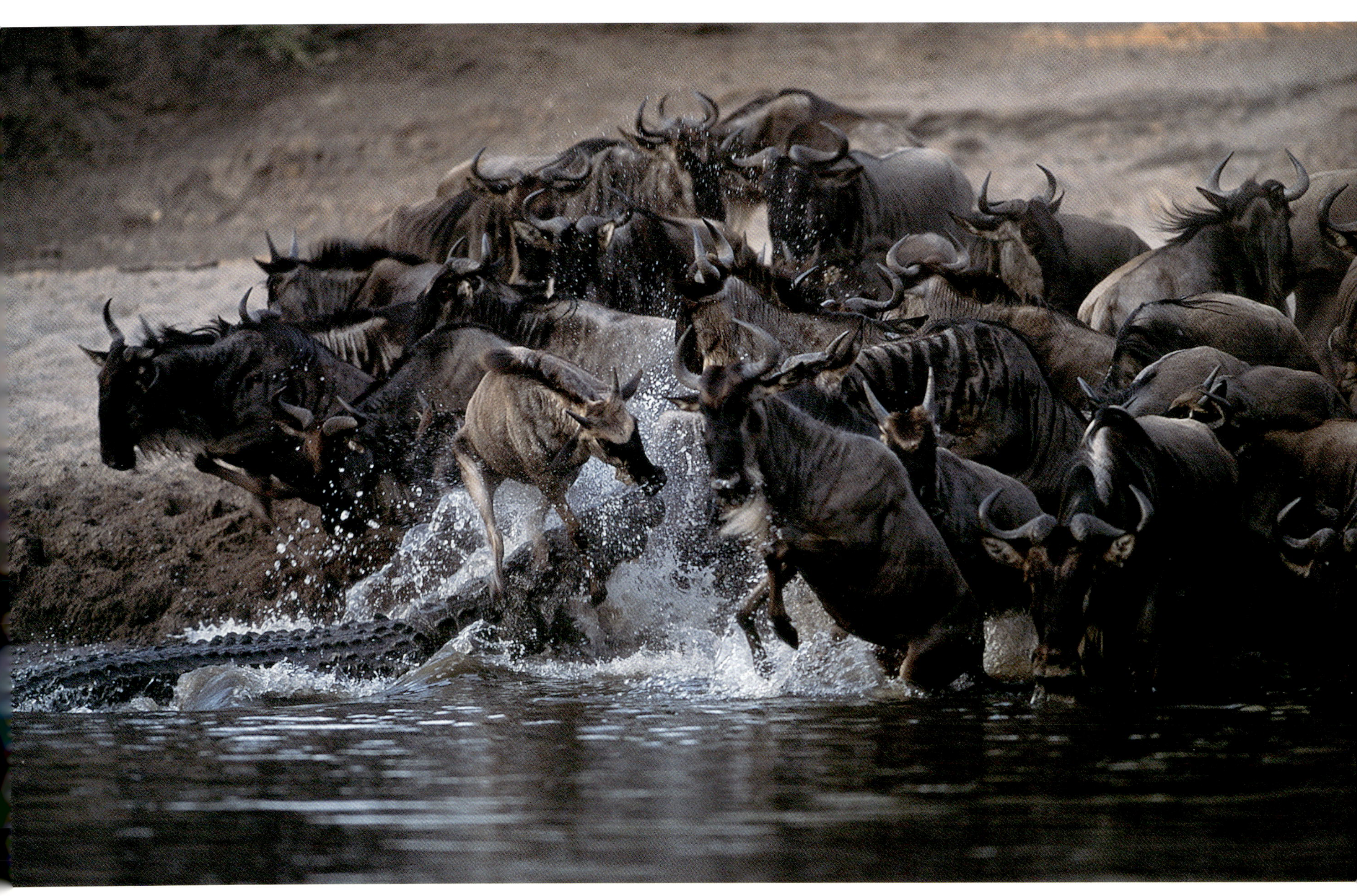

Opposite and above
Migrating wildebeests on the Serengeti-Mara plains of East Africa provide essential food for Nile crocodiles. To catch a wildebeest, the crocodile will approach totally submerged with only its eyes breaking the surface of the water until it gets within striking distance, at which point it will launch itself out of the water at the target. However, as seen here, crocodiles often miss.

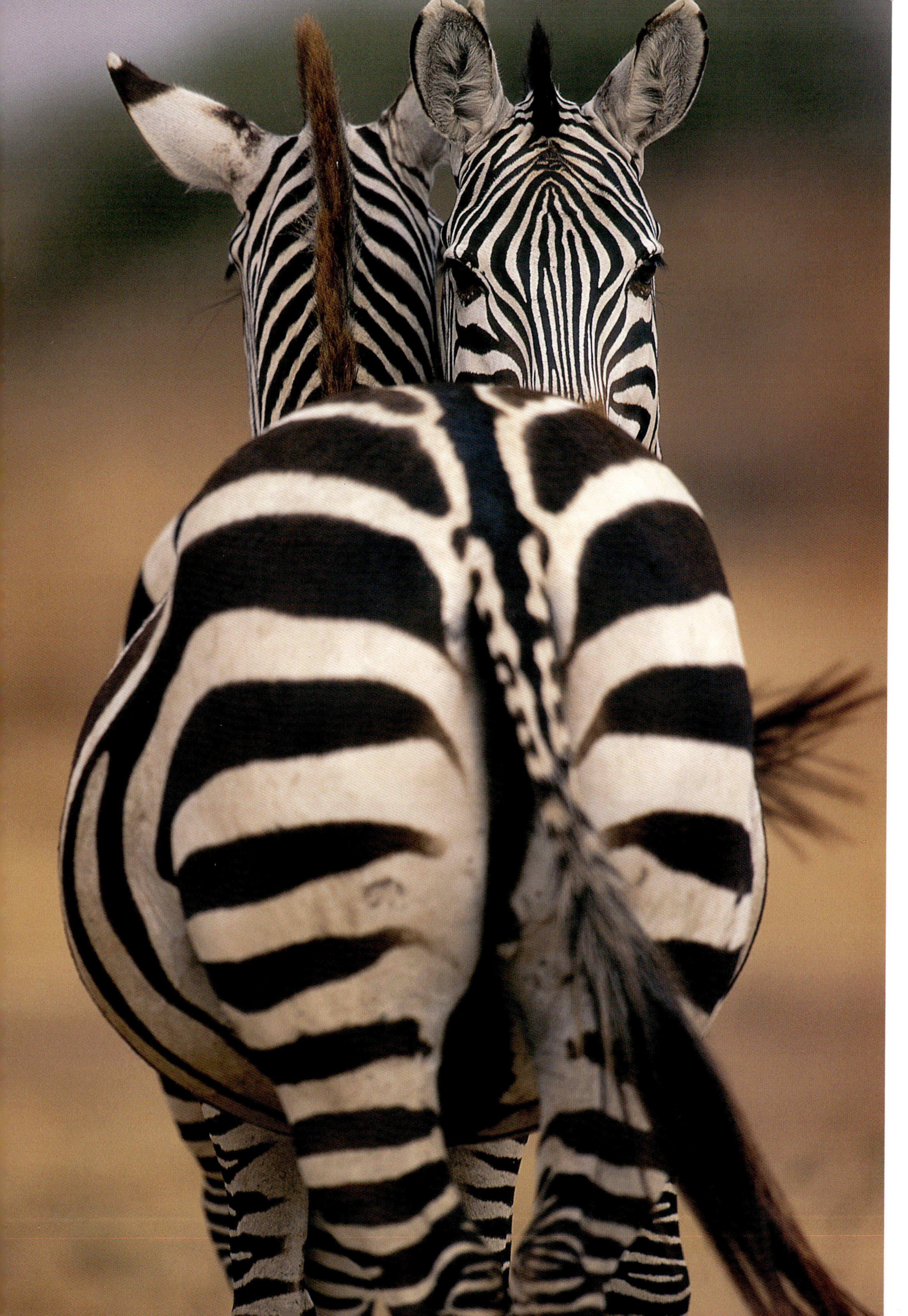

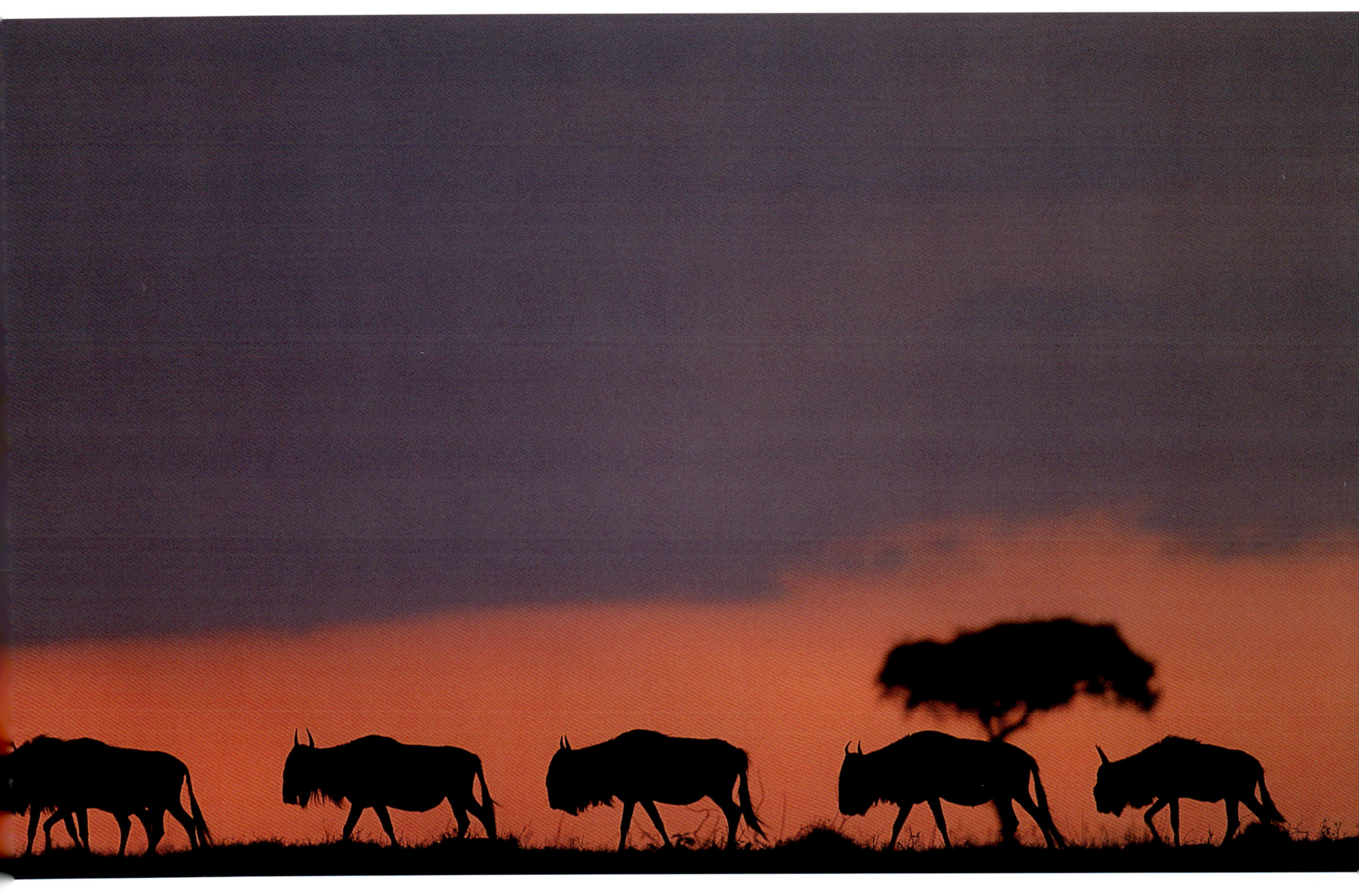

Wildebeests walking in single file at dusk. This is actually an anti-predation strategy: Were they to advance as a broad front, a predator concealed in the grass would have a greater chance of catching an individual animal by surprise.

Opposite
Two plains zebras engaged in mutual grooming. This stance enables them to cover a 360-degree perspective of their surroundings, making it difficult for a lion to approach undetected.

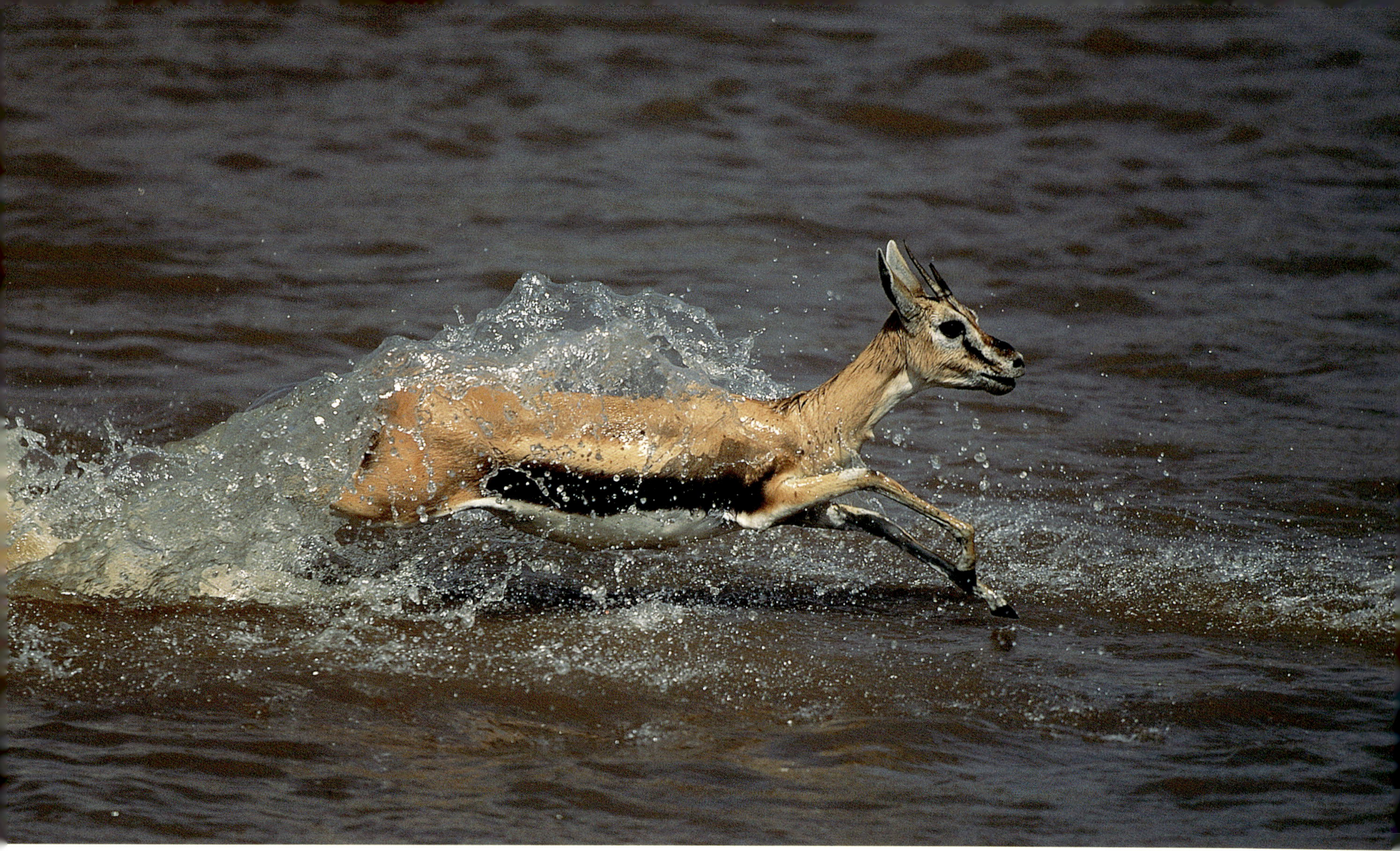

Thomson's gazelles do not cross rivers often, but when they do, usually in search of better grazing, they're rather awkward about it, splashing across in great haste.

Opposie, above
Having spotted a prowling cheetah in the vicinity, a Grant's gazelle raises its leg in readiness to stamp on the ground as a signal to the cheetah. Its whole body is conveying the message that it has spotted danger of a lethal kind. The cheetah will not attempt to attack this gazelle, having lost the advantage of surprise.

Opposite, below
A male eland escapes an attempt by male lions to catch it by surprise. While putting distance between him and them, it jumps to demonstrate to the lions that he has plenty of energy to spare. Considering the weight and bulk of an eland, it is not surprising that most big cats leave it alone.

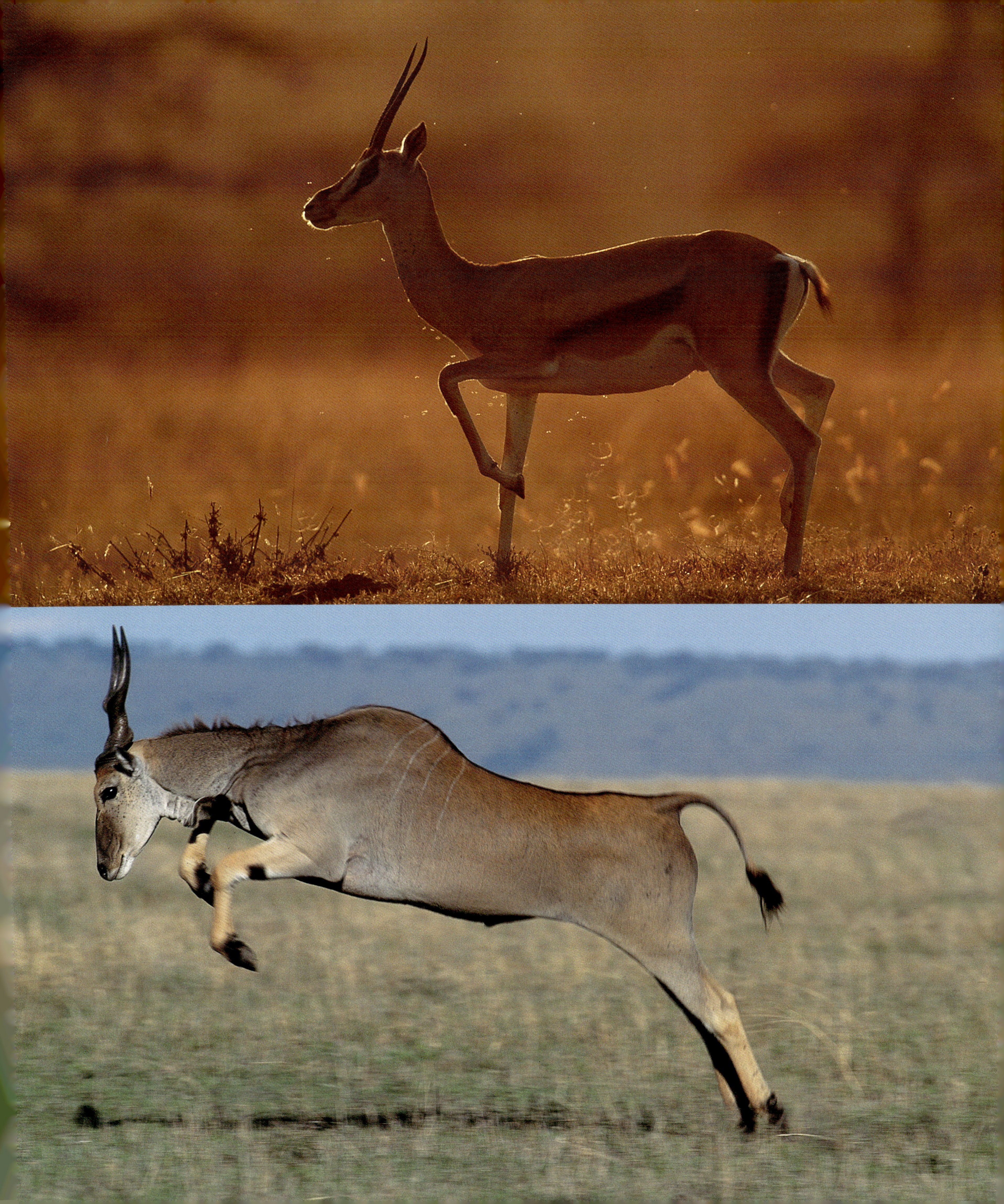

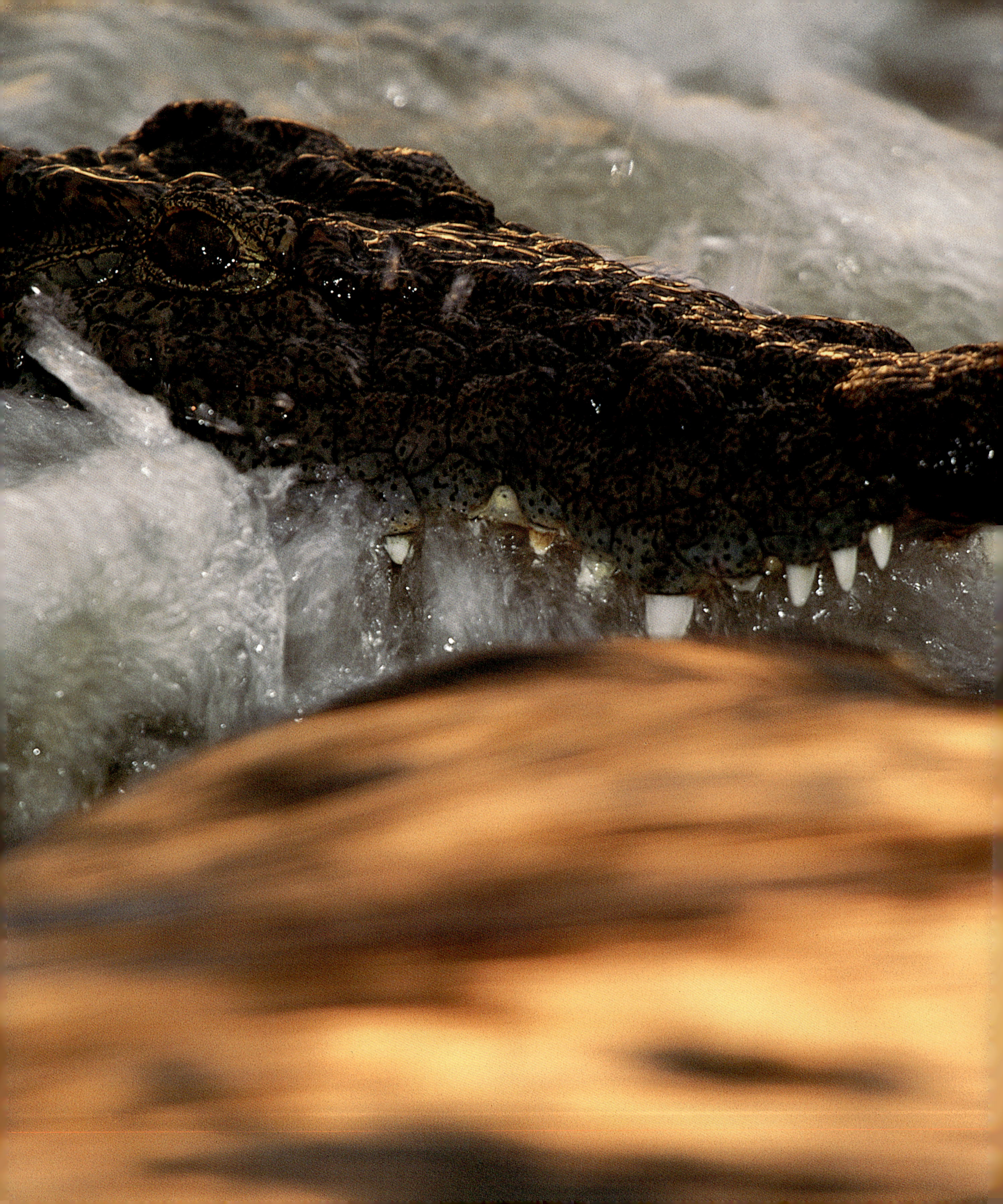

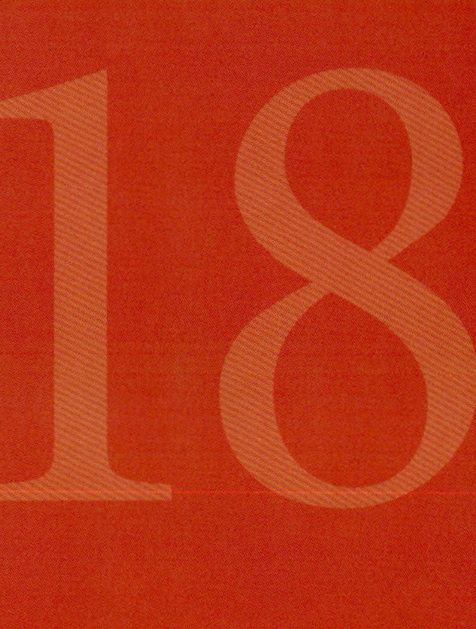

The Hunters

Most visitors don't come to the national parks of East Africa for the scenery. They come to see the large mammals – elephants, rhinos, giraffes, buffaloes, the spectacle of the large herds, the predators. Although there are nearly 30 species of mammalian predators perched high up on the pyramid of life, most tourists especially want to see the three big cats – lions, cheetahs, and leopards. Surprisingly, however, the big hunters are relatively rare sightings, compared to the herbivores.

Why should this be so? One answer lies in the fact that carnivore food is far more nutrient-rich than herbivore food, consequently carnivores don't need to spend as much time eating as herbivores. Every couple pounds of grass that a zebra eats contains less than an ounce of protein; every couple pounds of zebra flesh that a lion ingests is nearly all protein. Thus, herbivores spend most of their time feeding (18 hours a day for a zebra), whereas carnivores eat in spaced-out bouts, resting in between (18 hours a day for lions), usually in dark, shady cover.

Another answer lies in leakage of energy. Many herbivores die from causes other than predation, so the supply of food calories left for the carnivores is but a fraction of the total supply of herbivores. In addition, some of those food calories the carnivores do capture go toward helping their young to grow. Furthermore, much of the food eaten remains undigested and passes out as waste. It is not surprising, then, that it takes about a hundred gazelles to support a lion for one year.

Of course, a lucky tourist may get to see some action, but it is likely to disappoint, for titanic battles between predator and prey are rare. Predators are loathe to risk injury and are therefore cautious hunters. They go for the easiest meat: the young, the old, the lame, and the sick. Lions are careful to avoid zebra stallions in particular, as they are powerful and pack awesome karate kicks. They simply don't have the edge in firepower to pull off repeated successful killings if they continually attack the fit and strong. Lions that have been hungry enough to try, have often ended up with an injury, such as a dislocated jaw from a swift back kick. A seriously injured lioness cannot hunt and, if alone, faces starvation. Natural selection has seen to it that aggressiveness in lionesses is purged from the gene pool because such individuals would incur more than an average share of fatal injuries and thus leave fewer descendants. Most lions make do with the prey they can kill with minimal danger to themselves. When there is no choice and hunger bites, however, the risk-reward ratio changes and the big predators are driven to take on whatever is available.

We have implied that the number of herbivores determines the number of carnivores, but could it be the other way round? It has been observed that where predators are scarce, herbivore numbers are high. Perhaps predators do exert sufficient pressure to prevent population explosions in many prey species. Predators may be better herbivore managers than humans.

Pages 254–255
This Nile crocodile is a death trap. At the touch of a passing fish, the jaws will snap shut.

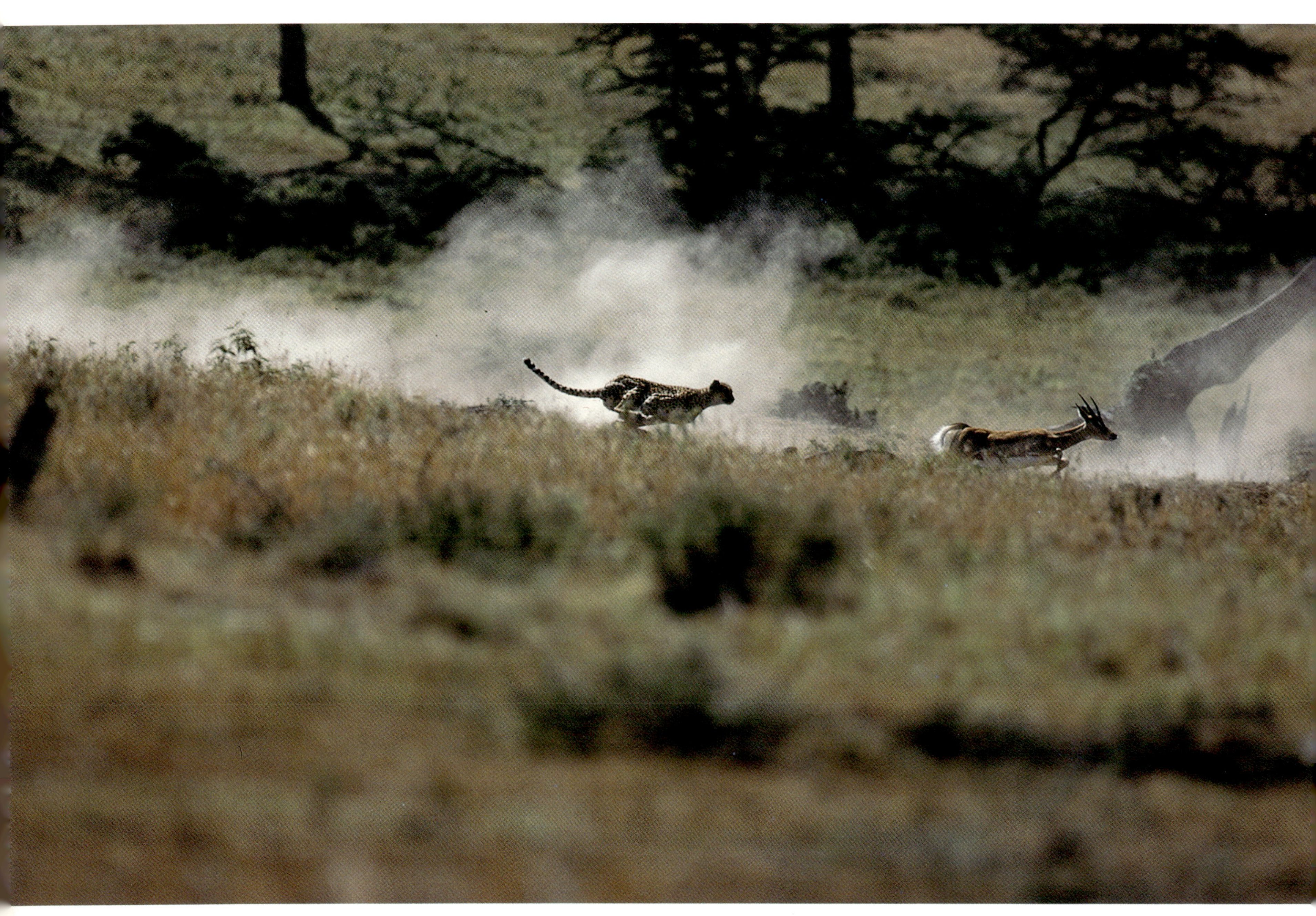

This female cheetah stalked her prey, then sprinted, quickly accelerating to top speed, and managed to bring down the fleeing animal on the run.

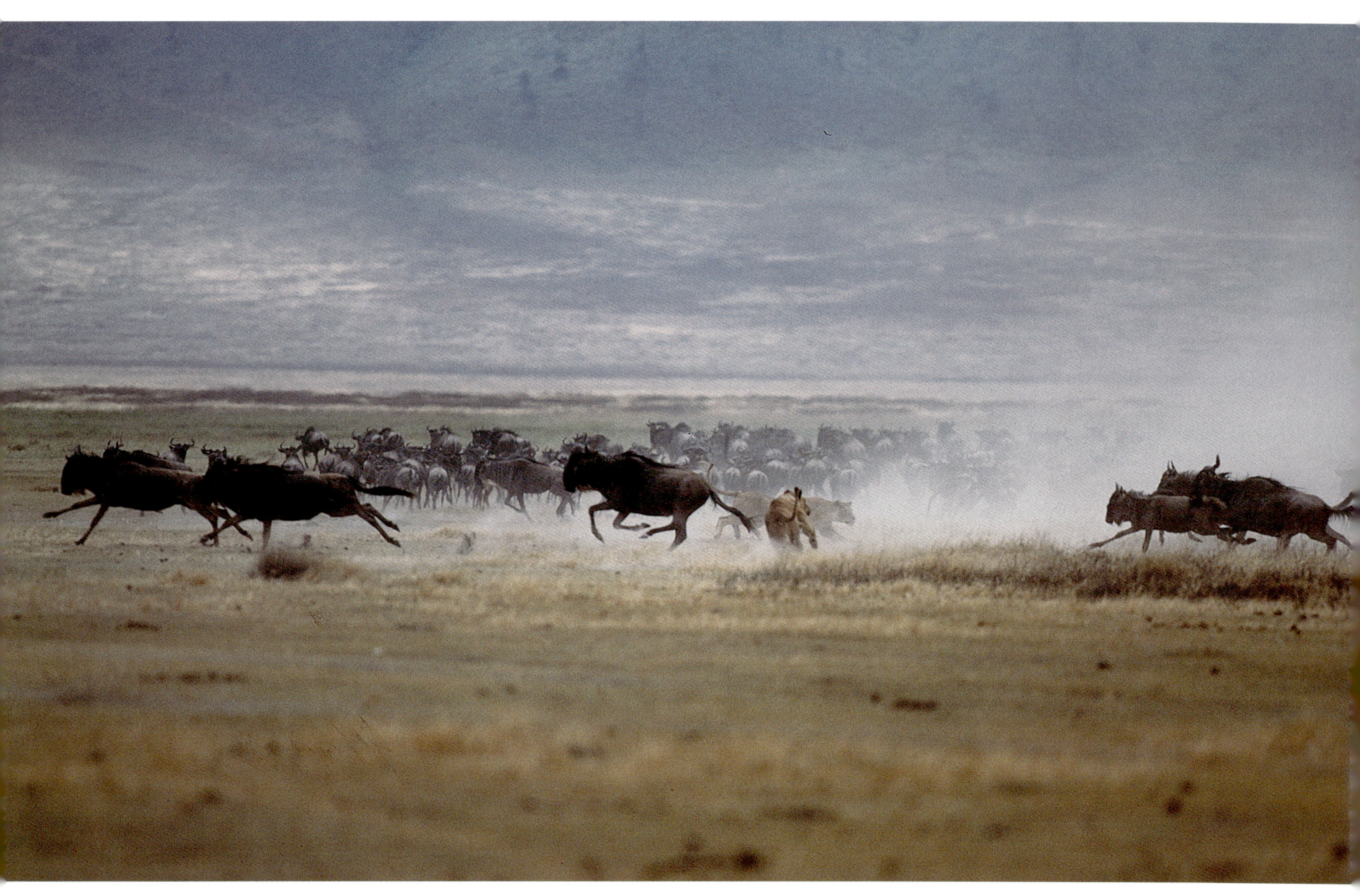

Lionesses waiting in ambush at a water source burst into this herd of wildebeests at an opportune moment. They ignore the adults in favor of weaker and slower calves.

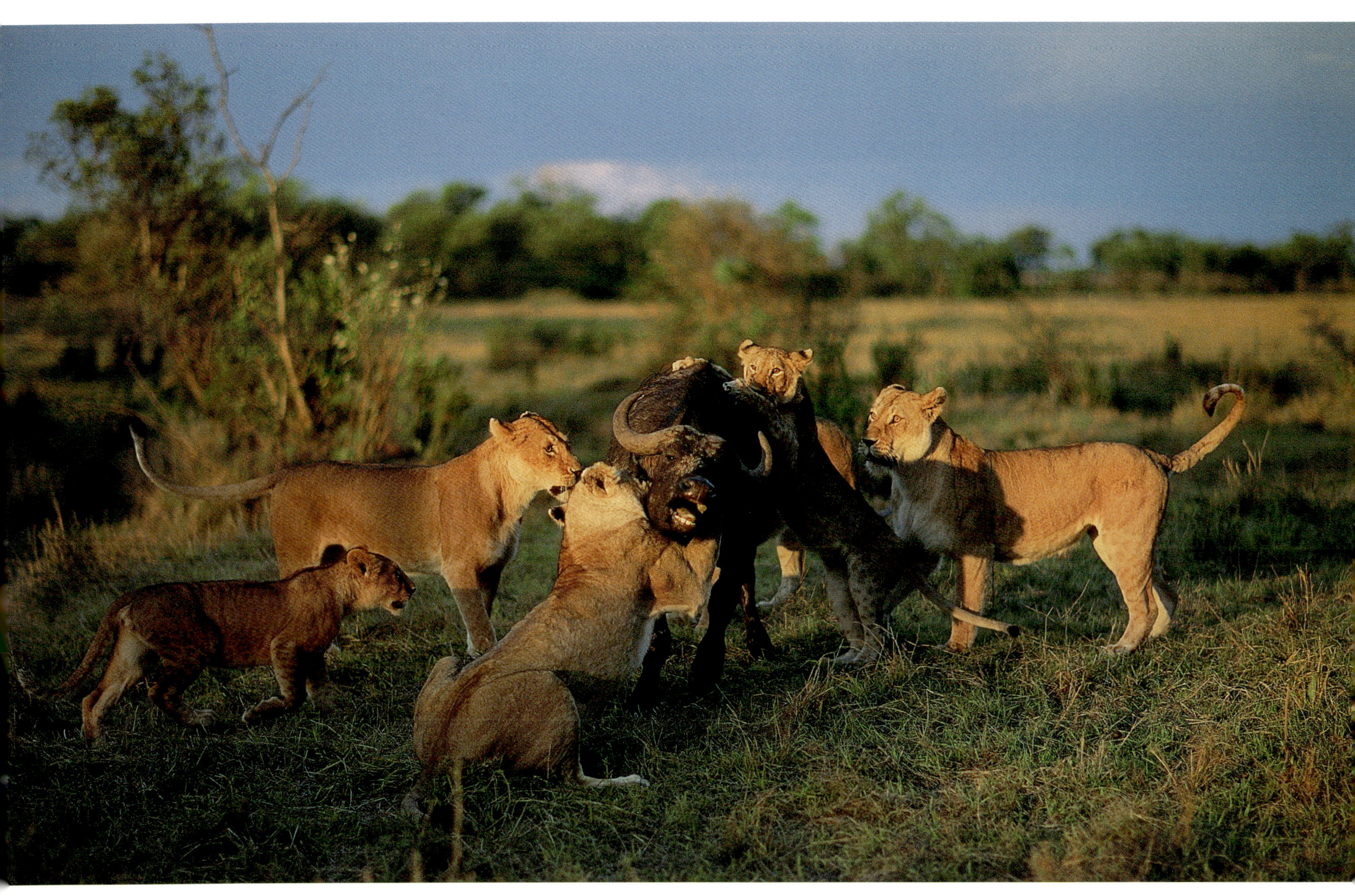

Lionesses of a pride subdue a Cape buffalo, which is moments away from death. By hunting in teams, lions, hyenas, and wild dogs command enough fire power to take on large prey animals should the need arise, although they usually avoid this rather risky behavior.

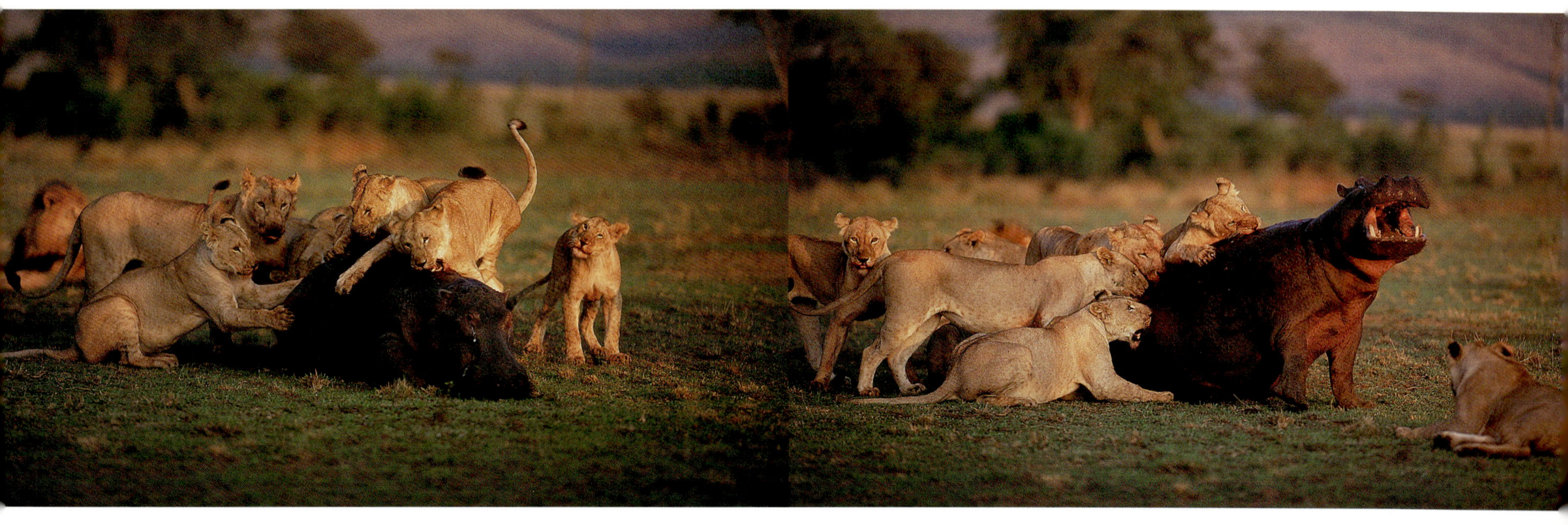

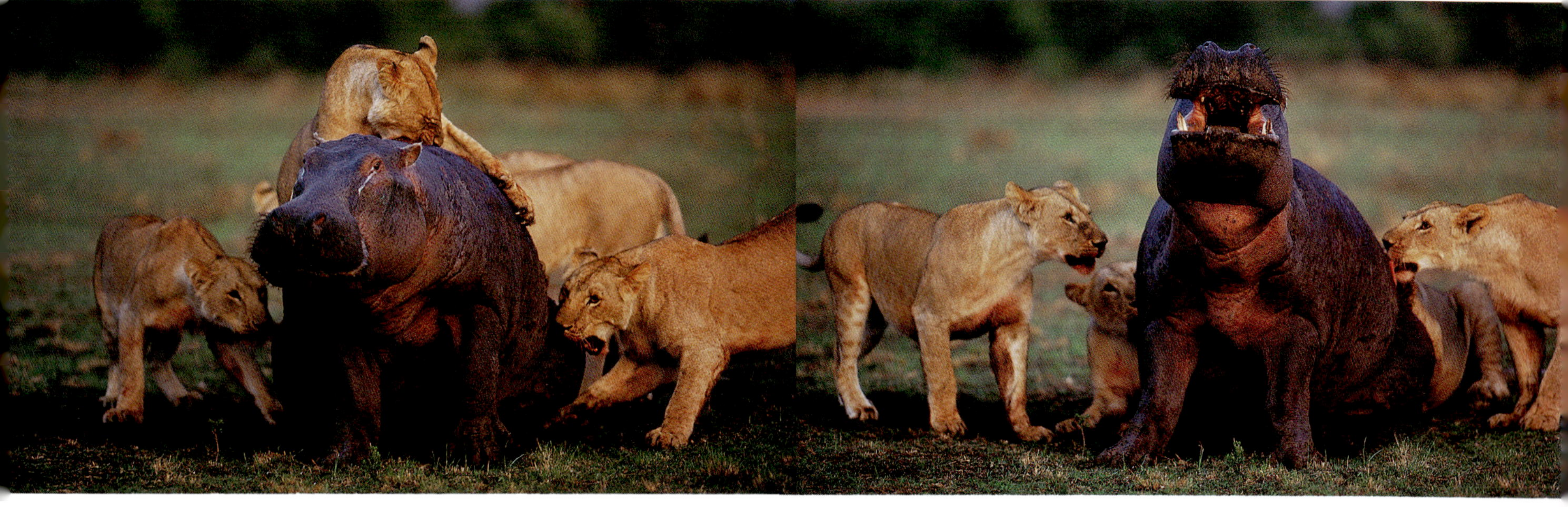

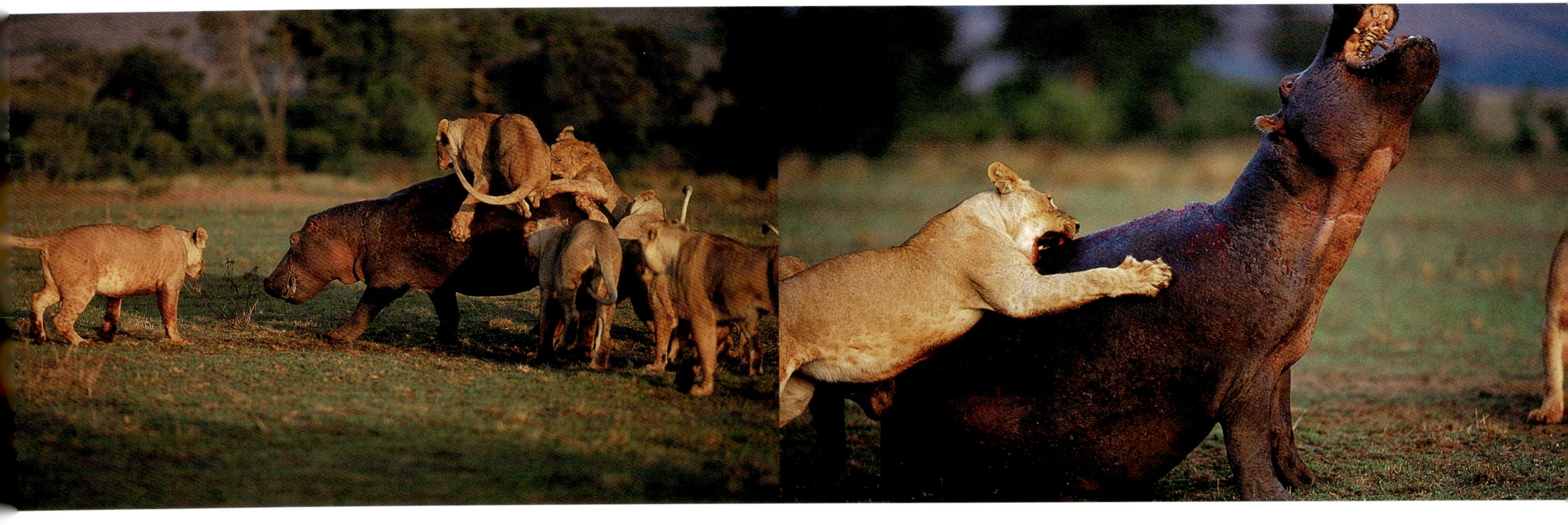

Opposite and above
It being the dry season, this young male hippo had wandered far during the night, in search of more grazing. On his return to the river at dawn, he was intercepted by a lion pride consisting of a male, four females, and ten adolescents. He broke free of the cordon, but in the melee a bite to one of his hind legs disabled him. Still, with great determination, the limping hippo tried to cover the remaining distance to the river, but the lions had other ideas. By this time the adult lionesses had lost interest, and despite the ingenuity of the teenagers, the hippo made it to the riverine bushes and then the riverbank where there were other hippos. The lions finally gave up at the sound of an approaching Maasai, but the hippo died a week later only two feet away from the water.

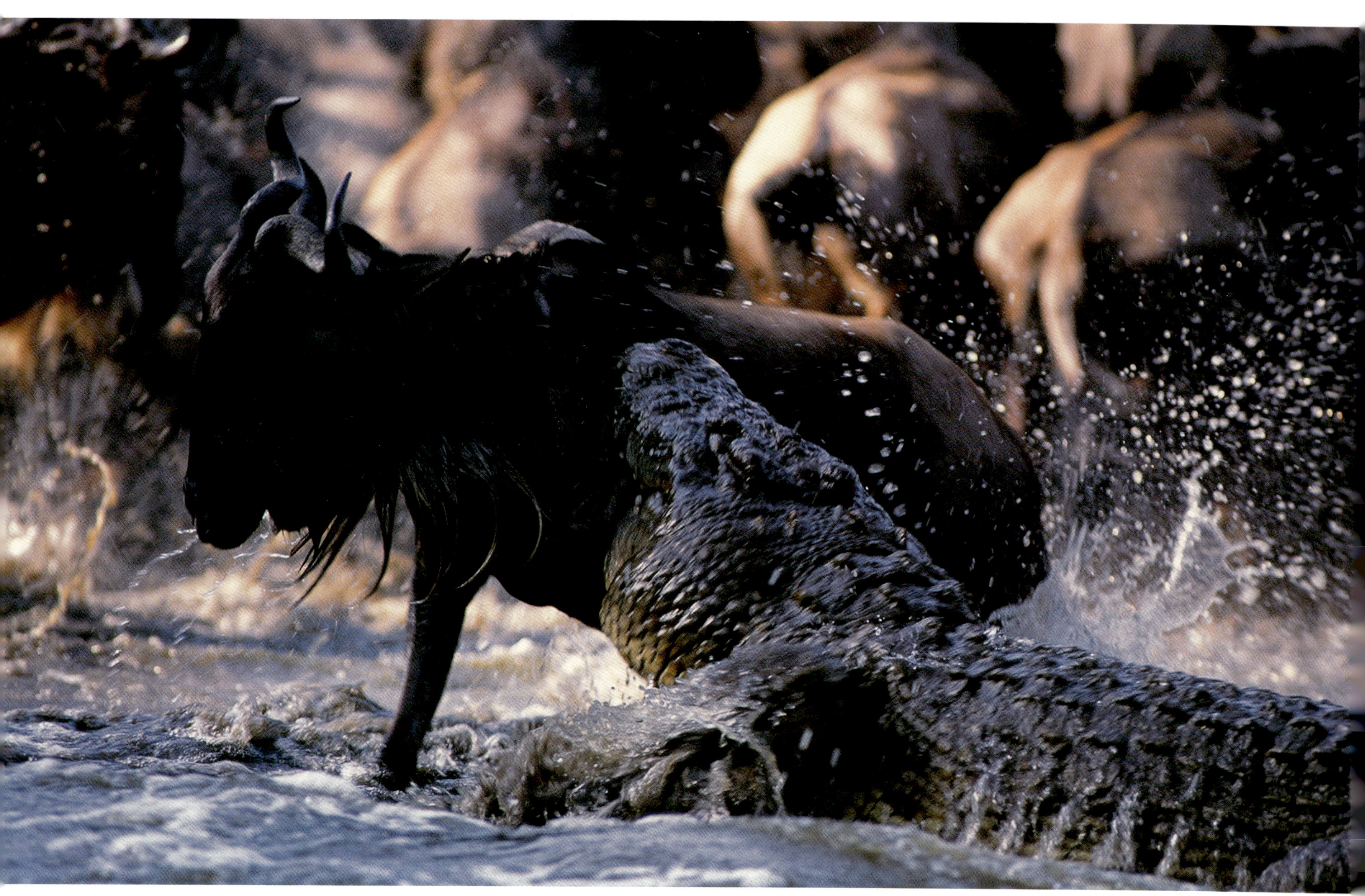

Although it was only 7 a.m., the thirsty wildebeests were already at the riverbank, nervously edging forward. The huge crocodile lying in wait remained undetected until it lunged. It pulled its victim into deep waters and killed it by drowning.

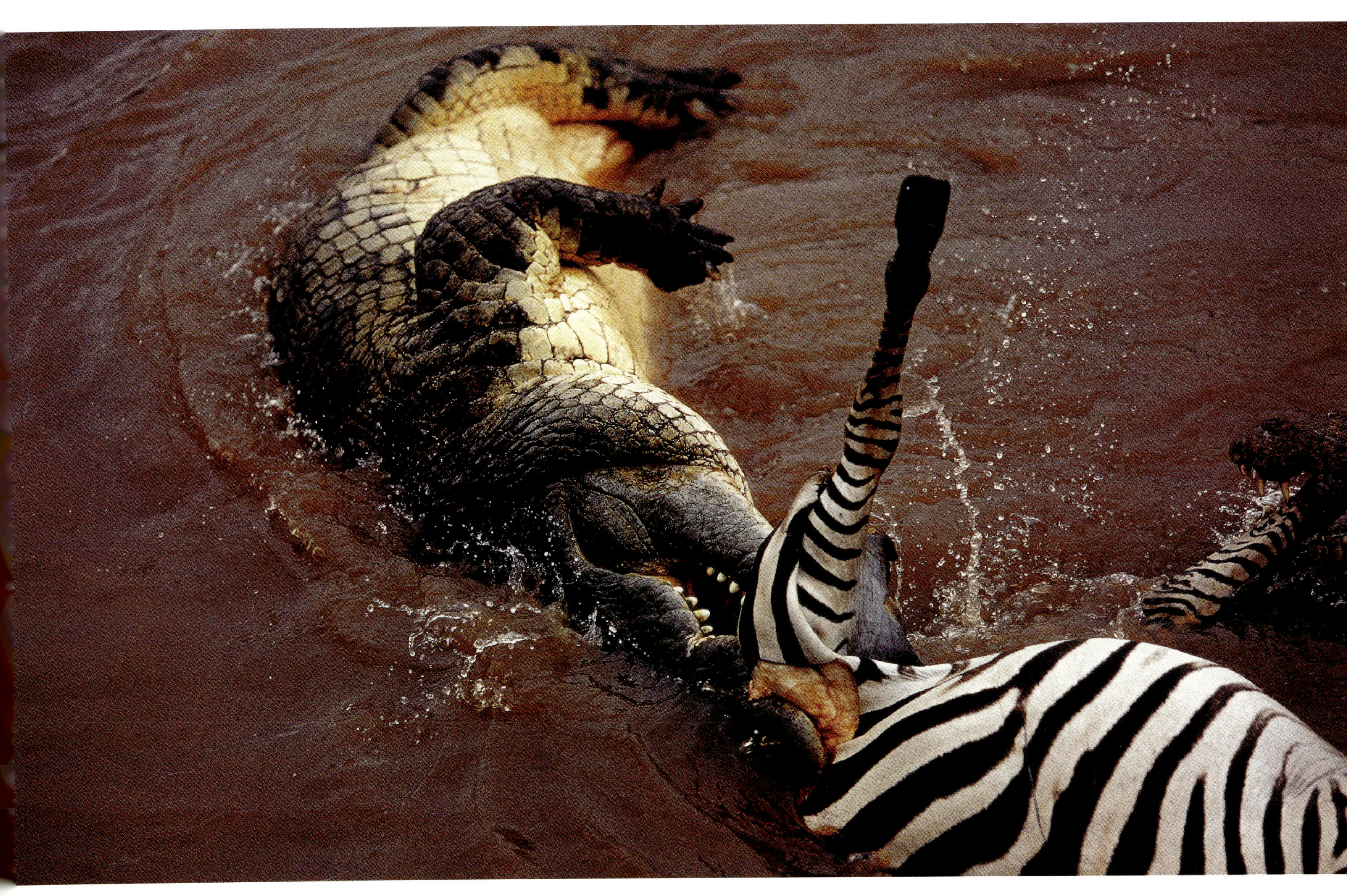

These crocodiles are cooperating with each other. One crocodile grips the carcass to hold it steady while another rolls with the bite, pulling off a chunk of meat. Large chunks of meat are swallowed whole.

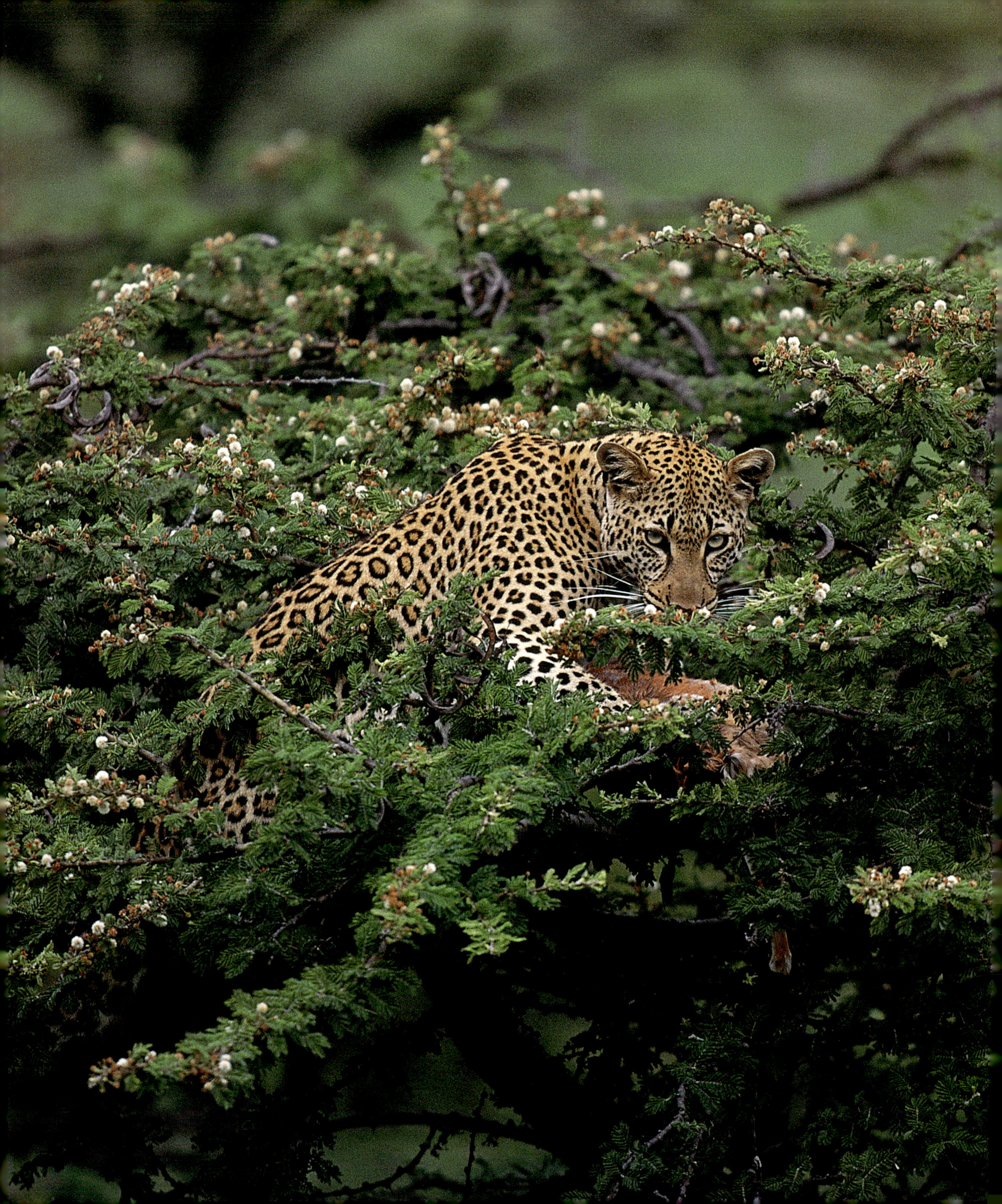

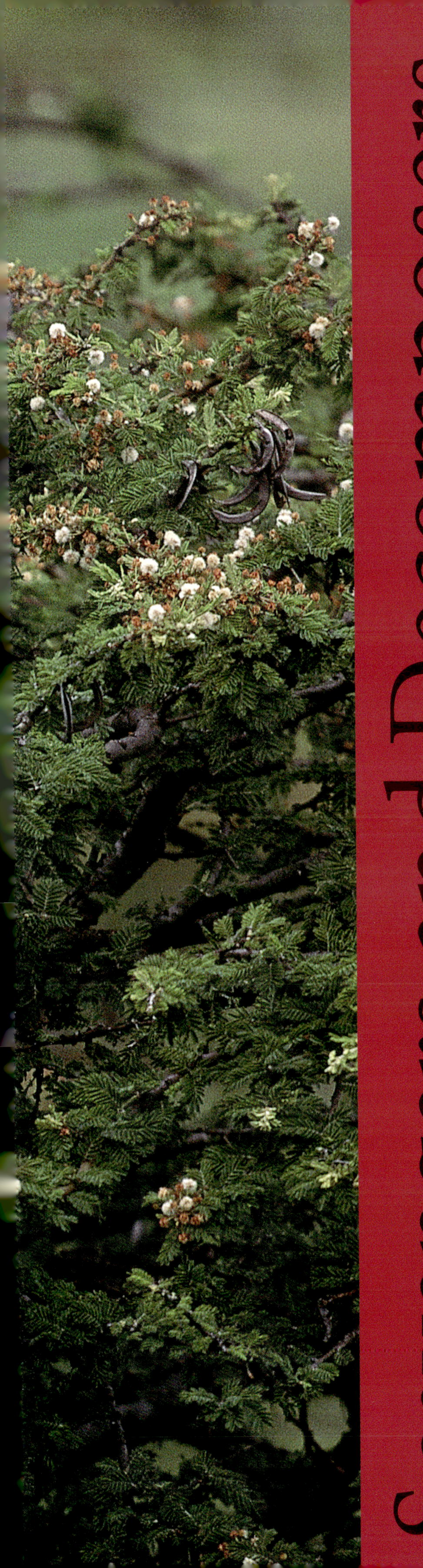

19

Scavengers and Decomposers

It was still dark when we left camp. Our headlights picked out a shoal of bright eyes that became a group of resting wildebeests held fast in the beams. We switched off the lights and the wildebeests moved off the track. At 6:45 a.m., just as the sun freed itself from the horizon, we reached the vast plains and scanned with binoculars to pick out a feeding pride of lions.

And we found them. You could tell lions had killed the wildebeests by the way the three dead bodies were spaced so close together – a lion could walk from one kill to the other in less than a minute. The pride had eaten a lot, but there was still some flesh left for the resident hyena clan waiting in the wings. A jackal pair was walking to and fro in an agitated manner, and some vultures had already descended from the skies and were perched on a convenient leafless tree, waiting patiently. A couple of marabou storks were also standing by. As soon as the lions left their kill, the scavengers moved in. First it was the hyenas with the nimble jackals darting in to snatch pieces of flesh, then the vultures rushed in to strip off every morsel of flesh. The carcasses quickly disappeared, leaving only rib cages and a scattering of other bones and horns as evidence.

Nearly all carnivores scavenge at one time or another, although there is some variation in the extent of scavenging. Vultures are full-time scavengers and the most specialized of all. They range over thousands of square miles, conserving fuel by soaring, skillfully navigating a route through thermal up-draughts and air rising on the windward side of hillsides. They also have the keenest eyesight of any diurnal savannah animal, and are able to see minute details on the ground from great heights. If a vulture spots something that captures its interest, it quickly swoops down, followed by other alert vultures. The story goes that a Maasai traversing a grassy plain decided to lie down and take a nap, and was roused awake by vultures landing nearby to investigate.

If the vultures around a kill were all alike, there would be a great deal of competition. However, selection pressure has resulted in a wide variety of species on the savannah. Vultures on a carcass may appear to be engaged in chaos (they do bicker for space), but there is an underlying order, with various species arriving on the scene of a kill at different times and feeding on different parts of the carcass, each using specialized parts of their anatomy. The white-headed vulture and the lappet-faced vulture are called rippers; the white-backed vulture and ruppell's griffon are gulpers; and the hooded vulture and the Egyptian vulture are scrappers. Thus, each vulture species occupies a distinct niche. Any aggression, usually ritualized, is predominantly between individuals of the same species.

After the predators have had their fill, the scavengers have dealt with the leftovers, and the dung beetles and maggots have done their work, all that remains of a carcass are the bones. But even these hard rem-

Pages 264–265
This young female leopard has stowed her kill, a young Thomson's gazelle, in a blooming acacia tree to escape a group of scavenging hyenas, which cannot climb trees.

nants are temporary furniture on the plains: Beetles enter bone cavities and gradually destroy them, while horn moths lay their eggs on the horns, their larvae tunneling into it as they feed on this tough material.

All the while, the true decomposers, fungi and bacteria, are hard at work bringing about the decay of any material they come across, converting it into carbon dioxide, water, and nutrients. These simple substances are utilized by the green plants, and the material circulates all over again through the pyramid of life. A vast array of creatures work diligently alongside the decomposers: locusts that eat live plants, army worms that can clear entire areas of grass in almost no time, quela birds whose numbers sometimes build up to the millions and who subsist on seeds, and termites and earthworms that consume dead vegetation. Termites, in particular, can quickly return tons of nutrients to the earth by ferrying dead wood and grass underground.

The savannah is such a busy place that 30 percent of all living material gets recycled every year compared with 8 percent in a rainforest. And since the recycling occurs at such a rapid rate, the savannah can support very large populations of living things.

So there we have it: An ecosystem in which material is constantly being resurrected in the form of new bodies as it travels from one level of the pyramid to another, forever circulating in the circle of life.

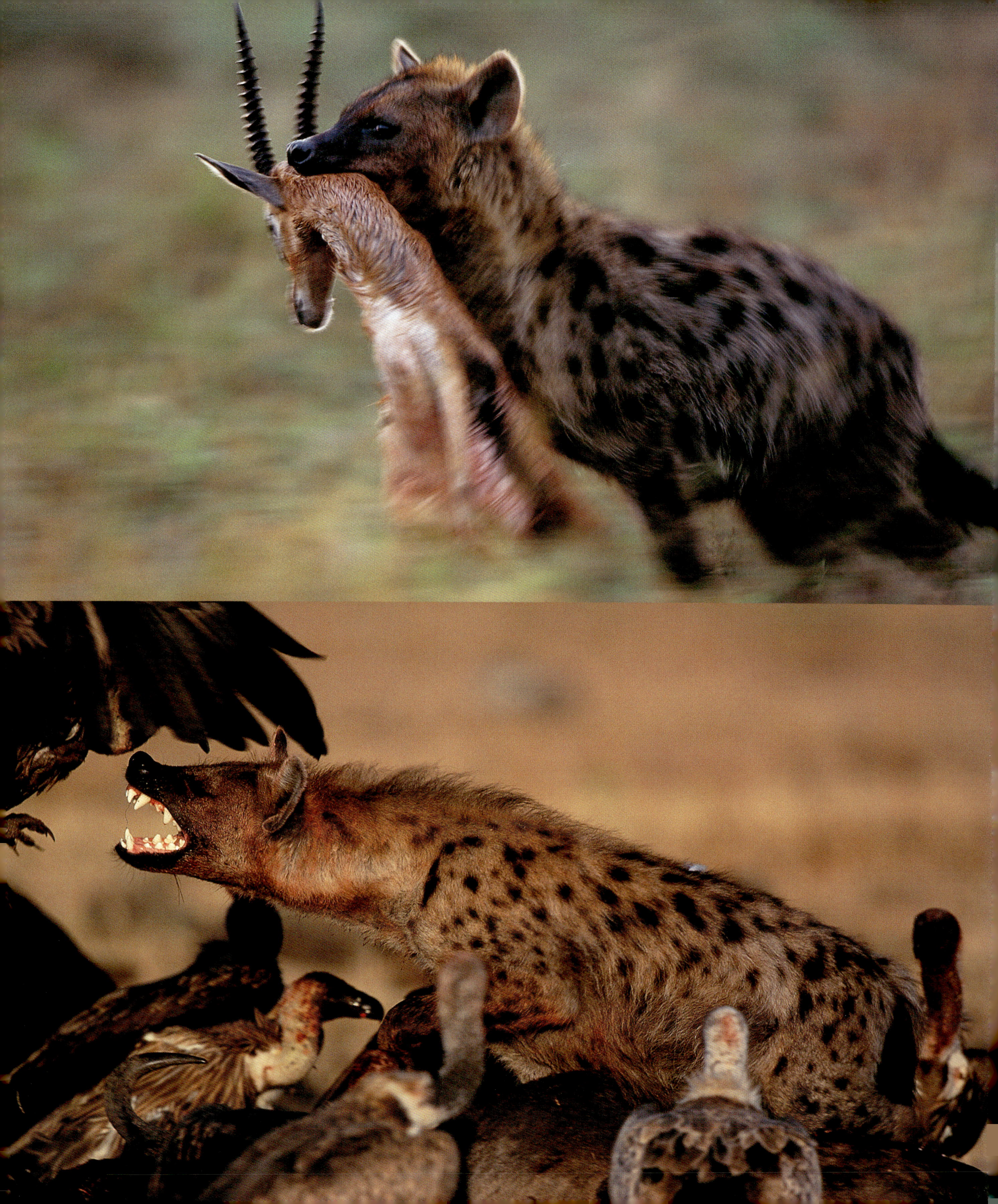

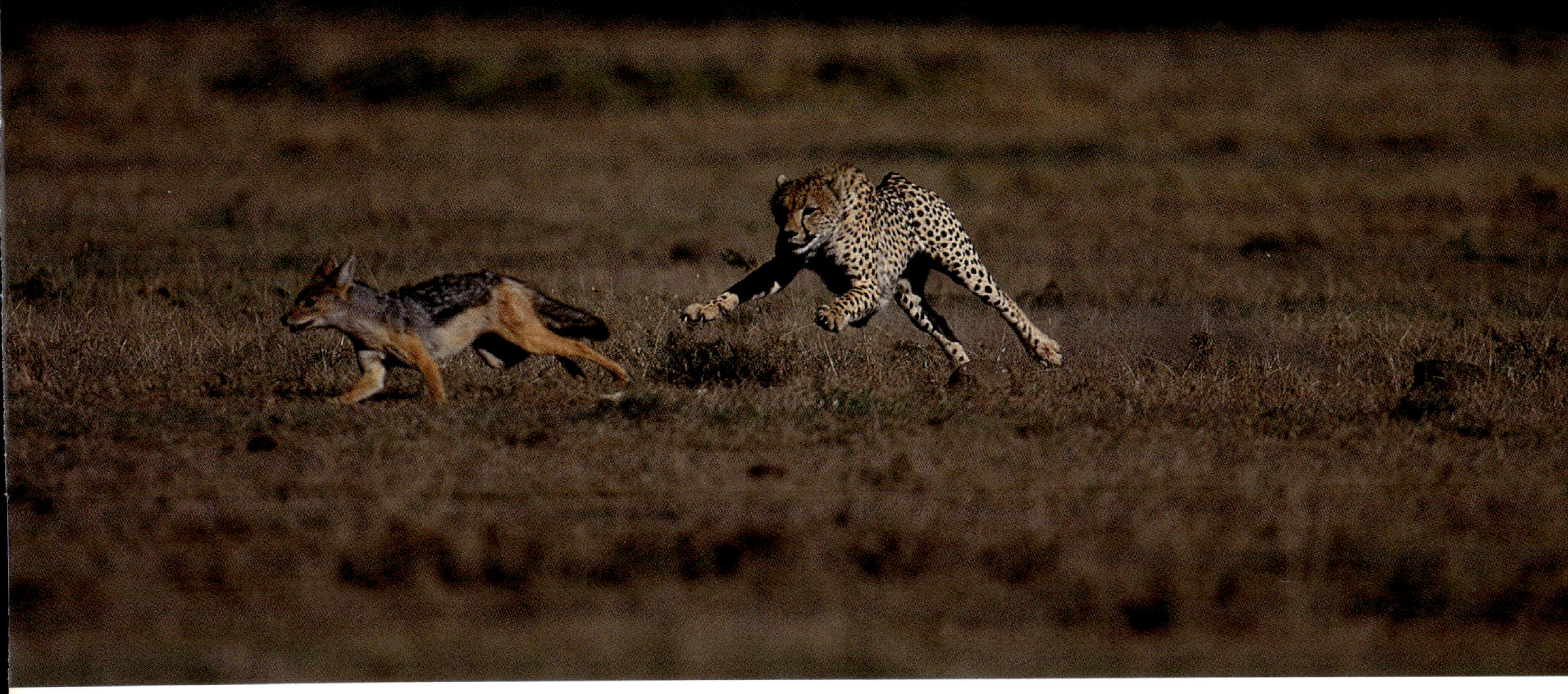

A cheetah chases a black-backed jackal from its kill. Although cheetahs are quite capable of catching jackals, they rarely hunt them due to their snapping jaws and sharp teeth. This persistent jackal returned to scavenge several times and was chased off on each occasion.

Opposite, above
A spotted hyena carries a gazelle carcass to its den. As gazelles usually prove too swift for the ungainly hyena, chances are this kill was poached from a cheetah.

Opposite, below
These bold, aggressive vultures have frustrated this lone hyena's attempt to eat in peace. The hyena's snarling grimace is a clear message to keep away.

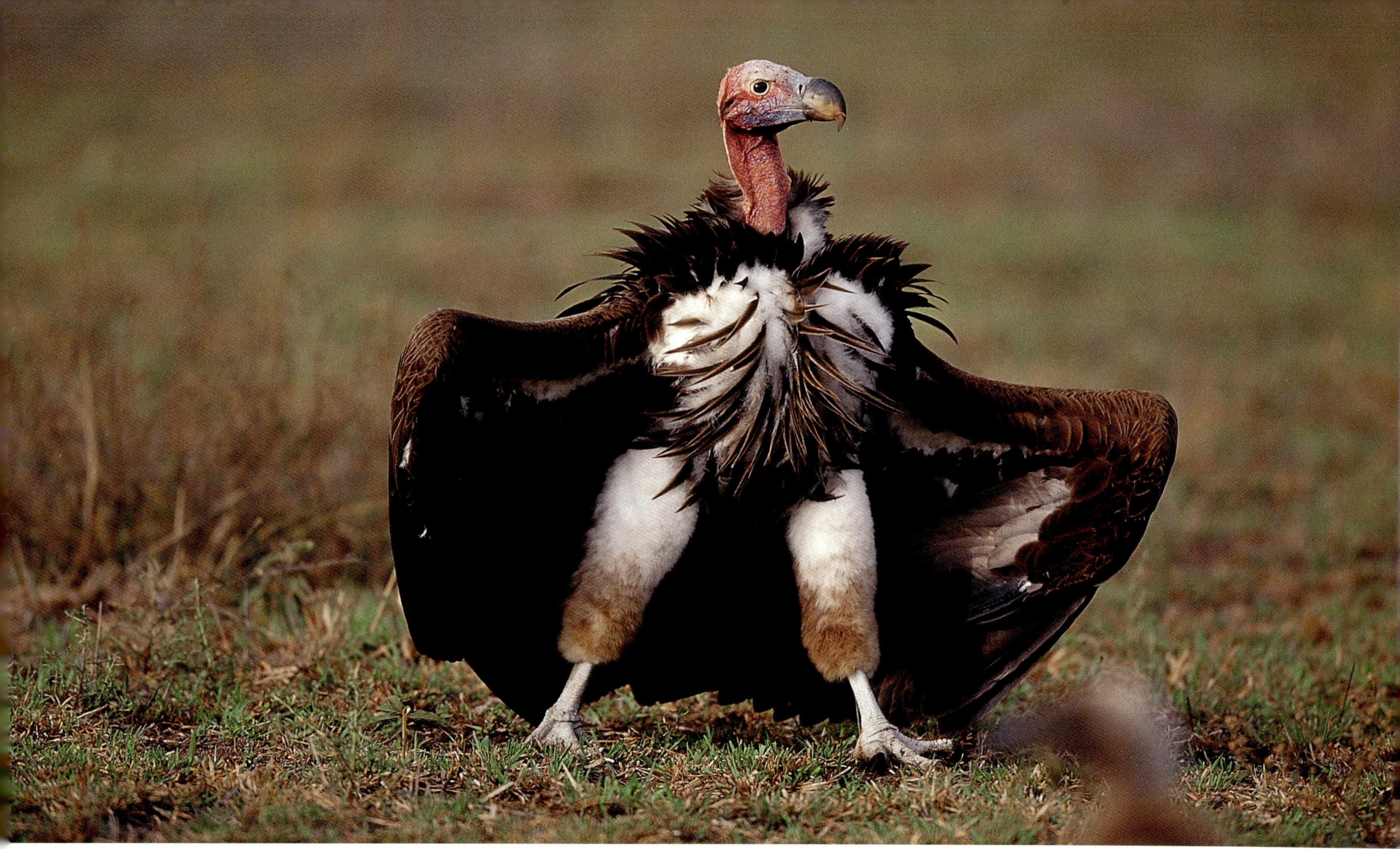

The lappet-faced (or Nubian) vulture is a huge bird with a wingspan of close to nine feet, a large skull, and a massive bill. At the kill-site it will try to make itself look even larger by prancing about in an exaggerated manner in order to intimidate the other vultures.

Opposite, above
A vulture gliding high in the sky can spot the slightest movement on the ground with its binocular vision, which is ten times keener than a human's. Coming in for a landing, this vulture checks its speed at around treetop height and hangs in the air for a moment, long shanks dangling, talons spread.

Opposite, below
This lone lappet-faced vulture descended quickly from the skies when it spotted a kill-site, but the mass of vultures already at the site wouldn't make room for it until it charged in at great speed with outstretched wings.

Pages 272–273
Two lappet-faced vultures take to the air, kicking out karate-style, in dispute over the prime feeding position at a kill-site. Hissing and squabbling occasionally over the next couple of hours, the vultures reduced the slain animal to little more than bloodstains and bone.

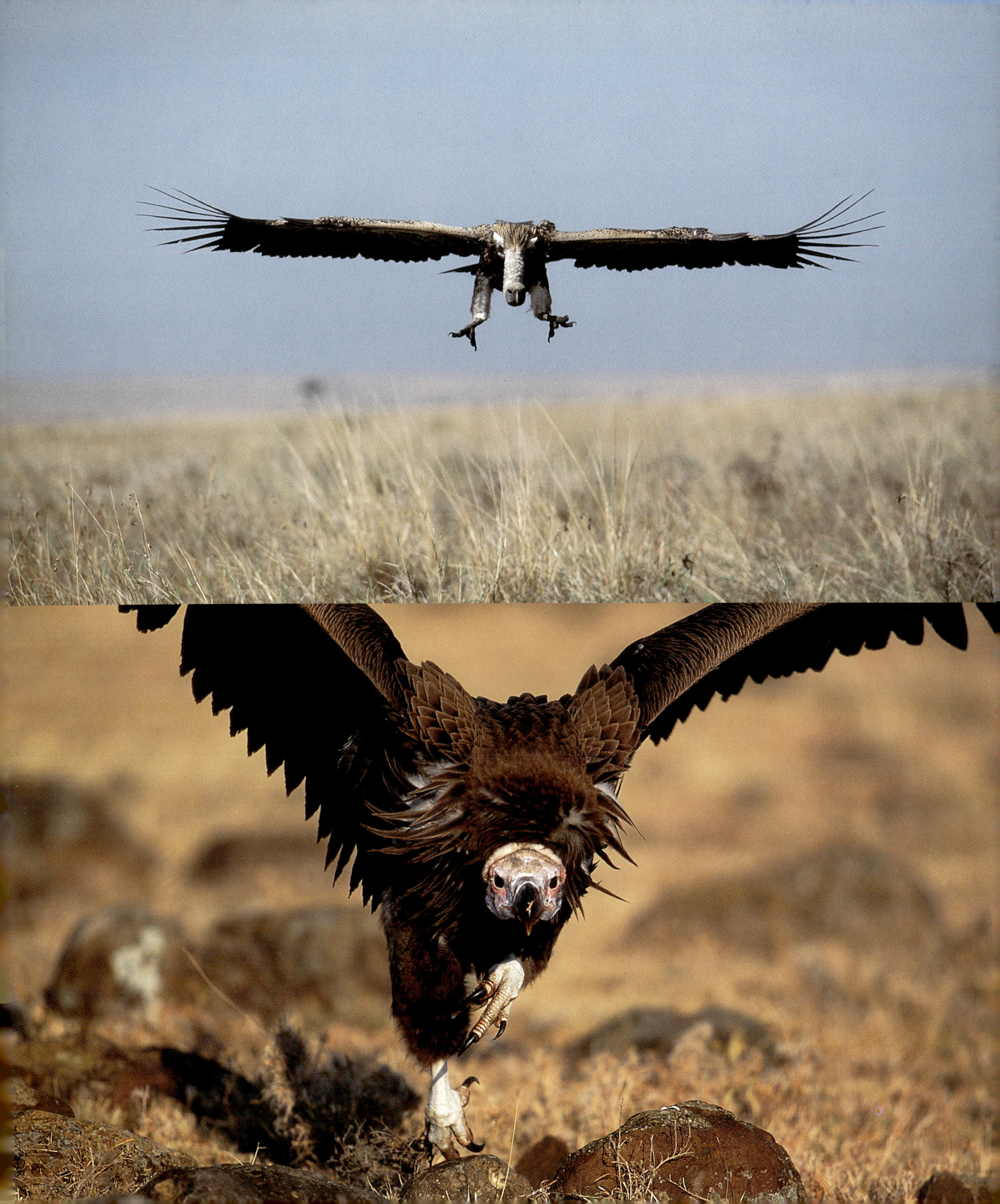

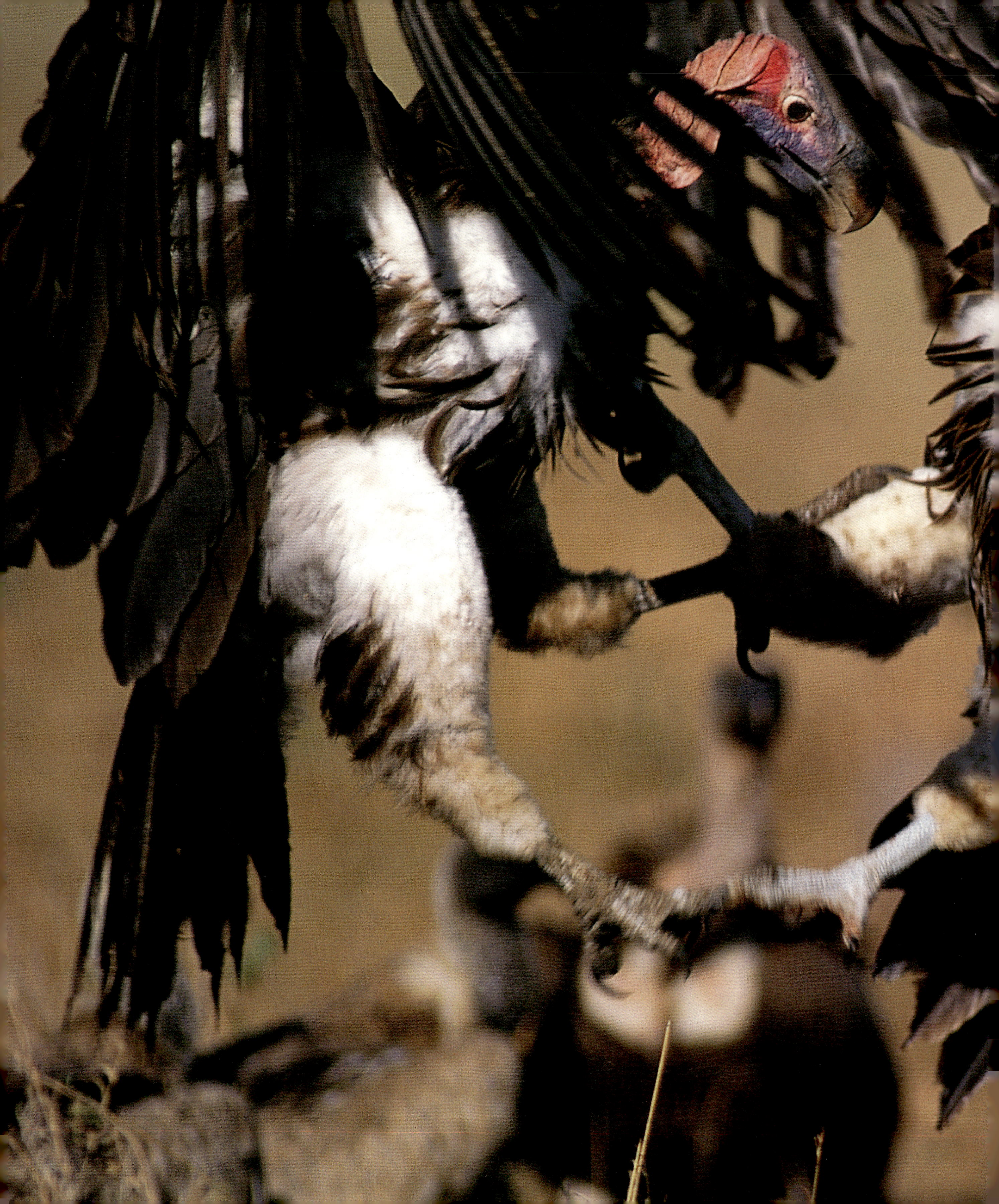

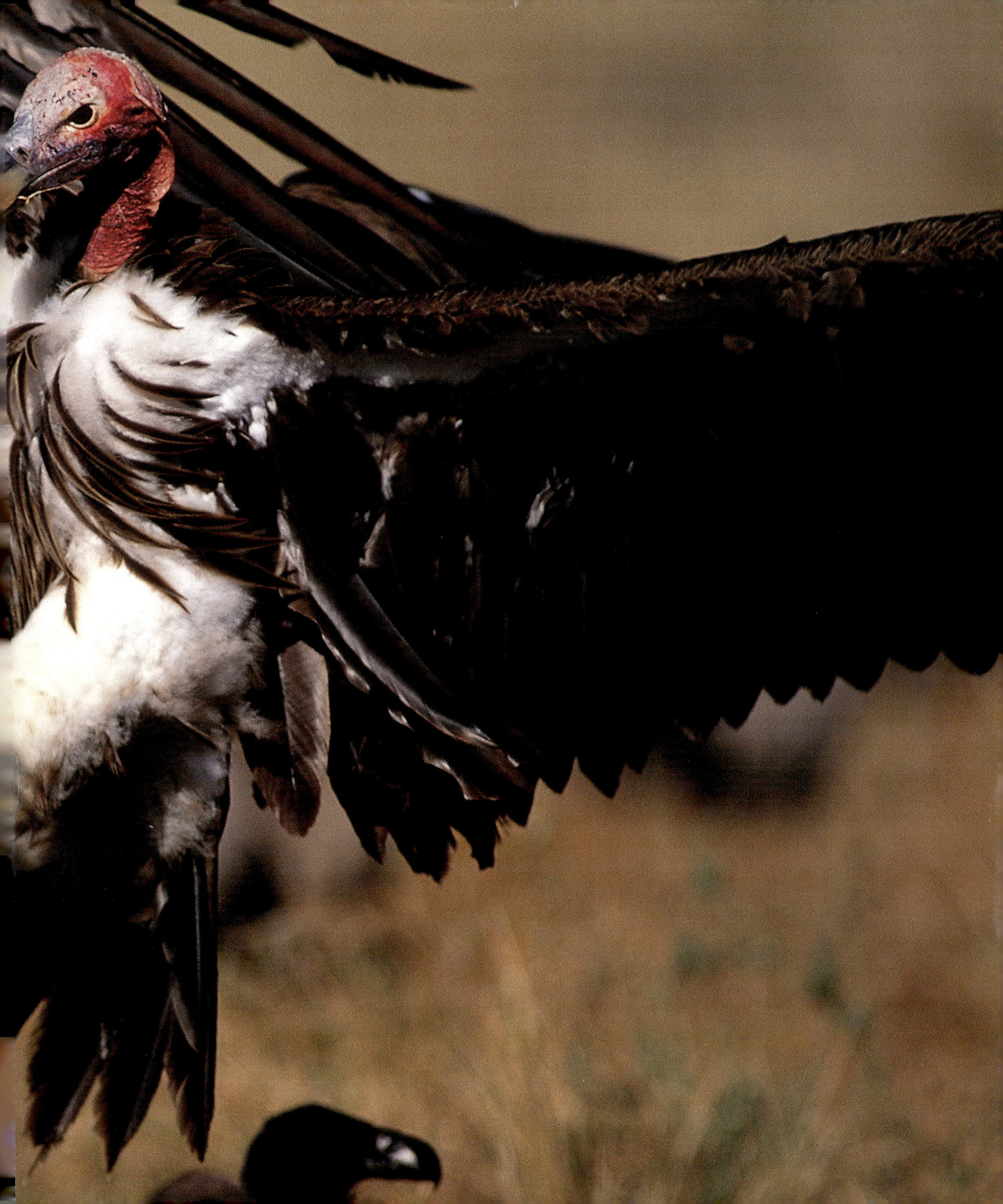